St Andrews Studies in Reformation History

Belief and Practice in Reformation England

Frontispiece Professor Patrick Collinson

Belief and Practice in Reformation England

A Tribute to Patrick Collinson from his Students

Edited by

SUSAN WABUDA and
CAROLINE LITZENBERGER

Ashgate

Aldershot • Brookfield USA • Singapore • Sydney

Published by
Ashgate Publishing Limited
Gower House
Croft Road
Aldershot
Hants
GU11 3HR
England

BR
375
.B45
1998

Ashgate Publishing Company
Old Post Road
Brookfield
Vermont 05036–9704
USA

The authors have asserted their moral right under the Copyright, Designs and Patents Act, 1988, to be identified as the authors of this work.

British Library Cataloguing in Publication Data

Belief and Practice in Reformation England: A Tribute to
  Patrick Collinson from his Students.
  (St Andrews Studies in Reformation History)
  1. Reformation—England.   2. Great Britain—History—Tudors,
  1485–1603.
  942'.05

Library of Congress Cataloging-in-Publication Data

Belief and practice in Reformation England: a tribute to Patrick
  Collinson from his students/edited by Susan Wabuda and Caroline
  Litzenberger.
    p.   cm. (St Andrews Studies in Reformation History)
  Includes bibliographical references and index.
  1. Reformation—England.   2. England—Church history.
  I. Collinson, Patrick.   II. Wabuda, Susan.   III. Litzenberger, C. J.
  IV. Series.
  BR375.B45 1998
  274.2'06—dc21   98–3164
                                                          CIP

ISBN 1 85928 430 2

This book is printed on acid free paper

Typeset in Sabon by Manton Typesetters, 5–7 Eastfield Road, Louth, Lincolnshire.
Printed and bound in Great Britain by MPG Books Ltd, Bodmin, Cornwall

Contents

List of figures and tables

Figures

Table

Notes on contributors

Patrick Carter was a Leverhulme Visiting Fellow in the Department of Modern History, University of St Andrews in 1997–98. He is the author of several articles on church finance in Reformation England.

John S. Craig is an assistant professor in the Department of History, Simon Fraser University. He is the author of articles on aspects of the English Reformation and co-editor (with Patrick Collinson) of *The Reformation in English Towns 1500–1640*, a volume in the Themes in Focus Series published by Macmillan.

David J. Crankshaw is a member of Robinson College and is completing his PhD at the University of Cambridge.

Seán F. Hughes was a junior research fellow at Trinity College, Cambridge from 1995 to 1998 and is completing his PhD at the University of Cambridge. From 1999 he will teach at the University of St Thomas, St Paul, Minnesota.

Arnold Hunt was a junior research fellow at Trinity College, Cambridge from 1994 to 1997 and completed his doctoral dissertation at the University of Cambridge in 1998.

Norman Jones is a professor of history and chair of the Department of History, Utah State University. His written work includes most notably *Faith by Statute: Parliament and the Settlement of Religion 1559* and *The Birth of the Elizabethan Age: England in the 1560s*. He is currently writing a social and cultural history of the English Reformation.

Beat Kümin is a research fellow of the Swiss National Science Foundation at the University of Berne. He is the author of *The Shaping of a Community: The Rise and Reformation of the English Parish c. 1400–1560* and editor of *Reformations Old and New: Essays on the Socio-Economic Impact of Religious Change c. 1470–1630*.

Caroline Litzenberger is an assistant professor of history at West Virginia University. She is the author of *The English Reformation and the Laity: Gloucestershire 1540–1580* , as well as several articles on aspects of the English Reformation.

Damian Nussbaum is a member of Queens' College, and completed his PhD thesis on 'The Reception of John Foxe's *Acts and Monuments*' at the University of Cambridge in 1998.

Kate Peters is a lecturer in archives and records management at University College London. She completed her PhD thesis on 'Quaker pamphleteering and the development of the Quaker movement, 1652–1656' in 1996 at the University of Cambridge.

Susan Wabuda is an assistant professor of history at Fordham University in New York. In addition to several articles on religious change in the sixteenth century, she is the author of the forthcoming book, *Preaching during the English Reformation*, a volume in the Studies in Early Modern British History series published by Cambridge University Press.

Alexandra Walsham is lecturer in history at the University of Exeter. She is the author of *Church Papists: Catholicism, Conformity and Confessional Polemic in Early Modern England*, and her Cambridge PhD thesis is to be published soon by Oxford University Press under the title *Providence in Early Modern England*.

Acknowledgements

This book is the fulfilment of a long-held aspiration, shared among all of Patrick Collinson's recent postgraduate students, to bring together a public profession of our gratitude for the lively encouragement, guidance and concern that he lavished upon each one of us. The nature of the many different academic positions Patrick occupied in his long and fruitful career, in London, Khartoum, Sydney, Kent, Sheffield and Cambridge, meant that he never had the opportunity to gather to himself as many students as he might have had reason to expect. We feel especially fortunate, therefore, to be part of the select group who benefited from the opportunity to be guided by him.

In addition to the obvious debt we owe to him, this book would not have appeared without the assistance of many who gave unstintingly of their time and resources. The editors wish to express their thanks to Norman Jones for his constant support, and gracious introductory chapter. We are indebted to Andrew Pettegree for his limitless encouragement. To Alex Walsham go our thanks for selecting and obtaining the cover illustration which is printed with permission from the British Library. Arnold Hunt gave much useful assistance in compiling the bibliography of Patrick's recently published works.

Our colleagues at the Departments of History at Fordham and West Virginia Universities have provided us with much needed support. In addition, we would be remiss if we did not signal our thanks to Michael Vargas. Other tokens of appreciation will be found in the notes of the chapters that follow.

This volume really began, however, when we were all research students at Cambridge, and we all share in our appreciation for the friendship extended to each one of us by Liz Collinson during that time and since. She was a constant source of reassurance and support. She opened not only her home, but also her heart, to us all. In the turbulence each of us felt in his or her own way (as students do), as we worked toward our degrees, she was our 'anchor to windward'.

What this book is, and what we will achieve in our careers, is a tribute to both Patrick and Liz Collinson, and this is a mere token of our esteem and thanks.

Abbreviations and conventions

Abbreviations

Libraries, archives and manuscripts

BL	British Library
CCCC, PL	Corpus Christi College, Cambridge, The Parker Library
CUL	Cambridge University Library
ChUL	Chicago University Library
CWA	Churchwardens' Accounts
GDR	Gloucester Diocesan Records
GL	Guildhall Library, London
GRO	Gloucestershire Record Office
ITL	Inner Temple Library
LAO	Lincolnshire Archives Office, Lincoln
LPL	Lambeth Palace Library
NRO	Norfolk Record Office
PRO	Public Record Office, London
SROB	Suffolk Record Office, Bury St Edmunds

Journals, series and record society publications

ARG	Archiv für Reformationsgeschichte
CS	Camden Society
DNB	Dictionary of National Biography
EETS	Early English Text Society
HJ	Historical Journal
HMC	Historical Manuscripts Commission
JBS	Journal of British Studies
JEH	Journal of Ecclesiastical History
LP	Letters and Papers, Foreign and Domestic, of the Reign of Henry VIII, 22 vols in 33 parts, (London, 1862–1910).
OED	Oxford English Dictionary
PS	Parker Society
SCH	Studies in Church History
SCJ	Sixteenth Century Journal
STC	A Short-title Catalogue of books printed in England, Scotland, and Ireland, and of English books printed

	abroad, 1475–1640, rev. edn, 3 vols (London, 1976–91).
TBGAS	*Transactions of the Bristol and Gloucestershire Archaeological Society*
TRHS	*Transactions of the Royal Historical Society*
Wing	*A Short-title Catalogue of books printed in England, Scotland, Ireland, Wales, and British America and of English books printed in other countries, 1641–1700*, 2nd edn, 3 vols. (New York, 1972–82).

Conventions

In quotations and titles the original spelling has been retained except for the pairs of letters, i and j, and u and v, which have been changed to adhere to modern usage. Additionally, dates have been standardized in the old style but with the year beginning on 1 January. Standard abbreviations have been silently expanded, and punctuation has been added where necessary to clarify meaning. The statutes cited in this volume are printed in A. Luders, T. E. Tomlins et al., (eds), *The Statutes of the Realm* (London, 1817, repr. 1963).

Known from their works: living and writing early modern English religious history

Norman Jones

Patrick Collinson examined my dissertation, but I was not his student. Yet I am his student. He has taught me, other scholars and, most of all, his students who have contributed to this volume, to think about early modern English religion as a human experience, not as arid theology, or as the superstructure of political and economic forces.

I suspect that Collinson learned at an early age that religion and the rest of life were inseparable. Like all historians, his sense of a 'right' explanation of human actions grows first from his experience and secondarily from the sources he has read. Notably, his sense of 'right' leads him to explain early modern religious experiences as inseparable from the intellectual, social or political milieus in which his subjects lived. That grounding of religious experience in the breadth of life gives his work a much wider applicability, and has created a band of students whose dissertations transgress a number of traditional historical boundaries.

All of this is to say that Patrick Collinson has changed the way we think about early modern England. Long before he returned to Cambridge as Regius Professor of Modern History he was known as the leading authority on Puritanism, but, to his credit, he was much more interested in the people who have been called Puritans than in Puritanism. In fact, he once proposed that the word Puritan be banished because it muddled our understanding of what was essentially an experiential state of mind rather than a theological or political position.[1]

His vision of religion has thrown the Reformation into confusing shadows by making it clear that it was experienced differently in each parish and in each mind. But at the same time he has encouraged a better understanding of how confusing the process of Reformation was. Clearly a believer in the 'long Reformation', Collinson is much more interested in Reformation 'from below' than from above, in the sense that his work

---

[1] Patrick Collinson, 'A Comment: Concerning the Name Puritan', *JEH*, 31 (1980), p. 463.

has taught us to pay attention to individuals and local communities, whether parishes or cathedrals. His curiosity about funeral sermons, diaries, authors' books, the Protestant family and the godly town leads us inexorably back to the reality of the Reformation experience. However, Collinson not infrequently confronts us with the reality that religion and politics are inseparable, and that 'below' and 'above' are parts of a loop. As he once said, an understanding of 9,000 parish councils amounts to an understanding of how a single political society was constructed.[2]

His students have replicated and magnified his interest in individuals and local institutions, as this volume attests. Collinson, like all masterful mentors, is open to many approaches to his subject, but underneath his students' broad interests, here sweeping across two centuries and varying from subtle theological parsing to hard sociological analyses of parishes, stands his insistence that people lived the Reformation. One of the virtues of his method is that the reader comes to know the people under discussion. In Collinson's hand the religious practices of early modern England spring to life with all the complexity of a Trollope novel – which is not surprising, given his love of Trollope.

Collinson's work, and much of his students' work, is moving us closer and closer to understanding what reformation meant to the people who lived through it. By asking how one lived whatever one's faith was in the early modern period, they have explored a range of sources and approaches. Theology and ecclesiology, wills and churchwardens, sermons and printed books, parish records and eulogies, all form part of the grist for their mills.

The chapters in this volume explore identity and definition. One theme is the compromise made by the leaders of the newly Protestant Church in order to protect the Queen who guaranteed Protestantism's safety in a world full of lurking papists and Scottish heirs. Another is the personal problem of a lived faith. What does a fervent desire to obey the law of God demand of a believer, in the face of a church that has found compromise *politique*? Yet another theme is the overwhelming problem of how to preserve community identity and institutions in the face of massive religious changes that provoke massive social realignments. Collinson's question about Canterbury Cathedral, 'what purpose did a Cathedral now serve?', is one he and his students have asked about all the other institutions and habits of the Old Church that carried into the New Church.[3]

---

[2] Patrick Collinson, *De Republica Anglorum or, History with the Politics Put Back* (Cambridge: 1990), p. 35.

[3] Patrick Collinson, Nigel Ramsay and Margaret Sparks (eds), *A History of Canterbury Cathedral* (Cambridge, 1995), p. 155.

Historiographical debate is associated with these themes, and Collinson has done his part here, as have his students. In particular, they are interested in how definitions and classifications are constructed by historians, and what impact those constructions have on the ways we understand the past. To denominate someone as a 'Puritan' or a 'Calvinist' requires an act of historical definition that needs careful attention.

The English Reformation was an act of state. That is an axiom, not subject to historiographical dispute. Monarchs in Parliament created the Anglican Church and imposed it through royal commissions sent to supervise the destruction of the old faith. This meant that the English church, now headed or governed by the monarch, was merged with the State. Retaining its medieval structure, its bishops, its courts, its cathedrals and its parishes, the English church had a new theology hostile to many of the practices of those establishments, throwing it into a confusion that lasted more than a century. This identity crisis induced a redefinition of the roles of churchmen and religious institutions. Several of the chapters in this volume explore facets of that redefinition. They demonstrate that over the 'long' Reformation the once semi-autonomous parishes fought to protect their identity and wealth from internal challengers and a rapacious government, that the bishops fought and lost a battle for a thoroughly reformed church in the 1560s, and that the now Protestant clergy were an important source of tax revenue for a Crown that played on their fear of a Catholic succession. By the time James I came to the throne, English religious society was splitting into patterns of conformity and resistance. Though fined for their faith, lay Catholics found the Crown winked at them as long as their priests were not seditious. This left room for them to fight among themselves in Archpriest Controversy. Among the Protestants those known loosely as Puritans hoped for further reform or were moving towards separatism. The arrival of the Scots king irritated all the sores. His rumoured hard line against Catholics and his positive response to the Millenary Petition, upset the tottering apple cart. James's attempts to bring all Protestant groups together at the Hampton Court Conference ultimately failed because conflicting ideals of both spirituality and ecclesiology could not be reconciled. And the Jesuit-led wing of the Catholics veered off into the Gunpowder Plot.

At the bottom of all this was the person in the pew, who experienced religion on the level of the parish. Surprisingly neglected as a subject of study, recent work on the operation of the parish has been stimulated by German scholarship.

One of the most important arguments about the German reformation is that its early stages were communal. Peter Blickle has suggested that the popular Reformation in German lands was a 'communal Reformation' [*Gemeindereformation*]. Opposing the 'princes' Reformation' that eventually carried the day, the communal reformers sought the common good, subordinating self-interest in the name of prosperity for all. It was the possibilities of communal freedom that attracted them to the message of Martin Luther.[4] Although this model of reform has been challenged from a number of directions, it has given rise to important studies of how local communities governed themselves. Beat Kümin has brought the question of a *Gemeindereformation* to English lands, arguing that the English equivalent of the German commune was the parish community. A geographically defined unit with certain collective responsibilities, the parish was a legal unit with legal rights of representation as well as legally imposed duties. Able to generate intense pride and loyalty, and subject to internal dissension and external attack, the parish embodied the corporate nature of late medieval religion.[5]

In his *The Shaping of a Community* Kümin asserts that the English parish developed as a part of the 'communalisation' of late medieval society. Perfectly suited to the nature of late medieval worship, it did not fare well in the Reformation. The Tudor state's interference undermined local religion and damaged communal worship. But the parishioners themselves were ambivalent. They traded cherished tradition for the prospect of increased lay control and parochial responsibility.[6] In the end they did not get the freedom they expected, but their choice makes perfect sense in the troubled context of the Reformation.

The attempts of parishes to maintain their independence and identity by aggressive legal action is the theme of Kümin's Chapter 1 in this volume. The communal authority of the parish, embodied in the churchwardens who governed it, was being redefined through its collisions and collusion with the law.

These shaping transactions began when the Crown moved to seize property given for 'superstitious uses' – prayers for the souls of departed parishioners. Across the realm people found institutions they cherished and property they owned needing protection. They could not save a chantry, but they could try to save their investments. For example, in the parishes of Llanfaredd and Llanelwedd in Radnor, Rees ap Gwyllim, Surveyor of Chantries, discovered that the parishioners

---

[4] Peter Blickle, *Gemeindereformation: Die Menschen des 16. Jahrhunderts auf dem Weg zum Heil* (Munich, 1985), translated into English as *Communal Reformation. The Quest for Salvation in Sixteenth Century Europe* (Atlantic Highlands, NJ, 1992).

[5] Beat Kümin, *The Shaping of a Community: the Rise and Reformation of the English Parish c. 1400–1560* (Aldershot, 1996), p. 2.

[6] Kümin, *The Shaping of a Community*, p. 263.

supported their two chantry priests on the rent of ten oxen. Producing about £17 10s. a year in rent, the plough team, purchased with proceeds from the sale of a broken bell in the early 1540s, was, in ap Gwyllim's book, property of the Crown under the Chantries Act 1549. The churchwardens, however, took action to keep the oxen in their parishes, deeding them over to other parishioners. Gwyllim took them to law, but it does not appear that the Court of Augmentations was ever able to collect the £11 the oxen were worth, or the £35 in back rent it claimed. The churchwardens stood together, and one gets the impression that they lied to the surveyors and the courts in the interest of their community.[7]

These activist churchwardens stood alongside the clergy, jointly sharing responsibility for the functioning of the Church. In a proto-typically Anglican way, the clergy of the Protestant Tudor church were treated as a separate establishment, just as in the days of popery. The nationalized church retained its own distinct voice in the new establishment. The bishops continued to sit with the other peers of the realm in Parliament and to constitute the Upper Houses of the Convocations of the provinces of Canterbury and York. In the Lower Houses of Convocation sat the representatives of the clergy. Charged with making policy for the Church in England, they met apart from, but at the same time, as Parliament. All that was new was the necessity of having their actions given statutory force by Parliament.

This structure immediately caused tension in the early Elizabethan church. In theory the bishops and the representatives of the clergy were the voice of the Church, and the experts on theology. Conciliar theory gave them that place. But like general councils of the Church in the fifteenth century, they were in a delicate political situation. Tudor Convocations repeatedly learned that they were the servants of the Crown no matter which ecclesiology they endorsed.

This semi-autonomous status imposed on the clergy contained confusing messages. On the one hand, the Church was responsible for the spiritual welfare of the nation and had the duty of imposing discipline. On the other, it was clear that the bishops were now servants of the Crown, unable to discipline without permission. It created an almost unendurable tension for the men raised to the episcopal bench by Elizabeth.

This tension came to a head in the mid-1560s when the Convocation of Canterbury set out to create and impose a new discipline for the newly restored Protestant Church of England. Part of the story is well

---

[7] PRO, SP46/3/1, fos 3–19.

known, brilliantly told by Patrick Collinson himself in his many books that show how the bishops, faced by opposition from clergy who refused to wear the prescribed clerical costume, were led into a fight with men who were otherwise their theological brothers. This battle cast the bishops in the role of the Queen's enforcers, costing them the respect of those who hankered after a more complete reformation.

The Vestiarian Controversy in the late 1560s created the ecclesiastical party known, for lack of a better term, as Puritans. Unfortunately, their experience with the bishops has overshadowed the early and middle years of that decade, leading scholars to see everything in terms of the disharmony between the bishops and Puritans. In his reconsideration of the Convocation of 1562–63, in Chapter 3, David Crankshaw shows just how misleading it is to see that dichotomy at work at the beginning of Elizabeth's years on the throne. He paints a picture of the bishops, led by Archbishop Parker, striving to create a church that was, at least in discipline, purely Protestant and in keeping with the desires of most of those who became Puritans.

Crankshaw, in a classical piece of *Quellenkritique*, demonstrates that there can be no doubt that Parker had a hand in the documents produced by Convocation as it sought to find a way to complete the English Reformation. He, not some proto-puritanical group among the lower house of Convocation, was behind the discipline. This is very important, since it drives what may be the last nail into the coffin of Sir John Neale's interpretation of the early Elizabethan political debate.

Neale believed that the watch spring of Elizabethan parliamentary politics was, from 1559 onward, a radical protestant party that was constantly striving to push the Church towards a Genevan model of discipline and government. Finding Puritans hard at work in 1559, he discovered them everywhere and taught his students to see them, too.[8] Neale's belief that Puritan pressure can explain the shape of the Elizabethan Settlement was undermined and destroyed in the early 1980s by Winthrop Hudson and myself.[9] However, William Haugaard's work on the Convocation of 1562/63 was not rejected at the same time, even though deeply influenced by the Neale thesis. Though many of us suspected that the drive for further ecclesiastical discipline was led by the bishops in that Convocation, there was no smoking gun. Now Crankshaw has found Archbishop Parker's fingerprints on the weapon and we can no longer doubt that the managerial concerns of the

---

[8] J. E. Neale, *Elizabeth I and her Parliaments 1559–1581* (London, 1953).

[9] Winthrop Hudson, *The Cambridge Connection and the Elizabethan Settlement of 1559* (Durham, NC, 1980); Norman Jones, *Faith by Statute. Parliament and the Settlement of Religion 1559* (London, 1982).

bishops, not a radical Puritan party, explain the Convocation's search for stricter ecclesiastical discipline.

Furthermore, Crankshaw's work underlines the difficulty of identifying camps within the new Elizabethan Settlement. The bishops shared many of the theological and disciplinary concerns of those who would later be called Puritans. Their ecclesiological differences did not appear in earnest until the 1570s, when the papal bull *Regnans in excelsis* and the *Admonition to Parliament* created clear threats from both the Catholic right and the Protestant left. Increasingly, conformity to the religious settlement identified a good subject of the Queen, making those who disagreed with the form of worship officially dangerous.

The Elizabethan bishops who planned further reformation of the Church in 1563 were blocked by the Queen, then, and again in 1566. None the less, the Queen gratefully accepted the subsidy granted to her by the Convocation of the Clergy of the realm in recognition of her 'most gracious bountifulness, principally for the setting forth and advancing of God's Holy Word'. Equally thankful for her defence of True Religion in France and Scotland, as well as mindful of the military costs that defence entailed, they gave her six shillings on the pound of value of their spiritual promotions, payable over three years.[10] They clearly knew, as Patrick Carter points out in Chapter 4, that they must support Elizabeth or they might see the True Church in England destroyed by another Mary. Already in 1559 Parliament had confirmed that Elizabeth owned the right to the first fruits and tenths of the Church and that she could exchange lands with bishoprics during vacancies.[11] And so secular taxes became an important part of clerical responsibility, and the government came to depend heavily on them.

As the reign advanced, this union of interest between the clergy and the Crown was cemented by crises spawned by critics on both ends of the spectrum. In 1571 the clerical subsidy was paid in thankful remembrance of the Queen's expenses in suppressing the Northern rebels, 'enemies to God'.[12]

Undoubtedly there were many clerics who were not as happy to pay as the acts confirming the subsidies of the clergy pretend, but the reality was that as Elizabeth's reign advanced, the defence of the Elizabethan Settlement was accepted as a necessary cost to the Church. In clerical eyes, Catholics, radical presbyterians and corrupt courtiers lusting after church property were equally dangerous to the Church and the State. And the State had an equal need to maintain their prosperity in order to

---

[10] 5 Eliz. I, c. 29.2.
[11] 1 Eliz. I, c. 4; c. 19.
[12] 13 Eliz. I, c. 26.2.

tax it. By the 1590s clergymen like William Harrison had abandoned sympathy for doctrines that undermined the institutions of the established Church and turned with thankfulness to a Crown that defended them – at a cost.[13]

For all religiously minded English people the years immediately after Elizabeth's accession were confusing. Although she was clearly Protestant, she provided no clear definition of what that meant. Her Convocation tried, but was rebuffed. It was not until 1571 that the Thirty-nine Articles spelled out the nature of her church. Others did not wait for an official decree to shape the lives of English Protestants. John Foxe was using history to do it.

Polemics of all genres were popular with Protestants in the Reformation, but they were generally broad and accessible to the masses. Poets like Luke Shepherd threw pointed verses at the heads of Catholic priests like 'Doctour Doubble Ale'. An ignorant, drunken priest who still keeps his bead-rolls and believes in Purgatory, Dr Doubble Ale represents the opposite of the ideal Protestant clergyman. 'Earnest in the cause of peevish popish laws', he cannot tell God's Word from the Devil's. Believing his own wit to be far above holy writ, he brings men to the gates of Hell.[14] In short, no man should respect or follow a priest of the Roman Church. Down with their authority! Down with their religion!

Once Catholic authority and religion were down, the Protestant propagandists had a different problem. No longer fighting to gain power, the Protestants needed role models for a faith that claimed to be primitive. In the 1550s a pan-European Protestant historiography began to emerge under the leadership of Matthias Judex and Matthias Flacius Illyricus, Lutheran scholars whose history of the Church century by century was designed to show how the True Church had survived the papal perversion. At the same time they celebrated the people who had clung to the truth, making heroes of former heretics like Wycliff. Dispatching book collectors throughout Europe in the 1550s they sought most particularly to find the history of heretics, telling their collectors not to collect the lives of the saints.[15] To their opponents their refusal to relate the

---

[13] G. J. R. Parry, 'The Creation and Recreation of Puritanism', in S. M. Jack and B. A. Masters (eds), *Protestants, Property, Puritans: Godly People Revisited, a Festschrift in Honour of Patrick Collinson on the Occasion of his Retirement* (Parergon, new ser. 14, 1996), pp. 49–50.

[14] Janice C. Devereux, 'Protestant Propaganda in the Reign of Edward VI: a Study of Luke Sheperd's "Doctour Doubble Ale"', in Eric Carlson (ed.), *Religion and the English People 1500–1620* (Sixteenth Century Essays and Studies, forthcoming 1998).

[15] Matthias Flacius Illyricus to Marcus Wagner, 5 March 1557, in Marcus Wagner, *Thüringen Königreichs, das es für und nach Christi geburth in Pagos getheilet gewesen etc.* (Jena, 1593), vol. 1, sig. L 4.

history of the saints made their purpose obvious. Conrad Bruno, for instance, condemned their history as a work of doctrine instead of history.[16]

In England a similar interest in martyrs appeared. Even in the 1540s John Bale had adapted the models provided by ancient martyrologists, declaring that martyrs provided necessary models of Christian constancy to be followed by others. In the preface to his *Examinations of Anne Askew* Bale argues that English martyrs were of two kinds. One kind, the Beckets of the world, were mostly monastery and chantry builders killed by kings. These were worshiped like idols. The other kind, the kind Anne Askew was, were preachers of the word of God killed by the Holy Spiritual Fathers for heresy and Lollardy. These were never honoured, not even with so much as a 'penny dirge or a grote mass of requiem'. Bale desired that these sorts of martyrs, who died for seeking the Lord, should not be forgotten.[17]

John Foxe, influenced by Bale and the Magdeburg Centuriators, set out to remedy the problem created by the disappearance of the role models provided by saints' lives. Of course his *Acts and Monuments* is an obvious attempt to create alternative paths to holiness, but Damian Nussbaum (Chapter 5) suggests that Foxe had intended to go even further. Not content to abolish saints, he wished to replace them in the liturgy with an alternative round of propers. Where once the deeds of the saints had been remembered by the faithful at mass, the Protestant preachers would remind their congregants of the heroes of their new faith.

Not surprisingly, this attempt to convert the old liturgical tools to new uses met with shrill criticism from all sides. Catholics were deeply offended by his presumption at putting heretics into the ecclesiastical calendar, while many Protestants were disturbed to see that there was a calendar, redolent of papistry, at all.

The quick disappearance of the calendar of martyrs from the *Acts and Monuments* marks another step in the meandering passage of the English brand of Protestantism towards a mature self-understanding. It would take many more experiences and experiments before it would jell into an Anglican mould.

Patrick Collinson reminds us that the early Elizabethan Church was 'an enforced coalition of contrary religious traditions and tendencies, crudely distinguishable as very protestant, not-so-protestant, and crypto-

---

[16] Conrad Bruno, *Adversus Novam Historiam Ecclesiasticam, quam Matthias Illyricus et eius collegae Magdeburgici per centurias nuper ediderunt, ne quisque illis malae fidei historicii novis fidat, admonitio catholica* (Dilingae, 1565), sig. B. 5; D. 5.

[17] Elaine V. Beilin (ed.), *The Examinations of Anne Askew* (Oxford, 1996), pp. 75–9.

papist'.[18] Caroline Litzenberger's offering in Chapter 6 demonstrates
the work of definition that occurred in the 1570s as the bishops and
their officers tried to maximize conformity. Recusancy rose, and not
just among Catholics. The shape of English Protestantism was sketched
by episcopal responses to those whose Protestantism ran contrary to the
official position of the Church. In a reciprocating motion the bishops'
attempts to impose conformity pushed more and more people over the
line into resistance to episcopal authority. As the piston of enforcement
rose and fell the various coalitions began to shake into place or fall
away.

Central to this process of definition was the creation of a new clerical
self-identity. The clergy of Elizabeth's church, more than any one else,
had an identity problem. By the time Elizabeth settled into her reign her
clergy had experienced a roller-coaster ride of ideological change that
left many confused at the least, and alienated at the worst. Priests
ordained before 1549 had, by 1560s, led worship in Latin twice and in
English twice. They had 'reformed' their church fabrics under Edward
VI, restored the altars and roods under Mary, and torn them out under
Elizabeth. Meanwhile the theological meaning of their roles and liturgies had boxed the compass. As Elizabeth's reign progressed the older
priests died, and the new young ministers, freshly minted graduates of
the universities, took their places and tried creating a new, preaching
ministry of the kind they had been taught to value. Believing absolutely
in the Word of God, they sought to understand and apply it in the
world.

These clergy, mostly nourished by Cambridge, combined in some
counties with the lay magistracy to form a potent alliance for the
advancement of God's cause. This was especially true in Suffolk, where,
as Collinson has pointed out, magistracy and ministry united to create
one of the first groups of English clergy to realize the reformed ideal of
a pastoral ministry. Nearly all of the Suffolk clergy were from Cambridge (30 were from St John's College alone), and during the 1570s
and early 1580s they maintained frequent contact with one another by
their attendance at the Bury St Edmund's combination lectures.[19] Designed to teach one another a clearer understanding of the Bible, the
lectures gave rise to a nasty civic conflict in the early 1580s as the
clerical disagreement over the proper role of the clergy spilled over into

---

[18] Patrick Collinson, *Archbishop Grindal 1519–1583: the Struggle for a Reformed
Church* (Berkeley, 1979), p. 167.

[19] Patrick Collinson, 'Magistracy and Ministry: a Suffolk Miniature', in R. Buick
Knox, (ed.), *Reformation Conformity and Dissent. Essays in Honour of Geoffrey Nuttall*
(London, 1977), p. 76.

ideological disputes between leading local families, some of whom were conservatives and others of whom supported a reformed religious position. Mixing into the conflict was Bishop Freke of Norwich, who was trying to control the combination lecturers because he feared they promoted nonconformity. Making matters even more confused, a group of Brownist heretics had been discovered in Bury, increasing episcopal scrutiny of the town.

Diarmaid MacCulloch's study of Suffolk under the Tudors reached the conclusion that Bury became the centre of religious controversy in the 1580s because a number of religious movements met and mingled in a town that had lost its traditional governmental structure when the Candlemas Guild was suppressed. In the absence of a single, overarching authority various local powers attempted to control the town, and to impose their ideas of order. In 1581 the Puritan faction interfered with Dr John Day's attempt to hold a commissary court in the bishop's name. The politics of the situation went from bad to worse, provoking Privy Council and archepiscopal interference against the reformers from Cambridge. The community was more and more split along ideological lines, with leading local Catholics using their influence to hinder the more puritanical in their duties. It even spilled over into the parliamentary election of 1584, when the choice went to Sir William Drury, a man of known anti-Puritan opinions.[20] It was into this very heated atmosphere that the irenic Reverend Thomas Rogers moved.

An Oxford man with moderate views, Rogers, as John S. Craig shows in Chapter 7, tried to find the middle ground amid the hostile 'Cambridge Boys'. For his pains he was condemned and excluded by his fellow clerics, embittering him and hardening his heart against those who refused the discipline of the established church. He learned to hate the schismatical nature of those who leaned toward Presbyterianism. Craig ends by asking if the Combination Lectures can be seen as the context for bitter disputes about the goals of the Church more than as times of collegial co-operation. Whatever the answer to his question, there is no question that these sorts of nasty local battles contributed to the definition of the English state church's conception of its place in the world.

Definitions demand exclusions as well as inclusions. Much of the excluding and including was *ad hoc*, appearing as local need forced decisions on to people previously uncommitted. The process had begun as soon as the Reformation, as Susan Wabuda reminds us in her discussion of female Bible reading in Chapter 2.

---

[20] Diarmaid MacCulloch, *Suffolk and the Tudors. Politics and Religion in an English County 1500–1600* (Oxford, 1986), pp. 198–215.

As long as the medieval Church's male clerical hierarchy was recognized as having powers and rights not given the unordained, the need for lay participation in biblical debate remained low. Biblical literacy required Latin and was an élite activity. In England Tyndale's translation and the arrival of the Reformation changed all that. Protestants of all stripes embraced the idea that scripture was the font of truth, and that every Christian could interpret it for *him*self. As Nicholas Ridley put it, scripture explained itself to the reader. Thus the reader, 'though he be a layman, fearing God, is much more fit to understand holy scripture than any arrogant and proud priest, yea, than the bishop himself, be he never so great and glistering in all his pontificals'.[21]

In the waning of the twentieth century we easily sense the contradiction such teaching presented to women. The patriarchal nature of Christian religion and Tudor society guaranteed that when Ridley said every layman could have as true a knowledge of scripture as a bishop, he did not ask himself whether that meant that every laywoman could have such a knowledge, too. But some women and men caught the logical imperative in an argument that declared that all humans would be saved only by faith and guided only by the Bible. If that was true, women had to read the Bible.

Equally, if scripture had to be followed, women had to be willing to invert the social order that demanded their obedience. Hugh Latimer, preaching in Epiphany of 1552, saw fit to drive home the necessary inversion of authority that went along with conversion. Christ, he pointed out, disobeyed his mother in God's cause when he stayed to dispute with the doctors in the Temple at Jerusalem. Arguing that a child is bound to obey its parents 'so far as the same may stand with godliness', Latimer said 'if they will have us go further, and pluck us from true religion and the serving of God', we should say 'we ought rather to obey God than men'.[22]

This was certainly the opinion of Sir Francis Hastings, who, counselling a female friend who wished to convert to Protestantism in spite of her Catholic parents, insisted on biblical authority that it was necessary to love Christ more than father or mother. 'Let neither loss of friends, loss of living, no nor loss of life draw you to deny the truth', he urged, 'for what can all the friends in the world do for you, if the Lord Jesus forsake you'?[23]

---

[21] Henry Christmas (ed.), *The Works of Nicholas Ridley* (Cambridge, 1841), p. 114.

[22] George E. Corrie (ed.), *Sermons and Remains of Hugh Latimer* (Cambridge, 1845), vol. 2, p. 158.

[23] C. Cross (ed.) *The Letters of Sir Francis Hastings, 1574–1609* (Somerset Record Society, 9, 1969), pp. 4–5.

The contradiction between social values of a patriarchal culture and the values of the reformed church created a tension that many are now exploring. Patrick Collinson has, in this as in so many other areas, pointed the way by his consistent awareness of the reality of women's influence in their families and communities. He is constantly attuned to the existence of people like Martha Higham, whose 35 years of widowhood were devoted to promoting God's cause. It was she, he suspects, who made Denham, her little corner of Suffolk, a bastion of Puritan faith.[24]

Martha Higham owned a Bible, read it, and liked to debate its meaning with her clerical friends and protégés. And it was parents like her who raised women like Grace Mildmay, whose hundreds of pages of meditations require a complete knowledge of scripture to understand. Clearly the woman with the distaff came to be included in the Reformation's insistence that God's word was the guide for each and every individual Christian.

Philip Stubbes's *Anatomie of Abuses* bears on its title-page a warning that all Bible literate people knew: 'I say unto you (saith Christ) except you repent, you shall perish.'[25] This familiar warning left Christian folk anxious to repent of their sin, but it also led them into the labyrinth of soteriology. How salvation works, what sin is, when it happens and what its magnitudes are, are problems that confuse and tantalize the faithful. And they were not questions the Elizabethan Church answered very directly.

The genius of the Elizabethan Settlement was its vagueness. Emphasizing the community of Christians, it remained carefully indistinct about the specific theological models that undergirded its liturgy, and which might have divided Christians from one another. This allowed the English to agree on justification by faith alone without defining how grace worked.

At the very beginning of Elizabeth's reign returning religious exiles tried to explain to their monarch the doctrine to which they subscribed. These men clearly believed in double predestination, knowing that 'predestination to life is the everlasting purpose of God', who chooses some men for election by grace while others are 'predestined to downfall'. Asserting this, however, raised complications they fully comprehended. God's purpose in this was a mystery that might be misconstrued by the ignorant. Therefore, they warned that this truth had to be carefully managed in their 'carnal age'. 'It were best', they wrote pragmatically,

---

[24] Collinson, 'Magistracy and Ministry', p. 83.
[25] Philip Stubbes, *The Anatomie of Abuses*, STC 23376 (London, 1583), title-page.

'that such articles be passed over in silence (indeed we do think discreet ministers will speak sparingly and circumspectly of them).'[26]

This circumspection is visible in the Thirty-nine Articles that define the Anglican faith. Written in 1563 but not enacted until 1571, they were to be subscribed by all clergy in the realm of England. Confirming the reality of predestination, article 17 hints at double predestination without forthrightly explaining it. Asserting that predestination to life is the everlasting purpose of God, the article stresses the happiness of the elect and the misery of the damned without clearly making damnation God's will. As David Cressy and Lori Anne Ferrell have observed, the article is 'practicably ambiguous'.[27]

This ambiguity bred a confusion that encouraged squabbles over predestination in the late sixteenth century. The classical statements on predestination made by Luther and Calvin were not accepted as canonical by Europe's theologians, who continued to ponder the working of this great mystery. Works like Girolamo Zanchi's *De praedestinatione sanctorum* of 1577 and Zacharias Ursinus's *Doctrinae christianae compendium* of 1584 refined and shaped the understanding of Calvin's doctrine of double predestination. English scholars took up the same issues, and disagreed loudly. Peter Baro and Laurence Chaderton disturbed Cambridge with their debates in the 1580s, while their colleague William Perkins attempted to schematize the operation of predestination in his *The Golden Chain* of 1590. Approaching the problem under the influence of Ramist philosophy, Perkins executed a precise act of 'Reformed scholasticism', subdividing the decrees of election and reprobation into a series of 'degrees'. Out of his analysis emerges a supralapsarian theology that makes it plain that our destinies are decreed by God before our births. Even babies might die reprobate, 'for the guilt of original and natural sin being left in God's secret judgement unto themselves' they die 'rejected of God' forever.[28] The most notable results of these debates and Perkins's arguments were the Lambeth Articles of 1595. Unapologetically predestinarian, the Lambeth Articles were considered to provide the definition of the seventeenth of the Thirty-nine Articles.

It was a definition that provoked bitter debate in the English church. Many English Christians remained uncomfortable with the immutable

---

[26] CCCC, MS 121, pp. 146–7.

[27] David Cressy and Lori Anne Ferrell, 'The Thirty-nine Articles, 1563', in D. Cressy and L. A. Ferrell (eds), *Religion and Society in Early Modern England* (London, 1996), pp. 63–4, 59.

[28] William Perkins, 'The Golden Chain' in D. Cressy and L. A. Ferrell (eds), *Religion and Society in Early Modern England* (London, 1996), p. 117.

decrees of predestination, leaning toward the rejection of supralapsarian predestination embodied by Jacobus Arminius. They preferred to believe that God had made our salvation contingent in some way on our choice, not simply upon the absolute, immutable decree of God before Adam met Eve in the Garden of Eden.

The battles that followed convulsed the English church, and historians tend to replicate them. Seán Hughes's discussion in Chapter 10 attempts to see through the smoke of seventeenth-century battles over predestination to discern what English Protestants really believed about this crucial dogma in the Elizabethan era. This is a healthy enterprise, reminding us that not all English theologians could be associated with Calvin's doctrine of predestination. Indeed, as Collinson has observed, 'The student who has only heard of "calvinism" must learn that English theologians were as likely to lean on Bullinger of Zurich, Musculus of Berne, or Peter Martyr as on Calvin and Beza.'[29] At the same time, Calvin was clearly the most read continental theologian in England in the later sixteenth century. His works went through 93 editions in English between 1559 and 1603, far outstripping Perkins's 68, Luther's 22 and Erasmus's 11 editions.[30] There was, as Nicholas Tyacke has observed, a 'Calvinist consensus' in England.[31]

Perhaps the proof of this consensus is that at the same time the Lambeth Articles were being defined, a delightful four-book attack on English Protestantism was written by William Reynolds, an English Catholic exile. His understanding of the theological position of his old colleagues is summed up by his title: *Calvino-Turcismus, id est, Calvinisticae Perfidiae, cum Mahumetana Collatio, et dilucida utriusque sectae confutatio.* Naturally Matthew Sutcliffe threw it back in his teeth with his *De Turcopapismo.*[32] In both cases, the argument was made that Antichrist is known by his works, and his works are identical in Islam and heretical Christianity.

This exercise in comparative discipline reminds us that the models of manners that mark theological debates and political uproars in

---

[29] Patrick Collinson, 'England and International Calvinism, 1558–1640', in Menna Prestwich (ed.), *International Calvinism, 1541–1715* (Oxford, 1985), p. 214.

[30] Andrew Pettegree, 'The Reception of Calvinism in England', in Wilhelm H. Neusner and Brian G. Armstrong (eds), *Calvinus Sincerioris Religionis Vindex* (Sixteenth Century Essays and Studies, 26, 1997), p. 282.

[31] Nicholas Tyacke, *Anti-Calvinists: The Rise of English Arminianism* (London, 1990).

[32] Thomas Reynolds, *Calvino-Turcismus, id est, Calvinisticae Perfidiae, cum Mahumetana Collatio, et dilucida utriusque sectae confutatio*, ed. William Gifford (Cologne, 1597); Matthew Sutcliffe, *De Turcopapismo, Hoc est, De Turcarum & Papistarum adversus Christi ecclesiam & fidem coniuratione, eorumque in religione & moribus consensione & similitudine ...* , STC 23460 (1599).

Elizabethan England are not, at their hearts, Calvinist in predestinary terms, though many credited their positions to Calvin. Andrew Pettegree concurs with Lake and Kendall that one could be a 'credal' Calvinist, using Calvin's theory of predestination without attempting to create a Christian community based upon it. Only 'experimental' Calvinists used double predestination as impetus for the creation of a godly community.[33]

Given the conflicting senses in which Calvin was deployed by an English church which was, in Collinson's phrase, anchored in 'the outer roads of the broad harbor of the Calvinist or (better) Reformed tradition', Hughes's argument that it is improper to assume that English theology on predestination was simply 'Calvinist' is important.[34] It is equally important to realize that there was no such thing as 'pure' Calvinism anywhere. The Dutch, the Scots, and even the Genevoises could not be said to practise pure Calvinism. (Naturally, Jean Calvin did not practise it either.)[35]

It might be argued that the reason it is difficult to classify the theology of the late Elizabethan churchmen is their failure to identify themselves clearly. They force us to use terms like 'Puritan' with shocking imprecision. If, as Alex Walsham argues in Chapter 8 of this volume, a man so intemperately puritanical as Philip Stubbes is only 'sometimes a kind of Puritan', our attempts at definition by theological party are probably doomed to fail. But not if we are dealing with Quakers. Unlike their forefathers, the people who followed George Fox acquired an identity very quickly in the 1650s. Kate Peters, in Chapter 11, finds them appropriating and proudly using the nickname 'Quaker' almost instantly. It gave them recognition, and a self-conscious cohesion, that many other movements lacked. Quakers were delighted to set themselves apart from the profane and ungodly who refused to recognize their inner lights.

Most religious sects failed to do this, providing historians ample opportunity for disagreement. Sometimes groups like the Ranters are dismissed as the creations of overheated minds, since no one can be found who admitted to being a Ranter. At other times the failure of individuals to appropriate titles in a consistent way means that the names in use for them only cause confusion, as 'Puritan' does.

As Patrick Collinson has taught us, it is very dangerous to think of religious history apart from the people who attempted to live the religion. The impossibility of putting people into specimen jars and affixing

---

[33] Pettegree, 'Reception', p. 283.
[34] Collinson, 'International Calvinism', p. 215.
[35] Pettegree, 'Reception', pp. 268–9.

labels is obvious when we look at the cases of Philip Stubbes and Laurence Chaderton.

The prima-facie case for Stubbes's Puritanism is made by his great diatribe, *The Anatomie of Abuses: contayning A Discoverie, or Brief Summarie of such Notable Vices and Imperfections, as now raigne in may Christian Countreyes of the Worlde: but (especiallie) in a verie famous Ilande called AILGNA: Together, with most fearfull Examples of Gods Iudgementes, executed upon the wicked for the same, aswell in AILGNA of late, as in other places, elsewhere. Verie Godly, to be read of all true Christians, everie where: but most needefull, to be regarded in Englande.* Expressly written to move England to repentance, its audience is very clearly the wicked. Stubbes knew the 'Godly' would help him overcome the 'maligne stomaches' of the wicked and perverse whose backs would be galled by his writing, and who would turn on him, disgorging their stomachs and biting him like rabid dogs. But he took the risk of writing because 'reformation of manners and amendment of life' – the suppression of pride – was never more needed.[36] Reformation was necessary, and Stubbes had the duty to prescribe the purgative that would cause it, for, as his own character says in the book, 'I will assay to do them good ... in discovering their abuses, and laying open their enormities, that they ... may in time seek to the true physician and expert surgeon of their souls Christ Jesus ... .'[37] If they do that, they will avoid the vanities of this world, cease wallowing in its pleasures and delights, and live forever in the Kingdom of Heaven.[38]

What follows is the most quotable catalogue of sin in the English language. Page after page, chapter after chapter, the horrors unfold in exquisite detail. But Alex Walsham asks if he really meant it. Is he the model of a Puritan? Or is he a man who understood his market and wrote a book that played to it? The complicated answer suggests he was both a stern moralist and a shrewd writer who could adopt and adapt traditional moral complaints to his audience's expectations. Moreover, he is a transitional figure, writing what amounted to updated and reformed hagiographical and moral pieces in the medieval tradition. Like John Foxe writing a calendar of martyrs to replace the calendar of saints, Stubbes created a modern moral polemic that owed much to earlier traditions. Even a committed reformer could not simply abandon the traditions of moral exhortation and piety in which he and his contemporaries were raised. Perhaps he was a Puritan (whatever that

---

[36] Philip Stubbes, 'The Epistle Dedicatorie' in P. Stubbes, *The Anatomie of Abuses*, STC 23376 (London, 1583).

[37] Stubbes, 'The Epistle Dedicatorie', sig. B.iiii verso.

[38] Stubbes, 'The Epistle Dedicatorie', sig. R.i.

means) but he was also a literary man writing for income and interacting with his profession.

Laurence Chaderton is another person who has been judged too simply. If Stubbes might be less a Puritan than usually assumed, Chaderton turns out to have been less a moderate than he appeared at the Hampton Court Conference. This ambiguity bred a confusion that encouraged squabbles over predestination in the late sixteenth century, as Arnold Hunt demonstrates. By the time the Conference took up the demands of the Millenary Petition for relief from the burden of human rites and ceremonies in 1604, he had been Master of Pembroke College, Cambridge for 20 years. The son of Catholic parents, he came of age in the troubled 1550s, converted to Protestantism while at Cambridge, holding a fellowship there until his death at 104 in 1640. When he went to Hampton Court he was 68 years old, the acknowledged conscience of the reformed party in England and a strong advocate for working within the system. Though he never wrote much, he was deeply respected in his era. None the less, he came back from the Hampton Court Conference tarred with the brush of moderation in such a way that made it hard for the younger, more radical folk to respect his position on obedience to the prince over conscience. Chaderton chose conformity after Hampton Court; his loudest critics chose separatism.

Choosing continued conformity, he had theological qualms, but he had conformed his entire adult life. He had promoted and led the Elizabethan reformers in their fights for Presbyterian ecclesiology and against papist surplices and signs, but he was of the generation that created the Elizabethan Settlement. Near the same age as Elizabeth herself, he came from a different time experientially than the younger folk. In his approach to reform he was equally committed, but he did not push his conscience beyond obedience to the Crown. When it became clear that James I would not further reform the Church, expecting instead greater conformity, the younger men denounced Chaderton, and the other three spokesmen at Hampton Court, as cats' paws of the prelates, stage players in the King's play, and, as was said of Chaderton, 'mute fish'.[39]

Chaderton's annotations show that he was well aware of the issues facing the Conference, and that he was walking a crafty, fine line between those who demanded conformity and those who took the more radical Puritan side. Thus to dismiss him as simply a moderate is too vague, too dependent on one historical episode. He was still living an

---

[39] Patrick Collinson, *The Elizabethan Puritan Movement* (Oxford, 1967; repr. 1991), pp. 458; 462–3.

earlier, Elizabethan, version of Protestantism that no longer conformed to the nonconformist trends among his younger brethren.

The complex, real lives of Stubbes and Chaderton take us back to Patrick Collinson's vision of religious history. For him religion is a lived experience that cannot be put neatly into labelled boxes. In the great range of his writings he has consistently paid attention to the human as well as the theological elements, and he has tempered his historical judgement with his sense of humanity's frailties and predilections. The problem of ideological definition that besets the study of those known as 'Puritans' has been in large part overcome by his insistence on seeing the people behind the ideas. Collinson has made us aware that early modern religion was experienced, and that ideas had profound meaning in the context of real peoples' lives. His students have learned this, and this volume testifies to his influence.

Once I climbed an island in the Cook Straight of New Zealand with Patrick, his wife Liz, and Glyn Parry. A bird sanctuary, the island is home to some of the rarest birds in the world, and we met most of the denizens. One parrot perched on the head of the Regius Professor of Modern History in the University of Cambridge. There Collinson stood, parrot capped and grinning. It is the same expression with which he greets the emerging lives of religious men and women in early modern England: happy tolerance mingling with delight.

CHAPTER ONE

Parishioners in court: litigation and the local community, 1350–1650[1]

Beat Kümin

The respective merits and pitfalls of the concept of 'community' continue to divide the historical profession. A quick search through library catalogues confirms its continuing popularity with students of all subjects and periods, but also the fear of a growing number of critics that it has become far too amorphous to convey any distinctive meaning.[2] A particular cause for concern seems to be the frequent association of 'community' with 'social harmony' and the suggestion of a broad ideological consensus. Scholars of the late medieval English parish, praising it as a 'means to lift people up',[3] as a focus for 'corporate' worship and a platform for many other unifying rituals, are singled out as prime culprits of such misrepresentations.[4] The concept of 'communalism', highlighted by Patrick Collinson as a potential tool in the quest for a 'new' social history,[5] has also been accused of downplaying oligarchical trends and inner tensions in central European towns and villages.[6] Far from getting

---

[1] I am grateful to John Craig, Katherine French and Neil Jones for their help with various aspects of this chapter.

[2] A random list of examples could include Ben Witherington, *Conflict and Community in Corinth: A Socio-Rhetorical Commentary on 1 and 2 Corinthians* (Grand Rapids, MI, 1995), Edgar Samuel, *The Portuguese Jewish Community in London, 1656–1830* (London, 1992), Marjorie Procter-Smith, *Women in Shaker Community and Worship: a Feminist Analysis of the Uses of Religious Symbolism* (Lewiston, ME, 1985); for a critical assessment of the term's proliferation see Christine Carpenter, 'Gentry and Community in Medieval England', *JBS*, 33 (1994), p. 340.

[3] Augustus Jessopp, 'Parish Life in England before the Great Pillage', *Nineteenth Century*, 43 (1898), p. 47.

[4] See for example Lawrence Stone's review of Eamon Duffy, *The Stripping of the Altars: Traditional Religion in England 1400–1580* (New Haven, CT, and London, 1992) in the *Guardian* (26 January 1993), p. 7.

[5] Peter Blickle, 'Kommunalismus: Begriffsbildung in heuristischer Absicht', in P. Blickle (ed.), *Landgemeinde und Stadtgemeinde in Mitteleuropa* (Munich, 1991), pp. 5–38; Patrick Collinson, *De Republica Anglorum; or, Social History with the Politics Put Back* (Cambridge, 1990), p. 16.

[6] André Holenstein, Beat Kümin and Andreas Würgler, 'Diskussionsbericht', in P. Blickle (ed.), *Landgemeinde und Stadtgemeinde in Mitteleuropa* (Munich, 1991), p. 490.

on with each other, peasants and burghers are said to have been constantly at loggerheads with each other, using even the most sacred religious rituals to enhance their positions.[7] Early modern people, we are reminded, were a litigious lot, whose daily life should not be idealized.[8]

The plentiful evidence for conflict in the English parish seems to substantiate this point. It would be difficult to see the behaviour of Alan Bugules, who threatened to kill the late fourteenth-century parson of St Just in Cornwall 'deuaunt toutz le ditz parochiens', as anything else but an indication of deeply strained local relations. An equally unpleasant character must have been Richard Ricard of Kennington in Kent. Described as 'a man of eville rewle and maliciows', he stood accused of a startling combination of murder, adultery, heresy, drunken debauchery and harassment. The testimony of his neighbours at a visitation in 1511 bears witness to a genuinely shocked and intimidated community.[9] In the course of the same century, more or less widespread anticlerical feelings (the intensity, of course, remaining a bone of contention) surfaced in many a *cause célèbre*, while incidents such as the stealing of the Host in London's St Botolph Aldersgate parish in 1532 do not seem to support the idea of a religious consensus either. Historians of nonconformity would probably extend the same verdict over the whole of our period.[10]

Conflict, furthermore, easily led to legal proceedings and the interference of external authorities. There is plenty of evidence for resentment of courts in general and lawyers in particular. When the Levellers called for the abolition of central jurisdiction and the passing of 'Judgements, or Convictions of life, limb, liberty, or estate, ... only by twelve sworn

---

[7] Corpus Christi processions are a famous example: Miri Rubin, *Corpus Christi: the Eucharist in Late Medieval Culture* (Oxford, 1991), ch. 4, and esp. pp. 266–70; cf. the struggles for precedence in parish rituals such as kissing the pax/sharing the holy bread, discussed in John Craig, 'Reformation, politics and polemics in sixteenth-century East Anglian market towns' (PhD, Cambridge, 1992), p. 138, and Caroline Litzenberger, *The English Reformation and the Laity: Gloucestershire 1540–80* (Cambridge, 1997), pp. 35, 39–40, 64–6, 101; and those about pews and seating: Margaret Aston, 'Segregation in church', in William Sheils and Diana Wood (eds), *Women in the Church* (SCH, 27, 1990), esp. pp. 250–54, 265–6.

[8] J. A. Sharpe, 'Enforcing the Law in the Seventeenth-Century English Village', in Victor Gattrell, Bruce Lenman and Geoffrey Parker (eds), *Crime and the Law: the Social History of Crime in Western Europe since 1500* (London, 1980), p. 102.

[9] William Baildon (ed.), *Select Cases in Chancery 1364–1471* (London, 1896), pp. 23–5; Katherine Wood-Legh (ed.), *Kentish Visitations of Archbishop Warham and his Deputies 1511–12* (Maidstone, 1984), pp. 203–5.

[10] Susan Brigden, 'Tithe Controversy in Reformation London', *JEH*, 32 (1981), pp. 285–301, and her *London and the Reformation* (Oxford, 1989), p. 18 (St Botolph); Margaret Aston, *Faith and Fire: Popular and Unpopular Religion 1350–1550* (London, 1993); Margaret Spufford (ed.), *The World of Rural Dissenters 1520–1725* (Cambridge, 1995).

men of the Neighbour-hood', they expressed a commonly held antipathy against professional judges and unintelligible Law French proceedings.[11] The title of William Cole's pamphlet *A rod for the lawyers: who are hereby declared to be the grand robbers and deceivers of the nation* (1659) also speaks for itself. There had always been a degree of outside supervision,[12] but the strength of feeling in the early modern period owed much to the 'increase of governance' by local justices of the peace and the growing degree of religious and moral regulation in Tudor and early Stuart England.[13] At the height of the Protestant Reformation under Edward VI, for instance, parishes saw up to 15 per cent of their annual expenditure absorbed by episcopal or royal visitations and other legal proceedings,[14] while social historians observe a parallel 'transition away from a local court system geared essentially to facilitating the settlement of interpersonal disputes to one which emphasized the control of the richer over the poorer villagers and which, ultimately, demonstrated the penetration of the state into the parish'. Strenuous efforts had to be made to prevent a total erosion of local autonomy.[15]

This chapter, however, proposes to examine the relationship between 'community' and 'conflict' from another perspective. It will not venture into anthropological or psychological territory, but will attempt to reassess the evidence for litigation in the English parish with an eye to its potential to *serve* parochial interests and strengthen the bonds between members. This is in line with a growing awareness among English and

---

[11] Art. XXV of John Lilburne et al. 'An Agreement of the Free People of England' (1649), in William Haller and Godfrey Davies (eds), *The Leveller Tracts 1647–53* (Gloucester, MA, 1964), pp. 326–7; cf. Christopher Hill, 'The Norman Yoke', in his *Puritanism and Revolution* (London, 1958), pp. 77–8, and Christopher Brooks, *Pettyfoggers and Vipers of the Commonwealth: the 'Lower Branch' of the Legal Profession in Early Modern England* (Cambridge, 1986).

[12] The Yatton churchwardens, for instance, paid a fine of 2s. 4d. to the manor court well before 1500: Taunton, Somerset Record Office, CWA of Yatton: D/P/yat/4/1/1, 1482–83.

[13] Anthony Fletcher, *Reform in the Provinces: the Government of Stuart England* (New Haven, CT, 1986), quote from heading to ch. 4; ecclesiastical authorities, too, were now 'able to oversee parochial life more thoroughly than had hitherto been possible': Martin Ingram, *Church Courts, Sex and Marriage in England 1570–1640* (Cambridge, 1987), p. 329.

[14] Beat Kümin, *The Shaping of a Community: the Rise and Reformation of the English Parish c. 1400–1560* (Aldershot, 1996), appendix 3; the Laudian years provide an equally striking example: Andrew Foster, 'Church Policies of the 1630s', in Richard Cust and Ann Hughes (eds), *Conflict in Early Stuart England* (London, 1989), pp. 193–223.

[15] Quote from James Sharpe, *Crime in Early Modern England 1550–1750* (London, 1984), p. 93; for popular strategies of containment see Beat Kümin, 'The Fear of Intrusion: Communal Resilience in Early Modern England', in William Naphy and Penny Roberts (eds), *Fear in Early Modern Society* (Manchester, 1997), pp. 118–36.

continental historians that early modern state-building was not only the result of aggressive central initiative, but also of popular encouragement of state involvement, at least in certain areas, and a widespread acknowledgement that stronger legal and administrative bodies could be a resource as well as a threat for the local community.[16] I hope to illustrate this 'positive' connotation of 'parishioners in court' by means of a broad survey of the evidence, written from a historical rather than a legal perspective. The chapter cannot endeavour to discuss procedural details or the merits of each individual case, not least because of the fact that sentences and other supporting documents have often been lost. The structure of the argument is thematic rather than chronological, partly to avoid repetition, but also to emphasize structural continuities before and after the English Reformations. After a brief sketch of the wide variety of courts and judges involved (in section I), we will look in turn at how such cases could help to (section II) define and (section III) defend the local community. Section IV will then offer some conclusions.

I

Europe's *ancien régime* offered two distinctive types of jurisdiction. At the lowest *ecclesiastical* level the parochial incumbent dealt with a range of disciplinary matters,[17] while his superiors heard cases at visitations, in a large number of archidiaconal, episcopal or provincial courts, and, up to the Reformation, even in the Roman curia.[18] More surprising, perhaps, are the countless points of contact between parishioners and *secular* jurisdiction, starting with that of the local lords.[19] In the court leet of Prescot in Lancashire, to take one random example, ecclesiastical matters appear with some regularity, not least because 13 of

---

[16] M. Braddick, 'State Formation and Social Change in Early Modern England', *Social History*, 16 (1991), pp. 1–17; Joan Kent, 'The Centre and the Localities: State Formation and Parish Government in England, c. 1640–1740', *HJ*, 38 (1995), pp. 363–404; Peter Blickle, 'Einführung: Mit Gemeinden Staat machen', in P. Bickle (ed.), *Gemeinde und Staat im Alten Europa* (Munich, 1998), pp. 1–20.

[17] The priest's disciplinary tools ranged from hearing confessions, ordering penance and making presentments at visitations to pronouncing sentences of excommunication: for the extent of his *jurisdictio* see Rosi Fuhrmann, 'Die Kirche im Dorf', in Peter Blickle (ed.), *Zugänge zur bäuerlichen Reformation* (Zurich, 1987), pp. 149–50.

[18] See the institutional surveys in Ralph Houlbrooke, *Church Courts and the People During the English Reformation 1520–70* (Oxford, 1979) and Ingram, *Church Courts*.

[19] As early as 1275, the attorney of the township of Graveley sued a mason in the court of the abbot of Ramsey in the fair of St Ives, which ordered him to rebuild a deficient wall in Graveley church: Frederic William Maitland (ed.), *Select Pleas in Manorial Courts* (London, 1888), p. 150.

the 30 churchwardens between 1523 and 1555 also held some form of manorial office.[20] As a first indication of the 'positive' potential of legal proceedings, offences against all sorts of agricultural regulations could benefit parishes in a straightforward, financial fashion. Examples for the allocation of fines to church repairs include a case from Littleport in 1325, where Henry Sweetgroom was presented for illegitimate mowing in the fens and ordered to pay 32d. in equal portions to the lord and 'to the men of the vill for the repair of the church', and one from Tintinhull (Somerset), where the churchwardens recorded the receipt of 3s. 4d. in 1436 from tenants who had trespassed on the marsh.[21] Royal jurisdiction, to move to the higher levels, offered proceedings before the justices of the peace, the Westminster common law courts of Common Pleas and King's Bench, as well as, from the late Middle Ages, the equity jurisdiction in Chancery, Star Chamber and the Court of Requests.[22]

Even a superficial glance at local records will reveal how frequently parishioners appeared in all of these forums. The quantitative analysis of a sample of ten sets of churchwardens' accounts suggests that between 1 and 6 per cent of total expenditure was earmarked for the purpose.[23] The records of All Saints, Bristol, for instance, contain a great variety of individual items, from modest fees for writing or sealing a deed to massive investments in lawsuits filed in the capital. The official of the ecclesiastical court quite literally 'sat' in its parish church on several occasions;[24] a suit against Roger Acton, knight, in the late 1430s involved the appointment of a man called Thornton 'to be our attorney in London'; the attempt of Thomas Fyler to contest his mother's bequest of a house in the High Street triggered legal action in 1467–68; the case between Richard Haddon and the church cost over £2 in 1473–74; while expenses for going to the 'chancellor' appear in the

---

[20] Francis Bailey (ed.), *A Selection from the Prescot Court Leet and Other Records 1447–1600* (Preston, 1937), pp. 96, 117, 131; cf. Warren Ault, 'The Village Church and the Village Community in Medieval England', *Speculum*, 45 (1970), p. 211.

[21] Frederic William Maitland and William Baildon (eds), *The Court Baron, Being Precedents for Use in Seignorial and Other Local Courts* (London, 1891), pp. 145–6; many more examples, incl. Tintinhull, in Warren Ault, 'Manor Court and Parish Church in Fifteenth-Century England', *Speculum*, 42 (1967), pp. 53–64; ecclesiastical judges occasionally imposed a similar splitting of fines: F. Ragg (ed.), 'Fragment of Folio MS of Archdeaconry Courts of Buckinghamshire, 1491–95', *Records of Buckinghamshire*, 11 (1920–26), pp. 63, 71 (concerning the breach of an arbitration arrangement and a defamation suit).

[22] John Baker, *An Introduction to English Legal History* (3rd edn, London, 1990); Richard Jackson, *The Machinery of Justice in England* (7th edn, Cambridge, 1977), pp. 1 ff.

[23] Category 'legal costs' in Kümin, *Shaping of a Community*, appendix 3.

[24] See for example Bristol Record Office, CWA of All Saints: P/AS/ChW/3a, 1533–34.

1520s.[25] The many such payments made at Ashburton (Devon) include a fee of 6s. 8d. paid to Master Baldwin Malet, armiger, for his 'advice' about the parish's claim on a number of disputed lands,[26] and the rural community of Yatton (Somerset) recorded its first legal expenses almost as soon as the accounts open.[27] The same source mentions a lengthy 'privy session suit' against a Mr Gybbys about the possession of church goods in 1499–1502, a journey to Bristol to secure 'Baker's lands' in 1521–22, the withdrawing of a Consistory Court case in 1536–37, and Queen's Bench proceedings in 1585–86. The London parish of St Botolph Aldersgate, in turn, prosecuted its 'estate agent' Gilbert Allenson for irregularities connected to the purchase of new properties in Blackhorse Alley, footed massive expenses claims of its wardens in 1552–53 'at suche tyme as they were arested' (including costs for 'copies of enditements, their attornayes & counsaylors fees') and may be excused for employing its own 'parish solicitor' by 1649.[28]

Around 1400, ecclesiastical judges were clearly the most frequent points of reference for a parish's legal activities, reflecting its core canonical and religious duties, but gradually, as the amount of landed property and local government emphasis increased, quarter sessions and equity courts absorbed an ever greater share.[29] But who acted for the community? While lay representatives are simply referred to as *fidedigni* at the time of the earliest visitation evidence in the thirteenth century, churchwardens normally played a very conspicuous part by the fifteenth. Sometimes they acted alone, on other occasions in conjunction with specially selected sidesmen or *viri probi*.[30] In late medieval

---

[25] Clive Burgess (ed.), *The Pre-Reformation Records of All Saints, Bristol. Part I: the Church Book* (Bristol, 1995), MS pp. 488, 547, 562; CWA of All Saints, 1520–21, 1528–29.

[26] Alison Hanham (ed.), *CWA of Ashburton 1479–1580* (Torquay, 1970), for example 1525–26.

[27] CWA of Yatton, 1450–51, 1453–54 (3s. 9d. for a suit at Wells; the earliest accounts date from 1445).

[28] GL, CWA St Botolph Aldersgate: MS 1454, 1516–17; GL, Vestry Minutes of St Botolph Aldersgate: MS 1453/1, f. 52r (a Mr Herne).

[29] See for example the Great St Mary's wardens' complaint 'this day made in open sessions' at the Cambridge Quarter Sessions: Cambridgeshire County Record Office, Audit Book of the Parish of Great St Mary's: P30/4/2, 15 July 1645, and Kent, 'Centre and Localities', *passim*.

[30] Similarly, in early cases concerning oblations, tithes, fabric repairs and ornaments before the provincial court of Canterbury, 'one or two of the parishioners', who may or may not have been the current churchwardens, 'sued for the rest or served as proctors for the group': Norma Adams and Charles Donahue (eds), *Select Cases from the Ecclesiastical Courts of the Province of Canterbury* (London, 1981), p. 79; cf. Wood-Legh (ed.), *Kentish Visitations*, p. xxi ('it seems that the churchwardens had not always been questioned at the visitation').

county courts, local communities tended to be represented by unspeci-
fied *iurati*, but it is clear that the regular parish officers could also be
present. In line with their growing statutory responsibilities, however,
wardens, overseers and constables became more and more prominent in
the course of the early modern period.[31] The evidence from churchwardens' accounts suggests that parishes were liable for costs of both
successful and unsuccessful actions initiated by wardens on their behalf,
but some made it explicit: should any legal expenses arise out of a
recent Poor Law dispute, to cite a decision of the vestry of Great St
Mary's, Cambridge, on 14 December 1641, they would have to be
borne by the common purse, with the same assurance repeated for the
wardens of 1646, 'the said officers first acquainting the Parish with
such suites that at any time shalbe commensed against them'.[32]

II

But how can we bolster the claim that there was a positive side to all
this litigation? For a start, court action played an important part in the
territorial definition of the community, particularly in the frequent attempts by localities to adjust the ecclesiastical network. Occasionally,
insufficient resources prompted calls for a union of parishes,[33] but more
often chapels initiated formal canonical proceedings to separate from
their mother church, almost invariably arguing that the distance and
difficult access from their hamlets posed serious problems for their cure
of souls.[34] Many a case, however, reveals strong local identity as an
equally important motive: the Vicar of Barton Stacey in the diocese of
Winchester protested that the inhabitants of Newton, a township of just
nine households, expected him to celebrate regularly in their own chapel,
even though it was only one Italian mile from the parish church and he
could see no reason that prevented them from coming thither.[35]

Social historians tend to agree that formal litigation in higher courts
allows us to see but the tip of the iceberg, as most conflict management

---

[31] Jeremiah Post, 'Jury Lists and Juries in the Late Fourteenth Century', in James
Cockburn and Thomas Green (eds), *Twelve Good Men and True* (Princeton, 1988), p.
68; Fletcher, *Reform in the Provinces*, pp. 127–30.

[32] Audit Book St Mary's, pp. 45, 74; 'wee will beare and pay ... the charges ... against
all opposers whatsoever': Edward Tomlinson (ed.), *A History of the Minories, London*
(London, 1907), p. 235 (1692).

[33] GL, Register William Gray, Bishop of London: MS 9531/5, fos 66v-7 (St Augustine
Pappay and All Hallows on the Wall).

[34] Examples discussed in Kümin, *Shaping of a Community*, pp. 175–8.

[35] J. Twemlow (ed.), *Calendar of Papal Letters* (London, 1912), vol. 9, p. 335 (1443).

took place informally and locally, with appeals to external authority considered only as a last resort.[36] It is clear that the English parish subscribed to the same principle, offering a number of options to resolve conflicts internally. Perhaps the most striking example is the London peculiar of Holy Trinity Minories, to which Patrick Collinson has repeatedly drawn our attention.[37] Described quite rightly as 'a miniature kingdom of its own', whose extraordinary liberties made the parson and inhabitants exempt from nearly all outside interference, it sturdily opposed attempts by the bishop to visit or the county to tax it. Most attention has been paid to its nonconformist credentials, but the fact that parishioners reserved the right to approve the execution of writs within their precinct, encouraged the practice of clandestine marriages and confidently asserted that 'nothing of publick business of ye pariss be done but according to antient and Customary ways of publick vestry summoned by the Churchwardens' reveals just how much informal 'jurisdiction' rested in the hands of the local population.[38] Most parishes had more limited powers, of course, but the right to try and fine certain offenders seems ubiquitous: St Botolph Aldersgate imposed penalties on those who failed to attend its annual audit; it held a clerk accountable for the costs of a mass chalice 'by hys neclygenes lost'; and it decided that a gentleman and former warden was 'to be called & to be chardged & annswerable' for an unauthorized sale of parish goods.[39] The Waterford borough customs empowered parish 'procuratours' to take action in certain church matters,[40] while arbitration facilities – documented for instance for St Dunstan, Canterbury, or St Mary Magdalen Milk Street in London – must have existed nearly everywhere.[41] Such 'legal' activities

---

[36] Bernard McLane, 'Jury Attitudes Towards Local Disorder', in Cockburn and Green (eds), *Twelve Good Men*, p. 64; Keith Wrightson, 'Two Concepts of Order', in John Brewer and John Styles (eds), *An Ungovernable People* (London, 1980), p. 30; and Sharpe, 'Enforcing the Law', p. 107.

[37] Patrick Collinson, 'London's Protestant underworld', in P. Collinson, *The Elizabethan Puritan Movement* (London, 1967), pp. 84–91; Patrick Collinson, *The Religion of Protestants* (Oxford, 1982), p. 142.

[38] Tomlinson (ed.), *Minories*, pp. 165, 239 (quotes), 175, 226–39; cf. H. Gareth Owen, 'A Nursery of Elizabethan Nonconformity 1567–72', *JEH*, 17 (1966), pp. 65–76. For the determination of the Gloucester parish of St Michael's to minimize the intrusion of outside officials see Litzenberger, *Gloucestershire*, pp. 13–16.

[39] CWA Botolph, 1486–87, 1510–11, 1551–52; in 1567–68 the wardens were fined 3s. 4d. for disbursing money over and above their spending ceiling.

[40] Mary Bateson (ed.), *Borough Customs* (London, 1906), vol. 2, p. 63 (1485–86).

[41] Examples from Herbert Maynard Smith, *Pre-Reformation England* (London, 1963), p. 124, and Ian Archer, *The Pursuit of Stability: Social Relations in Elizabethan London* (Cambridge, 1991), p. 80; for the ubiquity of arbitration panels cf. Fletcher, *Reform in the Provinces*, p. 67.

boosted the powers of parochial institutions and thus the strength of communal ties. In addition, municipal officers, as at York or Newcastle under Lyme, gradually acquired extensive control over many ecclesiastical benefices within their walls, regulating the life and morals of priests, fining offenders and assuming jurisdiction in cases which were clearly of a spiritual nature.[42]

The growth of parish resources and responsibilities soon stretched the potential of such internal conflict management. 'Going to law' became inevitable in ever more cases, but even this could strengthen the community. The need for written evidence, as it turned out, encouraged better record-keeping and storage; parishes were now acutely aware of how important it was to have constant and open access to their collective 'memory'.[43] The skilful exploration of all the available legal options, furthermore, helped to overcome the delicate status of parish communities and officers in common law courts.[44] The fundamental right to make levies and by-laws was upheld as early as 1370,[45] but the position with regard to property-holding was rather less favourable. Common lawyers distinguished sharply between incorporated bodies such as 'the dean and chapter' of a cathedral or 'the mayor and burgesses' of a borough (which needed the State to 'breathe life into [their] nostrils') and informal aggregates of people.[46] As one of the latter, the parish was allowed to hold goods, but not lands, and while churchwardens could act as custodians for ornaments, bells and other movables,[47] they lacked any legal capacity when it came to accepting or

---

[42] Katherine Wood-Legh, *Perpetual Chantries in Britain* (Cambridge, 1965), pp. 169, 179; Thomas Pape, *Newcastle-under-Lyme in Tudor and early Stuart Times* (Manchester, 1938), pp. 18 ff.

[43] A property dispute in 1469 seems to have prompted the parishioners of All Saints, Bristol, to keep better records and to store them more safely: Burgess (ed.), *Pre-Reformation Records*, p. xviii; for West Country examples of litigation over control of parish records see Katherine French, 'Local Identity and the Late Medieval Parish: the Communities of Bath and Wells' (PhD, Minnesota, 1993), pp. 237–40.

[44] For what follows see above all the Year Books evidence, containing – in Law French – reports on the discussions of judges and counsel in particular common law cases. Unless otherwise indicated, cases cited below can be found in *Les Reports des Cases en Ley: Edward II – 27 Henry VIII* (11 parts, London, 1678–80), and *English Reports* (London, 1900). A useful compilation also in Sir Edmund Coke, *First Part of the Institutes of the Laws of England* (London, 1670), esp. lib. I, cap. I, sect. I, f. 3a, c.

[45] 44 Edward III, fos 18–19.

[46] Frederick Pollock and Frederic William Maitland, *The History of English Law Before the Time of Edward I* (2nd edn, Cambridge, 1968), vol. 1, p. 490 and Frederic William Maitland, 'Introduction' to Otto von Gierke, *Political Theories of the Middle Age* (Cambridge, 1906), p. xxx (quote).

[47] William Lambarde, *The Dueties of Constables* (London, 1602), pp. 57–8, defines wardens as 'persons inabled ... to take moveable goods, or cattels, and to sue, and be

defending gifts of immovable property.[48] Bequests of lands and tenements, however, kept pouring in and parishes were thus forced to look
for alternative ways to secure control over such resources. The solution
was found in a kind of trust, enfeoffment to use, in which local notables
held the lands on behalf of the unincorporated community. The essential advantage lay in the fact that the emerging equity courts, Chancery
in particular,[49] protected such arrangements and that, as 'non-supersti-
tious', charitable endowments, many enfeoffed holdings even survived
the Reformation confiscations. This newly found ability to hold land as
a quasi-corporate body (and the readiness to defend the property at
law) was to have an invaluable share in the consolidation and expansion of the English parish.[50] Two examples may illustrate the practice.
In a case tried by the commissary of the abbot of Whalley in 1532, the
property of Thomas Varley of Pendle was vested in feoffees for the use
of the fabric and liturgical wherewithals of a new chapel dedicated to
the Blessed Virgin.[51] Not all trustees acted impeccably, but they, too,
could be held to account in Chancery: those of John Ferrour, for
instance, who had failed to respect instructions regarding lands and
tenements bequeathed to the church of Stanwell in Middlesex, were
sued by the churchwardens in the mid-fifteenth century.[52]

---

sued at Law, concerning such goods for the use and benefit of their parish'. 'Cest
communement use en cest place, que tiels Gardeins porteront appeales de tiels biens del
Esglise prises, & c.': 11 Henry IV, f. 12; 8 Edward IV, f. 6.

[48] 'Si terr soit done *Parochianis talis Ecclesiae* ad *inveniendum unum Presbiterum vel
huiusmodi, &c.* le done ne vault riens, p[ar]c[e]q[ue] il n'ad ascun chose corporate, q[ue]
puit prender estate': 10 Henry IV, f. 3b. In the city of London, however, parishes were
formally allowed to hold lands: Edmund Gibson (ed.), *Codex iuris ecclesiastici Anglicani*
(2nd edn, Oxford, 1761), pp. 215–16.

[49] The giving of land to unincorporate bodies 'was not a difficulty that troubled the
chancellor': J. L. Barton, 'The Medieval Use', *Law Quarterly Review*, 81 (1965), p. 576.

[50] These issues are explored in more detail in Kümin, *Shaping of a Community*, pp.
24–6, 207–8, and Neil Jones, 'Trusts: Practice and Doctrine, 1536–1660' (PhD, Cambridge, 1994); brief surveys on the advantages of equity jurisdiction in Baker, *Introduction*, pp. 112 ff, and Jackson, *Machinery*, pp. 5–6.

[51] 'Ad vsum edificacionis, reparacionis, sustentacionis et maintencionis noue capelle
beate Marie ... et necessariorum eiusdem ad vsum sustentacionis diuinorum in eadem
celebrandorum': Alice Cooke (ed.), *Act Book of the Ecclesiastical Court of Whalley
1510–38* (Manchester, 1901), p. 158; for one of the best-documented cases of the
accumulation of lands by 'feoffees to the uses of the parish church' see R. N. Worth (ed.),
Calendar of Tavistock Parish Records (Plymouth, 1887), pp. 11, 77, 85, 92 and *passim*.

[52] PRO, C1 1/28/146.

III

Once 'defined' and consolidated, there was an enormous range of threats against which parishes needed to be defended. Non-attendance of religious worship, heresy and magical practices are among the most powerful challenges to the *raison d'être* of a Christian community, but also among the most difficult to interpret and quantify. Did people fail to come to church because they were opposed to the theological doctrines of the day, because they were not expected to do so on the grounds of their social inferiority or simply because the rising population could no longer be accommodated in the nave?[53] What about the position of parishioners who disrupted proceedings? One suspects that those, at least, who were presented for talking in church had not endeared themselves to their neighbours.[54] As for heretics or sorcerers, were they brought to trial because of pressure by the authorities or – as the latter had no means to conduct their own investigations – do the presentments reflect genuine intolerance of unorthodoxy by those summoned to visitations?[55] How much enthusiasm was there, at the grass-roots level, for the prosecution of such offenders? Similar problems arise when dealing with moral and sexual offences, although it certainly looks as if certain categories of persistent, serious 'rogues' were readily presented by the local community and gladly removed 'to the housse of correction'. Some even urged their justices to permit them the construction of one closer to home.[56]

The motives and attitudes towards other areas of litigation are easier to gauge. Pride of place among those finding broad popular support belongs to the recovery of debts, for evasion of financial duties by one parishioner meant higher charges for all the rest. Many examples can be

---

[53] In an area covering 478 churches, 26 cases of non-attendance surfaced in one case study dating from 1499: Christopher Harper-Bill, 'A Late Medieval Visitation: the Diocese of Norwich in 1499', *Proceedings of the Suffolk Institute of Archaeology*, 34 (1980), pp. 35–47, and the number seems generally small; for an evaluation of the questions raised see Collinson, *Religion of Protestants*, ch. 5.

[54] Such as Alice and Johanna Marcroft from Trawden in 1517: Cooke (ed.), *Whalley*, p. 54.

[55] A mere two cases of idolatry and witchcraft surfaced in the archdeaconry of Oxford in 1520: 'Churchwardens' Presentments, 1520', *Reports of the Oxfordshire Archaeological Society*, 70 (1925), pp. 80, 95; the strength and importance of heresy is of course one of the main bones of contention in the ongoing debate on the English Reformation; from the point of view of ecclesiastical jurisdiction see Houlbrooke, *Church Courts*, ch. 8.

[56] In the 1499 case study cited in note 53 above, 123 sexual offences were brought to the attention of the visitors, i.e. one in every four communities: Harper-Bill, 'Visitation'; CWA Yatton, D/P/yat/4/1/4, 1588–89 ('rogues'); Kent, 'Centre and Localities', p. 389; for a more detailed discussion see Ingram, *Church Courts*.

found among the records of the visitation of the archdeaconry of Oxford in 1520, where wardens reported people for outstanding rents, contributions to the wages of parish employees or other customary payments. Thomas Tailor, for instance, owed a staggering £4 1s. 6d. to the parish of Fringford, while John and William Peryman were cited by the archdeacon of Buckingham in 1493 for withholding church goods and ordered to repay the parishioners.[57] The wardens of Linwood (diocese of Lincoln) implored an episcopal visitor in 1473 to force one particularly persistent offender to return their property, 'for with owt my lordys help they gete it neaver'.[58] Similarly unpopular were independent-minded chapels which dragged their feet when asked to help with the upkeep of their parish church. At Prescot, secular and ecclesiastical authorities were called upon again and again to remind Farnworth of its duties.[59]

Another very common cause for appeals for help were priests and clerks who, in one way or another, let their flock down. In 1386, Common Pleas awarded damages of 12 marks to John Salter and Richard Petre, wardens of Torbryan in Devon, who had sued the chaplain William Pile for removing an expensive mass book from their church.[60] All Saints, Bristol, in contrast paid 4d. 'to Hychekocke the Summoner to cite Master William Twyte, Sir Harry Colas and Sir Thomas Halleway for negligence of divine service' in 1438–39.[61] The jurors of Pendle in Lancashire complained in 1535 'that the curate failed to hear confessions properly, because of his absence'; a Hertfordshire parish sued a clerk in Chancery for failing to keep his promise to come and work in their church; while, rather intriguingly, the parishioners of Grayingham (Lincs) resented 'an image which Robert Conyng [their parson] had set up in a most inconvenient place, so that the parishioners could no longer see neither the elevation nor divine service performed in the said

---

[57] 'Churchwardens' Presentments', p. 83; Ragg (ed.), 'Archdeaconry Courts of Buckinghamshire, 1491–95', p. 199; further cases in Wood-Legh (ed.), *Kentish Visitations*, for example pp. 56, 147, 62, 87, 109, 153, 229.

[58] Edward Peacock (ed.), 'Extracts from Lincoln Episcopal Visitations', *Archaeologia*, 48 (1885), pp. 249–50.

[59] Francis Bailey, 'The CWA of Prescot 1523–1607', *Transactions of the Historical Society of Lancashire and Cheshire*, 92 (1940), p. 176.

[60] Morris Arnold (ed.), *Select Cases of Trespass from the King's Courts 1307–99* (London, 1987), vol. 1, pp. 171–2; another chaplain, unflatteringly described as a 'communis latro', stood accused of taking a book worth no less than £10, as well as 'unum calicem, precij xls. et alia bona' of the church of St Paul, Malmesbury, by a Wiltshire jury in 1383–84: Bertha Putnam (ed.), *Proceedings before the Justices of the Peace in the Fourteenth and Fifteenth Centuries* (London, 1938), p. 387.

[61] Burgess (ed.), *Pre-Reformation Records*, MS p. 488.

church'.[62] Pope Eugenius IV, finally, asked by 'all' the parishioners of
the parish church of Ilfracombe in the diocese of Exeter to stop the
rector from laying hands on the oblations of a newly built church,
assigned a quarter of them to the upkeep of the fabric and the purchase
of ornaments.[63]

Lay officials, of course, could ruffle communal feathers too. John
Drewe and Robert Melwaye, churchwardens of Bapchild in Kent, asked
the Court of Requests in 1553 to summon Salmon Wilkyn, the current
farmer of their parsonage, so that 'order & direccion' may be taken as
suggested by right and 'equytye' about his failure to provide the customary alms to the local poor.[64] Complaints against executors or feoffees,
who withheld lands or other bequests from the parish, gave rise to a large
number of Chancery proceedings, as illustrated above.[65] Not all churchwardens were models of conscientiousness either. From an early stage,
royal courts offered parishioners recourse to an action of account, if their
representatives acted to the disadvantage of the Church,[66] and local
jurisdiction provided further options: All Saints, Bristol, for instance, had
its employee John Webley tried by city judges for an offence committed
during the Edwardian reign.[67] Visitations also invariably produced a
number of presentments for irregularities in parish administration,[68]
although ecclesiastical courts were keen to discourage malicious prosecu-
tions by showing a strong disposition to 'decide disputes arising out of
the administration of their office in the wardens' favour'.[69]

Breach of parish custom triggered proceedings throughout our period,[70] but the flood of religious and administrative regulation in the

---

[62] Cooke (ed.), *Whalley*, p. 176; PRO, C1 6/603/50 (1520s); Baildon (ed.), *Chancery*,
pp. 126–7; (the fifteenth-century Law French text speaks of 'vne ymage que le dit Robert
ad fait mettre en vn lieu deinz lour esglise a graunt nusance des ditz parochiens').

[63] Twemlow (ed.), *Calendar of Papal Letters*, vol. 9, pp. 376–7 (1443).

[64] Isaac Leadam (ed.), *Select Cases in the Court of Requests* (London, 1898), pp. 196–
8 (their wish was granted, but no judgement is recorded).

[65] Further examples include PRO, C1 1/28/401, 1/38/274, 3/150/80, 4/309/56.

[66] See for instance 13 Henry VII, f. 10.

[67] CWA All Saints Bristol, 1549–50 (at a cost of well over £3).

[68] Twelve of over 200 Kentish parishes had cause for concern in 1511: eight officers
did not render proper accounts, others owed the parish some money: Wood-Legh (ed.),
Kentish Visitations, passim; cf. 'Churchwardens' presentments', pp. 79, 85, 97, 112.

[69] Walter Morgan, 'An Examination of CWA and of Some Disputes Concerning Them
Before the Consistory Court of St Davids', *Journal of the Historical Society of the
Church in Wales*, 8 (1958), p. 79, with particular reference to a Welsh diocese, but R.
Burn, *Ecclesiastical Law* (London, 1842), vol. 1, p. 294, suggests that the situation in
England was very similar.

[70] In a Chancery case touched upon above, Robert Conyng, Parson of Grayingham in
Lincolnshire, was also accused of stopping his parishioners from ringing the church bell

wake of the Reformation created ever more points of friction. The canons of 1604, for instance, which granted parsons a share in parochial elections, led to a great deal of litigation in the capital. At St Stephen Walbrook (5 James I) and St Thomas and St Ethelburga (15 Charles I), incumbents startled their communities by refusing to present the laity's choice as churchwarden to the archdeacon. The parishes reacted by seeking prohibitions, arguing that canons could not change custom, and it looks as if judges warmed to their argument.[71] To take a closer look at the case of *Churchwarden Warner* vs *Parson of Allhallows* (17 James I), it was said that the parishioners were used to elect a junior and a senior churchwarden each year, but:

> That such a choice being made in that Parish of the said Warner to be Churchwarden, the Parson withstanding that election, nominated one Carter to be Churchwarden, and procured him to be sworn in the Ecclesiastical Court ... ; and this by colour of the late Canons; That the Parson should have the election of one of the Churchwardens; And this being against the custom, a Prohibition was prayed, and a president [precedent] shewn in the Common Bench ... ; For it being a special custom, the Canons cannot alter it, especially in London, where the Parson and Churchwardens are a Corporation.[72]

Similar problems arose in connection with the office of parish clerk and efforts to harmonize procedural practice.[73] Individual parishioners attempted to challenge the traditional place, date or electorate involved in churchwardens' appointments, but evidence from a diocesan case study suggests that parish custom retained precedence over more recent central regulation.[74] The trend towards more oligarchical government by 'select vestry' did not go unchecked either. St Botolph Aldersgate witnessed a particularly acrimonious battle in the 1630s, when an 'Inquisition under the Great Seal' had to look into serious allegations against a select body established (by episcopal faculty) in 1607. Twenty-seven 'good and

---

to summon all tenants to the collection of their rents and to deal with 'autres choses touchant la gouernaile de la dite ville': Baildon (ed.), *Chancery*, pp. 126–7.

[71] *English Reports*, vol. 79, p. 1075 and vol. 82, p. 231.

[72] *The Second Part of the Reports of Sir George Croke* (London, 1682), f. 532.

[73] In a case concerning St Katherine Coleman Street (21 James I), King's Bench granted the parishioners a prohibition ruling that the election of the clerk by the vestry was a 'good custom': *Reports of Sir George Croke*, f. 670 (Jeremy's case); another example from the same parish in *English Reports*, vol. 79, pp. 580–81, 1106 (*Orme* vs *Pemberton*, 16 Charles I); detailed rules about parish administration, for example in the canons of 1571 and 1604: Edward Cardwell (ed.), *Synodalia* (Oxford, 1842), vol. 1, pp. 122–6, and Gibson (ed.), *Codex*, pp. 215–16.

[74] Walter Morgan, 'Disputes before the Consistory Courts of St Davids', *Journal of the Historical Society of the Church in Wales*, 3 (1953), pp. 90–99.

lawful men' asked the commissioners to ensure that 'the vestrie of the said parish may bee publique as hath bin alwaies anciently accustomed for the generall freedom and benefit of all the foresaid parishioners'.[75] The main bone of contention was an increase in customary fees and by the time of a survey of London parish government in 1636, the wardens of St Botolph reported to Bishop William Juxon that the conflict had led to 'a suite commenced against some of the said parish in the high court of Starr Chamber touching the said fees', that as a consequence of all the relevant documentation requested by the court 'they have forborne their meetings in the said vestry for orderinge their said Church affaires', that they 'have likewise for the same reason forborne ... to make upp their Accomptes' and that this state of affairs '(without Reformation) is like in tyme to begett greate disorder in their saide parishe'. By 1645 government had, at least temporarily, returned to a 'democratically' elected body of 24 inhabitants.[76] At St Katherine Cree in 1636, another select vestry had to admit to the fact that it was disliked 'by the generalitie of the parrishe, and controverted by suits now depending both in the Court of Arches, before his Lorde ... of Canterbury, And also in the high Court of Chancerie before the Lord Keeper'.[77]

Historians of crime have noted how much litigation was directed against 'outsiders' and thus those against which the community could most easily be united.[78] A striking early modern example is the fight against unwelcome poor and their potential claims on communal resources. One of the prime concerns of the seventeenth-century vestry of St Michael Crooked Lane in London appears to have been 'the removeing of Inmates & undersitters by presenting them at the sessions', and any look at local records will confirm just how keen parish notables were to get rid of vagrants and other 'intruders'.[79] The poor rate proved a particularly contentious issue, with prosperous parishes doing their utmost to minimize contributions to less well-to-do communities, and the latter appealing to the justices of the peace to enforce their lawful claims on such payments. In a lengthy dispute spanning over a decade, the parishioners of Great St Mary's, Cambridge, steadily refused to support their neighbours of St Giles and St Andrew's, pleading in a petition to the justices of assize in 1636 to be 'overcharged and ...

[75] GL, MS 10,910 (6 January 1630).

[76] LPL, Carte Miscellanee, vol. 7, no. 55 (1636–survey); GL, Vestry Minutes of St Botolph Aldersgate: MS 1453/1, 23 September 1645.

[77] LPL, Carte Miscellanee, vol. 7, no. 11.

[78] Sharpe, *Crime in Early Modern England*, p. 82.

[79] LPL, Carte Miscellanee, vol. 7, no. 109; for a detailed case study see the forthcoming essay by Steve Hindle, 'The Politics of Exclusion: Power, Poor Relief and Social Relations in Frampton (Lincs), c. 1600–1800'.

utterly unable to contribute' to churches which 'have impoverished themselves by erecting new cottages'. After a series of arbitrations, orders and unsuccessful settlements, the overseers of the city's poorer parishes complained to the Cambridge quarter sessions of September 1645 that they had still not received 'the same rates in contempt of the said orders', and it was not before March 1649 that the wardens of St Mary's finally conceded that 'ther shalbe a too monthes rate made and collected … towarde the payment of St Andrews and St Gillses'.[80]

Common thieves, of course, sparked even greater resentment. To take a King's Bench example, William Balderby, warden of St Michael, Hitcham (Buckinghamshire), accused Nicholas Burne of stealing a chalice, an ordinal, two missals, a corporal cloth and several other items to the total value of 20 marks from the goods and chattels of the church on the night of 19 October 1412. Nicholas, who was brought to the court by marshal John Preston, denied acting feloniously and the sheriff of Buckingham was charged with the summoning of a jury. On the day specified, 24 men appeared and swore that Nicholas was guilty. The defendant now pleaded benefit of clergy, read a book 'like a clerk' and was handed over to the ordinary of the abbot of Westminster. As for the stolen goods, the court decided 'that the said Willelmus Balderby shall reclaim the said goods and moveables'.[81] Twelve jurors presented William Oliver and William Kendal to the justices of Leicestershire in 1413 for 'noctanter' breaking into the church of St Mary at Kirkby Bellars and taking away three chalices, two full sets of vestments, three books and other items 'de bonis communibus' of the said village.[82] At Yatton in Somerset, a church goods robbery led to proceedings at Uphill, Wells and Ilchester in the early 1540s, for which the wardens parted with a handsome £1 4s. 10d. Whether this incident had any religious undertones is impossible to determine, although it coincided with a substantial investment of £11 in new vestments.[83]

Negligent builders, artisans and craftsmen could also be put in the dock. All Saints, Bristol, spent 4d. 'for entering a plaint on the false vestment-maker' in 1450–51, and the parish of Basingstoke complained

---

[80] Audit Book of St Mary's, pp. 64 ff. (26 March 1636, 26 September 1645 and 12 March 1649).

[81] George Sayles (ed.), *Select Cases in the Court of King's Bench* (London, 1971), pp. 207–9; for an earlier case in Common Pleas, where churchwardens were represented by attorney and successfully recovered damages for a book stolen by a chaplain cf. Arnold (ed.), *Select Cases of Trespass*, vol. 1, pp. 171–2 (1386).

[82] Putnam (ed.), *Proceedings before the Justices*, pp. 100–101, 105. Total damages amounted to almost £40, and there were later proceedings in King's Bench, which apparently resulted in an acquittal.

[83] CWA of Yatton, 1540–42.

to the Chancellor in the 1520s that one of its newly commissioned bells was out of tune with the rest of the peal. Also, in an *assumpsit* case heard in King's Bench in 1507, the wardens of the Norfolk parish of Folsham sued a builder called Yarman for his failure to construct their new *sedilia* according to specifications, although they had failed to secure a written agreement.[84] The producer, meanwhile, who refused to part with the profits of a play staged in the late fifteenth century, found himself cited by the Chancellor at the behest of a Bedfordshire parish.[85]

Resentment of 'outsiders' stretched beyond individuals to more powerful external authorities. In the 1540s, the parishioners of St Mary Redcliffe, Bristol, sued the city's mayor for his decision to close the Candlemas fair granted to them in 1529. The case is as remarkable for the supporting evidence as for its substance: to emphasize the broad popular support for the complaint, they collected 629 signatures (out of a total population of perhaps 10 000) and appended 'ther usuall seale of the seid Churche'. The town authorities defended their action by arguing that the success of the market had serious repercussions for trading elsewhere, but the parish countered by producing extracts from recent churchwardens' accounts. As they still showed a profit, however, the evidence failed to sway the judges and the fair was formally abolished on 10 June 1544.[86] We have already seen how parishes fought attempts by the ecclesiastical hierarchy to interfere with custom in the wake of the Reformation, and the same holds true for the twin threats to their financial well-being: royal taxation and confiscation. Whatever the religious preferences of the nation, 'conformity' should no longer be used to characterize grass-roots reaction to the *fiscal* implications of the ecclesiastical changes. Communities up and down the country combined concealment and litigation to minimize their losses of chantry, fraternity and parochial property.[87] Parishioners and incumbents

---

[84] Burgess (ed.), *Pre-Reformation Records*, MS, p. 514; PRO, C1 5/520/33; John Baker (ed.), *The Reports of Sir John Spelman* (London, 1978), p. 261; other parishes, however, clearly used written agreements: *Reports of Sir John Spelman*, pp. 260–61. *Assumpsit* was an action at law in which a plaintiff asserted that the defendant had failed to fulfil a promise to perform a certain act.

[85] PRO, C1 3/146/48.

[86] Isaac Leadam (ed.), *Select Cases before the King's Council in the Star Chamber* (London, 1903), vol. 2, pp. cxviii–cxxiv, 237–76.

[87] The wardens of All Saints, Bristol, who administered the Halleway chantry, had a long tradition of defending the rights of subparochial institutions. See for example Bristol Record Office, Halleway Chantry Accounts: P/AS/C/1, 1466–67 (costs of 6s. 3d. for a lawyer and entering a complaint) and 1473–74 (over £2 9s. to fund a rent dispute against William Canynges, one of the wealthiest and most influential Bristol citizens); cf. Burgess (ed.), *Pre-Reformation Records*, MS, p. 565 (4s. 8d. 'to the recorder and Roger Kemes to defend us against Canynges for John Pynner's place').

sometimes supported and sometimes fought each other in court to soften the impact of the Act of First Fruits and Tenths 1534, while in the wake of the Chantries Act, 1547, churchwardens like those of Long Melford in Suffolk lobbied commissioners and privy councillors with 'bylls of complaynte' to spare their resources, and villages such as Cratfield employed the local manorial court to 'launder' nearly all of their landed endowments from any 'superstitious' connections.[88] The leading parishioners of Ashburton, apart from concocting 'a highly artificial' return to the Edwardian commissioners, spared no costs to prevent a crown agent from reaping the benefits of the dissolution with a suit in Star Chamber, while London's St Botolph Aldersgate showed equal determination to keep as much as it possibly could from the royal Exchequer. When a renewed search of the parish archives uncovered substantial amounts of hidden property early in Elizabeth's reign, the wardens invested 5s. in a large-scale investigation in their own books as well as at Westminster to check once and for all 'whether the acte of parliament for the dissolucion of channtries entituled the ... late kinge Edwarde the vjth to the said quite rentes'. The odds were stacked against them and these properties disappeared from their reckonings – how many more they retained 'illegally', of course, was not explicitly recorded.[89]

IV

'Conflict', to recall an anthropological commonplace, 'is a feature of all human societies and, potentially, an aspect of all social relationships'.[90] English parishes, struggling to accommodate the most heterogeneous religious and secular interests, inevitably provide no exception to this rule; here too, disputes were always just around the corner. Even a pillar of local society such as John Ford at Ashburton, a wealthy and

---

[88] Patrick Carter, 'The Fiscal Reformation: Clerical Taxation and Opposition in Henrician England', in Beat Kümin (ed.), *Reformations Old and New: Essays on the Socio-Economic Impact of Religious Change c. 1470–1630* (Aldershot, 1996), pp. 92–105; David Dymond and Clive Paine (eds), *The Spoil of Melford Church* (Ipswich, 1989), pp. 41–2; Ken Farnhill, 'Religious Policy and Parish "Conformity": Cratfield's Lands in the Sixteenth Century', in Katherine French, Gary Gibbs and Beat Kümin (eds), *The Parish in English Life 1400–1600* (Manchester, 1997), pp. 217–29.

[89] H. Hanham, 'The Suppression of the Chantries in Ashburton', *Reports and Transactions of the Devonshire Association*, 99 (1967), pp. 111–37, quote: p. 118; CWA St Botolph, 1559–60; cf. Christopher Kitching, 'The Quest for Concealed Lands in the Reign of Elizabeth I', *TRHS*, 5th ser., 24 (1974), pp. 63–78.

[90] Kevin Avruch, 'Conflict Resolution', in David Levinson and Melvin Ember (eds), *Encyclopedia of Cultural Anthropology* (New York, 1996), vol. 1, p. 241.

influential figure who had contributed £10 to a new rood loft, advised the church on many practical matters and wrote its accounts from 1509 to 1532, could suddenly find himself at odds with his parish.[91] Given the high expectations in terms of co-operation and financial engagement, it must have been only too tempting for many humbler parishioners to try and evade their responsibilities. On the other hand, they had rights as well as duties, which were liable to violations by negligent clergymen, independent-minded chapels or secular authorities. Furthermore, not all of the merchants or workmen that parishioners did business with acted in the best communal interest. Some of them were incompetent, others refused to honour their contracts. Court actions thus took so many different forms that it is hard to generalize on their impact, even more so as the boundaries between the different jurisdictions were blurred. Leaking chancel roofs were presented to archdeacons, riotous behaviour to the Star Chamber, while the withholding of church dues could surface in King's Bench or Consistory Court cases, and failure to attend divine service in a borough leet or before a bishop's commissary. Some trials left the community scarred, others resulted from unwelcome intrusions, but almost all caused a considerable drain on parochial resources.

Litigation, however, was not *a priori* a bad thing. Courts had been established to offer non-violent forms of conflict resolution and were called upon quite voluntarily by parish representatives (often, but not always, churchwardens) to deal with disruptive members, strengthen parochial institutions, and allow for the enforcement of communal priorities. Conflict was endemic, but the parties made every effort to arrive at some form of ritual cleansing or reconciliation. Ashburton spared no cost to have its church reconsecrated by a whole array of ecclesiastical dignitaries after it had been 'polluted' by an assault of William South upon William Sampson within the building; and when Elizabeth Sharp formally ended a lengthy and acrimonious rent dispute in the Bristol parish of St Ewen's she confessed to be 'right glad of this good ende ... be twen my husbond and you and this churche' and offered her neighbours the holy bread and a 'fayre towel' to be used at their Easter communion.[92] Conflict management was an integral part of the system and an essential tool to preserve or re-establish internal stability. Patrick Collinson's work has reminded us of how resilient the

---

[91] Hanham (ed.), *CWA Ashburton*, pp. vii–viii, 1526–28 (a rent dispute).

[92] *CWA Ashburton*, 1525–27 (dealings with the suffragan bishop, archdeacon Richard Tollet, the bishop's registrary and commissary caused expenses of over £11); Betty Masters and Elizabeth Ralph (eds), *The Church Book of St Ewen's, Bristol 1454–1584* (Bristol, 1967), pp. 60–61 (1463–64).

local ecclesiastical community remained well beyond the Reformation; to find 'parishioners in court' so frequently may well be taken as another sign of its remarkable vitality.

CHAPTER TWO

The woman with the rock: the controversy on women and Bible reading[1]

Susan Wabuda

'Everie one in his calling is bound to doo somewhat to the furtherance of the holie building' of the Church, wrote the godly matron Anne Locke at the beginning of her 1590 translation of Jean Taffin's *Of the Markes of the Children of God*, and although she acknowledged that there were 'great things by reason of my sex I may not doo', she knew 'that which I may I ought to doo'.

Anne Locke, whom Patrick Collinson introduced to scholars of the Reformation as early as 1965, exemplifies part of the tension which lay at the heart of women's roles in the early modern period. Had she drawn a list of those 'great things' outside of her calling and precluded to her sex, ministry and preaching could have figured large, forbidden to women by a strict interpretation of the silence St Paul enjoined women to keep. Instead, like other women of her generation, she supplied the pulpit through her sustentation of Puritan preachers (including John Knox, and her husband Edward Dering), and the use of her pen. She translated Calvin's sermons too, and in printing her work, 'I have according to my duetie brought my poore basket of stones to the strengthening of the walles of that Jerusalem whereof (by grace) wee are *all* both citizens and members.'[2]

---

[1] For their helpful comments, I wish to thank Larissa Taylor, David Myers, and our colleagues who heard a preliminary version of this chapter at the Sixteenth Century Conference in St Louis, Missouri on 27 October 1996. I am also in the debt of Mary Erler and Norman L. Jones, who read this chapter at a mature stage. Patrick Collinson heard some previous work along these lines and, as usual, I wish my writing were a better reflection of his sound advice.

[2] From the dedicatory epistle written by Anne [Locke] Prowse, translator of Jean Taffin's *Of the Markes of the Children of God*, which was printed in no fewer than seven editions between 1590 and 1635 (STC 23622 ff.); Patrick Collinson, 'The Role of Women in the English Reformation Illustrated by the Life and Friendships of Anne Locke' (SCH, 2, 1965), pp. 258–72, quoted p. 272 (emphasis added); reprinted in Collinson, *Godly People; Essays on English Protestantism and Puritanism* (London,

The model for women as established by Paul was undoubtedly a complicated one. It stipulated that they keep silent in their churches, refrain from instructing men and live in obedience under the guidance of their husbands. Yet in his epistle to Titus, Paul entrusted matrons with the responsibility to teach uncorrupted doctrine to younger women, to instruct them how to be good. And he wrote of female 'helpers in Jesus Christ', including Priscilla (the wife of Aquila), whom the Acts of the Apostles records as having instructed a man named Apollos in the faith. Paul's summons for Christians to work towards edification, for the spiritual building of the Church through the promulgation of sacred teachings, was of such importance that it required the efforts of anyone, man or woman, who could bring their abilities to the task.[3]

Among the great themes inherent in the Christian Church is the idea that God may use a weaker vessel to confound or embarrass the stronger. For English women during the Reformation, the balance between silence and teaching was tested, especially when the appropriateness of Bible reading was at issue. The startling anomalies of children teaching their parents, of laypeople instructing the clergy, of women directing men, which accompanied the new availability of the Bible in English, represented potent threats to the usual economy of obedience and deference.[4] Flushed with the excitement of discovering William Tyndale's New Testament, Robert Plumpton sent a copy to his mother in the mid-1530s, with the admonition that it was now 'my dutie to instructe you'. Even if she were not his mother, 'I am bounde to write to you', he proclaimed, 'for everie man or woman that it shall please God to sende knowledge in the Scriptures is bounde to instructe theire brethren in the lovinge of the Gospell'.[5] When Catholic translators sought to counteract

---

1983), pp. 273–87. Cf. her translation of *Sermons of John Calvin*, STC 4450 (London, 1560), which was dedicated to Katherine, Duchess of Suffolk. For women and their support of preachers, see my essay 'Shunamites and Nurses of the English Reformation: the Activities of Mary Glover, Niece of Hugh Latimer', in W. J. Sheils and Diana Wood (eds), *Women in the Church* (SCH, 27, 1990), pp. 335–44.

[3] For edification, see Paul's Epistles, including Romans 15:2–4; 2 Corinthians 12:19; Ephesians 4:29. For women's silence: 1 Corinthians 14:34–5; 1 Timothy 2:9–15; Ephesians 522–33, based on Genesis 1:26 and 3:6. For older women teaching the young: Titus 2:3–5. For Priscilla: Romans 16:3; Acts 18:1–28 (and my thanks to Maria Dowling).

[4] Susan Brigden, 'Youth and the English Reformation', *Past and Present*, 95 (1982), pp. 37–67; A. G. Dickens, *The English Reformation* (2nd edn, London, 1989), pp. 334–8; Peter Lake, 'Feminine Piety and Personal Potency: the "Emancipation" of Mrs Jane Ratcliffe', *The Seventeenth Century*, 2 (1987), pp. 143–65; Diane Willen, 'Godly Women in Early Modern England: Puritanism and Gender', *JEH*, 43 (1992), pp. 561–80.

[5] Joan Kirby (ed.), *The Plumpton Letters and Papers* (CS, 5th series, 8, 1996), pp. 205–7; Thomas Stapleton (ed.), *The Plumpton Correspondence* (CS, 4, 1839), pp. 231–3; A. G. Dickens, *Lollards and Protestants in the Diocese of York 1509–1558* (London, 1982), pp. 131–7; and Dickens, *English Reformation*, p. 95.

the damage wrought by Protestant editions of the New Testament with their own orthodox English version in 1582, they observed that in the better era of the primitive church, 'the scholer taught not his maister, the sheepe controuled not the Pastor, the yong student set not the Doctour to schoole, nor reproved their fathers of error & ignorance'.[6]

My goal in this chapter is to push further our understanding of the theoretical basis for establishing (and also opposing) the view that English women could be permitted to read the Bible in the vernacular. The oscillations of the early years of the Reformation, as it unfolded in England in its own series of unique gyrations, are nowhere more apparent than in the alternating periods when holy scripture in the vernacular was either banned or promoted. Translations of the Bible were illegal under the terms of medieval heresy laws, which were reversed for the first time in 1534. Officially sponsored English Bibles were set up publicly in churches fitfully from 1536. In 1539, a royal proclamation disallowed the disruption of divine service by public Bible reading, and then the reading of holy scripture was forbidden to most women, and the lower social orders, by statute in 1543, a law that was reversed under Edward VI, when the English Bible was again made available to all levels of society. Then with the revival of the old punitive medieval laws under Mary, English Bibles were prohibited once again, until at last Elizabeth restored Edward's laws, and permitted the Bible to all who would read it.

For women, even more than for men, the extent to which they were to approach the mysteries of holy writ on their own was hotly contended, especially during the reign of Henry VIII, particularly because it spoke to the age-old problem of the role women were to exercise in the faith. If we wish to explore a small angle of that persistent problem of the extent to which the ideals for women's roles changed during the Reformation, then we could do worse than to look at Bible reading for some clues. We need to ask under what circumstances it was lawful for women to teach, and thus to take upon themselves a role that had been traditionally associated with the clergy. For as we will see, the 1543 Act for the Advancement of True Religion and for the Abolishment of the Contrary not only forbade women of the lower classes to read the Bible, but stipulated that not even noblewomen or gentlewomen should read it in the hearing of anyone, lest they inadvertently teach.

Potentially, this Act could affect every woman, though we know in practice that levels of literacy for women in general lagged behind those for men, even at the uppermost levels of society. The new celebration of

---

[6] *The Nevv Testament of Jesus Christ*, STC 2884 (Rheims, 1582), sig. a3v.

women's erudition by the humanists was a remarkable development that was beginning to bear fruit, especially in works like Margaret Roper's translation of Erasmus's commentary on the Paternoster.[7] Before the breach from Rome, it was never disallowed for any layperson, man or woman, to read the Latin Vulgate. Select portions were well known at every level of society. Women taught their children with English primers and other texts. This too was permissible and completely ordinary.

The mystical sanctity of the Bible was as much the essence of the problem as was the status of womankind. Its numinous power as a full text, even as the most precious of books, meant that it compared with the consecrated Host as an object of veneration. And like the Host, its divinity and powers were so profound that it had to be reserved to those worthy to come near it. In the pure and scrupulous Latin of St Jerome's Vulgate, it could do no harm. But once it was 'Englished' (and the difficulties, theologians agreed, of rendering an accurate and orthodox translation were immense), the dangers began. It could be abused, 'jangled', 'wrested', misinterpreted, handled irreverently, bandied about in alehouses, used falsely and inspire heresies. Worse, in this debased form it could reach greater numbers of people than had ever been able to approach it directly before, many of whom would be hard-pressed to understand the full theological complexity of its material. And as women were prone to error by the very nature they took from Eve, they were at greatest risk.[8]

In practice, the 1543 act had an immediate impact upon women of the upper classes, who enjoyed the best opportunities to acquire at least solid skills in the vernacular (if not the learned tongues), and were poised to wield the most influence in their own households and in the greater community.[9] They were clearly disadvantaged by the 1543 Act, as they were well aware. Its ultimate reversal meant that English women

---

[7] See Rita Verbrugge, 'Margaret More Roper's Personal Expression in the *Devout treatise upon the Pater Noster*' in Margaret Patterson Hannay (ed.), *Silent but for the Word: Tudor Women as Patrons, Translators, and Writers of Religious Works* (Kent, OH, 1985), pp. 30–42.

[8] Margaret Aston, 'Devotional Literacy', in her collected essays, *Lollards and Reformers: Images and Literacy in Late Medieval Religion* (London, 1984), pp. 101–33; Eamon Duffy, *Stripping of the Altars: Traditional Religion in England c. 1400–c. 1580* (New Haven, CT, and London, 1992), ch. 6; David Cressy, *Literacy and the Social Order: Reading and Writing in Tudor and Stuart England* (Cambridge, 1980), pp. 51–2; Miri Rubin, *Corpus Christi: the Eucharist in Late Medieval Culture* (Cambridge, 1991), pp. 335–42; Keith Thomas, *Religion and the Decline of Magic* (New York, 1971), pp. 45–6.

[9] Cressy, *Literacy*, especially chs 1 and 6 for women's learning, pp. 51–2; Maria Dowling, *Humanism in the Age of Henry VIII* (London, 1986), ch. 7.

were held to a less strict interpretation of the Pauline ideal. Women under Elizabeth had a clearer mandate than had been expressed before, not only to read the Bible, but to teach it.

The whole issue of women and Bible reading was frequently epitomized by a common emblematic figure of a woman at work, which we will see was linked with Tyndale's famous challenge, as recorded by his first biographer John Foxe, 'if God spared him life, ere many years he would cause a boy that driveth the plough, to know more of the Scripture', than even learned priests did (or, for that matter, the Pope himself).[10] And of course Tyndale's words were founded on Erasmus's clarion call to read the Gospels and apostolic Epistles in his *Paraclesis* of 1516, a passage that was so striking to his readers that we often find them underlined in surviving contemporary copies: 'I wold to god/the plowman wold singe a texte of the scripture at his plowbeme/ And that the wever at his lowme/with this wold drive away the tediousnes of tyme. I wold the wayfaringe man with this pastyme/wold expelle the werynes of his jorney.'[11] This aspiration was an encapsulation of one of the great promises of the movement of reform, that the Bible would be everywhere available, without distinction of rank because all of the restrictions that had prevented its translation and printing would be removed. And although the ploughman has been the focus of many important recent studies, it is rather startling to realize that the complementary symbol for women, the image of the woman with the rock, with whom the ploughman was most often paired, has not received serious attention until now.

---

[10] John Foxe, *The Acts and Monuments*, ed. George Townsend (London, 1843–49), vol. 5, p. 117. Cf. David Daniell, *William Tyndale: a Biography* (New Haven, 1994), pp. 1, 18, 44, 317 and pp. 92–107.

[11] 'Vtinam hinc ad stiuam aliquid decantet agricola, hinc nonnihil ad radios suos moduletur textor, huiusmodi fabulis itineris taedium leuet uiator.' Erasmus, *Paraclesis, id est, adhortatio ad sanctissimum ac saluberrimum Christianae philosophiae studium, ut uidelicet Euangelicis ac Apostolicis literis legendis, si non sola, saltem prima cura tribuatur* (Basle, February 1519), esp. pp. 8–9; reprinted in *Opera omnia* (Leiden, 1703–06; repr. 1961–62), vol. 5, pp. 138–43 and vol. 6, pp. 3–4. The quote is from the contemporary translation, *An exhortation to the diligent studye of scripture* [trans. W. Roy?], STC 10493 (Marlborow in the londe of Hesse: Hans Luft [Antwerp], 1529), unpaginated. A modern translation is found in John C. Olin (ed.), *Christian Humanism and the Reformation: Selected Writings of Erasmus* (New York, 1987), pp. 97–108. Examples of contemporary underlining of this passage can be found in the CUL copy of the 1519 edition cited above, S61.29.c.5.218(1), p. 8, with the marginal notation added: 'et euangelicis literis' in a sixteenth-century hand; and also in a 1522 edition, CUL, S61.29.d.5.7(7), sig. A4v.

Unlike much of the rest of western Europe, vernacular translations of the Bible had been prohibited in England by Church law in 1408, complemented by three statutes that were designed to check the native Wycliffite heresy, which was spreading through unorthodox preaching and books.[12] Of course the role of reading itself was already an important issue by the early fifteenth century, and it intensified as printing was developed, as acoustic reading (the most common means of reading before the modern era) was tantamount to teaching or even preaching. Reading was vocal and reading was social. To read was to pour the printed words into the ears of all those within hearing range. And the dangerous threat that women's reading represented in the accustomed sphere of their households was obvious.[13] It was in the close rooms, in the 'prive chambres and prive places', which were revealed by Hawisia Moon in 1430 as the centres for the Lollards' 'scoles of heresie'. Together they 'herd, conceyved, lerned, and reported' their unorthodox opinions. Even through the early years of the sixteenth century, the household remained the most common place for Lollard men and women to covertly memorize and repeat their illegal manuscript versions of the books of the New Testament.[14] Remarkably, Lollard women in their conventicles taught men to learn by heart long portions of their New Testaments. Early in the reign of Henry VIII, records preserved by Foxe show that one Agnes Ashford of Chesham had to be warned by a panel of bishops, because she had been teaching the Sermon on the Mount to the men of her acquaintance. The Lollards were the first in England to blur the distinctions between the laity and the clergy, and in depreciating the role of the priesthood, even Lollard women could annex the teaching functions of the sacerdotal office.[15]

---

[12] See the medieval laws against heresy: the 1408 Constitutions of Archbishop Thomas Arundel, printed in William Lyndwood, *Provinciale, (seu Constitvtiones Angliae)* (Oxford, 1679), p. 286. Statutes: (1382) 5 Ric. II, st. 2, c. 5; (1401) 2 Hen. IV, c. 15; (1414) 2 Hen. V, st. 1, c. 7. Reprinted in Thomas More, *The Apology, the Complete Works of St Thomas More*, ed. J. B. Trapp (New Haven, CT, 1979), vol. 9, appendix C. Cf. John Guy, 'The Legal Context of the Controversy: the Law of Heresy', in *The Debellation of Salem and Bizance, Complete Works of St Thomas More*, ed. John Guy (1987), vol. 10, pp. xlvii–lxvii.

[13] Margaret Aston, 'Lollardy and Literacy', in her *Lollards and Reformers: Images and Literacy in Late Medieval Religion* (London, 1984), pp. 193–217.

[14] The confession of Hawisia Moone of Loddon, 1430, printed in Anne Hudson (ed.), *Selections from English Wycliffite Writings* (Cambridge, 1978), pp. 34–7; Patrick Collinson, 'The English Conventicle', in W. J. Sheils and Diana Wood (eds) *Voluntary Religion* (SCH, 23, 1986), pp. 223–59. Also, Claire Cross, '"Great Reasoners in Scripture": the Activities of Women Lollards 1380–1530', in Derek Baker (ed.), *Medieval Women* (SCH, subsidia 1, 1979), pp. 359–80.

[15] Foxe, *Acts and Monuments*, vol. 4, pp. 224–5; Margaret Aston, 'Lollard Women Priests?', in her *Lollards and Reformers: Images and Literacy in Late Medieval Religion* (London, 1984), pp. 49–70.

By the end of the fifteenth century, official efforts against the Lollards were largely effective, and the Church's measures to instil in orthodox believers the rudiments of faith included the regular administration of the sacraments, pastoral preaching and also an astonishing range of pious literature which poured from English printing presses under the early Tudors. The Church always maintained that the Bible was lively food for the soul but, like the sacrament of the altar, had to be administered properly, by priests who understood the correct interpretations of scripture and taught orthodox views. Holy scripture was presented to the laity during the celebration of the mass, especially on Sundays, in ritual *tableaux* that highlighted its importance, during the readings of the Gospel and Epistles verses of the day, and also in the homily which followed, and many of the books the laity brought with them to church enabled them to follow along. Devotional works like primers were very common, and were designed to help the laity reach to the heart of their faith, especially through prayer, the shared experience of the parish mass, and through meditations on the crucifix. Improper translations of the Bible were lethal. In 1554, John Standish reminded his readers that many had been 'utterly poisoned with the letter of thenglysh Bible'.[16] Some devotional works struck an uneasy balance between encouraging the faithful and avoiding the pitfalls of heresy, mixing English and Latin, sometimes providing only fundamental material, like the Paternoster, in English.[17]

Tyndale's yearning for the Scriptures in his own language was expressed through his reference to the ploughboy, and Wycliffite reformers had also employed the symbol of the ploughman to criticize the Catholic priesthood.[18] The ploughman was a recurrent symbol in the sermons and writings of the time, and as Anne Hudson has argued, a *topos* of social and religious inversion, especially in his most familiar guise as Piers Plowman. He usually represented a challenge to authority of some sort, and an attack upon privilege, a sign that in due course the meek and deserving will overcome the haughty and unprincipled. The ploughman's very ubiquity as the most ordinary of labourers made his

---

[16] [John Standish], *A discourse wherin is debated whether it be expedient that the scripture should be in English for al men to reade that wyll*, STC 23207 (London, 1554), sigs D8r, I6v, E3v. Cf. More, *Apology*, pp. 12–14.

[17] Duffy, *Stripping of the Altars*, especially ch. 2; Patrick Collinson, 'The Coherence of the Text: How It Hangeth Together: the Bible in Reformation England', *Journal for the Study of the New Testament*, supplement series, 105 (1995), pp. 84–108; Aston, 'Devotional Literacy' and 'Lollardy and Literacy', pp. 101–33, 193–217.

[18] See Andrew McRae, 'Fashioning a Cultural Icon: the Ploughman in Renaissance Texts', in S. M. Jack and B. A. Masters (eds), *Protestants, Property, Puritans: Godly People Revisited, a Festschrift in Honour of Patrick Collinson on the Occasion of his Retirement* (Parergon, new series, 14, 1996), pp. 187–204.

defiance of convention all the more striking.[19] But we can also find that the symbol had some surprisingly long orthodox roots. Armed only with his faith and the Paternoster, in some tales the simple ploughman could pierce unscathed through purgatory to heaven, while the diligent clerk was seduced from the right way by his study.[20] The ploughman's popularity extended far beyond association with any single political or religious point of view. In the *Lytell geste howe the plowman lerned his pater noster*, a humourous poem printed by Wynkyn de Worde in 1510 (from origins in the sermons of the Franciscan saint, Bernardino of Siena), the ploughman was a stingy and stubborn man, who received his comeuppance when he was tricked into learning the Latin verses of the prayer by his parish priest. In this case, it was the virtuous cleric who provided the victory over ignorance and cupidity.[21]

The ploughman appeared alone in the *Lytell geste*, but an essential pairing occurs in other literary sources, not only in Erasmus, as we shall see, but also in Bishop John Fisher's famous Good Friday sermon. Fisher contrasted meditation and reading, arguing that the crucifix was a type of book which would bring more fruitful knowledge to all those who mused and marvelled on it than they could attain from any ordinary book. Every person, rich or poor, whether worshipping in a church or going about his or her customary occupations, could meditate upon the crucifix, to consider the full import of what Christ's sacrifice meant. Thus the poor labourer could contemplate upon it while working in the fields, 'when he is at plough'. Likewise, 'the poore women also in theyr businesse, when they be spinning of their rocks, or serving of their pullen' should reflect upon the sacrifice of Christ.[22]

And it is from Fisher that I have drawn my title, as the word 'rock' comes not from any scriptural reference to the 'Rock of salvation',[23] or

---

[19] Anne Hudson, 'The Legacy of *Piers Plowman*', in John A. Alford (ed.), *A Companion to Piers Plowman* (Berkeley, 1988), pp. 251–66.

[20] William Langland, *Piers the Ploughman*, trans. J. F. Goodridge (New York, 1966), p. 126.

[21] *Here begynneth a lytell geste howe the plowman lerned his pater noster*, STC 20034 (London, 1510); Duffy, *Stripping of the Altars*, ch. 2, especially pp. 84–5; A. G. Ferrers Howell, *S. Bernardino of Siena* (London, 1913), pp. 286–7; Hudson, 'Legacy', p. 258.

[22] John Fisher, *The English Works of John Fisher*, ed. John E. B. Mayor, Early English Text Society, extra series, no. 27 (1876), pp. 388–428, especially pp. 391–6. Eamon Duffy, 'Spirituality of Fisher', in Brendan Bradshaw and Eamon Duffy (eds), *Humanism, Reform and the Reformation: the Career of Bishop John Fisher* (Cambridge, 1989), pp. 214–15 (though 'rooks' here is a misprint). Also, Maria Dowling, 'John Fisher and the Preaching Ministry', *ARG*, 82 (1991), pp. 287–309. For the crucifix as a book, see Beryl Smalley, *The Study of the Bible in the Middle Ages* (Notre Dame, IN, 1964), p. 283, n. 3; Aston, 'Devotional Literacy', p. 104.

[23] Deuteronomy 32:15.

to Christ ('the Rock was Christ')[24] or even to St Peter ('upon this rock I will build my church')[25] but rather to the archaic word *rock*, of indeterminate origins, now almost completely disused and forgotten. It refers to the distaff, the common tool which women used to hold the unspun fibers of flax (or wool) before feeding them to the spindle and twisting them into thread. It is a word that was practically consigned to oblivion, along with the manual skills that it represented, once the preparation of yarn moved from the household to the industrialized spinning-mill.[26]

Culturally, ploughing and spinning were complementary archetypes for gender-specific work, and in England they were celebrated with their own rituals of sexual competition and fertility. In York, the shortest day of the year was marked with the public 'riding' of the figures of Yule and his wife. They scattered nuts into the crowd, and she carried a rock, ostensibly to warn the wives of the city to put aside their 'servile workes' to make preparations for the coming feast, but more probably as a symbol of misrule and disorder.[27] Even more to the point were the outrageous skimmington rituals that villagers used to shame husband-beating wives. Two male revellers rode together on the same horse, one playing the 'wife's' role in a parody of female dress, and the other as the 'husband', unmanned, facing the horse's tail as he plied his distaff. They rode in a noisy, drumming procession to the door of the unhappy household.[28] Here, the presence of the rock defined the breach of good order.

The end of the Christmas season was also celebrated by final bursts of sport and pleasure on Rock Day (also known as St Distaff's Day) and Plough Monday. St Distaff's Day was the first half-day of work on 7 January, and it was marked as young men and maids in their households rivalled each other to be the first to ready their respective implements in the morning. The young women strove to have a kettle on the fire before the men could hurry into the fields, and the losers paid a forfeit at Shrove-tide. Plough Monday came at the same time, following the first Sunday after Epiphany, better remembered now than Rock Day partly because its spirit of misrule had a public element. Young men

---

[24] 1 Corinthians 10:4.

[25] Matthew 16:18.

[26] See the second substantive meaning of the word 'rock' in the *OED*. For spinning in general, see Merry E. Wiesner, *Women and Gender in Early Modern Europe* (Cambridge, 1993), pp. 97–100.

[27] Alexandra F. Johnston and Margaret Rogerson (eds), *Records of Early English Drama: York* (Toronto, 1979), vol. 1, pp. 359–62; Duffy, *Altars*, pp. 581–2. My thanks to Lori Anne Ferrell and Gregory P. Ripple for these references.

[28] Anthony Fletcher, *Gender, Sex and Subordination in England 1500–1800* (New Haven, CT, 1995), pp. 201–3, 270–72, and plates 2 and 11.

raised funds by dragging ploughs in procession around their villages, soliciting donations for improvements to the fabric of their parish churches, or for the so-called 'plough-lights' which flickered before the great roods. The ploughs might actually be brought into the church for blessing (or rather for 'conjuring', as the Protestant polemicist John Bale sourly observed). Rock Day and Plough Monday balanced each other, the domestic and female with the male and public, each ultimately centred on the parish, where the maidens as a group also might meet the cost of candles. Even though lights were suppressed early in the Reformation, and Yule ridings and Plough Monday rituals came under assault, vestiges of the Plough Monday and Rock Day diversions survived into the seventeenth century (and skimmingtons longer still).[29]

Like Piers Plowman, the woman spinning appeared as a literary device on her own, but less frequently than her male counterpart. This in itself may be a reflection of the common appreciation of female dependence in society. She appears in her own story in the ribald *The gospelles of dystaves*, which appeared in English from the French around 1510. Six matrons met over successive winter nights for a spinning bee, one after another contributing her own 'gospel' of homely wisdom and dubious stories, recorded for posterity by a reluctant man whom they persuaded to sit among them. *The gospelles of dystaves* is the ultimate sixteenth-century collection of old wives' tales. Here the inversion takes a more traditional cast, finding humour in the narrator's predicament, stuck (and by implication unmanned), among the women, to whom formal learning or serious reading were practically unknown.[30]

The pairing of the ploughman with the spinner has an even more fundamental meaning devised to reflect the basic symmetry of society, where the woman is not merely an adjunct, but represents the female

---

[29] Duffy, *Altars*, pp. 13, 461; Barbara Hanawalt, '"Keepers of the Light": Late Medieval English Parish Gilds', *Journal of Medieval and Renaissance Studies*, 14 (1984), pp. 26–37; W. Carew Hazlitt, *Faiths and Folklore: a Dictionary*, in J. Brand, *The Popular Antiquities of Great Britain*, (rev. edn, London, 1905), vol. 1, p. 180; vol. 2, pp. 495–6; Ronald Hutton, *The Rise and Fall of Merry England: the Ritual Year 1400–1700* (Oxford, 1996), pp. 16–17, 50, 75, 87–8, 100, 114, 119–20; Charles Kightly, *The Perpetual Almanack of Folklore* (London, 1987), for 7 and 10 January, and 21 December (for the feast of Yule); Thomas Tusser, *Five hundred points of good husbandrie*, eds W. Payne and Sidney J. Herrtage (English Dialect Society, 21, 1878), pp. 180–82, 307–8; John Bale, *The Image of Both Churches* in *Select Works*, ed. Henry Christmas (PS, 1849), p. 528; Fletcher, *Gender*, pp. 200–202, 270–71.

[30] H. W[atson], trans. *The gospelles of dystaves*, from *Les evangiles des quenouilles*, STC 12091 (London, c. 1510), reprinted in *Distaves and Dames: Renaissance Treatises for and about Women*, ed. Diane Bornstein (Delmar, NY, 1978); Madeleine Jeay, *Savoir faire: une analyse des croyances des 'evangiles des quenouilles' (xve siècle)* (Montreal, 1982). I am indebted to Laura Doyle Gates for this reference.

half of the human equation, and together they symbolize the whole. Both are a development of the medieval expression: 'When Adam delved and Eva span, where was then the pride of man?'[31] As with Piers Plowman, there is always a measure of inversion involved in this couplet, an inherent criticism of privilege or wrongdoing. It shares deep resonances with the recurrent symbolism of the Christian Church, of the triumph of the poor or powerless through the intervention of God, including 'the rich He hath sent empty away', from the Magnificat; or how the 'stone which the builders rejected', became the Saviour of humankind.[32] The woman with the rock recalls not only the fault of Eve, but restitution in the domestic virtues of hard work, and suggests even sanctification and purity.[33] 'Who so fyndeth an honest faythfull woman?', asks Miles Coverdale's translation of the Book of Proverbs. 'She layeth her fyngers to the spyndle/& her hande taketh holde of the rocke.' A virtuous woman 'is moch more worth then perles'.[34] For Fisher too, the ploughman and the women with their rocks represented a type of inversion. Not only select members of society, including the wealthy or the ordained, could reach to the divine, but all people in every walk of life could approach the great mysteries of faith and redemption through prayer and devotion. These powers lay even within the grasp of the woman with modest means, who kept a run of chickens. For Fisher, every sinner could be made holy through the potency of the crucifixion, which was not dependent upon the ability to read.

And if the ploughman could be used to advance arguments for a variety of causes, so too could the woman with the rock be portrayed with a similar flexibility, beyond the levity of *The gospelles of dystaves*. Even inside the ranks of the humanists, in the writings of Erasmus and Juan Luis Vives, we see that the symbol was reinterpreted to reflect differing concerns. Fisher, inspired by the spirituality of St Francis of Assisi, held up the pattern of poor women spinning to increase in his listeners their appreciation for the sacrifice of God, and to draw the

---

[31] See the *OED* under the verb 'delve' for full references. Also, Tusser, *Husbandrie*, p. 155. For continental images of the ploughman and the woman with a distaff, see R. W. Scribner, *For the Sake of Simple Folk: Popular Propaganda for the German Reformation* (Cambridge, 1981), pp. 211–16; Simon Schama, *The Embarrassment of Riches: the Interpretation of Dutch Culture in the Golden Age* (New York, 1987), pp. 389–95, 416–17; Wiesner, *Women and Gender*, p. 98.

[32] Luke 1:53; Matthew 21:42.

[33] See Schama, *Riches*, ch. 6; John N. King, *Tudor Royal Iconography: Literature and Art in an Age of Religious Crisis* (Princeton, NJ, 1989), p. 190.

[34] Proverbs 31:10–23; and see these verses in Thomas Matthew, trans. [pseud. for Miles Coverdale, William Tyndale and John Rogers], *The byble, which is all the holy scripture*, STC 2066 (Antwerp, 1537).

faithful closer to Him.[35] Fisher's sermon was one of the finest exposi-
tions of the ancient commonplace that mimetic images are the books of
the unlearned. Vives and Erasmus drew upon different sources of inspiration, basing their allusions to women and spinning more closely upon
the epistles of St Jerome, the fourth-century Father of the Church who
first translated holy scripture from the original languages into the Latin
Vulgate.[36] When Erasmus revised his *Paraclesis* in 1523 as the *Exhortatio
ad studium Evangelicae lectionis*, issued as a preface before his paraphrase of the Gospel according to Matthew, he introduced the 'wedded
wyfe, when she sytteth at her dystaffe' to the ploughman, weaver, and
wayfarer, and advocated that she should have a companion or kins-
woman to read the Gospel to her as she spun, referring to Jerome as his
authority.[37] Erasmus helped to create the expectation that the laity
needed to approach the divine through the venue of words, not images,
and that women needed to read the Scriptures as much as laymen did.

Indeed, Jerome provided the original connection between women's
scriptural learning and her duties with the distaff. In his influential
Instruction of a Christen Woman, Vives quoted extensively from Jerome's
letter of advice to the matron Laeta concerning the education of her
daughter Paula. Paula was to learn large portions from both testaments,
including the Psalms, Proverbs, the Gospels, and the Acts of the Apostles, and Laeta was also to give her instruction in the art of how 'to
holde and occupie a rocke, with a wolle basket in her lappe, & turne
the spyndel, and drawe forth the threde with her owne fyngers'.[38]

---

[35] Duffy, 'Spirituality of Fisher', p. 215.

[36] See Lisa Jardine, *Erasmus, Man of Letters: the Construction of Charisma in Print*
(Princeton, NJ, 1993); Eugene F. Rice, *Saint Jerome in the Renaissance* (Baltimore, MD,
1985), especially ch. 5; Lily B. Campbell, *Divine Poetry and Drama in Sixteenth-Century
England* (Cambridge, 1959), p. 3; and also Collinson, 'The Bible in Reformation England', p. 108.

[37] Erasmus, *Epistola Nvncupatoria ad Carolvm Caesarem. Exhoratio ad studium
Euangelicae lectionis. Paraphrasis in Euangelium Matthaei* (Basle, 1523), sigs B2v, D7r,
E2v; translated into English in *An exhortacyon to the study of the Gospell*, STC 10494
(London, [1534?]), sigs G2r-v. Jerome to Demetria, *Opera omnia*, in J. P. Migne (ed.),
Patrologia cursus completus latinae (1877), vol. 1 (22), p. 130 (cols 1107–24). Cf. King,
Tudor Royal Iconography, p. 201.

[38] 'Discat et lanam facere, tenere colum, ponere in gremio calathum, rotare fusum,
stamina police ducere. Spernat bobycum telas, Serum vellera, et aurum in filia lentescens.'
Jerome, *Opera Omnia*, vol. 1 (22), p. 107, col. 875; quoted by Vives, *Instruction of a
Christen Woman*, trans. Richard Hyrde, STC 24856 (London, [1529?]), sig. C4r. For his
letters to female correspondents see Elizabeth A. Clark, *Jerome, Chrysostom and Friends:
Essays and Translations* (New York, 1979), pp. 35–106. And for Vives, see Valerie
Wayne, 'Some Sad Sentence: Vives's *Instruction of a Christian Woman*', in M. P. Hannay
(ed.), *Silent but for the Word: Tudor Women as Patrons, Translators, and Writers of
Religious Works* (Kent, OH, 1985), pp. 15–29.

Jerome, as much as Paul, set a crucial standard for Christian women. In his letters to his female correspondents, Jerome provided an interesting amplification of the usual Pauline epitome for women, developing in greater detail the apostle's recommendation that matrons should teach younger women.[39] In presenting a practical programme of readings for the education of girls by their mothers, and in his correspondence with women generally, Jerome helped to encourage the perception that women and learning were not inimical, though Paul's strictures continued to provide a brake upon what was usually considered permissible for women to do. The prohibitions against speaking in church and instructing men still held.

But for Vives, the teachings of Paul and Jerome balanced each other, and he gave them almost equal weight. Learning and virtue went together, and women needed to understand their subordinate place in the Church, in wedlock and in other aspects of life. Combined with reading, handwork was one of the ultimate badges of a woman's chastity. Let the maiden, he argued 'both lerne her boke, & beside that, to handle wolle and flaxe'. She should not be ignorant of these skills, he wrote with one eye on his patron Katherine of Aragon, 'no nat though she be a princes or a quene'.[40]

Jerome's syllabus was a close match for the material that was the common currency of Latin primers, and portions of the Gospels that were read by priests and expounded to the laity in the lessons of the mass and homilies. Vives too saw the value of devotional handbooks. Every woman, before attending mass, should 'rede at home the gospel and the epistole of the day, and with hit some exposition, if she have any'.[41] Writing originally in Latin for an international readership, this advice might at first seem unremarkable, as Eamon Duffy assures us that even unlearned members of the laity approached Latin texts with many degrees of comprehension, and macaronic primers were readily available.[42] But suddenly the reading list Vives supplied as being suitable for young girls might have acquired a new significance. Once the *Instruction of a Christen Woman* was itself translated into English by the late 1520s, his advice reached lower on the social scale. Vives's suggestion that 'every body knoweth' that the Gospels, the Acts of the Apostles and the Old Testament should be read, may have seemed somewhat avant-garde, as full scriptural translations were still prohibited. Vives

---

[39] Titus 2:3–5.

[40] Vives, *Instruction*, sig. C3v. For Katherine's skill with the needle, see Eric Ives, *Anne Boleyn* (Oxford, 1986), p. 175.

[41] Vives, *Instruction*, sigs C3v–D1r, D4v–E3r, F2r–v.

[42] Duffy, *Altars*, pp. 213–32.

made a strong case for their availability to women,[43] though this view fell far short of Erasmus's startling claim, in the revised *Exhortatio*, that as Christ had not kept any away from his voice, then no one should be kept from his books. Even harlots should read the gospel.[44]

Before the lifting of the old medieval heresy laws in 1534,[45] and until the passage of the Act for the Advancement of True Religion and for the Abolishment of the Contrary nine years later, theologians considered the appropriateness of women's reading, weighing Jerome against Paul, conservatives trusting in Paul, while the reformers built upon Erasmus's lead. The Bristol preacher Roger Edgeworth maintained that he had always believed that 'holie Scriptures shoulde be hadde in the mother tong', but admitted that he was deeply troubled by the implications that those who were not 'apt or mete' should take it in hand. And how could most women possibly fit the necessary criteria, given Eve's transgressions and Paul's strictures? Even Jerome's saintly correspondents had not been 'readers, preachers, or disputers of scriptures'. Indeed, God had given grace to such women solely 'to subdue their affections and lusts' so they were more disposed to understand what they read. It may have pleased Him to permit Priscilla to teach, but her example went against the common rule.[46] In contrast, the reformer Robert Wisdom preached in his Essex cure during Easter time in 1541 that parishioners should take the scripture in their hands when they met on Sundays and other holy days, to discuss it even at the alehouse. 'I trust to God to se the day, that maydes wil sing the Scripture at their wheles, and plowmen at their plow.'[47] And in 1536 a hopeful client of Cromwell's, a Suffolk clergyman named Thomas Wylley, wrote a play (which unfortunately has been lost) called 'The Woman on the Rokke', whose enthusiasm for the tenet of *sola scriptura* over the traditional intercessions can perhaps be appreciated from the brief description he included: 'yn the fyer of faythe a fynyng, and a purgyng in the trewe purgatory'.[48]

---

[43] Vives, *Instruction*, sigs C3v–D1r, D4v–E3r, F2r–v.

[44] Erasmus, *Exhoratio ad studium Euangelicae lectionis*, sigs B2v, D7r, E2v; *An exhortacyon to the study of the Gospell*, sigs G2r–v.

[45] They were repealed by 25 Henry VIII, c. 14; see Guy, 'Law of Heresy', in *The Debellation*, pp. xlvii–lxvii.

[46] *Sermons Very Fruitful, Godly and Learned by Roger Edgeworth: Preaching in the Reformation c. 1535–c. 1553*, ed. Janet Wilson (Woodbridge, Suffolk, 1993), pp. 136–40.

[47] BL, Harl. MS 425, fols 6r–6v, printed in John Styrpe, *Ecclesiastical Memorials*, vol. 1 (2), no. 115 (Oxford, 1824), pp. 473–4.

[48] PRO, SP 1/116, fols 158r–159v (*LP*, vol. 12 [1], no. 529); quoted in Paul Whitfield White, *Theatre and Reformation: Protestantism, Patronage, and Playing in Tudor England* (Cambridge, 1993), pp. 69–70, 102–3. (My thanks to the author for correspondence upon this matter.)

The strength of women's interest in scriptural reading gave rise to worries which ultimately were addressed in the 1543 law. To Anne Boleyn must go much early credit for being a tireless promoter of the English Bible. She advanced evangelical preachers, distributed English prayer-books to replace Latin primers and above all protected the illegal trade in prohibited books. She even put an English Bible on a desk for members of the court to read. Until she was superseded by Cromwell, the movement to bring about English reform owed a great deal to her.[49] For the first time, women began to read the Bible, not just in their households, but openly and in direct contravention of Paul and of the royal proclamations of 1539 and 1541. One Mrs Castle of St Andrew Holborn parish was known as 'a reader of the Scripture in the church', and she was cited by officers of Bishop Edmund Bonner of London for being a 'meddler'.[50] The gentlewoman Anne Askew read for a week in Lincoln Minster, undismayed by the clusters of priests who stopped to stare at her.[51] Edgeworth raised his alarm because he may well have witnessed Bristol women reading the Scriptures publicly.[52]

Laymen too were noted for disturbing congregations at church 'with loud reading the English Bible',[53] and the Act for the Advancement of True Religion and for the Abolishment of the Contrary was meant to stop such displays. With the renewed protection accorded to the mass in the Act of the Six Articles of 1539, and the fall of Thomas Cromwell, it marked the reinvigorated conservatism of Henry VIII in the late years of his reign. It forbade the reading of the Bible by any unauthorized persons, privately or openly, especially by any women or men beneath the degree of yeoman, and it prohibited scriptural discussions or arguments. Noblewomen or gentlewomen might read the Scriptures to themselves, but only in the greatest privacy, out of the range of the

---

[49] Maria Dowling (ed.), 'William Latymer's Cronickille of Anne Bulleyne', in *Camden Miscellany XXX*, (CS, 4th series, 39, 1990), especially pp. 61–3; and M. Dowling, 'Anne Boleyn and reform', *JEH*, 35 (1984), pp. 30–46: E. W. Ives, *Anne Boleyn* (Oxford, 1986), pp. 314–18, and 'Anne Boleyn and the Early Reformation: the Contemporary Evidence', *HJ*, 32 (1994), pp. 389–400.

[50] Paul L. Hughes and James F. Larkin (eds), *Tudor Royal Proclamations* (hereafter *TRP*) (New Haven, CT, 1964), vol. 1, pp. 284–6, 296–8. Foxe, *Acts and Monuments*, vol. 5, p. 444; Susan Brigden, *London and the Reformation*, (Oxford, 1989), pp. 343–4.

[51] John Bale (ed.), *The first examinacyon of Anne Askewe*, STC 848 (1546), reproduced in facsimilie edn in *The Early Modern English Woman*, vol. 1, sel. John N. King (Aldershot, 1996), fol. 33r; reprinted in Elaine V. Beilin (ed.), *The Examinations of Anne Askew* (Oxford, 1996), p. 56; Bale, *Select Works*, p. 173; Foxe, *Acts and Monuments*, vol, 5, p. 541.

[52] Martha C. Skeeters, *Community and Clergy; Bristol and the Reformation c. 1530–c. 1570* (Oxford, 1993), pp. 64–5.

[53] Foxe, *Acts and Monuments*, vol. 5, p. 443; BL, Harl. MS 425, fols 6r–v.

hearing of any other person.[54] The new law represented a reversal of previous policy and the strictest interpretation of Paul, for it went so far as to forbid women to read in the hearing of each other.

And it was upon this rendering of Paul that the law received some of its most persistent challenges, particularly by high-born women who believed that the apostle had meant for them to provide instruction to their sisters, if not to men. Paul's epistle to Titus, as well as St Jerome's letters, provided loopholes to exploit. Many women, uncertain as to the legality of reading the Bible, or themselves mindful of Paul's injunctions not to teach men, instructed only their daughters. Anne Locke's mother-in-law taught her three daughters (but not her sons) from 'good' English books smuggled from abroad 'very privately for feare of troble'.[55] Margaret Ambsworth, of St Botolph Algate parish in London, was cited as early as 1541 by Bonner's men, 'for instructing of maids, and being a great doctress'.[56] Indeed, when Askew was questioned in London about her Bible reading and sacramentarian beliefs in 1545, dissections of the implications of Paul's words were central. Bonner's chancellor rebuked her 'for uttering the scriptures: for St Paul (he said) forbade women to speak or to talk of the word of God'. But that was not Paul's meaning, she replied, for he had forbidden women merely 'to speak in the congregation by the way of teaching'. She had taught privately, and only women, to judge from the main witnesses against her, who testified that she had read from the Acts of the Apostles to support her criticisms of idolatry and transubstantiation. And under Paul's precepts, if not Henry's, that was allowed. She turned the tables upon her questioner by asking him 'how manye women he had seane, go into the pulpett and preache?' And when he admitted he had never seen any, she told him to 'fynde no faute in poore women, except they had offended the lawe': Paul's law, scriptural law, not the king's. The fault was not hers, but by implication lay with the Act for the Advancement of True Religion.[57]

---

[54] 34 and 35 Hen. VIII, c. 1, viii, x–xvi. Cf. Diarmaid MacCulloch, *Thomas Cranmer: a Life* (New Haven, CT, 1996), pp. 310–11.

[55] Maria Dowling and Joy Shakespeare, 'Religion and Politics in Mid Tudor England through the Eyes of an English Protestant Woman: the Recollections of Rose Hickman', *Bulletin of the Institute of Historical Research*, 55 (1982), pp. 94–102.

[56] Cf. the example of Brisley's wife in Foxe, *Acts and Monuments*, vol. 5, pp. 444, 448.

[57] See Acts 7:48 and 17:25. Bale, *First examinacyon*, fols 10r–v, 31v; reprinted in Beilin (ed.), *Examinations*, pp. 20–21, 29–31; Bale, *Select Works*, pp. 155–6; Foxe, *Acts and Monuments*, vol. 5, p. 538. Cf. Margery Kempe's defence during a similar line of questioning more than a century earlier: 'I preche not, ser, I come in no pulpytt.' Sanford Brown Meech (ed.), *The Book of Margery Kempe* (EETS, 112, 1940), pp. 126, 130–31. Derek Wilson's assertion that Askew's husband took away her Bible and forbade her to resort to the chained Bible in church is completely unsubstantiated by any evidence, and

Askew's case had important ramifications, especially in light of her links to evangelicals at court, including Katherine Parr. Perhaps heartened by Askew's release following this first examination, only a few months later the queen began to commission a translation of Erasmus's *Paraphrases upon the New Testament*. Her own deep interest in theological matters found expression not only in her patronage and scriptural reading, but in regular intense theological discussions in her privy chamber, among her ladies and gentlewomen, culminating in some frank (and ill-advised) exchanges with the king. They gave conservatives much needed ammunition in the summer of 1546 to try to dispatch leading reformers from positions of influence in the failing months of Henry's life. Askew was burnt, and Katherine was forced to make a humiliating submission to the king, affirming how 'very unseemly, and preposterous' it was for her or for any woman to presume to instruct her lord and husband. Damaging though these events were, paradoxically these sacrifices helped to ensure the ascendancy of the Protestants in time for the crucial juncture of Henry's death in January 1547.[58]

Many of the old trammels could now be removed. When Parliament assembled in the autumn of that year, the old Act for the Advancement of True Religion was under fire, with Katherine Parr and the godly Duchess of Suffolk leading a propaganda campaign against it. The printing of Katherine's *The lamentacion of a sinner* was timed to coincide with Parliament's meeting. Remarkable too as a milestone in women's spiritual writings, Katherine argued that scriptures should be made available to the wider public once more. How was it possible to 'allege the scriptures to be perillous learnyng, because certayne reders therof, fall into heresies'? Why withhold the Scriptures from the many, for the transgressions of a few? Such strong backing helped to remove the old law, and made the way clear for the implementation of evangelical policies. Bible reading for women, as well as men, was permitted once more.[59]

---

indeed is not an accurate representation of the meaning of the 1543 Act. D. Wilson, *A Tudor Tapestry: Men, Women and Society in Reformation England* (London, 1972) p. 164.

[58] Foxe, *Acts and Monuments*, vol. 5, pp. 553–61; Maria Dowling, *Humanism*, pp. 211–13, 219–43; MacCulloch, *Cranmer*, pp. 352–63; Susan Wabuda, 'Equivocation and Recantation during the English Reformation: the "Subtle Shadows" of Dr Edward Crome', *JEH*, 44 (1993), pp. 224–42. See the various dedications by the translators to Katherine and her ladies in *The first tome or volume of the Paraphrase of Erasmus vpon the newe testament*, STC 2854 (London, 1548/49), especially Nicholas Udall's before the gospel of Luke (dated 30 September 1545).

[59] Queen Katherine Parr, *The lamentacion of a sinner*, STC 4827 (London, 5 November 1547), sigs F2r–F4v; reproduced in facsimilie edn of STC 4822 in Janelle Mueller

Edward VI's reign also helped to publicly associate women with the Bible on a scale that had been unprecedented previously, especially in the burnished dedications to Katherine's evangelical ladies which appeared before the beginning of each part of Erasmus's *Paraphrases*, which in its turn was set up in parish churches for all to read. Of great influence, too, was Bale's edition of Askew's account of her ordeal. Such works shifted the whole tenor of the argument on Bible reading for women beyond general allusions to spinning. While references to the woman with the rock became less common, Jerome's letters remained an important point of reference. Bale's printed 'elucidation' of what was proper for a good Christian woman to do may even have exceeded Askew's own aspirations. He offered her as an example for all Christians, male or female, to emulate in reading the Bible. 'Christ commaunded all peoples, both men and women (Johan. 5.) to serche the scryptures, if they thynke to have everlastynge lyfe.'[60] Building again upon the model established by Jerome to the virtual exclusion of Paul's prohibitions, Bale stressed how, 'In the prymatyve churche, specyallye in Saynt Hieromes tyme, was it a great prayse unto women to be lerned in the scriptures.'[61] And when Askew's reading caused her to question many traditional tenets, and led her husband to drive her violently out of his house, Bale provided a novel interpretation of Paul's first letter to the Corinthians to argue that she was right to seek 'a dyvorcement' from him, rather than quoting the more standard caution that 'the unbelieving husband is sanctified by the wife'.[62] Bale culminated by placing a quotation from the book of Joel on Askew's title-page: 'I wyll poure out my sprete upon all flesh (sayth God) your sonnes and your doughters shall prophecye.'[63] Every woman who was empowered by

---

(ed.), *The Early Modern Englishwoman* (Aldershot, 1996), vol. 3, sigs F7r–G1r; 1 Edw. VI, c. XII, ii; John N. King, 'Patronage and Piety: the Influence of Catherine Parr', in M. P. Hannay (ed.), *Silent but for the Word: Tudor Women as Patrons, Translators, and Writers of Religious Works* (Kent, OH, 1985), pp. 43–60; King, *Tudor Royal Iconography*, pp. 246–9, 251–2.

[60] John 5: 39; Bale, *First examinacyon*, fol. 28r; Beilin, *Examinations*, p. 50; Bale, *Select Works*, p. 169.

[61] Bale, *First examinacyon*, fols 10v–11r; Beilin, *Examinations*, pp. 30–31; Bale, *Select Works*, pp. 155–6; John Bale (ed.), *The lattre examinacyon of Anne Askewe*, STC 850 (Marpurg in the lande of Hessen [Wesel], 1546), fols 43v–44r; reprinted in facsimile edn in *The Early Modern Englishwoman*, sel. John N. King; Beilin, *Examinations*, pp. 126–7; Bale, *Select Works*, pp. 222–3.

[62] 1 Corinthians 7:10–16; Askew, *Lattre examinacyon*, sigs 15r–v; Beilin, *Examinations*, pp. 92–4; Bale, *Select Works*, p. 199.

[63] Joel 2:28–9; title-page to Askew's *Lattre examinacyon*, reprinted in E. V. Beilin (ed.), *The Examinations of Anne Askew* (Oxford, 1996), p. 73; Bale, *Select Works*, p. 186. Cf. King, *Tudor Royal Iconography*, pp. 207–9.

God to speak His truth, or to teach with her pen, must be heard. On the authority of God himself, the severest interpretation of Paul was superseded.

Of course, under Mary such views of Askew were overturned by Catholic theologians, who saw her as a warning, not the triumphant martyr. Standish's *Whether it be expedient that the scripture should be in English* was meant to ventilate the issue as it came under consideration yet again by Parliament in 1554, when the revival of the medieval heresy laws were under review. 'How manye women heretikes have taken upon them thoffice of teachinge heresy in these yeares paste, and all contrarye to Paules doctrine?' As he had been among the theologians who had examined Askew, he felt he had a clear view of the extent of the damage. The English Bible had been responsible for the loss of too many souls. 'Therfor for Jesus sake away with it, let it kyll no moo.'[64] Or as the Bishop of London's chancellor told the book smuggler Elizabeth Young, 'It is more fit for thee to meddle with thy distaff, than to meddle with the Scriptures.'[65]

The very first act passed by Elizabeth's first Parliament settled the issue forever. By restoring Edward's laws, and making the Bible legal for all time, the way was also paved for a remarkable outpouring of spiritual writings by women. Askew was among the first to contribute to a growing style of religious writing, which consisted of a heavy reliance upon a wide array of quotations from especially the New Testament, to the almost complete exclusion of any other references. We see this style again and again in later works, including many of the letters of the Marian martyrs that were printed by Foxe.[66]

What the controversy on the woman with the rock and the mid-century arguments concerning women and Bible reading led to by the end of Elizabeth's reign was a modest clarification of women's roles. Paul's strictures against women speaking in church continued to be respected, at least for the time being, which still prevented most women from public ministry. But Jerome's model of the devout woman of letters, exercising herself in reading the Scriptures and singing the Psalms as she maintained her household and instructed her children and servants was invoked time and time again.[67] Anne Locke's erudite but self-effacing translations are representative of this change.

---

[64] Standish, *A Discourse*, sigs D8r, I6v, E3v; 1 and 2 Philip and Mary, c. 6.

[65] Foxe, *Acts and Monuments*, vol. 8, p. 541.

[66] Cf. Susan Wabuda, 'Henry Bull, Miles Coverdale, and the Making of Foxe's *Book of Martyrs*', in Diana Wood (ed.), *Martyrs and Martyrologies* (SCH, 30, 1989), pp. 245–58.

[67] See John Mayer's funeral sermon for Mrs Lucy Thornton of Suffolk in *A Patterne for Women*, STC 17742 (London, 1619), especially pp. 8–13, 19, 30 and the appendix

The Reformation had sought to extend the holiness that had previously been the reserve of the parish more intimately into the lives of the faithful, transforming each household into its own little church. In this sense, women did have a better defined role to play, in reading and instructing those in their care. The most sacred of all texts was now to fill their hands too. Thomas Becon reminded the readers of his *Catechism* that Paul 'most straitly commanded' women 'to preach and teach' in their own households, for 'every man and every woman is a bishop in their own house'. Women must still keep silent in the congregation, and not teach openly,[68] but once the Bible was correctly translated, it made no difference who uttered it, for it was God's voice speaking, beyond any rude human agency. And in the words that God addressed to comfort Paul, which Bale claimed for Anne Askew and the Church he believed her to represent: 'The strength of God is here made perfyght by weakenesse.'[69]

---

on Jerome, pp. 51–153. Also William Forde, *A Sermon Preached at Constantinople* at the funeral of Lady Anne Glover, STC 11176 (London, 1616), p. 76; Charles Fitz-Geffry's *Deaths Sermon Vnto the Liuinge* on Lady Philippe Rous of Cornwall, STC 10940 (London, 1620), pp. 3, 26. I owe these references to the kindness of Dell Twerell. Contrast these sources with Rice's view that appreciation for Jerome began to lag, in *Saint Jerome*, pp. 197–9.

[68] John Ayre (ed.), *The Catechism of Thomas Becon* (PS, 1844), pp. 376–7. Similarly, [Antonius Corvinus], *A Postill or Collection of Moste Godly Doctrine vpon Every gospell through the yeare, aswell for Holye dayes as Sondayes, dygested in suche order, as they bee appoynted and set forthe in the booke of Common Prayer*, STC 5806 (London, 1550), preface.

[69] 2 Corinthians 12:9; Askew, *First examinacyon*, fol. 9v; Beilin, *Examinations*, p. 13; Bale, *Select Works*, pp. 143–4.

CHAPTER THREE

Preparations for the Canterbury provincial Convocation of 1562–63: a question of attribution[1]

David J. Crankshaw

Sir Geoffrey Elton once observed that in attempting to make its contents more accessible the Public Record Office has committed many grave sins. Amongst the worst was the nineteenth-century practice of amalgamating papers from several discrete sixteenth-century collections into one chronological sequence conformable to the calendar then in progress. 'As a result', he wrote, 'the office papers of Thomas Cromwell, preserved for three centuries in a separate collection, are now broken up and redistributed; and while we may suppose, with good reason, that many memoranda and notes of the time came from that archive, we can no longer be sure.'[2] That was an extreme case, but the effect of archival dissolution is that the historian is often so gratified to have found any documentation bearing upon the matter in hand that questions of provenance tend to be overlooked unless there are intrinsic difficulties – such as over date, authorship or purpose – which must be addressed before the documents can properly be understood. Sometimes light can be shed on the problems of origin and transmission by an examination of surrounding materials. In this chapter it is argued that a failure to place certain documents in their archival context, rather than merely in their historical context, has seriously distorted our perception of the important Canterbury provincial Convocation of 1562–63. This distortion in turn has led to the imposition of a false dichotomy: of an episcopate seen as obstructive and even backsliding

---

[1] Throughout this chapter dates are Old Style, with 25 March taken to be the beginning of the year. I must take this opportunity to thank several people who in different ways have facilitated the research for, or writing of, this chapter: Professor Collinson, Tom Freeman, Tim Graham, Felicity Heal, Elisabeth Leedham-Green, the staff of the MSS Department of Cambridge University Library, the staff of the Parker Library at Corpus Christi College, Cambridge and last, but by no means least, my parents.

[2] Geoffrey Elton, *England 1200–1640, the Sources of History: Studies in the Uses of Historical Evidence* (London, 1969; repr., 1976), p. 72.

on the one hand and of a Puritan element held to be constituted as a party and possessed of a detailed and coherent programme for reform on the other.

The ecclesiastical equivalent to Parliament, which was broadly secular and with which it sat in parallel, the Convocation of the province of Canterbury, like its sister assembly in the province of York, was a law-making institution composed of the archbishop, his suffragan diocesan bishops, dignitaries such as archdeacons and deans, and elected representatives of the lower clergy.[3] Already discussed, to varying degrees, by historians from Gibson to Carlson, this particular Convocation of 1562–63 was the first to meet under the conditions of the Elizabethan Church Settlement of 1558–59, which had restored Protestantism in place of Catholicism as the State's confession of faith.[4] The Queen had initially licensed Archbishop Matthew Parker in November 1562 to summon the constituent members for 12 January 1562, the day after her second Parliament was due to begin, but the postponement of that opening by one day meant that Convocation did not settle down to its business until 13 January.[5] After a plenary session held in the Chapter House of

---

[3] This chapter is concerned exclusively with the Convocation of the province of Canterbury.

[4] Edmund Gibson, *Synodus Anglicana: Or, The Constitution and Proceedings of an English Convocation, Shown from the Acts and Registers thereof, to be Agreeable to the Principles of an Episcopal Church* (London, 1702), an edition of which (with the same title) was published by Edward Cardwell (Oxford, 1854). Many of the MSS relating to this Convocation are printed, not altogether accurately, in John Strype, *Annals of the Reformation and Establishment of Religion, and Other Various Occurrences in the Church of England, during Queen Elizabeth's Happy Reign: Together with an Appendix of Original Papers of State, Records, and Letters* (London, 1709; repr., 1824), vol. 1, pt 1, pp. 470–529, vol. 1, pt 2, pp. 562–8; John Strype, *The Life and Acts of Matthew Parker, The First Archbishop of Canterbury in the Reign of Queen Elizabeth ...* (London, 1711), Book 2, pp. 119–23; Edward Cardwell (ed.), *Synodalia: A Collection of Articles of Religion, Canons, and Proceedings of Convocations in the Province of Canterbury, from the Year 1547 to the Year 1717* (2 vols, Oxford, 1842); Walter Frere, *The English Church in the Reigns of Elizabeth and James I (1558–1625)* (London, 1904), pp. 96–102; William Kennedy, *Archbishop Parker* (London, 1908), pp. 168–79; Victor Brook, *A Life of Archbishop Parker* (Oxford, 1962), pp. 127–41; J. C. Barry, 'The Convocation of 1563', *History Today*, 13 (1963), pp. 490–501; Patrick Collinson, *The Elizabethan Puritan Movement* (London, 1967; repr., 1982), pp. 65–6; Patrick Collinson, *Archbishop Grindal 1519–1583: the Struggle for a Reformed Church* (London, 1979), pp. 161–2; William Haugaard, *Elizabeth and the English Reformation: the Struggle for a Stable Settlement of Religion* (Cambridge, 1968), where Strype's errors of transcription are corrected in Appendix I; and A. J. Carlson, 'The Puritans and the Convocation of 1563' in Theodore Rabb and Jerrold Seigel (eds), *Action and Conviction in Early Modern Europe: Essays in Memory of E. H. Harbison* (Princeton, 1969), pp. 133–53.

[5] Haugaard, *Elizabeth and the English Reformation*, p. 54. A copy of the writ of *mandamus* which Parker sent to Grindal is preserved as BL, Lansdowne MS 1031, fol.

St Paul's Cathedral in London, the two houses divided, meeting in a further 34 sessions until 14 April 1563, the Upper House (consisting of the bishops) mostly gathering in Henry VII's chapel at Westminster Abbey, whilst the Lower House (comprising all the other members of convocation) congregated in St Mary's chapel at St Paul's. On one occasion, when Parker was indisposed, the bishops met at Lambeth.[6]

There is agreement that apart from the approval of the ephemeral clerical subsidy, this Convocation's principal and lasting achievement was the promulgation of the Thirty-nine Articles of Religion, which essentially revised the Edwardian Forty-two Articles of 1553.[7] Admittedly, the Queen excised an article concerning eucharistic doctrine between the subscription of the new codification by members of Convocation and the publication of a Latin edition before the end of the year, but the omitted article was restored in 1571, when all 39 were confirmed by Convocation and sanctioned by parliamentary statute.[8] However, these achievements need to be seen in the context of what might have been achieved. Indeed, there is some justification for saying that this Convocation is as significant for what it failed to achieve as for what it succeeded in achieving. It is the aspirations of some of the participants in terms of alterations to the liturgy, reform of the Canon Law and improvements in the economic viability of benefices which are, indirectly, the subject of the present chapter; or at least the problem to be tackled here is that of attributing those aspirations to the correct group of participants.[9]

32r–v. Only a prorogation took place on 12 January 1562; formal proceedings began the following day. Nevertheless, the gathering of 12 January was still counted as the first session and the meeting on 13 January as the second: Gibson, *Synodus Anglicana*, pp. 193, 194.

[6] The locations of the sessions are discussed in Barry, 'Convocation', pp. 492–3.

[7] The articles are evaluated in Haugaard, *Elizabeth and the English Reformation*, pp. 258–72.

[8] Haugaard, *Elizabeth and the English Reformation*, pp. 253–55. During the Convocation of 1571 members of the Lower House subscribed a copy of the first Latin edition of the Articles of 1562, which had been published in 1563. This copy, together with its attached subscriptions, is now Bodleian Library, MS Arch. Seld. A76. The subscriptions are undated, but that they were affixed in 1571 is indicated by the fact that Anthony Russhe subscribed as Dean of Chichester (a benefice to which he was installed on 10 June 1570) and by the fact that John Briggewater subscribed both as proctor for the clergy of the Diocese of Rochester and as Archdeacon of Rochester (a dignity he had resigned by 10 July 1571): Walter Peckham (ed.), *The Acts of the Dean and Chapter of the Cathedral Church of Chichester 1545–1642* (Sussex Record Society, 58, 1959), p. 73; Centre for Kentish Studies, MS DRc/R8, fol. 121ar.

[9] This is not the place in which to undertake a detailed analysis of the proposals themselves, a task which must await the appearance of a proper scholarly edition of all the relevant material. In the meantime, the reader is referred, with some hesitation, to Haugaard, *Elizabeth and the English Reformation*.

We know what some of the aspirations were from the various responses to two separate invitations, one general and the other specific. In his opening address to both houses, Parker stressed the opportunity now presenting itself for the consideration of reform. This declaration, implicitly inviting proposals, was entirely conventional.[10] Then, during the third session on 16 January 1562, the archbishop started the ball rolling in the Upper House by explicitly calling upon the bishops to put forward written proposals for reform at the next session.[11]

Scholars have traditionally identified two papers attributed to Bishop Sandys of Worcester, one paper written by Bishop Alley of Exeter and two petitions presented by the Lower House as the surviving responses to Parker's invitations.[12] All of them contained radical suggestions. One of the papers associated with Sandys advocated the abolition of both the sign of the cross at baptism and of baptism by women. The petition consisting of 21 articles subscribed by 63 members[13] of the Lower House went much further: only ministers were to baptize, intending communicants were to be required to renounce the 'idolatrous' mass at the confession and non-communicants were to be obliged to withdraw from the church during the ministration of communion itself.[14] Superstitious images were to be removed from all public and private places and destroyed. Another petition, consisting of seven articles and bearing 34 signatures, insisted that the Psalms 'apoynted at common prayer' either be sung by the whole congregation or said by the minister alone, but that 'all curious singinge and playinge of the organs maye be removed'. Kneeling at communion was to be left to the discretion of the ordinary. The 'grave' and 'comelye' garment which ministers commonly wore when preaching was to replace the cope and surplice, whilst out-of-door clerical attire was not to be enforced. The petitioners wished to see the

---

[10] Haugaard, *Elizabeth and the English Reformation*, p. 55.

[11] Cardwell, *Synodalia*, vol. 2, p. 505; Haugaard, *Elizabeth and the English Reformation*, p. 56.

[12] ITL, Petyt MS 538/47, fol. 531r–v (statements attributed to Bishop Sandys); fols 448r–9v (Alley's paper, which is signed by the bishop at the top of fol. 448r); fols 581r–84v (the petition known as the 'Twenty-one Articles'); fols 576v–7v (the petition known as the 'Seven Articles').

[13] It should be noted that James Calfhill signed twice, so there are 64 signatures written by 63 individuals.

[14] Frere remarked that the proposed obligatory renunciation of the 'idolatrous' mass 'had little chance of success', for it 'would have contravened a policy on which the Church at this time was acting with considerable consistency, viz. that of not speaking against the mass itself, but only against the perversion of it as "private mass"': Frere, *English Church*, p. 98. For this erroneous statement he was taken to task by Charles Carter in 'The Real Matthew Parker', *The Church Quarterly Review*, 136 (1943), pp. 205–20.

thirty-third article concerning ceremonies mitigated and superstitious saints' days and holidays abrogated, or at least reduced to a mere commemoration for the better instructing of the people 'in historyes'. The climax to these moves famously came on 13 February 1562, the only day during this Convocation for which we have any detailed record of events in the Lower House, when the 'Six Articles' proposing changes to the Prayer Book were debated and defeated by the margin of a single vote.[15]

Convocation then appears to have turned from liturgical issues to questions of discipline. A *Liber de Disciplina* (i.e. 'Book of Discipline') was presented by the Lower House to the bishops on 26 February and referred to a committee of the Upper House presided over by Parker. On 1 March the 'prolocutor' (i.e. the 'speaker' in the Lower House and intermediary between the two houses) informed the bishops that the Lower House wished to have the book returned for the addition of new material. Although the amended book was again offered to the bishops on 5 March nothing more is heard of it.[16]

On the basis of the two petitions, the close February vote and the labours over the 'Book of Discipline', historians have tended to see proceedings in the Lower House not only as dominating this Convocation, but also as a formative experience in the emergence of the Elizabethan Puritan movement. Professor Collinson clearly locates the initiative 'downstairs', at the same time recognizing that 'the more forward of the bishops', amongst whom he singles out Parkhurst and Sandys, 'were evidently favourable to some at least of ... [the] proposed reforms'.[17] Haugaard too could write of 'the legislative struggle between the precisians and the more moderate reformers', manifest in 'the crucial course of events in the Lower House' and ending in 'the ruin of the reformers' programme'.[18] An interpretation which saw the Lower House as making most of the running dovetailed with Carlson's allegation that Parker was an incompetent manager.[19] 'Frustrated in Convocation', Professor Collinson continues, 'the radicals were bound to look to Parliament', where 'once again there were bishops who

---

[15] ITL, Petyt MS 538/47, fols 574r–5v, 588r. The catalogue of Petyt MSS does not enhance understanding by listing as separate items, and without cross-referencing, what are obviously parts of the same document: James Davies (ed.), *Catalogue of Manuscripts in the Library of the Honourable Society of the Inner Temple* (London, 1972), vol. 2, p. 882, items 307, 308 and 315.

[16] Haugaard, *Elizabeth and the English Reformation*, pp. 67–73.

[17] Collinson, *Puritan Movement*, pp. 65–6.

[18] Haugaard, *Elizabeth and the English Reformation*, pp. 53, 67.

[19] 'If the Archbishop had been able to manage Convocation in other matters [apart from the Articles of Religion] as well as William Cecil managed the House of Commons, events might have gone differently': Carlson, 'Puritans and Convocation', p. 140.

approved of their initiative'.[20] For Haugaard, it was entirely natural that the torch should pass (by means never elucidated) from the disappointed clerical element to their lay brethren in the House of Commons, no doubt adding grist to the mill of that 'Puritan Choir' of which Neale thought he had found trace.[21]

The story of these attempts by an inchoate Puritan body working within the Church's legislative assembly to bring England in line with continental practice was already familiar from the works of John Strype, who identified and printed many of the documents upon which it is founded. It was Haugaard's contribution to supplement and correct Strype's transcriptions, in particular reattributing to the precisian element in the Lower House two of the most significant papers (and by implication a third), one of which Strype had previously associated with Parker's establishment.[22] This was to invest that element with a considerable degree of organization before the Vestiarian Controversy of 1565–66, which had traditionally been accepted as the point at which Puritan opinion really coalesced in the face of a general assault on nonconformity. In Haugaard's words: 'If it can be maintained that the militant reformers of the Lower House of the 1563 Convocation formed a coherent party, then "General notes" served as its most complete official prospectus. It proposed a carefully articulated programme of reform in almost all aspects of Church life.'[23]

Haugaard's thesis of a church which reached a turning-point and failed to turn, largely because of the combined forces of an implacable Queen and an incipient 'Anglicanism', was greeted by mixed reviews. Patrick McGrath called Haugaard's book 'important', whilst emphasizing what it left unexplained and unexplored.[24] Elton was enthusiastic: 'Haugaard, following the fortunes of convocation through the first years of the reign, effectively rewrites the history of the new Church's formative period.'[25] But Claire Cross sounded a note of caution, accusing Haugaard not only of over-simplification, but also of Whiggishness.[26]

---

[20] Collinson, *Puritan Movement*, p. 66.

[21] Haugaard, *Elizabeth and the English Reformation*, pp. 73–8 and *passim*; John Neale, *Elizabeth I and her Parliaments 1559–1581* (London, 1953) and John Neale, *Elizabeth I and her Parliaments 1584–1601* (London, 1957).

[22] Haugaard, *Elizabeth and the English Reformation*, pp. 60–61, 68–73, 342–56. These papers are all discussed in detail below, where references to the MSS are given.

[23] Haugaard, *Elizabeth and the English Reformation*, p. 61. The document known as 'Generall notes' is described below.

[24] For McGrath's review, see *History*, 54 (1969), p. 422.

[25] Geoffrey Elton, *Modern Historians on British History, 1485–1945: a Critical Bibliography, 1945–1969* (London, 1970), p. 40.

[26] For Claire Cross's review, see *JEH*, 20 (1969), pp. 350–51.

In spite of this reception, the book has been absorbed into the critical apparatus of footnote and bibliography to the extent that its place in the canon of 'standard works' seems assured.[27] Even revisionism has hitherto left it relatively untouched. Neale's interpretation of the early Elizabethan Parliaments which so evidently influenced his thesis may have succumbed to the onslaughts of Elton, Hudson, Jones and Sutherland, but Haugaard's account of the 1562–63 Convocation was tacitly endorsed by Collinson in 1979 and by Jones himself in 1982 and 1993.[28]

The time is ripe for a reassessment. Haugaard's whole thesis essentially turns upon the status of a number of documents. Although he was the first to move beyond Strype's editions to look at the manuscripts themselves, Haugaard severely damaged his argument when he admitted, 'I came to many of my conclusions about the relationship of the documents to one another before examining the originals.'[29] Professor Cargill Thompson warned us of Strype's unreliability, yet in this case Strype appears to have been substantially correct.[30] The present author's careful

---

[27] Wallace MacCaffrey, *Queen Elizabeth and the Making of Policy, 1572–1588* (Princeton, NJ, 1981), pp. 41–2; Rosemary O'Day, *The Debate on the English Reformation* (London, 1986), p. 208; John Guy, *Tudor England* (Oxford, 1988), p. 524; Christopher Haigh, *Elizabeth I* (London, 1988), p. 177; Diarmaid MacCulloch, *The Later Reformation in England 1547–1603* (Basingstoke, 1990), p. 175; Christopher Haigh, *English Reformations: Religion, Politics, and Society under the Tudors* (Oxford, 1993), p. 341; Wallace MacCaffrey, *Elizabeth I* (London, 1993), p. 466.

[28] John Neale, *Elizabeth I and her Parliaments 1559–1581* (London, 1953); Geoffrey Elton, 'Parliament in the Sixteenth Century: Function and Fortunes', *Historical Journal*, 22 (1979), pp. 255–78, reprinted in Geoffrey Elton, *Studies in Tudor and Stuart Politics and Government, III: Papers and Reviews 1973–1981* (Cambridge, 1983), pp. 156–82; Collinson, *Grindal*, p. 162; Winthrop Hudson, *The Cambridge Connection and the Elizabethan Settlement of 1559* (Durham, NC, 1980); Norman Jones, *Faith by Statute: Parliament and the Settlement of Religion 1559*, (Royal Historical Society Studies in History Series, 32, 1982), p. 170; Geoffrey Elton, *The Parliament of England 1559–1581* (Cambridge, 1986); Nicola Sutherland, 'The Marian Exiles and the Establishment of the Elizabethan Regime', *ARG*, 78 (1987), pp. 253–86; Norman Jones, *The Birth of the Elizabethan Age: England in the 1560s* (Oxford, 1993), pp. 288–9, where, although acknowledging that Haugaard's book is 'flawed' by its dependence on Neale's thesis, Jones remarks that it is 'still extremely useful for the study of the early Elizabethan church'.

[29] Haugaard, *Elizabeth and the English Reformation*, p. ix. In fairness it should be admitted that Haugaard did later inspect the original MSS and discovered errors in Strype's transcriptions.

[30] William Cargill Thompson, 'John Strype as a Source for the Study of Sixteenth-Century English Church History', in Derek Baker (ed.), *The Materials, Sources and Methods of Ecclesiastical History* (SCH, 11, 1975), pp. 237–47, reprinted in William Cargill Thompson, *Studies in the Reformation: Luther to Hooker*, ed. Clifford Dugmore (London, 1980), pp. 192–201, 251–3.

scrutiny of the original manuscripts, together with his discovery of a new one, shows that far from originating in the Lower House and constituting the precisians' programme for reform, as Haugaard would have us believe, several Convocation papers should properly be attributed to Parker's circle, as Strype supposed, a reversal which must call into question almost every aspect of the prevailing interpretation. In the remainder of this chapter I will (in section I) examine the generally known manuscripts, (in section II) introduce a newly discovered document, and (in section III) explore episcopal initiatives, before (in section IV) drawing some conclusions from this analysis.

I

Before engaging with the current interpretation it is necessary to introduce our cast of principals in some detail, which for the purposes of this chapter consist of three undated and anonymous documents.

As we shall see, the earliest of the three is that bearing the integral and contemporaneous heading 'Certen Articles in substance, desired to be granted by the Quenes maiestie'. There are two versions of this document, only the first of which was known to Haugaard: one, a draft (ITL, Petyt MS 538/47, fols 450r–53r), which I shall call 'Certen Articles' A, and the other, fair-written (LPL, MS 2002, fols 17r–20v), which I shall call 'Certen Articles' B. In its final form this document consists of ten numbered articles, which can be summarized as follows: first, a single book should be published under the Queen's authority containing articles of doctrine extracted from 'the boke of Apollogie' (that is, Jewel's *Apology*); those holding opinions to the contrary were to be proceeded against by the ordinaries, who were to invoke the heresy laws; secondly, there should be one catechism (that being written by Dean Nowell) which should be used in all schools, universities and private houses; thirdly, rules and rubrics in the Book of Common Prayer concerning rites and ceremonies should be 'reduced as nighe as maye be to edeficacon & to the godlye puritie and simplicitie used in the primityve Churche' as long as the substance of the book remained unchanged; fourthly, ministers should wear one prescribed form of external apparel, and those holding benefices who refused to conform to this prescription were to be deprived from their livings after three warnings; and fifthly, the imposition of the penalties prescribed by laws and injunctions for non-attendance at church should on no account be frustrated. The sixth article specifies that new laws should be devised in order to suppress adultery, fornication, incest and abuses concerning marriage, in the execution of which ordinaries were not to be hindered by prohibitions issuing from the Queen's courts.

The seventh article recommends that ordinaries should be empowered to investigate allegations of simony, which, if found to be true, would lead to the minister being disabled for seven years from holding a living and to the patron losing his right of presentation for that turn. The eighth article advocates that impropriators of town livings should augment the stipends of the vicars and, if necessary, the ordinary should join the Justices of the Peace in levying some form of taxation upon the parishioners for that purpose. The ninth article insists that impropriators should make a yearly allowance towards the repair of church chancels unless they were already ruinous and unused, in which case they should be demolished and the materials used for repairing the remainder of the church. The last article proposes that the granting of dispensations for plurality, non-residence and marriage without banns should be reformed.[31]

The second paper was contemporaneously entitled 'Generall notes of matters to be movid by the Clergie in the nexte Parliament & Synod'. Again, there are two versions of this document: one, a draft (ITL, Petyt MS 538/47, fols 435r–46r), which I shall call 'Generall notes' A, and the other, fair-written (ITL, Petyt MS 538/47, fols 419r–25v and 430r–32r), which I shall call 'Generall notes' B. In amplifying many of the suggestions adumbrated in 'Certen Articles', whoever composed 'Generall notes' sounded a note of strident radicalism. Some of the more interesting points are these: 'the use of vestmentes, Copes and Surplesses' was to be 'frome hensfurth taken awaye'; fasting and holy days were to be specified by name in the Prayer Book 'and the open observers of the Abrogated dayes ... punished'; the use of organs was to be discontinued and there was to be no more 'Curious Singinge' and 'sup[er]fluous Ringinge of Belles'; peculiar jurisdictions were to be extinguished; thrice weekly divinity lectures, to be delivered in English and attended by the cathedral clergy and singing men, were to be instituted in each of the cathedrals; cathedral clergy, as well as non-preachers who had been admitted to benefices, were to be required to study the Scriptures or risk removal; there was to be a grammar school in every cathedral; pluralism was to be restricted to preachers and graduates, whose livings were to be situated no more than 12 miles apart; benefices over a certain value were only to be held by ministers who could demonstrate a knowledge of Latin; all those holding livings who were not priests were required either to become priests within a specified time-scale or face deprivation; benefices over a certain value were only to be held by licensed preachers; patrons were not to grant rights of presentation to

---

[31] ITL, Petyt MS 538/47, fols 450r–53r, printed imperfectly in Strype, *Annals*, vol. 1, pt 1, pp. 522–5 and discussed in Haugaard, *Elizabeth and the English Reformation*, p. 345; LPL, MS 2002, fols 17r–20v. I quote the heading from the fair-written version.

any third party in advance of a vacancy; no dispensations for non-residence were to be granted for periods in excess of six months, except in cases of sickness; there was to be a rural dean in every deanery; all leases of parsonages were to be terminated in three years time and the parsonages annexed to the vicarages; patrons found guilty of participating in 'Symoniacall pactes' were to lose their rights of patronage for life; and the 'univ[er]sall subtraction of pryvie or p[er]sonall tythes' was to be remedied either by the institution of a poll tax or by the imposition of a rate based upon property rents, as established in London.[32]

Originally untitled, the third paper was subsequently headed 'Articles drawn out by some certain, and were exhibited to be admitted by authority; but not so allowed'. Known as 'Articles for Government', this document, of which only one text is thought to be extant (CCCC, PL, MS 121, pp. 267–355), is too long to be summarized here.[33]

In order to establish the chronology of these three papers we must start in the middle and work both backwards and forwards. The title of 'Generall notes' explicitly states that it was composed in advance of, and preparatory to, 'the nexte Parliament & Synod'. Since its first recommendation was that 'a certen forme of doctrine ... be conceyved in Articles and ... published and auctorised', the paper must have preceded the drawing up and adoption of the Thirty-nine Articles in the Convocation of 1562–63.[34] 'Generall notes' refers to the catechism commissioned from Alexander Nowell, the Dean of St Paul's, as 'alredye draw[n]', whereas 'Certen Articles' describes it as 'well nye finished'.[35] Thus there can be little doubt that 'Certen Articles' preceded 'Generall notes'. Both documents must have been composed before Convocation was convened and neither can have constituted a response to Parker's request for suggestions for reform.[36] Haugaard's work shows very clearly

---

[32] The draft is ITL, Petyt MS 538/47, fols 435r–46r, whilst the fair-written version is ITL, Petyt MS 538/47, fols 419r–25v and 430r–32r. The fair-written version is printed imperfectly in Strype, *Annals*, vol. 1, pt 1, pp. 473–84. Both versions are discussed in Haugaard, *Elizabeth and the English Reformation*, pp. 346–52, where Haugaard corrects and supplements Strype's transcription. Haugaard notes that Strype gave 'no indication that he knew of the draft' of 'Generall notes', that is to say of 'Generall notes' A: Haugaard, *Elizabeth and the English Reformation*, p. 346.

[33] CCCC, PL, MS 121, pp. 267–355. The headings of some of the articles (together with the occasional summary) are printed in Strype, *Annals*, vol. 1, pt 2, pp. 562–8. The MS, and Strype's treatment of it, are discussed in Haugaard, *Elizabeth and the English Reformation*, pp. 354–5.

[34] ITL, Petyt MS 538/47, fol. 419r ('Generall notes' B).

[35] ITL, Petyt MS 538/47, fols 419v ('Generall notes' B) and 450r ('Certen Articles' A) respectively.

[36] This important point is lost on Barry, who includes 'Generall notes' and 'Certen Articles' amongst the 'flood of suggestions' submitted in response to Parker's invitations:

that 'Articles for Government' drew to varying degrees upon the provisions of both 'Certen Articles' and 'Generall notes', developing certain points whilst adding entirely new ones.[37] We can say with considerable confidence, therefore, that 'Articles for Government' was the latest of the three papers, although that is not to say that it too must have been composed before Convocation began.

The historiographical tradition (actually more of a muddle) concerning these (and other) convocation documents is set out in Table 3.1. Attempts at comprehending 'Certen Articles' and 'Generall notes' in particular can be resolved into two key questions: who composed them and for whom were they intended?

Strype remarked that 'Certen Articles' A had been 'composed by a secretary of the archbishop's' and 'mended and added to in some places by the archbishop's own hand, and in some places by bishop Grindal's'.[38] Haugaard assumed that Strype had made this observation on the basis of his familiarity with early Elizabethan hands, but did not assess its veracity.[39] Kennedy repeated Frere, who, together with Brook and Barry, relied upon Strype, none of them displaying any evidence of acquaintance with the manuscripts themselves.[40] In fact no less than four hands appear on 'Certen Articles' A, one being Parker's and another Grindal's, whose role as annotator at the very least has been confirmed by his latest biographer.[41] The hands may be designated I to IV. Hand I (unidentified), distinctive in its rightward slant and formation of t, h, y and g characters, has written the whole of the main text, becoming less distinctive towards the end of the document, perhaps a sign of increased urgency. The wide line-spacing demonstrates that this manuscript was always intended to be a draft, which was then annotated, in this order, by Hands II (Parker), III (Grindal) and IV (unidentified).[42] The

---

Barry, 'Convocation', p. 497. Jones too obfuscates when he includes 'Generall notes' amongst those papers 'prepared in convocation': Norman Jones, 'Religion in Parliament', in David Dean and Norman Jones (eds), *The Parliaments of Elizabethan England* (Oxford, 1990), p. 120.

[37] Haugaard, *Elizabeth and the English Reformation*, pp. 68–73, 354–5.

[38] Strype, *Annals*, vol. 1, pt 1, p. 522.

[39] Haugaard, *Elizabeth and the English Reformation*, p. 345.

[40] Frere avoided the whole question of authorship and annotation, but cited Strype for the documents connected with this Convocation: Frere, *English Church*, pp. 97, 109. Kennedy only remarked upon the corrections made by Parker and Grindal, citing Strype as an 'authority': Kennedy, *Parker*, pp. 170, 179. Brook turned Parker's 'secretary' into his 'chaplain' (a not improbable combination), otherwise following Strype: Brook, *Parker*, p. 136. Barry, turning him back into a 'secretary', had nothing else to say about 'Certen Articles', even neglecting to mention its title: Barry, 'Convocation', p. 497.

[41] Collinson, *Grindal*, p. 162.

[42] The order in which the annotations were made is established as follows. Grindal's

Table 3.1 Variant chronologies proposed for some documents relating to the Convocation of 1562–63[1] (The documents are listed in the order in which each historian, either explicitly or implicitly, suggests that they appeared. Any matter which is conjectural is indicated by means of square brackets.)

PERIOD	STRYPE 1709	FRERE 1904	KENNEDY 1908	BROOK 1962	BARRY 1963	HAUGAARD 1968	CARLSON 1969	CRANKSHAW 1998
Before Convocation	'Generall notes'□	'Certen Articles'? 'Generall notes'?	'Certen Articles' [□] 'Generall notes' [□]	'Generall notes'?		'Certen Articles'* 'Generall notes'**	'Certen Articles'?	'Certen Articles'□ 'Generall notes'□ 'The Commentary'[2]
During Convocation	Sandys 1□ 7 Articles* 6 Articles [*] Sandys 2□ AG□ 21 Articles□ 6 Questions□ Alley□ 'Certen Articles'□	Sandys 1 & 2□ Alley□ 21 Articles* 7 Articles* 6 Articles [*] BD/AG*	Sandys 1 [& 2]□ Alley□ 21 Articles* 7 Articles* 6 Articles [*] BD/AG* 6 Questions□	Sandys [1 & 2]□ Alley□ 'Certen Articles'□ 21 Articles* 7 Articles* 6 Articles [*] BD/AG* 6 Questions□	6 Articles [*] 21 Articles* 'Generall notes'? 'Certen Articles'? Sandys 1□ 7 Articles* Sandys 2□ Alley□ BD/AG? 6 Questions□	Sandys 1 & 2□ Alley□ 7 Articles* 6 Articles* 6 Questions□ BD/21 Articles* AG [*]	21 Articles* 7 Articles* 6 Articles* Sandys 1 & 2□ Alley□	21 Articles*[3] 6 Articles* 7 Articles* ['Sandys'] 1 & 2□ Alley□ 6 Questions□ AG□ BD□

Key:
AG = 'Articles for Government'
Alley = Bishop Alley's proposals
BD = 'Book of Discipline'
Sandys 1 and 2 = Two sets of proposals attributed to Bishop Sandys

□ = A document held to have originated amongst the episcopate
* = A document held to have originated either in the Lower House of Convocation or amongst precisians who became members of that House
? = A document, the origin of which is not stated

Notes:
1 References to 'Certen Articles', 'Generall notes', 'The Commentary', the 'Twenty-one Articles', the 'Seven Articles', the 'Six Articles', the papers associated with Bishops Sandys and Alley, and 'Articles for Government' are all provided in the main text. The document here referred to as the '6 Questions' (headed 'Articles to be inquired of in the lower howse of Convocation' and broadly concerning the economic viability of benefices) is not discussed in the present chapter because there is no doubt of its episcopal origins. It survives as ITL, Petyt MS 538/47, fol. 587r and is printed from another source (with slight variations) in Gibson, *Synodus Anglicana*, pp. 210–11. Any documents concerning the articles of doctrine (the Thirty-nine Articles, the Catechisms, the Homilies and the clerical subsidy are omitted from this table.
2 It is argued in the main text that 'The Commentary' originated neither with the Upper House nor with the Lower House, but with a legal expert or experts.
3 I shall be discussing the status and chronology of this and the following two sets of articles elsewhere.

annotations consist of a few deletions, but mostly of insertions of new words or phrases, Grindal also adding a marginal comment not intended for incorporation in the main text.[43] Once the annotations were complete, most of the document, with two or three significant changes, was neatly rewritten by Hand I as 'Certen Articles' B.[44] Although the narrower line-spacing suggests that extensive further revision was not expected, the copyist made some minor slips which had to be corrected, most notably the incorporation of Grindal's marginal comment, subsequently struck out.[45]

Brook wrote that he could find no evidence that 'Certen Articles' was ever presented to the Queen, but such a notion betrays a fundamental misunderstanding of the document.[46] It is inconceivable that in its highly corrected state 'Certen Articles' A could ever have been shown to

---

annotations on ITL, Petyt MS 538/47, fols 450r (line 8, 'errors'), 451r (line 4, 'and incestes') and 452r (line 3, '& other proprietaries') show that he began his interlinear annotations directly above the insertion mark and continued to the right. On fol. 450r (line 7, '& punisshed'), however, there is only one insertion mark, entirely to the left of which Grindal entered his annotations. This was because Parker's annotations ('bi the ordinaryes') already occupied the space Grindal would normally have used. So, whoever wrote this document went straight to the top for comments. On fol. 450r (at the bottom) the further annotations to Grindal's annotations demonstrate that the Bishop of London was not the last man to be permitted to scrutinize the text.

[43] ITL, Petyt MS 538/47, fol. 450v.

[44] For example, Article 3 of 'Certen Articles' A originally read:

> It[e]m that some fewe imperfections escaped in the Boke of Service as well in choise of the chapters, as of the psalmes, w[i]t[h] other suche thinges concerninge the Rites and Ceremonies in the church maye be reduced to edeficacon as nye as maye be, to the godlie simplicitye used in the primityve churche.

This text was then annotated, those annotations being incorporated in the revised version of Article 3 presented in 'Certen Articles' B:

> It[e]m for that the choise of Chapters maye be better considered in ye Boke of service, and that certen Rules and Rubrickes in the saide Booke of comon prayer concerninge certen Rites and Ceremonies in the Churche maye be reduced as nighe as maye be to edeficacon & to the godlye puritie and simplicitie used in the primityve Churche.

However, one sentence was added to the end of Article 3 of 'Certen Articles' B which had appeared neither in the original text of 'Certen Articles' A nor in the annotations to it: 'The wholle substance of the saide Boke notwithstandinge, remayninge untouched.' The annotations to Article 8 of 'Certen Articles' A were not incorporated in the corresponding article of 'Certen Articles' B. Moreover, the last article of 'Certen Articles' A is entirely omitted from 'Certen Articles' B even though (in contrast to Article 9) it has not been struck through.

[45] LPL, MS 2002, fol. 17v.

[46] Brook, *Parker*, p. 136.

the Queen, and doubtful whether even 'Certen Articles' B would have been exhibited. Besides, the title itself discloses that this document was never intended to be placed before higher authority; it was the substance of the articles rather than the particular form of words which was to be propounded to Elizabeth, although the means by which that substance might be conveyed was not elucidated. The resounding silence amongst contemporaries, together with the absence of any contemporaneous copies, suggests that 'Certen Articles' never left the possession of its authors – we know that there was more than one because Hand I wrote 'We thinke' – and in all probability this was because it was immediately superseded by 'Generall notes', which develops most of its points.[47]

'Generall notes' A is a complex manuscript, understanding of which is not helped by the fact that it is currently bound out of order, as Haugaard recognized.[48] Once rearranged it will be seen that the text follows the order of treatment proposed at the outset, namely 1) concerning the drawing up, authorization and publication of articles of doctrine; 2) concerning reform of the Prayer Book; 3) concerning the drawing up of a code of discipline for both the clergy and the laity; and 4) concerning the augmentation of the value of livings. This reconstitution also establishes that one of the folios bound into 'Generall notes' A has been omitted from the original numeration.[49]

The main text is written in two hands, or possibly the same hand under quite different conditions, but the variations are sufficiently great as to suggest that the former was the case.[50] The lion's share, hurriedly and even carelessly written by Hand V (unidentified), has been subject

---

[47] For the words establishing multiple authorship, see ITL, Petyt MS 538/47, fol. 450r and LPL, MS 2002, fol. 17r ('Certen Articles' A and B respectively).

[48] Haugaard, *Elizabeth and the English Reformation*, p. 347, where he prints a table clarifying how the folios of 'Generall notes' A should be reorganized. Haugaard tells us that he worked on the basis of the order of sections specified at the outset: ITL, Petyt MS 538/47, fol. 435r. In fact the document has its own distinct foliation in the top left-hand corner of each recto, which is older than the current foliation (in the top right-hand corner) in respect of the whole volume: see ITL, Petyt MS 538/47, fols 435r (indistinct), 439r (2), 440r (3), 441r (4), 442r (5), 443r (6), 444r (7), 445r (8), 446r (9), 437r (10), 438r (11). This numeration shows that Haugaard's reconstitution is correct.

[49] ITL, Petyt MS 538/47, fol. 436r–v, which is discussed below. The omission may well mean that this folio does not belong to 'Generall notes' A at all.

[50] For Haugaard, the draft was written 'either by several hands or by the same hand under varying conditions': Haugaard, *Elizabeth and the English Reformation*, p. 346. Two completely different ways of forming 'f', 'h' and 's' characters are apparent between various sections of the document: see, for example, ITL, Petyt MS 538/47, fols 439r and 440r. It is difficult to see how more than two hands could have been involved in writing the main text, as implied by Haugaard's use of the word 'several'.

to considerable emendation in the same hand.[51] The remaining portions are neatly written by Hand VI (unidentified) and hardly corrected at all.[52] Strangely, the divisions between the hands do not correspond exactly to the divisions between the four parts of the document. Thus, part one (concerning the articles of doctrine) begins in Hand V, covering the verso of one folio, but continues in Hand VI for the recto of the next folio.[53] This same hand then wrote the whole of part two on the verso of the folio.[54] After that, parts three and four are written throughout in Hand V, with the exception of one folio belonging to part three which appears in Hand VI.[55] The two hands differ markedly in terms of line-spacing. Hand V varies considerably between compressed text in which hardly any room is left for interlinear annotations and widely spaced lines which were evidently intended to accommodate them. By contrast, Hand VI adopted a uniform and relatively narrow line-spacing. Since Hand VI always appears on its own folios, all of this evidence points to the conclusion that these folios were later insertions, replacing earlier leaves which had probably been so extensively corrected that an immediate redraft was unavoidable.

Hand V occasionally glossed the text it had written. For example, against the recommendation that articles of doctrine be set forth, this hand wrote 'm[emoran]d[um] that thies articles be drawn w[i]t[h] spede'.[56] It was probably once the insertion of rewritten folios had been

---

[51] See, for example, ITL, Petyt MS 538/47, fol. 442v. This hand also wrote an interesting memorandum, hitherto overlooked, which appears to indicate some connection with Parker's establishment:

> To thinke upon suche a one as is mete to be prolocutor & to no[m]i[n]ate ij or iij to chose one owte of them for that rowm / there must be iij also chosen to present the same p[ro]locutor when he is chosen to my L. of Cant grace / The p[ro]locutor maketh an ovation at ... the tyme that he is p[rese]n[ted] & so doth one of them that doth present him. (ITL, Petyt MS 538/47, fol. 447v)

Who but the archbishop and president of Convocation was in a position to nominate two or three men as prolocutor, from whom the Lower House would choose one? The memorandum is consistent with what we know of Parker's great interest in discovering the correct procedures observed in Convocations: Haugaard, *Elizabeth and the English Reformation*, p. 342.

[52] Hand V was responsible for ITL, Petyt MS 538/47, fols 435r-v, 440r-43r, 444r-5v, 437r-8v. Hand VI wrote fols 439r-v and 446r. It should be noted that fols 443v and 446v are blank, whilst fol. 436r-v (written in Hand V) is the folio omitted from the original numeration and the exact position of which must be conjectural.

[53] ITL, Petyt MS 538/47, fols 435v, 439r.

[54] ITL, Petyt MS 538/47, fol. 439v.

[55] ITL, Petyt MS 538/47, fols 440r-45v, 437r-8v. The exceptional folio is fol. 446r.

[56] ITL, Petyt MS 538/47, fol. 435v.

effected that the manuscript was viewed by Grindal, for his annotations (Hand III) appear on portions written by Hand V and by Hand VI.[57] Although there is no sign here of Hands I (unidentified) or II (Parker), the archbishop is mentioned in a marginal note: '*Addantur annotationes D. Cantuar. ad dom. secretarium*', which suggested to Haugaard that Parker 'may have dictated the comments after the document had been given to him for his perusal'.[58]

'Generall notes' B is no less complicated than its predecessor. This time bound correctly,[59] it reproduces the text of 'Generall notes' A, incorporating its many emendations, but also, rather oddly, replicating the marginal comments.[60] Two hands were responsible for the main text. All of it is written by Hand I (unidentified) except for the introductory *schema*, the first portion of part one and the whole of part four, which were penned by Hand VII (unidentified). Both hands adopted a relatively narrow line-spacing, indicating that further revision was not

---

[57] ITL, Petyt MS 538/47, fols 439v, 440v.

[58] ITL, Petyt MS 538/47, fol. 437r, where the annotation is not easy to distinguish. Examination of the same annotation on 'Generall notes' B (ITL, Petyt MS 538/47, fol. 420r) suggests that Haugaard may have misread 'dnu' (with an abbreviation mark above it) as 'dom.': Haugaard, *Elizabeth and the English Reformation*, p. 346. If 'dnu' stands for 'dominum', then is it possible that 'dnu Secretar' meant 'master Secretary'; in other words, Secretary Cecil?

[59] Both 'Generall notes' A and B are bound the same way; that is to say the sections into which the document is divided follow the same sequence. Because Haugaard correctly perceived that 'Generall notes' A is misbound according to the table of contents at the beginning (confirmed by the original numeration not noticed by Haugaard), he assumed that 'Generall notes' B must also currently be bound out of order. Consequently, when he printed a corrective table for 'Generall notes' A he indicated how 'Generall notes' B should be reconstituted along the same lines: Haugaard, *Elizabeth and the English Reformation*, p. 347. But the assumption is false. 'Generall notes' B has its own pagination in the top left-hand corner of most leaves, which is older than the foliation (in the top right-hand corner) in respect of the volume. This older numeration shows that the present arrangement is the historic arrangement. Here I give the older numeration in brackets after the current foliation: ITL, Petyt MS 538/47, fols 419r (unnumbered or very faintly numbered), 419v (2), 420r (3), 420v (4), 420*r (unnumbered), 420*v (6), 421r (7), 421v (unnumbered), 422r (9), 422v (10), 423r (11), 423v (12), 424r (unnumbered), 424v (unnumbered), 425r (15), 425v (16), 430r (unnumbered), 430v (18), 431r (19), 431v (20), 432r (21). In most (if not all) of these cases the folio is probably not unnumbered: the number is simply concealed in the binding. All of this demonstrates that whereas in 'Generall notes' A certain folios were probably rewritten and an attempt was made to maintain the original arrangement, when 'Generall notes' B came to be written the task was entrusted to two scribes, but the division of labour did not coincide exactly with the various sections of the text and no attempt was made subsequently to maintain the original arrangement. It was in this disordered state that 'Generall notes' B was dispatched to the commentator: see below.

[60] Haugaard, *Elizabeth and the English Reformation*, p. 346.

envisaged here. However, as before, the portions written by the different hands appear on discrete folios.[61] The marginal comments of 'Generall notes' A were probably transferred to 'Generall notes' B once these two discrete sections had been joined together, because they appear in Hand VII regardless of whether the main text had been written by that hand or by Hand I.[62] 'Generall notes' B was subsequently read by Archbishop Parker, who frequently wrote the word *'delibe[ra]t[u]r'* (Haugaard's expansion) or *'delibe[re]t[u]r'* (Strype's expansion) in the margins of the earlier folios.[63] Although 'Generall notes' B is neatly written, the fact that the marginal comments of 'Generall notes' A were reproduced exactly indicates that the later manuscript could not have been considered a formal document fit to be presented to higher authority. Parker's annotations establish that the next stage was to be the renewed consideration of specific points.

Let us summarize our conclusions so far. 'Certen Articles' A is a draft text, scrutinized and annotated by Parker, Grindal and one other person before being fair-written and amended as 'Certen Articles' B. There is no evidence to suggest that it was intended to be submitted to the Queen and most of its advice was taken up and developed in 'Generall notes'. 'Generall notes' A is a composite manuscript, heavily corrected, probably partly rewritten, and certainly scrutinized by Grindal. Having been wholly rewritten in two different hands as 'Generall notes' B, it was read by Parker, who hoped that further discussion would ensue. The main texts of 'Certen Articles' A and B and 'Generall notes' B are all either wholly or mostly written in the same hand: Hand I (unidentified), which surely proves that they originated in the same circle.

Before proceeding it is necessary to attend to the single folio omitted from the original numeration of 'Generall notes' A.[64] Like most of that manuscript, this leaf is written in Hand V (unidentified), whilst the contents bear some affinity with part four: concerning the augmentation of the value of livings. Haugaard thought that the leaf might have belonged to 'Generall notes' A 'at some stage'.[65] However, the text is not now represented in 'Generall notes' B, which presents us with

---

[61] Hand VII wrote ITL, Petyt MS 538/47, fols 419r–20*v (pp. [1]–6 of the original pagination), whilst Hand I wrote fols 421r–5r, 430r–32r (pp. 7–21 of the original pagination).

[62] ITL, Petyt MS 538/47, fols 419v (the marginal memorandum about the drawing of the Articles, which appears in Hand VII on a folio written by Hand VII) and 421v (at the foot, where the annotation appears in Hand VII on a leaf generally written by Hand I).

[63] ITL, Petyt MS 538/47, fols 422r, 422v, 423r, 425r; Haugaard, *Elizabeth and the English Reformation*, p. 346; Strype, *Annals*, vol. 1, pt 1, pp. 476, 477, 478.

[64] ITL, Petyt MS 538/47, fol. 436r–v.

[65] Haugaard, *Elizabeth and the English Reformation*, p. 347.

several possibilities: either it was not available to be copied and was only later restored, or it was deliberately excluded, or it was copied but that part of 'Generall notes' B has since been lost. The composite nature of both 'Generall notes' A and B, together with the fact that the former is misbound and the latter divided by the interpolation of unrelated later material, indicates that the first and third possibilities cannot be ruled out.[66] On the other hand, the fact that this leaf is omitted from the original foliation surely argues that it never belonged to 'Generall notes' A in the first place, which explains why it was not copied into 'Generall notes' B. Most likely it should be associated with the later working party investigating these issues.[67]

II

All previous accounts of this Convocation have ignored another anonymous document, bound in the same volume, which is an important contemporaneous point-by-point commentary upon 'Generall notes'.[68] Written in an unidentified hand, it evaluates the proposals from an authoritarian legalist-conservative perspective, approving of some measures but strongly rejecting others, whilst at the same time making explicit some of the assumptions inherent in the earlier document. Thus, for example, 'Generall notes' recommends that Nowell's *Catechism*, new articles of doctrine based upon the Edwardian articles and a revised version of Jewel's *Apology* should be joined together in one book 'by commen Authoritie to be authorised'.[69] The commentary reveals that 'commen Authoritie' was taken to mean parliamentary statute: careful consideration was to be taken not only over the book, but also over the 'pe[n]nyng of ye statute therunto to be a[n]nexed'; that is to say, whoever was responsible for organizing the contents of the projected book was also expected to draft the accompanying bill.[70]

---

[66] 'Generall notes' B is separated into two portions by the interpolation of material dating from 1572: ITL, Petyt MS 538/47, fols 426r–9v.

[67] I intend to publish an article about these important episcopal working parties elsewhere.

[68] ITL, Petyt MS 538/47, fols 564r–8r.

[69] ITL, Petyt MS 538/47, fol. 419v ('Generall notes' B). There was a precedent for joining together complementary works in the parliamentary addition in 1552 of the Ordinal to the Prayer Book, which were then issued in a single volume. Whether that volume was subsequently considered to consist of one work or two was of critical importance in 1559 in relation to the validity of Parker's consecration as archbishop: Brook, *Parker*, pp. 81–4.

[70] ITL, Petyt MS 538/47, fol. 564r.

In other respects, however, the commentator displayed little sympathy for the priorities of advanced thinkers. 'Wilfull & publicke tra[n]sgressours of ye lawes & Inju[n]ctyons', who had abandoned singing, surplices, copes and organs were to be punished. Although favouring the revival of the Henrician commission to reform the Canon Law, he objected to the suggestion that the measures adumbrated in 'Generall notes' should be 'established' in the meantime. His disapproval of several measures betrays two overriding concerns: not to tie the Queen's hands and to protect existing privileges, clerical as well as lay. Hence the dispensing powers of the Crown were not to be restricted, nor were earlier dispensations to be invalidated. The extinguishing of peculiar jurisdictions and the assumption of control over all churches in a diocese by the bishop was denounced as

> verey Injuryous perillous & ambityous & unreasonable / Injuryous to ye owners ... & their subjectes / perillous for by lyke example ye prynce ... owght to have all exempte & pryviledged places fro[m] bysshopp[es] univ[er]sytyes townes & incorporatyons as ye yle of Ely ye bisshoprych of Durh[a]m & subjecte them to ye co[m]mune gov[er]neme[n]t of others ...

Proposals designed to prevent patrons from granting away rights of next presentation provoked the retort that it was 'm[ar]veylous yt ye patrone may neyther geve nor sell his awne enherytau[n]ce'.[71] Overwhelmingly the sentiment is one of 'don't rock the boat': ensure the proper enforcement of existing laws before the precipitate enactment of any new ones. Moderate reforms intended to buttress the Act of Uniformity, the Prayer Book and the Royal Injunctions are commended, but radical departures are vigorously opposed.

There is a strong correlation between the articles in 'Generall notes' B against which Parker wrote '*delibe[ra]t[u]r*' or '*delibe[re]t[u]r*' and those to which the commentator most objected.[72] Since the commentator engaged with the whole of the document and not simply those particular items, it seems likely that his scrutiny preceded Parker's annotations. In any case, Parker would surely not have requested a commentary upon articles he had already indicated were unsatisfactory. This suggests that once 'Generall notes' B had been assembled it was dispatched

---

[71] ITL, Petyt MS 538/47, fols 565v, 566r, 566v, 567r.

[72] Judging by the order in which he made his comments, it is clear that the commentator read 'Generall notes' B rather than 'Generall notes' A and that he saw the former in the same arrangement in which it is now bound. It might be thought that the correlation breaks down in that Parker did not mark for further consideration any paragraph in part four (concerning the augmentation of the value of livings), about which the commentator had a great deal to say. However, the whole of that section was later assigned to a working party and its report scrutinized by Parker.

for legal opinion, following which Parker made a marginal note of those articles requiring further attention.

III

Both the commentary and this chronology help in the attribution of 'Certen Articles' and 'Generall notes'. The Acts of the Upper House record that on 19 January the prolocutor, Alexander Nowell, appeared before the bishops and announced that some members of the Lower House had introduced papers concerning things to be reformed ('*reformanda*'). It had been agreed, he explained, that these papers should be handed over to a committee composed of members of the Lower House, who were to reduce the papers into chapters and to exhibit them before him at the next session.[73] Implicitly, any proposals receiving the assent of a majority of the Lower House would thereupon be presented to the bishops in the form of a petition bearing subscriptions, which was the normal *modus operandi*.

Haugaard maintained that 'Certen Articles' and 'Generall notes' probably constituted two such *reformanda* because several of the proposals they contain were incorporated into the later petitions which manifestly did issue from members of the Lower House. Parker's and Grindal's annotations were explained in terms of advance and informal attempts to test the water, which itself seemed to argue for a considerable degree of organization on the part of the precisians.[74] But there is absolutely no evidence to support this construction, and indeed everything points the other way. The prevailing attribution may be doubted on four grounds: diplomatic, content, treatment and location.

If 'Certen Articles' and 'Generall notes' were amongst the *reformanda* then it is hard to see why any committee should have been required to reduce them to chapters. Both are clearly and logically organized into either numbered articles or paragraphs sequentially identifying problems and offering remedies. As we have seen, 'Generall notes' had even been drafted in four distinct chapters concerning doctrine, liturgy, discipline and finance.

More significantly, Hand I (unidentified), which was responsible for writing all of 'Certen Articles' A and B and most of 'Generall notes' B,

---

[73] Haugaard, *Elizabeth and the English Reformation*, pp. 57–8. According to Carlson's reading of the Acts, it was on 19 January that the prolocutor submitted to the bishops reform articles which had already been reduced into chapters by the Lower House committee: Carlson, 'Puritans and Convocation', p. 141.

[74] Haugaard, *Elizabeth and the English Reformation*, pp. 57, 60–61, 345–7.

appears in quite independent manuscripts associated with Archbishop Parker. It wrote, for example, the copy of a royal signet letter of 22 January 3 Elizabeth [1560], addressed to Parker and other ecclesiastical commissioners, which is preserved amongst the archbishop's papers.[75] It wrote what was evidently a briefing document, prepared for the archbishop's use, telling him who constituted the early Elizabethan nobility and how they should be addressed.[76] Moreover, this hand also wrote a letter from Parker to Cecil dated Bekesborne, 3 June [1564], to which the archbishop added a holograph postscript.[77] Who but one of the primate's own staff – a secretary and/or chaplain – would have been in a position to copy an incoming royal letter and to pen an outgoing archiepiscopal one?

The papers' contents hardly suggest non-episcopal origins. The full title of 'Generall notes' provides a clue: 'Generall notes of matters to be movid by the Clergie in the nexte Parliament & Synod'. Who but the bishops was in a position to 'move' anything in both Parliament and synod? Who, for that matter, but the bishops, as representatives of the clerical estate, could have used the all-inclusive term 'the Clergie' in this context? Moreover, the authors showed themselves to be remarkably well informed. They cite the statute of 25 Henry VIII which had authorized the King to nominate 32 commissioners to revise the Canon Law, and were aware that the results of the Edwardian commissioners' labours were still extant.[78] Since in 1545 Cranmer himself had shown less than a perfect knowledge of earlier Henrician efforts towards reform of the Canon Law, it is scarcely credible that members of the lower clergy

---

[75] CCCC, PL, MS 121, pp. 389–91 (according to Parker's pagination). The text of the letter, which concerns alterations to the lessons in the Book of Common Prayer, is also preserved in LPL, MS Register of Archbishop Parker, I, fol. 215r, from which it is printed in Edward Cardwell (ed.), *Documentary Annals of the Reformed Church of England; being A Collection of Injunctions, Declarations, Orders, Articles of Inquiry, &c. From the year 1546 to the year 1716; with Notes Historical and Explanatory* (Oxford, 1839), vol. 1, pp. 260–63 and John Bruce and Thomas Perowne (eds), *Correspondence of Matthew Parker, D.D. Archbishop of Canterbury. Comprising Letters Written by and to him, from A.D. 1535, to his Death, A.D. 1575* (PS, 1853), pp. 132–4; also noticed in Walter Frere (ed.), *Registrum Matthei Parker Diocesis Cantuariensis A.D. 1559–1575* (The Canterbury and York Society, 35, 1928), vol. 1, pp. 331, 365. Very likely the original letter would have been sent to Parker as the senior commissioner, who would have had a copy made for himself before circulating the original to the other commissioners.

[76] CCCC, PL, MS 114A, pp. 109–112 (according to Parker's pagination).

[77] PRO, SP 12/34, fols 40r–41v, printed in Bruce and Perowne (eds), *Parker Correspondence*, pp. 214–17.

[78] ITL, Petyt MS 538/47, fols 440r, 422r ('Generall notes' A and B respectively). The statute in question was 25 Henry VIII c. 19: 'An Acte for the submission of the Clergie to the Kynges Majestie'.

should have known all this and felt emboldened to outline interim laws.[79] The authors were acquainted with the state of progress of Nowell's *Catechism*, yet it is reasonable to ask whether that information would have been known outside the circle which commissioned it and before Convocation assembled. Finally, if 'Certen Articles' and 'Generall notes' inspired the lower clergy's petitions, why then did those petitions omit so many of the earlier suggestions and why did they introduce articles which had formed no part of the preliminary papers?

The treatment of the documents is inconsistent with known Elizabethan practice. In a strictly hierarchical society, and with an archbishop sensitive to questions of propriety, it seems implausible that members of the lower clergy, however intimate they may have been with some of the future bishops whilst in exile, would have offered draft proposals for scrutiny by the most senior members of Convocation in advance of the first session. Furthermore, if the chronology outlined above is correct, once 'Generall notes' A had been transcribed as 'Generall notes' B, partly by a clerk in Parker's service, the transcript was examined by a legal expert before Parker made his annotations. This suggests that the referral to the expert was done at the archbishop's behest, or at least by someone in his household. But would the archbishop have allowed the copying and referral of a document composed by men other than his episcopal brethren and sent to him informally for his suggestions? Far from it. As Gibson observed in 1702, it was recognized that the bishops had 'a separate Power to advise with Counsel either in the *Common* or *Civil* Law, upon any difficulty in the Course of their Proceedings; in Cases, more especially, where there is any danger or appearance of their interfering with the *Statutes* and *Customs* of the Realm'. Giving examples drawn from Convocations held between 1419 and 1662 (excluding that of 1562–63 but including the Convocation of 1586), he noted that this consultation could be effected either by

---

[79] Cranmer apparently knew neither the names of the men whom the King had appointed to revise the Canon Law nor the whereabouts of the book they had written, but he expected Bishop Heath of Worcester to know these things: Archbishop Cranmer to King Henry VIII, Bekisbourne, 23 January 1545: PRO, SP 1/213, fols 144r–5r (final version) and 149r–v (draft), (*LP*, vol. 21, pt 1, items 109 and 110), quoted in F. D. Logan, 'The Henrician Canons', *Bulletin of the Institute of Historical Research*, 47 (1974), p. 101, where printed editions of the letter are cited. This ignorance is all the more surprising given Cranmer's evident interest in reform of the Canon Law: Paul Ayris, 'Canon Law Studies': Appendix IV to Paul Ayris and David Selwyn (eds), *Thomas Cranmer: Churchman and Scholar* (Woodbridge, 1993), pp. 316–22 and Diarmaid MacCulloch, *Thomas Cranmer: A Life* (New Haven, CT, and London, 1996), pp. 119, 121, 290, 294, 301, 327, 351, 377, 449, 476, 483, 494, 499–504, 512, 517–18, 520, 524–5, 533–5, 540, 541, 610–11, 618, 620, 624.

admitting lawyers to the debates of the house or by appointing certain bishops to explain to them the perceived difficulties and to solicit their opinions. No such obligation was held to attach to the motions of the lesser clergy.[80] There can be little doubt that, although unknown to Gibson, the commentary upon 'Generall notes' B is the product of just such a consultation, being particularly concerned with the relationship between the recent proposals and the existing legislation.

Finally, the current attribution entirely fails to account for the fact that both the draft and the fair-written versions of 'Generall notes' are found together. What is more, not only are they located amongst papers which evidently once belonged to Parker, but these Parkerian papers, together with many other miscellaneous documents, almost certainly later passed into the possession of John Selden, the famous jurist and antiquary, and constitute much of that part of Selden's library which historians have hitherto thought was destroyed by fire in the late seventeenth century.[81] How these documents descended to William Petyt (1637–1707) is still rather mysterious, but some discussion is necessary here in order to prevent any misapprehension about their ultimate provenance.

First, it is important to recognize that part of Parker's archive is 'missing'. The archbishop bequeathed the bulk of his manuscripts to his *Alma Mater*, Corpus Christi College, Cambridge, on conditions stringent enough to have ensured that most of them remain there.[82] The date at which they were removed from Lambeth, where he died, is a matter of uncertainty, but there is agreement that no contemporaneous list of what was taken survives.[83] We know that much cognate material was gathered up and bound during Parker's lifetime, yet there is no evidence to suggest that everything in his possession was necessarily conveyed to

---

[80] Gibson, *Synodus Anglicana*, pp. 140–46.

[81] Dr Barratt remarked that most of Selden's historical MSS 'cannot now be traced' and that 'the rumour that they perished in a fire is the only explanation which has been offered, and seems a likely answer': Dorothy Barratt, 'The Library of John Selden and its Later History', *The Bodleian Library Record*, 3 (1950–51), pp. 128, 134–5, 136, 142.

[82] Samuel Kershaw, 'Archbishop Parker, Collector and Author', *The Library*, new series, 1 (1900), pp. 379–83; Montague James (ed.), *A Descriptive Catalogue of the Manuscripts in the Library of Corpus Christi College, Cambridge* (Cambridge, 1912), vol. 1, pp. xiii–xxv; E. C. Pearce, 'Matthew Parker', *The Library*, 4th series, 6 (1926), pp. 209–28. For MSS annotated by the archbishop but not now in the Parker Library, see Sheila Strongman (ed.), 'John Parker's Manuscripts: an Edition of the Lists in Lambeth Palace MS 737', *Transactions of the Cambridge Bibliographical Society*, 7 (1977), pp. 1–27.

[83] Although it was formerly believed that the removal had taken place in the 1590s, Professor R. I. Page has recently found evidence to suggest that it might have occurred in 1576, within a year of Parker's death. I am grateful to Tim Graham for communicating this news to me.

Cambridge.[84] Late material, as yet unsorted or unbound, together with papers thought to be 'official' and of continuing value to his successors, may well have been left behind.[85]

One curious feature of the archbishop's incoming correspondence preserved at Cambridge is that it contains nothing dated later than May 1572; that is to say there is nothing for the last three years of his life.[86] I have argued elsewhere that the disappearance of the post-1572 petitions for dispensations can perhaps be explained as a consequence of Parker's reform of procedure in the Faculty Office.[87] Yet the disappearance of the later incoming letters not petitioning for dispensations has remained unexplained.

Apart from the odd stray, some of which entered the British Library, there are two main groups of papers which at some point became separated from the rest: those at Lambeth Palace Library and those at the Inner Temple Library. The letters collected in a volume at Lambeth clearly once formed part of Parker's archive since they consist of original incoming letters and draft replies and fall entirely within the temporal scope of the Cambridge volume.[88] The letters at the Inner Temple are also original incoming letters and draft replies, dating not only from every year between 1559 and 1571 except 1568, but also extending to 1572, 1573 and 1574.[89] Interspersed with these letters are

---

[84] Many of the volumes in the Parker Library are paginated in Parker's distinctive red pencil. At the beginning of these volumes is a contemporaneous table of contents arranged according to this pagination and laid out in columns ruled by a red pencil: see, for example, CCCC, PL, MSS 121, 122.

[85] Bill implicitly recognized that some of Parker's archive was left behind when he wrote that 'many' of the archbishop's papers were 'gathered into his own library': Edward Bill (ed.), *A Catalogue of Manuscripts in Lambeth Palace Library MSS. 1907–2340* (Oxford, 1976), p. ix.

[86] Richard Barnes, Bishop of Carlisle, to Archbishop Parker, Rose Castle, 14 May 1572, together with the archbishop's draft reply dated Lambeth, 22 May [1572]: CCCC, PL, MS 114A, bound after p. 401. This is not the location (between pp. 421 and 423) implied by James's catalogue: James, *Catalogue*, vol. 1, p. 260. It should be added that many of the letters in this MS are undated or only partially dated.

[87] David Crankshaw, 'The Elizabethan Faculty Office and the Aristocratic Patronage of Chaplains', in Claire Cross (ed.), *Patronage and Recruitment in the Tudor and Early Stuart Church* (York, 1996), pp. 20–75.

[88] These letters, dating from 1558, 1559, 1560, 1561, 1563 and 1571, are printed from LPL, MS 959 in Bruce and Perowne (eds), *Parker Correspondence*, pp. 49, 50–53, 57–63, 65–6, 68–71, 74, 114–15, 161–2, 176–7, 196, 387.

[89] These letters are printed from ITL, Petyt MS 538/47 in Bruce and Perowne (eds), *Parker Correspondence*, pp. 108, 124–7, 129–32, 146, 148–9, 151–2 (surely a stray from Cox's archive), 156–160, 172–6, 201–2, 223, 243–5, 284–5, 309–16, 355–8, 375–6, 378–9, 381–2, 384–7, 390 (either a stray from the Duchess of Suffolk's papers or, more likely, an original letter which was never sent), 434–5, 444, 444–5, 451–2, 474–7.

non-epistolary documents of a markedly official character. Here, for instance, is a document which digests the vitriolic *Admonition to the Parliament* of 1572 and was evidently intended to brief whoever commissioned it.[90] These letters and papers, some relating to ongoing controversies, are carelessly scattered throughout the volume and were probably still unbound at the time of Parker's death, which was why they were excluded, intentionally or otherwise, from the batch removed to Cambridge. It is in the Petyt fragment of Parker's archive that 'Certen Articles' A and 'Generall notes' A and B are to be found. Yet Parker's 'missing' archive alone cannot have supplied the vast number of Tudor ecclesiastical documents scattered throughout Petyt's huge composite volumes.

Earlier attempts to explain this accumulation have not proved convincing. Riley declined to speculate at all, whilst Macray conjectured that Petyt had acquired 'the official papers of ... one of the law-officers of the Court of Arches, possibly those of Dr Richard Cosin', but Cosin, who was Dean of the Arches and Vicar-General of the province of Canterbury, died in 1597, whereas many of the papers date from between 1598 and 1603.[91] Davies argued that sixteenth-century documents might have passed from Robert Bowyer via Henry Elsynge, both of whom were Keepers of the Records in the Tower. But whilst this notion is plausible in respect of Petyt's parliamentary records, it can hardly account for any ecclesiastical papers, which were not kept in the Tower and about which neither Bowyer nor Elsynge seem to have been at all curious. Having refloated the Cosin hypothesis, Davies remarked that some of the manuscripts, including 'the correspondence of Matthew Parker, Edmund Grindal, and John Whitgift', 'might equally well have come from Doctors' Commons or the Queen's Advocate's Office', but he was finally driven to admit that it was 'difficult to suggest a plausible source for the many hundred original ecclesiastical documents

---

[90] ITL, Petyt MS 538/47, fols 426r–7r, 462r, 464r, 466r–7v.

[91] Henry Riley (ed.), 'The Petyt Manuscripts: Inner Temple', *Second Report of the Royal Commission on Historical Manuscripts* (London, 1874), pp. 151–6; William Macray (ed.), 'Report on MSS. in the Library of the Inner Temple', *The Manuscripts of the Duke of Leeds, The Bridgewater Trust, Reading Corporation, The Inner Temple, &c.* (HMC, 11th repr., appendix, pt 7, 1888), p. 228. Some transmission of Matthew Parker's papers to Cosin is not at all impossible, for John Parker, the archbishop's son, gave him MSS of Bede and of Gregory's 'Decretals' in 1585 and 1596 respectively, as well as a copy of his father's *De antiquitate Britannicae ecclesiae & priuilegiis ecclesiae Cantuariensis, cum archiepiscopis eiusdem 70*, STC 19292 (1572), of which an English edition appeared in STC 19292a (1574). Strongman notes that this copy of the 'Decretals' might be the one marked as missing by John Parker in the register of the archbishop's bequest to Corpus Christi: Strongman (ed.), 'John Parker's Manuscripts', pp. 15–16.

of the reign of Elizabeth I which ... seem a little remote from the main fields of Petyt's interests'.[92]

Of course Petyt might have acquired these papers if they belonged to a much larger collection which did include material close to his interests. One such collection was that accumulated in what became known as the 'paper study' of the Archbishops of Canterbury at Lambeth.[93] This was quite distinct from the archiepiscopal library founded there in 1610.[94] Doubtless the contents were occasionally depleted in accordance with the provisions of various archbishops' wills.[95] Nevertheless, an inventory compiled from September 1633, probably coinciding with the arrival of Archbishop Laud, shows that the holdings of the study were both voluminous and varied.[96]

Whereas the archiepiscopal library was taken to Cambridge for safe-keeping at the beginning of the Civil War, it was only in the middle of the century, once Lambeth Palace had been sold by Parliament, that the papers from the 'paper study' came into Selden's custody. A substantial, though unquantifiable, proportion of Selden's library passed to Matthew Hale, one of his executors, and then disappeared from view until Mr James Fairhurst discovered it this century. 'Certen Articles' B is located in a Fairhurst manuscript restored to Lambeth Palace in the 1960s.[97]

---

[92] Davies, *Catalogue*, vol. 1, pp. 42–7. Davies notes that Petyt's correspondence gives no hint of the source of those MSS which were not his own transcriptions.

[93] The name 'paper study' was used to identify a room at Lambeth Palace in 1633, although whether that room was then in regular use or was merely a place of deposit for the archiepiscopal muniments is uncertain: Bodleian Library, Tanner MS 88, fols 20r, 57r (modern pencil foliation). The name has been employed by modern historians: see, for example, Barratt, 'Library', p. 137.

[94] Edward Bill, 'Lambeth Palace Library', *The Library*, 5th series, 21 (1966), pp. 192–206.

[95] It is not clear whether or not the 'paper study' ever contained books as well as manuscripts, but for Grindal's books see Collinson, *Grindal*, pp. 36, 44, 56, 70, 82, 96, 146, 243–4, 280–81, 314, 319–20. Professor Collinson corrects the erroneous statement in Sears Jayne, *Library Catalogues of the English Renaissance* (Berkeley and Los Angeles, 1956), pp. 20, 125 that Grindal's books no longer survive.

[96] The inventory, now Bodleian Library, Tanner MS 88, fols 20r–56r and 57r–9v (modern pencil foliation), is currently misbound. The correct arrangement can be reconstructed by means of the original ink pagination which appears in the bottom right-hand corner. Although fol. 57r is not so paginated, the discolouration shows that it was once exposed as the first leaf of a gathering, whilst fol. 58r is paginated as p. 3. This gathering runs to fol. 59v, which is p. 6. Thereafter the inventory resumes at fol. 20r (or p. [7]), which is also heavily discoloured, the text continuing until fol. 56r (or p. [78]), although this gathering continues a little further as blank and unnumbered leaves. The date 16 September 1633 appears on fol. 57r and '1634' on fol. 20r. A thorough edition of this inventory is highly desirable.

[97] Barratt, 'Library', pp. 128–42. Dr Barratt prints the list of Selden's miscellaneous MSS drawn up *c.* 1655 (Bodleian Library, MS Selden supra 111, fols 1r–12r) as Appen-

Since the Fairhurst manuscripts can certainly be traced back to the archbishops' study, and since we know that Parker and his officials kept cognate material together, it hardly seems too far-fetched to suggest that the Convocation manuscripts which passed to Petyt had come from the same place. That there was once a discrete collection of Convocation papers is vouchsafed by another folio in Petyt MS 538/47 which bears the single word '*Synodalia*' in a contemporaneous italic hand.[98] '*Synodalia*' is the name of the volume in the Parker Library containing not only the directory of Convocation procedure and 'Articles for Government', but also, as we have seen, a manuscript written by Hand I.[99]

In fact the provenance of Petyt's Convocation documents is placed beyond all doubt by entries in the 1633–34 Lambeth inventory. This discloses that 'Bundell P' on shelf number 32 contained 'Certaine Articles desired to be granted by the Queene', which is a slightly abbreviated version of the title of 'Certen Articles'.[100] Meanwhile, 'Bundell GG' on shelf number 12 contained 'Gen[er]all notes of matters to be moved by the Clergie in the next p[ar]liem[en]t or Sinode w[hi]ch I conceave was in the beginning of Q Eliz. tyme'.[101] That same bundle contained 'Actes in the lower house of Convocation in ffebr 1562', which is clearly Petyt's manuscripts recording the division of 13 February 1562, whilst the document described as 'The Requestes of the Clergie in ye lower house of Convocation under their handes' is evidently that now known as the 'Twenty-one Articles'.[102] Examples could be multiplied.

There was certainly a 'Bundle P' in Selden's library, the inventory of which, dating from *c.* 1655, unhelpfully says that it consisted merely of 'divers letters & negotiations'. Although that inventory lists bundles AA to FF (without, for the most part, specifying their contents), there is no entry in respect of a bundle 'GG'. However, that does not mean that bundle GG was not in the library in some form or other. Many of the inventory's entries are vague, perhaps even incomplete, presumably

---

dix C to her article, Barratt, 'Library', pp. 256–74. For Appendices A and B, see Barratt, 'Library', pp. 208–13; Edward Bill, 'Records of the Church of England Recently Recovered by Lambeth Palace Library', *Journal of the Society of Archivists*, 3 (1965), pp. 24–6; Bill, 'Lambeth Palace Library', pp. 201–2; Bill, *Catalogue*, p. ix.

[98] ITL, Petyt MS 538/47, fol. 527*r/531*v (the folio is numbered twice).

[99] CCCC, PL, MS 121. It is difficult to know how old this name is. The volume is paginated in red pencil and the vertical lines forming the table of contents on the first (unpaginated) leaf are also ruled in red pencil, but the text there fails to mention the word '*Synodalia*'. The volume was certainly known by this name by 1715: Thomas Bennet, *An Essay on The Thirty Nine Articles of Religion Agreed on in 1562, And Revised in 1571* ... (London, 1715), p. 176.

[100] Bodleian Library, MS Tanner 88, fol. 43v (modern pencil foliation).

[101] Bodleian Library, MS Tanner 88, fol. 35r (modern pencil foliation).

[102] Bodleian Library, MS Tanner 88, fol. 35v (modern pencil foliation).

because, as Dr Barratt pointed out, 'the Selden catalogue was written by a clerk who did not always understand what he was copying'. Moreover, it is not impossible that the contents of some of the bundles had been mixed up: one entry reads 'Process of the mariage of H: 8: Bundle EE & other things', another reading 'Letters of the Lords of the Councell and proceedings in Ecclesiasticall Causes & antient Charters in the Bundle EE'.[103]

Quite how and when Petyt's Lambeth documents became separated from the portion which Fairhurst was to discover is still obscure, but that there was some transfer of materials from Selden's library to Petyt tends to be confirmed by the latter's possession of a draft of Henry Elsynge's 'Modus tenendi Parliamentum' annotated by Selden himself. Petyt also owned two transcripts of Selden's 'Touching Jurisdiction in Parliament'.[104] Some investigation into contact between Selden, Hale and Petyt, all lawyers and antiquaries, may well prove fruitful. Whatever light that enquiry sheds upon particular routes of transmission, it remains highly probable that we possess in the Petyt manuscripts papers from Selden's library which did not descend to Hale, or at least if they did descend to Hale, were distinct from the portion found by Fairhurst.[105]

---

[103] Barratt, 'Library', pp. 256, 259–60 (item 57 for 'Bundle P' and items 68–70, 79, 82, 83 and 85 for 'Bundles AA–FF'). It is important to distinguish between the Lambeth material identified by means of letters (especially double letters) and Selden's own *collectanea* which was identified in the same way. Dr Barratt reported that 'in a notebook which had belonged to Selden, Hale listed the contents of eight volumes of Selden's collectanea labelled AA-HH, all of which can be traced'. In 1950–51 volume GG, 'containing mainly notes of creations of peers', was said to be in the possession of Mr Alan Keen: Barratt, 'Library', p. 139 (including n. 7). Not only is this description inconsistent with the Lambeth material designated 'GG', but it is apparent that Hale was listing volumes, whereas the Lambeth material and those items in Selden's library labelled 'AA–FF' were manifestly bundles of unbound documents. It was clearly because the Convocation documents remained unbound, certainly in 1633–34 and probably c. 1655, that they could be divided between the Petyt and Fairhurst collections. Presumably they were bound up either whilst in Petyt's possession c. 1655–1707 or once they had passed to the Inner Temple, but by that stage the original arrangement by bundle had largely dissolved, which was why the documents were so often misbound and cognate material was dispersed between several composite volumes.

[104] Davies, *Catalogue*, vol. 1, p. 39.

[105] It is worth adding that apart from the Convocation documents there is another instance of cognate material occurring in both the Petyt and Fairhurst MSS. The great corpus of papers in the former collection concerning the activities of the English Catholic missionary community, then convulsed by the Archpriest Controversy, are clearly related to the papers written by the same individuals on the same subject and at the same time preserved in the latter collection. Additional papers survive in Westminster Cathedral Archives: ITL, Petyt MSS 538/38, 538/47 and 538/54, catalogued in Davies, *Catalogue*, vol. 2, pp. 817–33, 857–83 and 899–908 respectively. Selected documents are printed in Thomas Law (ed.), *The Archpriest Controversy: Documents Relating to the Dissensions*

IV

Now even if there was nothing unusual in the submission of draft proposals by Haugaard's precisians to Parker and Grindal, there is something distinctly odd about the continued presence of those papers in the 'paper study' at Lambeth. Drafts offered for comment and duly annotated logically leave the custody of those making the annotations, passing either to another annotator or back to the authors. If the first

---

of the Roman Catholic Clergy, 1597–1602 (2 vols, CS, new series, 56, 1896 and 58, 1898); LPL, MSS 2006, 2007 and 2014 (Fairhurst Papers), catalogued in Bill, Catalogue, pp. ix–xi, 37–45, 60–65. Neither editor conjectures the papers' provenance although both indicate which items have been printed by Law; Westminster Cathedral Archives, MSS Westminster III, IV, V, VI and VII and Stonyhurst Anglia MS IX. Pollen misleadingly referred to the Petyt papers as 'Dr Bagshaw's dossier' and suggested that it was given to Bishop Bancroft when Bagshaw left England in 1601, then passing into the custody of 'some official, probably an ecclesiastical lawyer of the Court of Arches': John Pollen, The Institution of the Archpriest Blackwell: a Study of the Transition from Paternal to Constitutional and Local Church Government among the English Catholics, 1595 to 1602 (London, 1916), p. viii. However, that these manuscripts once all belonged together was established by Renold, who found endorsements and annotations in the hands of Bishop Bancroft and an unknown collaborator on all three portions: Penelope Renold (ed.), The Wisbech Stirs (1595–1598) (Catholic Record Society, 51, 1958), p. xix. We know that a number of Appellant priests, notably Bagshaw, Bluet and Colleton, colluded with Bishop Bancroft of London against the Archpriest, to the extent that Bancroft and the Government facilitated the secret printing of Appellant books within England: Arnold Meyer, England and the Catholic Church under Queen Elizabeth, trans. J. R. McKee (London, 1916), pp. 437, 454–5, 458; Philip Caraman, Henry Garnet 1555–1606 and the Gunpowder Plot (New York, 1964), pp. 282, 285–8, 292, 295, 299, 314, 323; John Bossy, The English Catholic Community 1570–1850 (London, 1975), pp. 44, 47; Adrian Morey, The Catholic Subjects of Elizabeth I (London, 1978), pp. 204–6, 213; Arnold Pritchard, Catholic Loyalism in Elizabethan England (Chapel Hill, 1979), pp. 68, 125, 170, 226–7, 227 n. 90. Jenkins relates contemporary suspicions that Bancroft was orchestrating the pamphlet warfare and amply demonstrates from typographical evidence that 'the finger of contemporary suspicion, pointing at Bancroft, was right': Gladys Jenkins, 'The Archpriest Controversy and the Printers, 1601–1603', The Library, 5th series, 2 (1948), pp. 180–86. On Bagshaw, Bluet, Cecil, Colleton and Mush, see Godfrey Anstruther, The Seminary Priests: a Dictionary of the Secular Clergy of England and Wales, 1558–1850, I: Elizabethan 1558–1603 (Ware and Durham, [1969]), pp. 13–17, 42, 63–8, 82–5, 240–41 respectively. It seems reasonable to conclude that what we have here is Bancroft's dossier derived from those priests with whom he was colluding, supplemented by intercepted communications, but artificially, perhaps even accidentally, divided between the Petyt, Fairhurst and Westminster collections. Presumably the dossier had originally been housed in the bishop's palace at Fulham, where Bluet (at least) enjoyed Bancroft's hospitality (John Bossy, 'Henri IV, the Appellants and the Jesuits', Recusant History, 8 (1965–66), p. 83), but when Bancroft was translated to Canterbury in 1604 his papers were no doubt removed from Fulham to the 'paper study' at Lambeth. Selden's library certainly contained material relating to the Archpriest Controversy: Barratt, 'Library', p. 257 (item 11).

annotator retains anything at all it is a fair-written copy of the final version, probably sent by the authors as a matter of courtesy. For the annotator to have retained both draft and fair-written versions makes no sense at all unless the documents actually originated in his circle. That these papers were generated by the bishops and engaged Parker's attention need occasion no surprise. If the archbishop was proactive enough to have commissioned a directory of Convocation procedure and to have prepared a preliminary recension of the Edwardian articles with the assistance of some of his suffragans, then there is no reason why this or a similar episcopal working party could not have been responsible for drafting 'Certen Articles' and 'Generall notes'.[106] Given that the papers call for a thoroughgoing reformation in almost all aspects of the Church, it might be objected that they could have been the work of a clique of bishops, formerly exiles, acting independently, whose proposals were only subsequently disclosed to Parker. But the archbishop's annotations to texts written by one of his servants and retained amongst his own papers implies that the whole enterprise was sponsored from above, which is not to say that Parker necessarily agreed with all of the recommendations.

This interpretation makes much more sense of a letter to Cecil drafted by Parker shortly after 14 April 1563, the day Convocation dissolved, a letter generally misrepresented through selective quotation:

> in consideration of yester nightes talke, calyng to remembrance [what] the qualyties of all my bretherne bi in experyenc of our co[n]vocation socyeties I see som of them to be *pleni rimarum[,] hac atque illac effluunt*[107] [i.e. unable to keep a secret]: although in dede the Q. m^tie maye have good cause to be well co[n]tented w[i]th hir choyce of ye most of them/ very few excepted amongst who[m] I count my[self]/ and furdermore though we have done amongest ourselfes lytle in o[u]r own causes,[108] yet I assure youe our mutuall conferencys have taught us such experyence that I trust we shal all be the better in governance for herafter/ and wher the Q. highnes doth note me to be to soft and easye I thinke dyverse of my bretherne wil rather note me ... to sharpe and to ernest in moderatio[n] w[hi]ch towardes them I have used, & wil

---

[106] Two stages of revision have been discerned in Parker's MS of the Thirty-nine Articles. It is generally agreed that the first stage was complete by the time the Upper House began discussion of the articles on 19 January. Bishop Gheast of Rochester is usually associated with Parker in producing the preliminary revisions: Brook, *Parker*, p. 130; Haugaard, *Elizabeth and the English Reformation*, p. 248.

[107] Parker here misquotes Parmeno in Terence's 'Eunuchus' (i.e. 'The Eunuch'): 'plenus rimarum sum, hac atque illac perfluo ... ': J. Sargeaunt (ed.), *Terence with an English Translation* (The Loeb Classical Library, 1, 1912), pp. 244–5. I am indebted to Elisabeth Leedham-Green for this identification.

[108] This passage originally read 'lytle in o[u]^r conferencys', but this was struck out.

stil do tyl mediocrytie shalbe receyved amongest us. though toward
them *qui foris sunt* [i.e. who are in public life] I ca[n] not but
shewe cyvil affabylitye & yet I trust inclyning to no grete cowardnes
to suffer wilful heedes to escape to easely/ *Sed ista pererga*[109] [i.e.
but these things are secondary].[110]

Fraught with internal tensions the bishops may have been, but what
was 'o[u]r own causes', in which Parker claimed they had made little
progress, if not the programme outlined in 'Certen Articles' and 'Generall
notes'?

This attribution to an episcopal working party might explain another
much quoted, though otherwise opaque, exchange. Writing in 1567, the
Nonconformists George Withers and John Barthelot declared that 'many
things of the greatest advantage to the church, which had been adopted
by the last convocation but one [that is to say in 1562–63], were
suppressed, and never saw the light'. Accordingly

> Our case was also proposed to the convocation at the last meeting
> [in other words in 1566] by a certain most learned man connected
> with the bishop of Norwich; but one of the bishops interrupted
> him, saying, 'What are these things to you? We begun this matter,
> and we will make an end of it.'

At this the first speaker replied, 'We thought the queen was the author
of this business, but we now perceive that you yourselves are.' 'And so',
the account continues, 'they would not suffer the matter to be brought
forward'.[111] Historians have hitherto concentrated upon the last sentence, interpreting it to mean that whereas the precisians had supposed
that it was the Queen alone who had ordered the drive against nonconformity over vestments, they now saw that the bishops themselves were
implicated. However, this sentence needs to be read in the light of the
unidentified bishop's claim that 'we begun this matter'. In what sense
could the bishops be said to have 'begun this matter', especially since
'this matter' evidently referred to 'Our case'? The answer, I submit, is to
recognize that here is an admission that far from being obstructive, the

---

[109] Parker has written 'pererga', but this should read 'parerga'. I am most grateful to
Elisabeth Leedham-Green for pointing this out to me.

[110] Draft letter from Archbishop Parker to Sir William Cecil, no place, [*c*. 14 April
1563]: ITL, Petyt MS 538/47, fol. 326v, a modernized version of which is printed in
Bruce and Perowne (eds), *Parker Correspondence*, p. 173 (where 'pererga' is silently
corrected to 'parerga').

[111] George Withers and John Barthelot to Henry Bullinger and Rodolph Gualter, no
place, August 1567, printed in Hastings Robinson (ed.), *The Zurich Letters, (Second
Series) Comprising the Correspondence of Several English Bishops and Others with
some of the Helvetian Reformers, During the Reign of Queen Elizabeth* (PS, 1845), p.
150.

bishops had themselves been proponents of further reformation in the Convocation of 1562–63. In 'Certen Articles' and 'Generall notes' we have ample evidence of their plans.[112] Unfortunately, many of the bishops, including Parker, Jewel, Cox, Berkeley and, reluctantly, Grindal, somewhat compromised their integrity by bowing to royal pressure to pursue the cause of uniformity.[113] They had seen in the Vestiarian Controversy the dangers of allowing the tail to wag the dog; or to put it another way, they appreciated that they could not run with the hare and hunt with the hounds. No wonder that the scandalized precisians would ever afterwards castigate the bishops, or at least a substantial number of them, for backsliding.

The reattribution of 'Certen Articles' and 'Generall notes' must affect our perception of 'Articles for Government', which was so evidently indebted to those earlier works. There is, unfortunately, no space here to discuss this and the other Convocation papers which have hitherto either been ignored, misidentified or misattributed,[114] but there can be little doubt that 'Articles for Government' constitutes a preliminary attempt at some disciplinary Canons intended to serve as a stopgap until a comprehensive revision of the Canon Law could get underway.[115]

---

[112] It is difficult to know whether 'Our case' signified the precisians' arguments against vestments or broader proposals for ecclesiastical reform. 'Generall notes' shows that the bishops were in agreement over vestments, for the first recommendation in the section devoted to reform of the Prayer Book is 'That the use of vestmentes, Copes, and Surplesses be frome hensfurth taken away': ITL, Petyt MS 538/47, fol. 421v ('Generall notes' B).

[113] Collinson, *Puritan Movement*, p. 73.

[114] I shall be discussing these other Convocation documents elsewhere, possibly as an introduction to an edition of 'Articles for Government'.

[115] As 'Generall notes' makes clear, the intention was to petition the Queen and Parliament for the appointment of new commissioners to carry forward the Edwardian revision of the Canon Law; Convocation's immediate task was to 'establish' interim 'lawes or orders': ITL, Petyt MS 538/47, fol. 422r ('Generall notes' B). Norman Jones recently discovered amongst the Hastings MSS in the Huntington Library a draft bill, containing a short enacting clause, which sought to revive the Edwardian legislation permitting the sovereign to appoint another commission: Norman Jones (ed.), 'An Elizabethan Bill for the Reformation of the Ecclesiastical Law', *Parliamentary History*, 4 (1985), pp. 171–87. Jones found that the bill could not be dated with certainty, although internal evidence 'militates against a 1559 dating', which means that it was not the bill 'for makyng of eccliasticall [sic] lawes by xxxii persones' introduced in the House of Commons on 27 February 1558 but killed in the Lords after a single reading on 22 March 1558. He therefore concludes that it was 'probably a sister of the famous "alphabetical bills" ... generated by Convocation in 1563, introduced into Parliament in 1566, and revived in 1571'. Because the author 'was aligned with those who wished to complete the Reformation in England, but ... had faith in the established religious hierarchy', Jones thinks that 'the bill is more likely to have come from among the moderate reformers than from the admonition Puritans'. Indeed 'the bishops ... may

We need to look again at its title: 'Articles drawn out by some certain, and were exhibited to be admitted by authority; but not so allowed'. When 'Certen Articles' and 'Generall notes' were attributed to the precisians it made sense to identify the 'authority' here cited as the bishops. But now that those preliminary papers are fathered upon the episcopate, this 'authority' must be sought higher still, and surely in the Supreme Governor herself. Hence the Queen demonstrated as early as 1562–63 her obstinacy in the face of calls for reform. Hence, too, the supreme irony of her later statements that Parliament was an inappropriate forum for the discussion of ecclesiastical matters when she had already thwarted episcopal initiatives manifest in the Church's own legislative assembly. This treatment explains why the 'Alphabet Bills' were introduced covertly by the bishops in the House of Commons during the Parliament of 1566. Sir Geoffrey Elton strongly attacked Neale's notion that these bills represented an unofficial drive planned by Puritan zealots. 'The Queen well knew', he wrote, 'that there had been mitred backing' for Bill A, which proposed to give statutory authority to the Thirty-nine Articles. 'She accused some of the bishops of having put the bill into the Commons, and though Parker himself claimed not to have known about this nor even to have heard the single reading in the Lords, she was most probably right.' Parker told Cecil that Elizabeth objected not so much to the bill itself, and certainly not to the articles, but to the 'hugger-mugger way in which it had been started, in an effort, she implied, to outflank her unwillingness to have Parliament legislate for the Church'. If the bishops could play this sort of game in respect of Bill A, then it hardly seems improbable that they could have done the same in the case of the other 'Alphabet Bills', many of which owe something to the programme outlined in 'Certen Articles', 'Generall notes' and 'Articles for Government'.[116] Despite all of this, the Queen managed to retain the upper hand. Yet we can see in these Convocation papers significant attempts by the bishops not only to reassert the authority of the clerical estate, but also to put the Church's

---

have been the authors'. There is one piece of evidence, not mentioned by Jones, which strengthens his argument that the Hastings bill may have been drafted for the Parliament of 1562–63 but not introduced for lack of time: perhaps it was one of the draft statutes which Parker and Grindal were dealing with in January 1563, after Parliament had been prorogued: 'I send your grace herewith also a temporal man's draft for two statutes to be considered': Bishop Grindal to Archbishop Parker, no place, 2 January 1563: ITL, Petyt MS 538/47, fol. 525r, printed in Bruce and Perowne (eds), *Parker Correspondence*, pp. 201–2.

[116] John Neale, 'Parliament and the Articles of Religion, 1571', *The English Historical Review*, 67 (1952), pp. 510–21; John Neale, *Elizabeth I and her Parliaments 1559–1581* (London, 1953), pp. 166–170, 173, 194, 196–7, 203–7, 209, 216–18, 238; Geoffrey Elton, *The Parliament of England 1559–1581* (Cambridge, 1986), pp. 99–100, 205–7.

own house in order. If these attempts had been successful, then the later history of the Elizabethan Church, not least in terms of the development of the Puritan movement, might have been very different indeed.

CHAPTER FOUR

'Certain, continual, and seldom abated': royal taxation of the Elizabethan church

Patrick Carter

During the course of Elizabeth's reign, the gap between the English crown's expenditure and its ordinary income widened inexorably. In particular, the military confrontation with Spain after 1585 placed unprecedented demands upon the fiscal resources of the Elizabethan state – a crisis compounded by costly campaigns in Ireland during the last decade of the reign. Through taxes, loans and military levies the Church carried its share of the ever-increasing expenses of war and government. Reflecting upon the burden of royal taxation borne by the clergy, the Essex rector William Harrison wrote in 1577 that 'the Church of England is no less commodious to the prince's coffers than the state of the laity, if it do not far exceed the same, since their payments are certain, continual, and seldom abated'.[1] While clergy sometimes resented the administrative and fiscal obligations placed upon them by clerical taxation, the leadership of the established church appreciated the importance of clerical financial support in strengthening the bonds between church and crown. For the continuing safety of the Elizabethan regime was crucial to the survival of the Gospel and of the existing ecclesiastical order, and the English clergy both prayed and paid for its preservation and protection.

Like their Tudor predecessors the Elizabethan clergy owed the crown three separate taxes: first fruits, tenths and subsidies. The first two had been imposed by Parliament from 1535 as permanent levies upon benefices.[2] Payable by all new incumbents, first fruits were equal to one

---

[1] William Harrison, *The Description of England* (Ithaca, 1968), p. 31. I am grateful to Professor Jim Alsop for reading and commenting upon an earlier draft of this chapter.

[2] 26 Henry VIII, c. 3. On clerical taxation see Felicity Heal, 'Clerical Tax Collection under the Tudors: the Influence of the Reformation', in Rosemary O'Day and Felicity Heal (eds), *Continuity and Change: Personnel and Administration of the Church of England 1500–1642* (Leicester, 1976), pp. 97–122; and Patrick Carter, 'Royal Taxation of the English Parish Clergy, 1535–58' (PhD, Cambridge, 1994). A recently published article by Sybil Jack, while unreliable on many details of clerical tax collection, provides

entire year's income less the annual tenth. Rather than paying the entire sum immediately, most clergy took advantage of the allowance to compound for their first fruits, entering bonds guaranteed by several sureties, promising to pay in instalments over two years. All beneficed clergy also owed annual tenths, due at Christmas and collected each spring by diocesan officials who accounted in the Exchequer. As part of her effort to reverse the ecclesiastical policies of her father and brother, in mid 1555 Mary Tudor abolished first fruits and assigned tenth revenues to the Church to cover the cost of pensions paid to the ex-religious. This generosity towards the Church proved only temporary, however. Anxious both to replenish crown coffers and to reinforce the royal supremacy, the new Elizabethan regime moved quickly in early 1559 to resume collection of first fruits and tenths. A bill to recover the ecclesiastical revenues alienated by the Crown was introduced in Parliament in January 1559, and first fruits compositions began anew five months later. The 1559 act contained one major innovation, however. Henceforth almost one-third of benefices (rectories worth £6 13s. 4d. or less and vicarages valued at £10 or less) were excused from first fruits payments: a considerable concession which alleviated the plight of many poorer incumbents.[3] Tenths were restored as an annual royal tax save in the dioceses of Ely and Oxford, where they were regranted to the sees as partial compensation for the inequitable exchanges of lands which Elizabeth had extracted from her bishops.

Unlike first fruits and tenths, which were imposed by the Reformation Parliament without clerical consent, the Elizabethan clergy assembled in their two provincial Convocations of Canterbury and York retained the power to grant the Crown subsidies, parallel to but separate from those offered by the laity in parliament. Since the 1534 submission of the clergy, however, all acts of Convocations required royal approval; in the case of clerical subsidies this was accomplished through the confirmation of clerical grants by parliamentary statute. Until the 1590s beneficed clergy generally paid clerical subsidies at the

---

a valuable analysis of the legal records of the Exchequer relating to clerical taxation: Sybil M. Jack, 'English Bishops as Tax Collectors in the Sixteenth Century', in S. M. Jack and B. A. Masters (eds), *Protestants, Property, Puritans: Godly People Revisited, a Festschrift in Honour of Patrick Collinson on the Occasion of his Retirement* (Parergon, new series 14, 1996), pp. 129–63.

[3] 1 Elizabeth, c. 4; PRO, E 334/7; Norman L. Jones, *Faith by Statute: Parliament and the Settlement of Religion 1559* (London, 1982), pp. 160–62. On Mary's reign, see Rex H. Pogson, 'Revival and Reform in Mary's Church: a Question of Money', in Christopher Haigh (ed.), *The English Reformation Revised* (Cambridge, 1987), pp. 139–56; and Patrick Carter, 'Mary Tudor, Parliament and the Renunciation of First Fruits, 1555', *Historical Research*, 69 (1996), pp. 340–46.

rate of two shillings per pound per year (i.e. equivalent to an additional annual tenth); thereafter two or more subsidy payments were usually required each year – a response to the costs of war in Ireland and against Spain. Stipendiary clergy and chaplains contributed on a sliding scale, from 6s. 8d. to 13s. 4d. per year, deducted from their wages. Grants were offered first by Canterbury Convocation, which met in London at the same time as Parliament. A committee composed of bishops and proctors of the lower house would assemble (as in the Great Hall at Lambeth in December 1566) to determine the size of the subsidy and agree upon the wording of the grant. Copies of the prepared subsidy book were then read and approved in both houses of Convocation, generally without additional debate. One of the notable exceptions came in February 1589, with the first grant of a double clerical subsidy. Between 12 and 26 February Convocation devoted five sittings to the subsidy proposal, followed on 28 February by an extraordinary conference at Lambeth involving bishops and some of the lower clergy at which an agreement was at last hammered out.[4] After Canterbury's assent a copy of the grant was sent north to York to be approved by the clergy of the northern province. At around the same time the archbishop introduced in the House of Lords a bill incorporating the text of the Canterbury grant. The clerical subsidy bill received only formal consideration in Parliament, often given several readings on the same day, with only the preamble and confirming clause read aloud.[5]

The residual fiscal autonomy of the clergy was unequivocally expressed through the public presentation of the subsidy to the Queen, notably before parliamentary confirmation of the clerical grant. One such ceremony took place on 7 December 1566, when a delegation of five bishops led by Archbishop Parker went to court to deliver the Canterbury grant directly to Elizabeth. Several members of the lower house of Convocation accompanied them but were refused admission to the royal chamber owing to the Queen's indisposition. The supreme governor was evidently well enough, however, to read through the text of the grant and express her gratitude to the clergy for their subsidy.[6] A similar presentation on 27 February 1585 degenerated into a heated

---

[4] David Wilkins, *Concilia Magnae Britanniae et Hiberniae* (4 vols, London, 1737), vol. 4, pp. 251, 335.

[5] See for example *Journals of the House of Commons* (London, 1852), vol. 1, p. 91. The 1601 clerical subsidy bill received three readings in the Lords on a single day, when the clerk noted 'that, at the second and third reading of the said Subsidy, the body of the Grant was omitted to be read (according to the accustomed Manner); and only the Preface and Confirmation of the grant were read' (*Journals of the House of Lords* (London, 1846), vol. 2, p. 252).

[6] John Strype, *Annals of the Reformation* (4 vols, Oxford, 1824), vol. 1, pt 2, p. 239.

debate on the relative value of clerical and lay contributions to crown coffers, as well as the shortcomings of the Elizabethan episcopate.[7] In accepting the grant offered by representatives of Canterbury Convocation, the Queen thanked the clergy for their generosity: 'and the rather for that that came voluntarily and frankly wheras the Laity must be intreated and moved therunto'. Irritated by this pointed comparison, Lord Treasurer Burghley dismissed the clerical subsidy: 'Madame, these men come with mites, but we will come with pounds.' His comment drew a sharp retort from the Queen: 'I esteeme more of their mites, than of your pounds, for that they come of themselves not moved, but you tarry till you be urged thereunto.' Whether individual clergy were any more inclined to liberality than their lay brethren is debatable, but Elizabeth evidently saw an opportunity to encourage Parliament by highlighting the actions of Convocation. Nor did clerical generosity remain unrewarded: such fiscal support of the Crown helped to ensure Elizabeth's protection of the established church against attacks both from within and without Parliament. Yet while promising to silence their Puritan critics, the Queen nevertheless took the opportunity afforded in February 1585 by the presence of bishops and other senior clergy (as well as leading lay councillors) to criticize various ecclesiastical abuses. Having raised the subject of unsuitable ministers and lax episcopal supervision, an acrimonious argument ensued between Burghley and Archbishop Whitgift on the best remedies for the shortage of preaching ministers and the responsibility of lay impropriators, which was finally terminated through a timely royal intervention. As in parliamentary consideration of lay taxation, discussions of clerical subsidies could easily be diverted to broader issues of church and commonwealth.

The preambles of Elizabethan clerical subsidy grants emphasized the Crown's effort to advance the cause of true religion, as well as the expenses incurred in the defence of the realm of which the clergy underwrote their share. Like the preambles to lay subsidy statutes (which fulfilled a similar propaganda purpose), clerical subsidy grants were couched in general terms, and adhered even more closely to a single template with little variation from one grant to the next.[8] The first Elizabethan clerical subsidy grant (1563) acknowledged the recent progress in promoting the Gospel in England and the costs of interventions in

---

[7] PRO, SP 12/176/69. On the significance of this meeting for the struggle between Whitgift and the Puritans in Parliament, see Patrick Collinson, *The Elizabethan Puritan Movement* (Oxford, 1967; repr., 1990), p. 284.

[8] For a comparable analysis of Elizabethan lay subsidy statute preambles, see Richard W. Hoyle, 'Crown, Parliament and Taxation in Sixteenth-Century England', *English Historical Review*, 109 (1994), pp. 1192–3.

France and Scotland to end religious persecution, as well as the debts
inherited by Elizabeth from her half-sister Mary.[9] The eight succeeding
grants followed the pattern of 1563, with only minor additions, deletions
or alterations in phrasing: that of 1571 referred to the expense of subdu-
ing the Northern Rising, that of 1581 to rebellion in Ireland, while that
of 1589 recalled 'the rare and wonderfull preparacion of the Spanishe
forces readie to have invaded this Realme the last yeare'.[10] In contrast to
lay grants with their repeated references to the charges of civil defence
and the manifold benefits of the Queen's just and benevolent rule, clerical
subsidy grants stressed the preservation of true religion and the necessity
of defeating those dedicated at home and abroad 'to the extirpation and
rooting out of the sincere profession of the Ghospell of Christ'. Oddly,
the 1597 clerical grant departed entirely from this usual script. With
scarcely a reference to religious motivation, the grant extolled the many
blessings of the Queen's rule and recognized the great charges incurred in
maintaining this 'most godly and happy government'. In 1601 the draft-
ers of the clerical subsidy grant (the longest yet) returned to earlier
religious themes, while employing more florid language than in the past.
The clergy once more acknowledged the Crown's support against the
Church's opponents (both papist and Presbyterian) during the preceding
years: 'for who hath or should have a lyvelier sense or better remembrance of your Majesties princelie courage and constancie in advancinge
and protecting the free profession of the Gospel within and without
youre Majesties Dominions ... then your Clergie'.[11] Together with the
offering of state prayers and the preaching of obedience to the temporal
powers, the granting of subsidies was a tangible public demonstration of
clerical support for their supreme governor. With the puzzling exception
of 1597 (when the clergy may perhaps have sought to imitate lay subsidy
grants by limiting religious references), clerical subsidy grants concentrated upon the Crown's role in promoting protestantism. Elizabeth's
support of her churchmen elicited the gratitude of the clerical estate,
which was expressed through both fiscal and political support of her
regime.

The purchase price of royal protection paid by the clergy to their
supreme governor was substantial.[12] During the early 1560s average

---

[9] 5 Elizabeth, c. 29.

[10] 13 Elizabeth, c. 26; 23 Elizabeth, c. 14; 31 Elizabeth, c. 14.

[11] 39 Elizabeth, c. 26; 43 Elizabeth, c. 17; David Dean, *Law-Making and Society in Late Elizabethan England: the Parliament of England, 1584–1601* (Cambridge, 1996), p. 54.

[12] Total royal ecclesiastical revenue includes first fruits, clerical tenths, clerical subsidies and temporalities of vacant bishoprics. These figures are based upon Frederick C.
Dietz, 'The Exchequer in Elizabeth's Reign', *Smith College Studies in History*, 8 (1923),
pt 2, pp. 80–89; and PRO, AO 1/1207/20, 21; AO 1/1208/22.

annual clerical revenues, swelled by the first fruits of the fresh bench of Elizabethan bishops and the revenues of vacant sees, amounted to over £39 000 per annum and accounted for almost 14 per cent of total Exchequer receipts. In contrast, during the succeeding two decades annual revenues fluctuated between £20 000 and £25 000, and by the early 1580s constituted less than 9 per cent of Exchequer receipts. With the demands of war from 1585, however, clerical tax revenues rose dramatically to average over £37 000 per annum by the later 1590s, largely because of the introduction of multiple subsidy grants. Throughout the reign annual tenths receipts remained relatively constant, at between £11 500 and £12 500, while as casual revenue first fruits receipts were more erratic, ranging between £5 000 and £10 000 per annum. Subsidy revenues, subject to the size and frequency of grants, naturally varied. Their annual value to the Crown rose markedly during the 1590s, however. During the preceding decade clerical subsidies yielded over £9 000 per annum on average, while after 1590 their annual value soared, reaching a peak of almost £20 000 in the year ending at Michaelmas 1599.

In the face of this ever-increasing fiscal burden, the continued employment of a tax assessment of clerical incomes completed in 1535 offered some relief to incumbents whose real incomes rose throughout the later sixteenth century in step with agricultural prices. Recognizing this widening gap between nominal and real values of benefices, various proposals were floated for a comprehensive reassessment in order to maximize royal revenue from clerical taxation. One such scheme sought to divert the resulting additional tenth receipts from crown coffers to the laudable object of maintaining preaching ministers and augmenting impoverished livings 'as are [too] meane for learned pastors'.[13] However, most such plans originated with private projectors who proposed to collect the increased clerical taxes, sharing the additional revenue with the Crown. Naturally the clergy appreciated the advantage offered by the underassessment of benefices (similar to that enjoyed by many contributors to lay subsidies) and fiercely resisted any attempt to increase clerical assessments. William Harrison had complained that threats of enhanced assessments were unfair: 'as if our livings were not racked high enough already'.[14] A scheme advanced in early 1585 to increase assessments and lease clerical tax revenues to laymen prompted one bishop to appeal to Archbishop Whitgift to scuttle the plan.[15] Already

---

[13] BL, Add. MS 48 064, fols 198v–9r.

[14] Harrison, *Description*, p. 31.

[15] Bodleian Library, Tanner MS 459, fols 116r–17r. The author may have been William Wickham, Bishop of Lincoln.

heavily taxed in comparison with the laity, any increase would hinder clerical recruitment by discouraging the study of divinity 'when they see the reward of their Labors waxeth worse and worse, and is dayly sought to be diminished'. The unidentified bishop concluded by criticizing the unreasonable lay expectations entertained of the clergy, who were to be learned and generous in hospitality while leading lives of apostolic poverty. He suggested that the promoters of the scheme were animated more by jealousy and hostility towards the clergy than by concern for the Crown's finances.

Prompted by this appeal Whitgift prepared a lengthy memorandum to Lord Burghley rehearsing these and other arguments against allowing a reassessment of the leasing of clerical tax revenue.[16] Clergy compounding for first fruits would have greater difficulties arranging for sureties if the taxes were increased, while current incumbents of benefices could find themselves liable for any additional tenths and subsidies due from their predecessors. The Crown would also lose out, since a more realistic assessment of bishops' incomes would almost certainly result in lower taxes, while a fixed annual farm for first fruits (a tax whose yield varied from year to year) could cost the Crown considerable revenue. Any increase would be a disincentive to the study of divinity, and foster dangerous clerical discontent with the tax regime. According to the archbishop, higher taxes would further lower the living standards of English clergy, many of whom were already worse off than Thames watermen. Finally, Whitgift sought to conjure up the spectre of a Puritan conspiracy by hinting darkly that the scheme to ensure lay control over the collection of clerical taxes was but one element in a wider plot to undermine the established church and the privileges of the clergy, 'that they which could not prevayle in Parlement may this way be revenged'. Energetic lobbying succeeded in protecting one of the few tax advantages enjoyed by the clergy; no general reassessment of benefices was ever undertaken. In consequence of this failure to secure a more realistic assessment, the only avenue open to the Crown to increase clerical subsidy revenue was to seek multiple grants (the same solution adopted for lay taxation beset by similar problems of assessment).

Royal taxation imposed administrative as well as fiscal burdens upon the English church. The new Elizabethan bishops inherited responsibility for clerical tax collection (and arrears) from their deprived Marian predecessors. In early 1559 collection of the third instalment of the 1555 subsidy and the first instalment of the 1558 subsidy were in

---

[16] BL, Lansdowne MS 45, fols 184r–5r.

progress, with three further instalments of the latter still due. Some Marian bishops, like Henry Morgan of St David's, oversaw recovery of arrears and the conclusion of their subsidy accounts in the Exchequer after their deprivation. At the same time their Protestant successors, including Pilkington of Durham and Grindal of London, challenged Exchequer efforts to extract Marian subsidy debts from them. Yet as late as the mid-1560s the Durham collector faced demands for tenth receipts due a decade earlier, while Bishop Cox of Ely was at last compelled in 1573 to pay Marian arrears out of his own pocket. During the 1560s and 1570s Archbishop Parker himself received repeated requests for tenth arrears due from the estate of cardinal Pole. Parker protested that Pole's executors had obtained an acquittance from the exchequer covering the disputed sums; in his efforts to settle the matter the primate even sought testimony from one of the cardinal's former servants at Leuven. He laboured in vain, however, for as late as November 1579 the Exchequer was issuing process against Parker's own executors in order to recover Marian arrears.[17]

In selecting diocesan tax collectors, bishops and cathedral chapters turned most often to their own officials, especially registrars: trusted and reliable men like John Martiall and Richard Franklyn at York, Edward Cole at Winchester and Alban Stepneth at St David's. At Canterbury Archbishop Grindal chose his chief steward John Scott, while his successor Whitgift employed his secretary Abraham Hartwell. During a vacancy in their see Durham cathedral appointed the capitular registrar Simon Comyn, who later served a second term as collector in conjunction with his work as receiver-general of the bishopric. Appointments of family members to the office of diocesan collector, while relatively rare, were often a source of scandal, as in the mid-1580s when Bishop Goodwyn of Bath and Wells granted the collectorship to his son Thomas, and the corrupt brother of Bishop Barnes of Durham served as diocesan subsidy collector.

If bishops sometimes displayed poor judgement in selecting their officials, in mitigation it must be remembered that their freedom to choose was frequently sharply circumscribed by competing interests and personalities. In the first place, although all collectors' patents expired upon the death or translation of the bishop (life grants of collectorships had been prohibited since 1553 owing to a succession of scandals), dislodging an incumbent collector could prove difficult. The experience of the first Elizabethan bishop of Coventry and Lichfield,

---

[17] PRO, E 179/21/112; SP 46/27, fols 84r, 191r; SP 46/29, fol. 256r; Durham University Library CC Bprc 23/11–16; LPL CM I/73a, 73c, 78.

Thomas Bentham, is instructive. Thomas Bolt, a Staffordshire clerical pluralist and the incumbent collector in 1560, refused to make way quietly for his successor. Having promised Bolt's post to an Exchequer receiver, the bishop's problems were compounded when he was approached by the privy council on behalf of another candidate. Anxious not to offend the council, Bentham was nevertheless unwilling to withdraw his own previous offer; in the end Bolt managed to retain his position (perhaps as a compromise candidate), although relations between bishop and collector remained strained. Bentham was particularly concerned that Bolt would employ receipts from any fresh collections to cover debts already incurred. Similar external pressure was brought to bear by Robert Cecil upon the dean and chapter of Exeter during a vacancy in 1597. Henry Locke, one of Cecil's agents and possessed of an unsavoury record of indebtedness, lobbied hard for the collectorship, but his efforts were vigorously resisted. Locke proposed to continue to employ the same local deputies, but understandably neither they nor the dean and chapter wanted anything to do with him.[18]

Some collectors exploited lax episcopal supervision to enrich themselves through fraud, with severe consequences for the diocesan bishops involved. The unhappy experiences of Bishop Parkhurst of Norwich are well known in this regard. The bishop inherited from his predecessors a careless and untrustworthy collector, George Thimelthorpe, who accumulated considerable arrears and tampered with records to escape responsibility. To his horror Parkhurst found himself heavily indebted to the Crown and without effective legal recourse against his delinquent deputy. The bishop succeeded in discharging his debt to the Crown before his death, albeit at considerable cost to both himself and his see. At Exeter his colleague Bishop Bradbridge left debts of over £1 200 at his death in 1573, incurred through the sharp practices of his collector Henry Boroughs. Accused of forging the bishop's signature and deceiving Bradbridge into giving him his discharge before he had concluded his account in the Exchequer, Boroughs was imprisoned for debt but managed to return as collector after 1585. The Exeter collector was also deeply unpopular among clergy and parishioners across the diocese, owing to his alleged readiness to seal church doors for late payment of subsidies and his reluctance to excuse those paying first fruits from contributing to subsidies. He was accused of showing greater

---

[18] Rosemary O'Day and Joel Berlatsky (eds), *The Letter Book of Thomas Bentham, Bishop of Coventry and Lichfield, 1560–1561* (CS, 4th series, 22, 1979), pp. 195–6, 198, 203, 209, 224–5, 228–9; R. Roberts and E. Salisbury (eds), *Calendar of Salisbury Manuscripts at Hatfield House* (24 vols, London, 1883–1976), vol. 7, pp. 347, 382, 406, 422.

concern to extract the maximum personal fees than to collect the Queen's money.[19]

The Exchequer relied upon the sound judgement of bishops in appointing their deputies, a system which left the Crown with limited direct control over the gathering of its clerical tax revenue. Collectors were episcopal rather than crown agents, and bishops endeavoured to maintain their clerical autonomy. As a result, smooth collection of tenths and subsidies depended upon harmonious relations among diocesan officials; where these were lacking problems were sure to arise. Such was clearly the case at Coventry and Lichfield in the late sixteenth century, where a bitter dispute between Bishop William Overton and his chancellor, Thomas Becon, polarized the diocese and created administrative chaos.[20] By mid-1585 personal and professional relations between the two men had reached their nadir. Under a grant from Overton's predecessor Becon had been overseeing tax collection in the diocese, prompting the bishop to circulate letters to his clergy forbidding them to pay the chancellor, and to appoint his own collector Thomas Fitzherbert. Anxious to ensure prompt collection of the Crown's revenue, Lord Treasurer Burghley brokered a deal under which Becon and Fitzherbert agreed between them that the latter should serve as collector.[21] Yet Overton's continued hostility to Becon and the poisoned atmosphere within the diocesan administration soon compelled the Lord Treasurer to intervene once more. Both sides traded accusations: Becon claimed that Overton was continuing to interfere in the collection (rather than allowing Fitzherbert to cooperate with him), while the bishop now suggested that the Chancellor was manipulating the allegedly innocent Fitzherbert for his own evil ends. The dispute rumbled on unresolved through late 1585; at Westminster there was growing alarm (well founded) that the new collector Fitzherbert was handling subsidy receipts without having lodged the required security. Eventually, weary of the dispute and declaring that Coventry and Lichfield was the source of more problems than the entire remainder of the English church, Burghley shrewdly washed his hands of the matter and referred it to the Chancellor of the Exchequer Sir Walter Mildmay for adjudication.[22]

By the end of December Mildmay had concluded another agreement between Becon and Fitzherbert, whereby the latter would continue as

---

[19] Felicity Heal, *Of Prelates and Princes: a Study of the Economic and Social Position of the Tudor Episcopate* (Cambridge, 1980), pp. 251–2; Ralph A. Houlbrooke (ed.), *The Letterbook of John Parkhurst, Bishop of Norwich* (Norfolk Record Society, 43, 1974–75); BL, Lansdowne MS 20, fol. 153r; PRO, SP 46/16, fol. 171r; E 135/11/14.

[20] Heal, *Of Prelates and Princes*, p. 254.

[21] PRO, SP 46/33, fols 291r, 293r.

[22] BL, Lansdowne MS 45, fol. 111; PRO, SP 46/33, fols 317r, 332r, 345r.

collector and the Chancellor formally be discharged from any further financial obligations to the Crown. Realizing that the bishop's difficult personality lay behind some of the trouble, Burghley urged that the Exchequer endorse this settlement regardless of Overton's views. Yet Fitzherbert proved a poor choice as collector; implicated in several financial scandals and criminal conspiracies, he had been replaced by 1587 and in 1591 was being prosecuted for debt. The suggestion that Overton's fractiousness contributed to the difficulties at Coventry and Lichfield is supported by his subsequent behaviour. For example, when the Exchequer issued process against the bishop for clerical tax arrears in 1594, Overton reacted violently. The recipient of one of the bishop's intemperate letters declared that it was 'suche as I thinke neither Bishopp nor anie other modest man should have written ... nor the most pacient and charitable man can well beare'.[23] So long as the Crown relied upon diocesan bishops and their officials for the collection of its clerical revenues, its ability to ensure smooth tax collection was strictly circumscribed. Personal rivalries and conflicts could complicate royal revenue administration, whether within the county communities, the Exchequer, or the Church.

Despite the salutary example offered by such notorious scandals, some bishops continued to be unfortunate in their choice of deputies or careless of their collectors' activities. The inevitable problems which followed encouraged those who sought to wrest complete control of collection from the bishops. To this end one parliamentary bill, dating perhaps from the early 1580s, attributed the problems to the negligence of some bishops and their collectors, which 'leave her highnes longe unanswered of her dewe and their successors greevously charged and encumbered therewith'. It proposed to assign to the Crown the power to appoint collectors, who might or might not be the diocesan bishops and their deputies. Another plan aimed to ensure that all collectors lodged the sufficient security in the Exchequer first required under Edward VI, while reserving to the Lord Treasurer the power to appoint collectors, particularly where accounts were more than two years in arrears.[24] Such moves to limit episcopal control over clerical tax administration drew a forceful defence of the existing system from Archbishop Whitgift. He noted (accurately) that diocesan collectors' debts paled in comparison with those of some other delinquent royal financial officials (including the remembrancer of first fruits and tenths

---

[23] PRO, SP 46/33, fols 338r, 340r; SP 46/38, fol. 3r; SP 46/39, fol. 33r. For Fitzherbert's subsequent career, see Peter W. Hasler, *The House of Commons, 1559–1603* (3 vols, London, 1981), vol. 2, pp. 125–6.

[24] PRO, SP 12/147, fol. 201r; BL, Lansdowne MS 105, fol. 220r.

Sir Christopher Hatton, who owed the Crown over £40 000 at his death), and that adequate securities were already demanded. More rigorous enforcement of existing regulations was required.[25] Plans to deprive bishops of responsibility for tax collection would further discredit the episcopate and leave the clergy vulnerable to extortion by lay officials. While some harried bishops may secretly have yearned to be released from responsibility for tax collection, Whitgift was uncompromising. As with proposals to reassess benefices and lease clerical taxes, the archbishop portrayed the attempt to reorganize clerical tax collection as a covert assault upon the established church by its critics at Court and in Parliament, motivated by lay greed and a desire to weaken the power of the ecclesiastical estate.[26]

Contemporary criticism of the system of episcopal collection and an emphasis upon fraud and debt in much of the surviving correspondence have encouraged historians to highlight the system's weaknesses. Yet for every dishonest official there were others like Simon Comyn, registrar to the dean and chapter of Durham and diocesan subsidy collector during the later 1580s. An industrious collector, Comyn was also regularly employed in London on other capitular business, particularly fighting attempts by the Archbishop of York to exercise diocesan jurisdiction during vacancies in the see. His credit with the Durham chapter was demonstrated in 1588, when the exchequer fees demanded exceeded his collector's allowance by three shillings. For his efforts on their behalf the dean and chapter granted him 40 shillings in reward and compensation.[27] Equally assiduous was Richard Massy, Ely diocesan tenth and subsidy collector during the 1560s and 1570s. Massy had purchased the office from his predecessor, and prudently settled the outstanding account before taking over. At Ely tenth receipts were paid not to the Crown but to the bishop, who received his revenue directly from Massy, while the certificates of subsidy non-payment were returned on time in to the Exchequer, with the assistance of the collector's London friends.[28] Nor did collectors lack sympathy for the plight of poorer clergy. Against the noxious Exeter example of Henry Burroughs, judged too willing to seal churches of delinquent clergy and extract the maximum fines for non-payment, should be set the Winchester collector George Acworth. In May 1568 Acworth interceded with the sheriff of Hampshire on behalf of poorer

---

[25] PRO, AO 1/1207/21.

[26] LPL, MS 3470, fol. 225r.

[27] Durham Chapter Register 5, fol. 161r–v; Durham Chapter Post Dissolution Papers 3152, 3159, 3282, 3285, 7122.

[28] CUL, EDR F/5/39, fols 120r, 136r–9r; PRO, SP 46/28, fol. 81r.

incumbents against whom process had recently been issued for clerical subsidy arrears. Acworth urged the Exchequer to defer the debts until after Michaelmas, when the harvest would have been gathered in. In the interim the solicitous collector promised personally to indemnify the sheriff if he would delay executing the writs.[29] Finally, in some cases the essential co-operation between bishop and collector (notably absent at Coventry and Lichfield) was rooted in close personal friendship. There can be no better example of such warm relations than those between Bishop Bullingham of Lincoln and his collector and agent William Collinson in the 1560s. The bishop's letters mix instructions on various business matters with concern for Collinson's children, furnishing their absent father with affectionate descriptions of their antics and advice on their rearing.[30]

The Crown's desire to maximize clerical tax revenue sometimes came into conflict with its protection of the Church and clergy, particularly in the pursuit of debt. The Elizabethan Exchequer made periodic efforts to recover a portion of the ever-increasing arrears of clerical taxes (especially first fruits), some of which dated from the reign of Henry VIII. In one such campaign against crown debtors the remembrancers of first fruits and tenths dispatched hundreds of writs to sheriffs in early 1562 ordering them to levy clerical tax debts, yet as late as the mid-1580s more than £8 000 remained outstanding from the years before 1555.[31] The greater part of this sum was of course unrecoverable, yet these outstanding obligations attracted individuals prepared to pursue debtors at their own expense in return for a share (usually one-half) of any money collected. Such schemes offered the Crown both the potential of profit at little direct cost and an additional means to reward servants and courtiers. In 1571 Henry Middlemore secured a royal patent to search out lands of dissolved monasteries and chantries concealed from the Crown, as well as sums collected for clerical taxes but illegally retained by collectors. Originally for a term of seven years, Middlemore's grant was cancelled after three years at the instigation of the Privy Council, perhaps because of clerical concerns at his activities. Similar grants were later made, however, including one to Richard Wingfield for six years in May 1584.[32] The patentees' activities were deeply unpopular, although they offered the Crown income which was

---

[29] PRO, SP 46/32, fol. 64r.
[30] LAO, Cor/F/1, fols 11r, 12r, 15r, 19r.
[31] PRO, QAB 1/1/21; AO 1/1207/20.
[32] *Calendar of Patent Rolls, Elizabeth I* (9 vols, London, 1939–86), vol. 5, p. 167; vol. 7, p. 432; PRO, SP 12/277/45. Middlemore later complained that he lost at least £500 through the cancellation of his patent (BL, Lansdowne MS 64, fol. 143r).

otherwise lost. In the early 1570s Hugh Earthe was granted a patent to search for subsidy money collected from stipendiary clergy but never paid into the Exchequer. From the Crown's perspective the scheme was a success since 'thereby some profitt came to her Majestie for one moyties which otherwise ... would not have benne found out nor answered'. Yet Earthe's activities caused anxiety among bishops fearful that accounts already audited in the exchequer might now be reopened. Worse, Bishop Horne of Winchester was encouraged to believe that he and his collectors (including his son-in-law the diocesan chancellor George Acworth) would be spared scrutiny if a debt of £40 owed by Earthe to a diocesan official were forgiven. Moreover the patentee was allegedly pressuring the bishop to grant him one of the fatter benefices in the diocese in exchange for halting his investigations.[33] It is doubtful how far such freelance agents truly served the Crown's interests (rather than their own); there is no question however that such sharp practises reinforced fears about any attempt to place control over clerical taxation in lay hands.

Even as Whitgift and his colleagues complained of the excessive charges levied upon the clergy and the danger of allowing the laity control over clerical tax administration, defenders of the established ecclesiastical order (engaged in a polemical struggle against radical reformers) realised the strategic value of clerical contributions to crown coffers. Some Puritan critics denounced the payment of first fruits and tenths (together with crown impropriations) as a diversion of precious resources needed to support preachers. In this vein Walter Travers cited with approval the earlier criticism of first fruits by the reformer Martin Bucer.[34] Even if some clergy may privately have assented to this view of royal exactions, defenders of the Elizabethan settlement strove to turn the issue to their advantage. In their anti-Presbyterian polemic Richard Bancroft and Matthew Sutcliffe regularly employed a dual argument: attacks upon first fruits and tenths undermined the royal supremacy upon which the taxes were founded, while in turn the general Presbyterian assault upon the supremacy threatened the Crown's fiscal interests by removing the chief justification for payment of clerical taxes. Sutcliffe claimed that Puritan calls to end all clerical payments to the Crown (including impropriated tithes and temporalities of vacant sees, as well as clerical taxes) would reduce total royal revenues by one-third. Despite repeated declarations of their willingness to pay all lawful taxes,

---

[33] PRO, SP 46/40, fol. 146r; BL, Lansdowne MS 18, fol. 48r.

[34] *A parte of a register* ... STC 10400 (Middleburg, 1593), pp. 16, 177, 219; Walter Travers, *A Full and plaine declaration of Ecclesiastical Discipline*, STC 24184 (London, 1574), p. 116.

Puritans were vulnerable to conformist efforts to portray payment of first fruits and tenths as a litmus test of loyalty toward the established church and its supreme governor.[35]

The Crown did not hesitate to summon the clergy to assist in the defence of the Protestant faith abroad, through collections and extraordinary levies. Bishops were regularly asked to solicit funds from their diocesan clergy for the relief of continental coreligionists. Usually the council addressed a letter outlining the particular need to the Archbishop of Canterbury, who in turn informed his episcopal brethren of the circumstances. Requests succeeded one another with regularity, as Bishop Grindal of London remarked wryly in July 1568, in response to one such demand 'for the same cause [as three months earlier] saving thatt the matter is now remooved in place from Frawnce to Flawnders'.[36] The importance of additional contributions increased with the advent of war with Spain in 1585, and the heightened perils which confronted the realm thereafter. In early 1587 the clergy responded to the emergency by offering a benevolence to supplement the regular clerical subsidy. In thanksgiving for 'the free exercise of our mynistery and function, the true preachinge of God, and the syncere admynistringe of His holly Sacraments (to us farre more deare than our lyves and lyvinges)', Convocation granted the Crown three shillings in the pound upon all livings payable over three years. Employing the regular machinery of diocesan collectors, the benevolence (in reality a subsidy which lacked parliamentary confirmation) raised almost £15 000 between late 1587 and late 1591.[37]

More direct military assistance was also expected, but proved less readily forthcoming. In January 1586 the Privy Council required individual bishops to levy 'lance money' to pay for horsemen to be sent to the Netherlands, 'in regard to the common cause of Religion as also for the safetie of our selfe and state (wherein your interest is great)'. The lists of expected clerical contributors supplied by the council proved unrealistic, however, making collection slower than anticipated. For example neither Peterborough nor Exeter cathedrals could pay the sums demanded, and the Bishop of Peterborough was allowed to reapportion the levy more equitably. The clergy of Hereford diocese met their £300 assessment, but collection was slow owing to the many

---

[35] Albert Peel (ed.), *Tracts Ascribed to Richard Bancroft* (Cambridge, 1953), pp. 30, 36, 59; PRO, SP 12/245, fol. 135r; Matthew Sutcliffe, *A Treatise of Ecclesiasticall Discipline*, STC 23471 (London, 1590), pp. 102, 181.

[36] LPL, MS 2002, fol. 118r.

[37] PRO, AO 3/344; E 336/21; Dietz, 'Exchequer', pp. 86–7; G.W. Kitchin (ed.), *The Records of the Northern Convocation* (Surtees Society, 113, 1907), pp. 262–3.

small payments. Nevertheless by June 1586 £6 650 had reached the Exchequer.[38]

Clergy were reluctant contributors to the 1586 levy. Not surprisingly this was nowhere more true than in the troublesome diocese of Coventry and Lichfield, where Bishop Overton encountered considerable clerical resistance. Derbyshire clergy demanded to see the council's letters for themselves and rejected the bishop's warrant as invalid since it lacked the episcopal seal. They also wished to know the total diocesan assessment to ensure that they were not being unfairly burdened. In Warwickshire only one incumbent was willing to pay his share; all others pleaded their poverty. An attempt to mollify hostility by soliciting voluntary contributions in place of the assessed sums proved a dismal failure, raising scarcely one-tenth of the total required.[39] Despite two personal visits to his diocese, by mid-June 1586 Overton had collected only half of the £400 expected. Writing to secretary Walsingham, he complained bitterly about his clergy who were 'most unwillinge to shewe themselves readie and dutifull in any good service and specyallye yf it touche theire purse never so lytle'. The bishop believed that much of the blame lay with the council, which had agreed to reduce the assessment of a powerful member of the Lichfield cathedral chapter, who in turn encouraged others to seek favourable treatment for themselves: 'he doethe annimate all that come to him and they come to him thicke and threefolde for counsell and advise howe to shifte of this payment and to save themselves'. Overton begged the councillors not to further undermine his authority, and lamented the lack of support by the Earl of Leicester in encouraging contributions from his clerical clients in Warwickshire. In response the council merely urged Overton to greater efforts, while lamenting the 'unduetifullness' of the Lichfield cathedral clergy. By November some clergy had promised to pay next spring, while others remained obdurate. A petition from the cathedral chapter was referred to the council by Overton, endorsed with a caution against further concessions since 'the favor shewed to one castethe back all the reste'. The council replied with further injunctions to gather the sums outstanding and bind remaining recalcitrant clergy to appear in person at Westminster.[40]

---

[38] Bodleian Library, Tanner MS 78, fol. 20; PRO, SP 12/188/4, 36; SP 12/195/44; BL, Lansdowne MS 49, fol. 53r; J. R. Dasent (ed.), *Acts of the Privy Council, New Series* (46 vols, London, 1890–1964), vol. 14, p. 54.

[39] PRO, SP 12/188/6, 33. Such collections were only one of the responsibilities assigned to the 'learned preachers' in each Derbyshire deanery (Collinson, *Elizabethan Puritan Movement*, pp. 184–5).

[40] PRO, SP 12/149/37 (misdated 1581); SP 12/195/29; *Acts of the Privy Council*, vol. 14, pp. 166, 265.

The indifferent success of the 1586 levy seems to have prompted a shift in royal fiscal policy, with efforts concentrated upon those clergy best able to bear the burden of contributing and most amenable to the bishops' influence. Smaller groups were also more manageable and easier to approach. To supply and equip horsemen for the Irish wars of the 1590s larger sums were demanded from fewer clergy (particularly wealthy pluralists). Thus in October 1595 Archbishop Whitgift was required to arrange for armour and horses from Canterbury to be sent to Chester for embarkation to Ireland by the following March; an attempt by the Bishop of Norwich to reduce his diocese's contribution was dismissed by Lord Burghley who argued that Norwich was already lightly assessed in comparison with other sees.[41] Further levies for Ireland followed. In July 1598, for example, 20 horses were demanded from Canterbury and a further ten from York province (at a cost of £30 each). Bishop Bilson of Winchester, a less than enthusiastic contributor, noted to Robert Cecil his concern that 'we know not how often these employments may come'. Such suspicions proved well founded, for during the later 1590s they did indeed grow into regular demands. For his part Archbishop Whitgift warned that the 1598 request

> will be taken very hardly of the clergy, as well in respect of the late burden they sustained by the last sending into Ireland which was very great, as also for that they willingly consented to pay the first payment of the subsidy ... in hope that they should not be further charged extraordinarily.[42]

Wealthier clergy also contributed to the successful privy seal loans of the 1590s. In Gloucestershire in 1597, for example, at least five parish clergy loaned £20 each (the minimum), while the Archdeacon and Dean of Gloucester each subscribed £50. In the city of London at least a dozen clergy made loans, including both Lancelot Andrewes (£30) and John Donne (£20); the Bishop of Durham Toby Matthew paid £200 and Archdeacon Pilkington of Durham £30.[43] Given the fiscal and military burdens upon the Elizabethan state during the 1590s, clerical resentment towards the Crown's incessant demands is readily understandable. Nor should it be forgotten, as Whitgift reminded the privy council, that these extraordinary levies were in addition to unprecedented subsidies (as well as regular first fruits and tenths payments). The bishops also bore their

---

[41] LPL, MS 3470, fols 168, 173, 178, 179. Bishop Overton also complained of clerical obstruction in raising the 1591 Privy Seal loan at Lichfield (BL, Lansdowne MS 68, fol. 56v).

[42] Roberts and Salisbury, *Calendar of Salisbury Manuscripts*, vol. 8, pp. 264–5, 279, 281–2, 296–7.

[43] PRO, E 401/2583, fols 16v, 29v, 79v (information supplied by Professor Jim Alsop).

share of the increased administrative burden placed by the Crown upon local élites in organizing and funding military campaigns. Few clergy during the 1590s could have measured up to the ideal of George Herbert's country parson who 'when he is set at an armour or horse, he borrows them not to serve the turn, nor provides slight and unuseful, but such as are every way fitting to do his country true and laudable service'. In reality Elizabethan clergy pleaded and prevaricated, complained and contested the Crown's extraordinary demands. Moreover they stoutly resisted any attempt to integrate them into the general system of military levies. Led by Archbishop Whitgift the English clergy vigorously asserted the same measure of autonomy in military contributions which they enjoyed in their other fiscal relations with the Crown.[44]

A close political relationship existed in Elizabethan England between the clergy and the Crown, for the established church enjoyed the (largely) benevolent protection of its supreme governor. Yet this came at considerable cost. Clerical contributions to crown coffers truly were 'certain, continual and seldom abated', both through regular taxes and the increasingly frequent military levies of the late sixteenth century. In addition to this substantial fiscal burden, bishops too often found their energies diverted from necessary pastoral work to the demands of financial administration: collecting tenths and subsidies, pursuing debtors and rendering accounts. Harried by incessant Exchequer demands and fearful of defaulting (given the traumatic experience of Bishop Parkhurst), some bishops grew disillusioned and began to despair. In a 1574 letter to Lord Burghley Bishop Horne of Winchester, who had earlier endured stormy exile at Frankfurt and a troubled tenure as Dean of Durham, lamented his administrative trials as a royal financial agent. Paraphrasing St Paul, he wrote that

> were it not for conscience sake to godward, and my duety to her Majestie, I wolde rather live and ende my life in poore and privat estate then, being a bishopp in a churche professing Christes religion, to be made as we all are, *spectaculum mundo, uno veluti excramentum mundi, omnium rejectamentum* ... I think more of this, then of mine accompts in thexchequer.[45]

---

[44] John J. N. McGurk, 'The Clergy and the Militia, 1580–1610', *History*, 60 (1975), pp. 198–210; Richard B. Wernham, *After the Armada: Elizabethan England and the Struggle for Western Europe, 1588–1595* (Oxford, 1984), pp. 565–7; F. E. Hutchinson (ed.), *The Works of George Herbert* (Oxford, 1941), p. 252. In 1588 the council rebuked Whitgift that his certificates for the 1586 levy offered only 'in parte excuses of the parties taxed and in parte promises to make up the somes required by some other waie' (LPL, MS 3470, fol. 95r).

[45] BL, Lansdowne MS 18, fol. 48r–v ['a spectacle for the world, like the refuse of the world, rejected by all ... '].

The costs of clerical taxation to the Elizabethan Church were high, and more than merely fiscal. Yet while an undesirable drain upon ecclesiastical resources, these payments and the energies devoted to their collection helped to ensure the survival of the established church and its supreme governor, against threats emanating from foreign powers and domestic critics alike.

CHAPTER FIVE

Reviling the saints or reforming the calendar? John Foxe and his 'kalendar' of martyrs[1]

Damian Nussbaum

Nothing quite like John Foxe's calendar of martyrs had ever before appeared in English. In Foxe's version, which prefaced his *Acts and Monuments*, the content of the medieval calendar was completely re-cast. Instead of the familiar array of medieval saints and festivals, there appeared an army of martyrs, most of them Protestant, and many unknown. This incursion into a traditional symbol of religious piety provoked an outraged response from defenders of the Catholic faith. Subsequently murmurings of disquiet at Foxe's presumption were heard even from within the Church of England itself.

The calendar was deceptively simple. On the surface, the martyrologist had discovered a novel weapon with which to ridicule the veneration of the saints, and to attack the papal power which instituted and sup-ported the practice. Foxe's innovation was to adopt a new approach to two familiar targets of Protestant polemicists, the papacy and the saints, by appropriating the very framework which the Catholic Church itself used to structure the cult. There were however other, deeper levels to Foxe's creation. Embedded in Foxe's enterprise was a positive intent to reshape and further reform the Church of England.[2]

---

[1] Earlier versions of this chapter were presented to the Religious History of Britain seminar at the Institute of Historical Research, and to the Early Modern British History seminar in Cambridge. I am grateful to all those present for their comments, suggestions, and encouragement.

[2] At least three different clusters of sacred calendars are considered in this chapter. First, there are the calendars of the pre-Reformation Catholic Church (here referred to as either the 'medieval', 'traditional' or 'Catholic Church's calendar'). Secondly, there are the calendars produced by the Church of England after the break with Rome, and particularly those printed under Edward and Elizabeth (here cited as the 'Church of England', 'English Church's', or 'Prayer Book calendar'). Since both Catholic and Church of England calendars were issued with the express consent of the Church authorities, they are also referred to as 'official'. Alongside the 'official' calendars, there also existed the unofficial 'alternative' versions, including Foxe's creation (here identified as the 'Foxeian' or '*Acts and Monuments* calendar', or the 'calendar of martyrs').

The calendar in *Acts and Monuments* was unusual but not unique. It fitted into a wider European tradition of 'alternative' calendars, in which Protestant martyrs took the places of medieval saints. Like Foxe's calendar, these creations were intended to purge the reformed churches of a lingering Roman presence, and to attack the 'popish' attachment to degenerate – or even non-existent – saints. Yet whilst the names of the old saints were discarded, the familiar outline of the calendar was retained and rededicated to a new task. Through the accepted and commonplace genre of the Church calendar, a largely uninformed readership was introduced to the newly constructed Protestant past. True, much of this anti-papal history was unknown territory, but the familiarity of the form in which it appeared might potentially encourage readers to welcome this dark continent as their religious heritage and spiritual home. In effect, Foxe's calendar was both reformed *and* reforming: it offered a critique of the Church's past, and a design for its future.[3]

I

In later sections we will turn to the reception which greeted the appearance of Foxe's calendar. But before considering the responses of Catholics and Protestants to the martyrologist's creation, we need to look more closely at the calendar of martyrs itself, and indeed the tradition which lay behind it.

In its widest sense a 'calendar' could include any system which defines the length of the year and divides it into smaller units. Traces of the Roman, Jewish and early Christian calendars were all apparent in the calendars of early modern Europe.[4] Amongst sixteenth-century English calendars, there is a useful, albeit imprecise, distinction to be drawn between primarily *sacred* and essentially *secular* calendars. Both of course followed the usual division of years into months and weeks, and both adopted the convention of attaching the names of saints to particular days. Yet there were differences. In secular calendars, notably almanacs, the saints' names were used to direct readers to the days on

---

[3] Foxe did not actually devise the calendar, as he himself was swift to point out. Since the creator is not named, I have used the shorthand 'Foxe's calendar' throughout this chapter. Not only is this convenient but also justifiable on the grounds that although Foxe did not design the 1563 calendar himself, he did choose to take responsibility for it thereafter, and to defend its implications against its detractors. See John Foxe, *Acts and Monuments*, 2 vols (London, 1583), vol. 1, pp. 581–3.

[4] For a brief survey of the subject and the secondary literature, see R. C. D. Jasper and Paul F. Bradshaw, *A Companion to the Alternative Service Book* (London, 1986), pp. 45–67.

which fairs were held, or when the legal terms began. In sacred calendars, such as primers and prayer-books, saints' days structured the liturgical year, designating when the faithful should feast, fast and toil. Despite the differences, there remained a considerable area of overlap, and as we shall see, much of the controversy regarding the calendar in the English church centred on these imprecisions and ambiguities.[5]

Foxe's calendar was traditional, at least in structure. It was based on the 20 or so fixed festivals of the Church year which, having survived Henry VIII's depredations, went on to appear in later Prayer Book calendars.[6] These ancient festivals were preserved because of their supposed scriptural warrant, and included the feasts of the Apostles and the early martyrs, as well as the days connected with the great high points of the Church's year, such as Christmas.[7] The spaces between the ancient saints were filled with the names of Protestant martyrs, together with the date of their suffering and the year of their death. Some were celebrated figures such as Bishop Hooper, Bishops Ridley and Latimer, Bishop Farrar of St David's and, of course, Archbishop Cranmer.[8] Many of them were quite unknown outside their communities however, and some were anonymous even locally. In December there appeared the names of William Tracy, Peter Sapience, 'a scholer', 'a Jew', 'Two gray Friers' and 'an old man of Buckinghamshire'.[9]

If recent victims predominated in Foxe's calendar, room was also kept for earlier martyrs. Considerable space was devoted to the Lollards of the fifteenth and early sixteenth centuries, and Wyclif was given a prominent position at the start of the year, on the second of January. Nor were continental martyrs and confessors forgotten. Both John

---

[5] See Bernard Capp, *Astrology and the Popular Press: English Almanacs 1500–1800* (London, 1979), p. 62; and Eamon Duffy, *The Stripping of the Altars: Traditional Religion in England c.1400–c.1580* (New Haven, CT, and London, 1992), pp. 46–52.

[6] For the 1536 Act abrogating many holy days see Duffy, *Stripping of the Altars*, pp. 394–5.

[7] The only non-scriptural saint to remain was Saint George, partly because he was already a red-letter saint at least in some calendars, and partly because of his influential connections with the monarchy, with the chapel at Windsor to which he gave his name, with the order of the Garter founded in his honour, and with England, whose patron saint he had become. See David Hugh Farmer, *The Oxford Dictionary of Saints* (3rd edn, Oxford, 1992), pp. 197–8.

[8] See the calendar entries for 23 February, 19 and 20 October, 26 February and 23 March in *Acts and Monuments* (1583), sig. §2ᵃ–§4ᵇ.

[9] The 1583 calendar was similar in content to the 1563 version, but not identical in its *mise-en-page*. The most significant change concerned the sharpest point of connection: the red-letter martyrs. Whereas in 1563 all red-letter entries had been printed in the same way, in 1583 the typography changed to distinguish ancient saints honoured with a holy day by the English church from more recent Protestant martyrs picked out by Foxe.

Hus and Jerome of Prague found spaces (2 May and 1 June respectively). On occasion the arrangement of names made for rather unexpected bedfellows. The humanist Erasmus shared a day with Luther's associate Philip Melanchthon, and with them on 30 December the Strasbourg reformers Martin Bucer and Peter Martyr were also honoured.

Given the novelty of Foxe's calendar of martyrs, and the ubiquitous popularity of the form which he was commandeering, it was unsurprising that responses were swift and their tone acrimonious. Even before publication in 1563, the mere rumour of the calendar's imminent appearance provoked vigorous criticism. Foxe himself recounted contemporary Catholic expressions of indignation, in particular the outrage felt at his presumption in omitting the saints, martyrs, confessors and virgins of the ancient church from their traditional home, and importing new martyrs and confessors in their places.[10]

Catholic critics of Foxe, both in 1563 and later, perceived the martyrologist's invention as a crude parody of their own church's calendar (or at least presented it as such). The first full-length Catholic rebuttal of the *Acts and Monuments*, penned by Nicholas Harpsfield, homed in on the calendar of martyrs as the most offensive element in the Protestant text, and this first assault set the tone and tactics for later Romanist critics of the martyrologist. Harpsfield, the former Archdeacon of Canterbury, was enraged at Foxe's audacity in seizing and exercising a power which no pope or heretic had previously claimed: the right to make martyrs. According to Harpsfield 'that new Pope', as he mockingly called Foxe, had created so many feast days and new apotheoses of martyrs, and so many marvels that readers did not: 'know whether to marvel at the man's impudence and impiety or his folly'.[11]

In the view of the former archdeacon, Foxe had committed a double crime when he had chosen to have the names of his Protestant martyrs printed in red ink. Bad enough was his disregard for the Church authorities, who alone had the right to institute feast days. Worse still, he had mocked those saints who had previously been placed in the medieval calendar and given special honour by being picked out in red-letter for particular reverence. Harpsfield perceived in the absence of these traditional saints a fundamental lack of respect for hagiographical

---

[10] See the preface 'ad doctum lectorem' in *Acts and Monuments* (1583), sig. *1^b–*2^b, and the loose translation provided by J. F. Mozley, *John Foxe and his Book* (London, 1940), pp. 132–4.

[11] Nicholas Harpsfield, *Dialogi sex* (2nd edn, Antwerp, 1573), p. 601. The final – and longest – of the six dialogues is directed against Foxe, pp. 543–741.

inheritance of the Church, and he was eloquent in his condemnation of the perpetrator.[12]

Harpsfield dwelt on the individual exchanges which had taken place, accumulating a casualty list from the Sarum calendar of those ancient saints who had been lost for the sake of including Protestant martyrs. Saint Matthew had been superseded by Hooper; Alexander, Bishop of Alexandria and opponent of the Arians, had been supplanted by Farrar; a host of African martyrs, victims of the Arians, had been replaced by Cranmer.[13] Harpsfield's choice of lost saints was by no means accidental, for it reinforced the notion that the Protestants were the present-day successors of heretical groups in the early church. Harpsfield inspired the later cohorts of Catholic critics who sketched out an alternative history for Protestantism from Foxe's own materials, a history showing the reformed faith to be rooted in ancient heresies which even Protestants claimed to abhor.[14]

Foxe was certainly not without defenders within the Church of England. Matthew Sutcliffe, Dean of Exeter, writing in the early seventeenth century, argued that in the calendar of martyrs, Foxe was simply emulating the practices of the early church. Adapting the ancient adage that it was the cause which made the martyr and not the punishment, Sutcliffe argued that it was the cause which made the martyr, not the Pope, and so it required no papal decretal to 'register saints in heaven'. It was Sutcliffe's view that Foxe had known the causes which made his sufferers into martyrs, and these causes would have made them true martyrs whether or not they were recorded in his calendar.[15]

By the 1630s however, voices of dissent were to be heard even from within the Church of England itself. Archbishop Laud berated a calendar similar to Foxe's, deriding it as 'a base Business' and a 'notorious abuse' which 'left out all the Saints, Apostles and all'.[16] Laud's chaplain, John Pocklington, went even further. He complained bitterly at this

---

[12] Harpsfield, *Dialogi sex*, pp. 602, 625.

[13] Harpsfield, *Dialogi sex*, p. 603.

[14] Other Catholic attacks on *Acts and Monuments* were launched by Thomas Harding, Edmund Campion and, notably, Robert Persons, English Jesuit and most active of early seventeenth-century Catholic polemicists. Taking up where Harpsfield had left off, Persons attempted nothing less than the fundamental demolition of Foxe's work, using Foxe's calendar as the structure for his attack. See Robert Persons alias N. D. *A treatise of three conversions of England* (St Omer, 1603–04), tomes ii and iii.

[15] Matthew Sutcliffe, *A threefold answer* (London, 1606), pp. 242–6 and esp. p. 245.

[16] See W. Scott and J. Bliss (eds), *The Works of William Laud* (7 vols, Oxford, 1847–60), vol. 4, p. 265; and John Browne, clerk to the House of Lords, in Maurice F. Bond (ed.), *The Manuscripts of the House of Lords: Addenda 1514–1714* (London, 1962), pp. 427–8.

work in which: 'the Holy Martyrs, and confessors of Jesus Christ, (... whose names are written in heaven) are rased out, and Traitors, Murderers, Rebels, and Hereticks set in their roomes'.[17]

In his answer to Harpsfield and the other early Catholic critics of the calendar of martyrs, Foxe was typically robust, flatly denying that he had parodied the medieval calendar, or even that he had created a calendar at all. Forcibly he made the point in 1563 that the so-called 'calendar' in *Acts and Monuments* was in fact an index, recording the month and year in which the martyrs had met their deaths, and was purely for the private use of his readers.[18] He repeated his defence in 1570 and amplified it. His calendar was intended, he said, 'for no other purpose, but to serve the use only of the reader, in stead of a table, shewing the yere and moneth of every Martyr, what time he suffered, &c', and was no more harmful than Harpsfield's table at the end of his Dialogues.[19]

How plausible was this defence of Foxe, that his calendar was no more than a helpful prefatory tool, to record the names and dates of his martyrs? First impressions were rather against him, since his 'catalogue' was unambiguously entitled 'The Kalender', and its typography closely mimicked the *mise-en-page* of the traditional calendar, right down to the use of red-letter, and the inclusion of the Golden Number. In any case, the 'catalogue' could not function as a table in the traditional way, lacking page numbers and any other means of locating individual martyrs in the main text. Foxe himself was so unsure of the calendar of martyrs, that even whilst defending it against his critics in principle, he abandoned it in practice, removing it from the 1570 edition of *Acts and Monuments*. He replaced it with an alphabetical list of martyrs, and the page numbers where they could be found. The addition effectively undermined the claim he was still making, that his calendar was nothing more than a table of martyrs. How could it be only a table when here, in 1570, was the genuine article?[20]

Whatever Foxe's denials on other matters, even the martyrologist had to confess that his calendar might give the appearance of setting up new red-lettered holy days. The martyrologist himself remained adamant

---

[17] John Pocklington, *Altare christianum* (2 edns, London, 1637), p. 92 (1st edn); p. 114 (2nd edn).

[18] 'Quanquam à me quidem non aliter Calendarium hoc institutum est, nisi ut *pro Indice* duntaxat suum cuiusque Martyris mensem & annum designante, ad privatum Lectoris serviret usum'. *Acts and Monuments* (1583), sig. *2ª.

[19] *Acts and Monuments* (1583), vol. 1, p. 581. Foxe was here translating his earlier Latin defence.

[20] See the table entitled, 'The names of the Martyrs in this booke conteyned' in John Foxe, *Acts and Monuments* (2 vols, London, 1570), vol. 1, sig. C2ª–3ª.

that he did not intend to 'appoint out holy dayes and working daies by colours of red and blacke, in my ... Calendare, to be observed'.[21] Yet he had to admit that appearances were against him, that the use of red-letter for certain of the more prominent Protestant martyrs such as Cranmer, Latimer and Ridley, might give the opposite impression, might even give Harpsfield's accusation 'some blush of credite'.[22] If these new red-letter days were not intended as new feast days, which they clearly were not, then at least one of their effects was to question the validity of the Catholic Church's calendar, and the pattern of holiness which it structured and sustained.[23]

II

The significance of Foxe's creation was profound. Later we will consider its implications for the Church of England, but first we look at its more obvious target. It struck at the very heart of traditional piety. The Catholic calendar, whose status the calendar of martyrs put into question, was one of the principal pillars upholding the cult of the saints.

Medieval calendars provided a form of appointments diary. They regulated the days on which the saints were to be celebrated, distinguishing the feasts as single or double according to their rank. In the Sarum rite, the days of the greater non-scriptural saints were marked by long sequences, retelling the exploits of the saint. On 6 December, the story of the day's saint, St Nicholas, was related with typical weight given both to his holiness and his efficacy in answer to prayer. Saintly he had been even as a nursing babe, having 'fasted while an infant', yet still managing 'at the very breast to merit joys on high'. In later life he had performed the valuable service of saving a virgin's honour, before beginning a second career after his death as a saintly intercessor. On appeal to Nicholas, disease would recoil, and stormy seas subside. Every year in the annual mass dedicated to St Nicholas, believers were reminded in this narrative both of the saint's history and his resultant powers to help and to heal by his intercession.[24] Similar 'sequences'

---

[21] *Acts and Monuments* (1583), vol. 1, p. 582.

[22] *Acts and Monuments* (1583), vol. 1, p. 582.

[23] Other than the red-lettering, the offending days were not accompanied with any of the necessary paraphernalia of holy days, in particular gospel, epistle and collect. Foxe himself directed readers to the accompanying preface, to dispel any suspicion that his red-letter days had been intended to set up new holy days. *Acts and Monuments* (1583), vol. 1, p. 582.

[24] F. E. Warren (ed.), *The Sarum Missal in English* (2 vols, London, 1913), vol. 2, pp. 252–3.

marked the masses dedicated to St Vincent and St Alban, to the translations of St Martin and St Osmund, to the feasts of St Anne and St
Katherine.[25] If the hearers were eager to know more, they could refer to
other sources of information. Foremost amongst the printed material
was the *Golden Legend*, which used the calendar as its structuring
principle. Like other collections and individual narratives of saints'
lives, the *Legend* was produced in the more accessible vernacular.[26] The
ubiquitous primers, whose prayers encouraged recourse to saintly me-
diation, also contained the calendar to shape their saintly piety.[27]

The calendar was the structural principle behind the cult of the
saints. It showed where the devotion of believers should be directed on
each succeeding day of the year. In effect, the medieval calendar provided a daily investment guide for the spiritual capital of the faithful.
The calendar itself was not the force motivating the believer to dedicate
so much time, energy and wealth to the relationship with the saint. The
principle source of dynamism was the belief in saintly efficacy: the
power of the patron to intervene on behalf of the petitioning client.
Take away veneration, and devotion to the saints was likely to wane.
Yet the calendar still provided a vital facilitating role, in ordering,
shaping, and prompting the outpouring of religious fervour. And it was
the calendar which Foxe had requisitioned in order to fashion a potent
weapon against his Roman opponents.

In the past, the medieval calendars had drawn on a common pool of
saints, mutually recognized and respected. There had always existed
differences between local calendars of course. Sarum and York had
differed considerably in the saints given places of honour, and this was

---

[25] See Warren (ed.), *Sarum Missal*, vol. 2, pp. 278–9, 374–5, 397–8, 409–10, 424–5,
583–4.

[26] Between 1483 and 1527 nine full editions of the *Golden Legend* were produced in
English. Jacobus de Voragine, *The Golden Legend* (London, 1483, 1487, 1493, 1498,
1504, 1507, 1512, 1521 and 1527). The spread of Voragine's influential hagiography is
considered in Brenda Dunn-Lardeau (ed.), '*Legenda aurea*': *sept siècles de diffusion*
(Montreal and Paris, 1986). Its impact is assessed by Helen C. White, *Tudor Books of
Saints and Martyrs* (Madison, 1963), pp. 31–66, and more recently by Sherry L. Reames,
The 'Legenda aurea': a Reexamination of its Paradoxical History (Madison, 1985), esp.
pp. 197–209.

[27] Some 127 editions of the Sarum primer have survived for the period from 1477 to
1535 – an output of about two per year, suggesting a high demand for these books of
private prayer. For the development of the primer see Edgar Hoskins, '*Horae beatae
Mariae Virginis*' *or Sarum and York Primers with Kindred Books and Primers of the
Reformed Roman use* (London, 1901), and Helen C. White, *The Tudor Books of Private
Devotion* (Madison, 1951). The primers' style of piety is outlined by Duffy, who also
compares the Sarum texts to the later 'Wayland' primers, and finds much to admire in
these versions produced after the restoration of Catholicism under Mary. See Duffy,
Stripping of the Altars, pp. 209–98, 537–43.

a pattern reflected across medieval Catholic Christendom.[28] Foxe on the other hand had drawn from a different pool altogether, substituting Protestant martyrs for Catholic saints, implicitly rejecting those he had excluded and denying their worth. By extension, he denied their individual expertise, and even their collective ability to mediate the prayers of the faithful. In Foxe's calendar, the network of welfare, which the saints had traditionally provided from the cradle to the grave, was wilfully torn apart.

The calendar of martyrs also provided a new lever to dislodge that traditional target of Protestant polemic, the Pope and papal authority. After examining the history of the previous 500 years, Foxe wondered aloud why he might not have: 'as good cause to celebrate these [martyrs] in my Calendar, which lost their lives and were slain, principally for the cause of Christ and of hys word: as the pope hath to celebrate his double and simple feasted saintes in hys Calendar'.[29] By side-lining the traditionally laborious process of selecting new saints, and disregarding the powers which participated in it, Foxe challenged the Catholic authorities, and especially the Pope, in one of the most significant areas of ecclesiastical jurisdiction.

III

Catholic howls of protest at Foxe's excesses in creating a calendar of martyrs have tended to drown out the full range of the martyrologist's criticism. In fact Foxe was not directing his criticism exclusively at the Catholic Church's calendar: the martyrologist also had the Prayer Book calendar in his sights. The Church of England's official calendar had undergone a series of fundamental changes since the 1530s, which from a moderate Puritan perspective had pared off some of the more objectionable saints and suppressed the more offensive practices, especially veneration. But vestiges of the medieval calendar remained, and in two ways the 'reformed' Prayer Book calendar still caused Foxe acute disquiet, despite the corrective surgery which had been performed on it. The revised Church of England calendar was unacceptable, for two reasons – partly on account of the holy days it continued to regulate, and partly because of the version of ecclesiastical history it implicitly upheld. Its model of piety and of the past were equally unwelcome to stricter Protestant tempers.

---

[28] The variety of medieval rites is considered by G. J. Cuming, *A History of Anglican Liturgy* (2nd edn, Basingstoke and London, 1982), pp. 12–14.

[29] *Acts and Monuments* (1583), vol. 1, p. 582.

In the case of the holy days, the fundamental break with the saintly past had come in 1549, when Cranmer's first Prayer Book dispensed with almost all the non-scriptural saints. However, there still remained a bare skeleton of holy days, comprising Christmas, Easter, and Whitsun, the feast days of the apostles, the evangelists, John the Baptist, Mary Magdalene and the virgin Mary.[30] Theologically the remaining saints were assigned an entirely new role. No longer were they primarily cast in the part of mediators to God on the believers' behalf, able to prevail with the deity through Christ's merits. In Lutheran style, believers were now encouraged to emulate the devotion of the saints, and to praise God, from whom the saints' qualities had come. The new roles of the saints were encapsulated in the collects for the feast days, rewritten by Cranmer. St Peter, in the new collect, was described as a man commanded to feed God's flock, whose example should inspire 'all bishops and pastors diligently to preach thy holy word, and the people obediently to follow the same'. In the collect for All Saints' day, the faithful were urged to follow the saints as paradigms of 'all virtues, and godly living'.[31] Instead of acting primarily as a lever for humans to work on God, the saints were now exclusively a lever for God to work on humanity.

Already in the 1550s many English Protestants wished to go further. The saints, and the sacred calendars which structured their commemoration, were remnants of the old faith, having provided the foundations for many Catholic observances such as veneration, pilgrimage and the honouring of relics – all practices detested by the reformed camp. In some Protestant quarters there was a desire to expunge every remaining trace of the saints from the liturgy, and every feast day from the Church's year. Whilst Cranmer cut back the Prayer Book calendar to focus only on scriptural saints, and to structure a strictly commemorative form of holy day, the foreign churches resident in London adopted a different course. In John a Lasco's liturgy of 1550, and the subsequent translations into French, Italian, Dutch and German, the saints played no part in the individual services, which were a sober mixture of preaching and prayers. Indeed the *Forma et ratio* of 1550, contained no calendar at

---

[30] These were also the saints whom Foxe used as the outline for his own calendar in 1563. The 1549 reforms reflected the scope of change amongst continental Protestants, who, finding themselves pulled between popular traditional attachment to festivals and personal theological aversion, frequently retained a few holy days to celebrate scripturally grounded saints. Bucer for instance supported an absolute abrogation in principle, yet retained some saints' days in practice. See Robert Stupperich (ed.), *Martin Bucers Deutsche Schriften* (5 vols, Gütersloh, 1960–78), vol. 1, 262–8; vol. 4, 238–9.

[31] Joseph Ketley (ed.), *The Two Liturgies of Edward VI* (Cambridge, 1844), pp. 72, 75.

all, so that all trace of the saints had been eradicated.[32] After Edward's death and the end of the great Protestant experiment in England, many reformers fled to the upper Rhine and Switzerland, where they encountered a range of simpler liturgies. By now most reformed churches on the Continent had long since abandoned celebrating saints' days and using the sacred calendar which recorded them.[33] In Zurich, the town council had narrowed down the acceptable feast days to Sundays and the holy days dedicated to Christ.[34] The expectation must have been considerable that in the event of the re-establishment of Protestantism in England a similar course would swiftly follow.

With the accession of Elizabeth came a return to the Edwardine settlement of religion in most of its details.[35] In the sacred calendar few changes were made, and the version issued in 1559 and underpinned by the Act of Uniformity followed the earlier model of the 1552 Prayer Book. The pre-Marian Protestant calendar was re-established, and there was no sweeping away of the Church calendar and its associated saints' days in the style of the Swiss reformed churches, or the Stranger churches in London. In this instance, as in many others, the continental Protestant churches had moved on, whilst the English church had remained in a ten-year time-warp.[36]

Foxe's opposition to feast days pre-dated his return from exile in Germany and Switzerland. He had taken a leading role in the discussions in Frankfurt which had proposed two liturgies, but found no

---

[32] John à Lasco, *Forma ac ratio* (Frankfurt and Emden, 1554?). Translated versions of the *Forma* appeared in Dutch (Emden, 1554 and 1563), French (London, 1552; Emden, 1552; and Frankfurt, 1556), German (Heidelberg, 1565), and Italian (Zurich, 1551?). See STC 16571a–16576.

[33] For an outline of the changes in the reformed Churches see Kaspar von Greyerz on Switzerland, and Wiebe Bergsma on the Low Countries, in Bob Scribner, Roy Porter and Mikulás Teich (eds), *The Reformation in National Context* (Cambridge, 1994), pp. 30–46, 67–79, esp. pp. 33 and 69.

[34] The final blow against saints' days in Zurich came in 1550, in the *Grosse Mandat* issued by the city council. See Anton Largiadèr, 'Das reformierte Zürich und die Fest- und Heiligentage', *Zwingliana*, 9 (1949–53), pp. 497–525, esp. pp. 512–13.

[35] An account of the changes, with the European dimension given its due weight, is provided by Diarmaid MacCulloch in *The Later Reformation in England 1547–1603* (London, 1990), pp. 27–43. Cf. Norman L. Jones, *Faith by Statute: Parliament and the Settlement of Religion 1559* (London, 1982), esp. pp. 83–159.

[36] The position of the reformed churches was to harden still further in the following years. Its classic formulation was expressed by Bullinger in the General Synod of Herborn of 1586. Article 48 stated that all saints' holy days were to be abrogated, and only Sundays and the feasts of Christ were to be retained. See Wilhelm Niesel (ed.), *Bekenntnisschriften und Kirchenordnungen der nach Gottes Wort reformierten Kirche (BSKORK)* (2nd edn, Zurich, 1938), p. 296. By the 1580s such a position had become commonplace amongst reformers of the Swiss persuasion.

place for saints' days or the calendar.[37] On his return to England, Foxe made a strong and only slightly veiled attack on the continuance of holy days in the English Church. In a preface to the *Acts and Monuments* condemning the use made by the Roman Church of the calendar and saints, he commented that in his opinion it would be better if holy days were abandoned altogether, leaving the sabbath alone, to be celebrated with due solemnity.[38]

Foxe's views were far from unusual within the English church. The observance of holy days proved an enduringly popular target for Puritan polemicists. In the grand litany of grievances against their half-reformed Church of England, the practice of celebrating saints' days was roundly condemned along with the use of vestments, rings in marriage and kneeling at communion. Saints' feast days were perceived as derogating from the dignity and importance of the Sabbath, which should have been the only focus of Christian worship – the only red-letter day. At worst holy days provided scope for a mistaken understanding of the saints' limited role in a reformed church, and could open the door to idolatry. Even at their best, they suggested the existence of days equal in importance to the Lord's day. Reform of holy days – preferably their abolition – was high on the Puritan list of demands. Even Archbishop Parker sought to soften the prohibition on working on holy days, only to see his attempts founder in both Convocation and Parliament. Foxe's calendar, published for the first time in 1563, was part of this campaign of the early 1560s to eliminate the cycle of saints' days from liturgical practice in the Church of England.[39]

---

[37] For the committee which included Foxe alongside Knox, Whittingham, Gilby and William Cole, and recommended the adoption of an adapted Genevan service, see Cuming, *Anglican Liturgy*, p. 88. A second proposal put forward by the Knoxians and based on the 1552 Prayer Book, is contained in Harry S. Witherspoon and George W. Sprott (eds), *The Second Prayer Book of King Edward the Sixth and the Liturgy of Compromise Used in the English Congregation at Frankfurt* (Edinburgh and London, 1905), pp. 203–60. A contemporary account of the conflict is contained in *A brieff discours off the troubles begonne at Franckford* (Heidelberg, 1575). Also see Patrick Collinson, *The Elizabethan Puritan Movement* (London, 1967, repr. 1991), pp. 33, 72, 153.

[38] See the preface 'ad doctum lectorem' in *Acts and Monuments* (1583), sig. *2ᵃ, where Foxe states, 'Festorum dierum iam plus satis erat in mundo'.

[39] Horton Davies, *The Worship of the English Puritans* (Westminster, 1948), pp. 75–6. Some Puritans even went so far as to attribute holy days, along with a host of other ceremonies and practices, to the malign influence of the Antichrist. *A parte of a register* (Middleburg, 1593?), p. 64. Rather less stridently, an anonymous petition of 1603 on the accession of James I, listed amongst the usual range of requests that 'the rest upon holydays [be] not so strictly urged'. See 'The Millenary Petition', summarized by Edward Cardwell in *A history of conferences ... connected with the revision of the Book of Common Prayer, 1558–1690* (Oxford, 1840), pp. 130–33. For Parker's lack of enthusi-

Foxe was to be disappointed in his vision for a reformed role for the saints. Not only did saints' days remain, and survive right up until the Civil War, but if anything the tide turned against Foxe and those who thought like him, bringing back into the official Church of England calendar offensive material, which had previously been expunged. In 1561 the black-letter saints' days, absent from the Edwardine calendars, returned to the Prayer Book calendar. Some 60 new saints were scattered throughout the year, resulting in a radical transformation in the contents of the official calendar. The criteria for choosing which saints to include and which to abandon remain obscure, though certain patterns emerge. There was a tendency to emphasize the heritage of the English church, including its connections with the Saxon church, and the primitive churches of both western and eastern Christendom. Amongst those saints who found a place in the new Prayer Book calendar were Augustine of Canterbury and Pope Gregory the Great, as well as the Saxon saints Etheldreda, Edmund and Edward. Some additions were particularly unwelcome in Protestant eyes. Hugh of Lincoln had been a Carthusian monk, and Richard of Chichester a champion of priestly celibacy. Neither seemed to have much to recommend his recruitment to a supposedly 'reformed' calendar.[40] Richard, it is true, was also a writer of simple, heartfelt piety, including the famous prayer: 'O most merciful redeemer ... may I know thee more clearly, love thee more dearly and follow thee more nearly, day by day', which more recently was to provide the lyrics for a song in the West End musical 'Godspell', but this contribution to popular culture came too late to rescue his reputation amongst Reformation Protestants.[41]

The precise role envisaged for the black-letter saints remained undefined. Instructions accompanying this new Prayer Book calendar made it plain that there should be no communal celebration of the black-letter saints, with a stern warning that only the named red-letter days were to be observed 'and none other'. This rubric guarded against a return of the traditional black-letter saints to their former pre-eminence. But if the black-letter saints were not to regain their full

---

asm for a strict observance of saints' days see Ronald Hutton, *The Rise and Fall of Merry England: the Ritual Year 1400–1700* (Oxford, 1994), p. 123, and Kenneth L. Parker, *The English Sabbath: a Study of Doctrine and Discipline from the Reformation to the Civil War* (Cambridge, 1988), p. 51.

[40] The 1561 calendar is included in W. K. Clay (ed.), *Liturgical Services. Liturgies and Occasional Forms of Prayer set forth in the Reign of Queen Elizabeth* (Cambridge, 1847), pp. 47–52. On the ambiguities of the 1561 calendar, also see William P. Haugaard, *Elizabeth and the English Reformation: the Struggle for a Stable Settlement of Religion* (Cambridge, 1968), pp. 117–19.

[41] See Farmer, *Dictionary of Saints*, pp. 238–9, 416–17.

dignity as minor feast days, what was their role to be? Did the early Elizabethan church hierarchy, which had reinstated the black-letter saints, view them merely as reference points for readers to navigate their way around the sacred calendar, or as something more?

The medieval calendar's traditional role in structuring the celebration of feast and fast days can obscure its commemorative function. Yet Sarum and other similar calendars had a vital secondary purpose: to register the names and hence preserve the memories of the saints, albeit without holding a separate holiday in their honour. In the early 1540s Cranmer had pinpointed this commemorative function of the calendar as ripe for reform. His intention, he said, was to excise the 'names and memories' of all non-scriptural and non-patristic saints.[42] Twenty years later in 1561, it was precisely these former targets of the Archbishop which had been reinstated in the official Prayer Book calendar. To many Protestants the dangers were obvious. Accounts of the saints from printed legenda might no longer be read during divine services, but plenty of hagiographical woodcuts, images and chapbooks still remained in circulation. Increasingly this material became clandestine, available only by illegal import, yet from an earnest Protestant perspective, the ongoing presence of the black-letter saints in the Church of England's calendar did nothing to discourage a continuing addiction to the old saints.[43]

The potential ambiguity of the black-letter saints soon became apparent. In an official calendar produced in 1564 and reprinted three times thereafter Latin verses were added to the entry for each month, celebrating the most prominent saints. During the year this included saints Valentine, George and Catherine, and in December mention was made of saints Nicholas, Anne and Lucy. Not only were Anne and Lucy mentioned, but passing reference was also made to their miraculous – from a Protestant perspective superstitiously miraculous – lives. These were hardly the expected occupants of a fully reformed calendar.[44]

---

[42] David Wilkins, *Concilia Magnae Britanniae et Hiberniae* (4 vols, London, 1737), vol. 3, p. 863. Cf. Duffy, *Stripping of the Altars*, p. 432.

[43] Tessa Watt records the continuing appearance of saints (though somewhat secularized) in ballads, and of a warning in 1579 against the import of Catholic woodcuts depicting the saints. See Tessa Watt, *Cheap Print and Popular Piety, 1550–1640* (Cambridge, 1991), pp. 110–11, 213–14, 179–81.

[44] In an 1851 edition of the *Preces privatae*, the editor W. K. Clay quotes a health warning allegedly attached to the original calendar, confining the uses of the black-letter saints within set limits. The saints were to perform a purely secular service, marking days of particular importance in the same way as the dog days and signs of the zodiac. The warning is not immediately apparent in any of the four editions of *Preces privatae* that I have consulted. Its authenticity is questionable, especially given that the only other

The black-letter saints hovered precariously between the secular and the sacred worlds. The confusion apparent in 1564 was less pronounced in the crucial 1561 calendar, which became the standard Prayer Book calendar right through to the Civil War, but it was none the less evident. On the one hand no explicit encouragement was given to readers to celebrate the memories of the black-letter saints. But on the other, since only a certain selection were deemed worthy of inclusion, it could easily be assumed that these saints possessed particular significance, beyond their simple secular role as date-markers. Certainly, there was nothing to prevent the black-letter days being interpreted as commemorations, celebrating the saints canonized by the Pope and preserving their memories into the era of a supposedly reformed Protestant Church.

Early Elizabethan Protestants differed on whether the medieval Catholic heritage was to be embraced, albeit selectively, or to be wholly rejected. Churchmen such as Archbishop Parker were quite content, even eager, to point to their medieval Catholic forebears, and the link they provided to the early church, in order to establish the antiquity of the reformed English church and the legitimacy of its clerical orders. On one level, including the black-letter saints in 1561 encapsulated the kind of ecclesiastical history Parker espoused, tracing back the English Church to its origins through the Roman, Saxon and medieval saints. Parker expanded on the idea a decade later, when he published his *De antiquitate Britannicae ecclesiae*, a history (and celebration) of his 69 predecessors as Archbishops of Canterbury and the Church they had served from the earliest times, with all the emphasis on continuity, rather than on the idea that the Reformation marked a watershed or break with the medieval past.[45]

Others were less enthused by the idea of such a medieval Catholic past. In a telling exchange between John Whitgift, newly appointed to the see of Canterbury, and a group of Chichester Puritans summoned before the archbishop for refusing to subscribe to the Book of Common Prayer, the confusion and lack of precision in the Church of England calendar was all too apparent. One of the principal objections raised

---

reference to the same quotation is found in the works of William Prynne, that often inventive polemicist. See the prefatory material to the *Preces privatae* in W. K. Clay, *Private prayers put forth by Authority during the reign of Queen Elizabeth* (Cambridge, 1851), and William Prynne, *A briefe survay and censure of Mr Cozens his couzening 'Devotions'* (London, 1628), pp. 34–5. There were four distinct editions of the *Preces privatae* (London, 1564, 1568, 1573 and 1574).

[45] Matthew Parker, G. Acworth and J. Josseline, *De antiquitate Britannicae ecclesiae & privilegiis ecclesiae Cantuariensis, cum archiepiscopis eiusdem 70* (London, 1572–74). Criticism of Becket's overreaching ambition was tempered with praise for the archbishop's personal holiness, see pp. 118–23.

against the Prayer Book was its calendar, and the black-letter saints in particular. It was not an attack that Whitgift found easy to counter. The Chichester group complained of the calendar's ambiguity, arguing that: 'it putteth in the popishe saints, and so retaineth an opinion of holines in them'. The archbishop countered that this did not matter in deciding whether to conform and subscribe, since: 'The Kalendars are not of the substance of the booke.' The Puritans would have none of it: 'they are a principall part of the book, and have a chief interest in the directions therof. And the statute calleth it a part also, primo Elizab'. Whitgift, apparently stumped, accepted the point by default. He fell back on an argument of convenience: the Church was free to legislate on matters indifferent for the edification of the people. 'The popish saints are not put in the Kallendars to norish any superstition as you saye, but to express the usuall tymes of payments, and the tymes of the courts and their returnes in both lawes.' But this was a line drawn in the sand. There was no sanction to prevent these secular boundaries being breached, and the black-letter saints being commemorated.[46]

Foxe did not reject all of the medieval saints. He praised St Chad's godly conversation, St Gregory's discretion and St Swithun's piety. Foxe's approbation for their holy lives was coupled with incredulity when faced by their miracles. Commenting on the marvels accredited to St Swithun he remained steadfastly unimpressed. 'But as concerning the miracles which are read in the Churche of Winchester, of this *Swythinus*, them I leave to be read together with the *Iliades* of *Homere*, or tales of Robenhood.'[47] Such instances are important, not only because Swithun, Chad and Gregory formed part of the medieval Catholic heritage of the English church: they were also honoured with places in the post-Reformation Church of England calendar. Foxe, who had ejected these black-letter saints from his own calendar, proved to be distinctly reserved about their very claim to sainthood, resting as it did on miracles whose veracity he rejected.

Foxe questioned the validity of the individual saints in the official Prayer Book calendar, and the history which collectively they implied and embodied. The martyrologist rejected the 'official' route to the past through the clergy and structure of the medieval church, in favour of a poor, persecuted remnant, scattered in every time and place. In much of *Acts and Monuments*, Foxe was concerned with lining up some fairly

---

[46] See 'A Breife and true reporte of the proceedinges againste some of the ministers and prechers of the diocese of Chichester for refusinge to subscribe to certaine articles', in Albert Peel (ed.), *The Seconde Parte of a Register* (2 vols, Cambridge, 1915), vol. 1, 209–20, esp. 211–12.

[47] *Acts and Monuments* (1583), vol. 1, 117 (Gregory), 137 (Swithun).

disparate elements into a convincing and credible alternative to the concrete clarity of a medieval church which, though it may have been corrupt, had undeniably existed. Foxe's calendar was another means to discredit the 'official' vision of the past. It was directed not only against Catholic opponents, but also against that rival version of the past that was still relied upon by some sections within the English church, and whose outline was reflected within the Prayer Book calendar.

IV

Was the intention behind Foxe's calendar exclusively negative? From the story so far, the calendar of martyrs was destructive in character, aiming to pull down Protestant commemoration of the saints as much as Catholic veneration. But was there also a positive note to Foxe's martyrological creation? Was his calendar an attempt to build up a new status for the martyrs, even as it tore down the former prestige of the saints?

Part of the answer lies in the fact that this kind of revision was not entirely new. Foxe was contributing to a tradition which in England had been initiated by George Joye in his Protestant primer of 1530. In iconoclastic mode, the Protestant exile Joye had removed all the non-scriptural saints from the calendar, and then added one name of his own: Thomas Hitton, a Protestant exile, who in the year of the primer's publication had been arrested, tried and burnt on a brief missionary trip to England.[48]

On the Continent there were similar innovations. Concern with the past, and enthusiasm for the Church calendar, were recurring preoccupations amongst the first generation of Lutheran reformers. Luther himself championed the cause of history and even turned his hand to martyrologies, producing a whole series of vivid pamphlet accounts of the earliest martyrs.[49] Melanchthon was an even more ardent supporter

---

[48] Joye's career and publications are considered by Charles C. Butterworth and Allan G. Chester, *George Joye, 1495?–1553: a Chapter in the History of the English Bible and the English Reformation* (Philadelphia, 1962). For Joye's primer and its novel design, see Cuming, *Anglican Liturgy*, p. 31, and Butterworth and Chester, *George Joye*, pp. 60–67.

[49] Luther composed five martyrological pamphlets in response to the early burnings of Henry of Zutphen, George Winkler, Leonhard Kaiser, Robert Barnes, and the Brussels martyrs. For these, and the preface he wrote for Hus's prison letters, see David Hugh Farmer, Karl Hausberger, Christian Hannick and Frieder Schulz, 'Hagiographie', *Theologische Realenzyklopädie*, 14 (1985), pp. 360–80, esp. p. 378. However, Luther's views altered significantly during the subsequent two decades. For the reformer's changing – and increasingly ambivalent – attitude towards martyrdom see David Bagchi, 'Luther and the Problem of Martyrdom', in Diana Wood (ed.), *Martyrs and Martyrologies* (SCH, 30, 1993), pp. 209–19.

of histories of all kinds. He urged his readers to consult the sacred calendar every morning, so that from church history they should be encouraged and spurred onward.[50] Only in the 1550s did a full-scale calendar of martyrs appear in the shape of Paul Eber's Latin *Calendarium historicum*. The Wittenberger's amalgam of sacred and secular history proved popular, running to six editions between 1550 and 1582.[51]

Another 'alternative' calendar was created in the later 1550s. Published in Frankfurt in 1559, the year in which Foxe himself was returning from continental exile, Goltwurm's *Kirchen Calendar*, or church calendar, prefigured Foxe's production rather more closely than did Eber's. It contained a similar hybrid of ancient and modern, with 13 pre-Reformation and 49 post-Reformation martyrs amongst the conventional selection of apostles and early saints. Goltwurm selected his witnesses, teachers and confessors from the pages of Rabus and Crespin, two continental martyrologists whose works had been published in the 1550s. The *Kirchen Calendar* was a poor man's martyrology, intended, Goltwurm said, to strengthen the faith and to improve the lives of his readers, especially if they could not manage the length or the Latin of the original stories.[52]

Some or all of these 'alternative' Lutheran calendars were probably familiar to Foxe. In general the martyrologist took a close interest in the

---

[50] C. G. Bretschneider (ed.), *Philippi Melanchthonis opera quae supersunt omnia* (Halle and Brunswick, 1834–60), vol. 24, p. 351.

[51] See Paul Eber, *Calendarium historicum conscriptum a Paulo Ebero Kitthingensi* (Wittenberg, 1550). For studies of Eber's calendar see Robert Kolb, *For all the Saints: Changing Perceptions of Martyrdom and Sainthood in the Lutheran Reformation* (Macon, GA, 1987), pp. 27–33; and Annemarie Brückner and Wolfgang Brückner, 'Zeugen des Glaubens und ihre Literatur. Altväterbeispiele, Kalenderheilige, protestantische Märtyrer und evangelische Lebenszeugnisse', in W. Brückner (ed.), *Volkserzählung und Reformation* (Berlin, 1974), pp. 520–78, esp. pp. 540–56.

[52] See Kaspar Goltwurm, *Kirchen Calendar* (Frankfurt, 1559), esp. the title-page and prefatory material. Five further editions of the calendar were printed up to 1612. Goltwurm's historical work is considered by Bernward Deneke in 'Kaspar Goltwurm. Ein lutherischer Kompilator zwischen Überlieferung und Glaube', in W. Brückner (ed.), *Volkserzählung und Reformation* (Berlin, 1974), pp. 124–77, esp. pp. 144–52. Crespin and Rabus produced martyrologies in French and German respectively, which roughly parallel Foxe's *Acts and Monuments*. See Jean Crespin, *Histoire des martyrs* (Geneva, 1570), and Ludwig Rabus, *Historien der Martyrer* (Strassburg, 1571–72). These, and other European martyrologies, are surveyed in Jean-François Gilmont, 'Les martyrologes protestants du xvie siecle' (unpublished Master's thesis, Université catholique de Louvain, 1966); Gilmont, 'Les martyrologes du XVIe siècle', in Silvana Seidel Menchi, H. R. Guggisberg and Bernd Moeller (eds), 'Ketzerverfolgung im 16. und frühen 17. Jahrhundert' (Wolfenbütteler Forschungen, 51, 1992); and A. G. Dickens, 'Weapons of Propaganda: the Martyrologies', in A. G. Dickens and John M. Tonkin, *The Reformation in Historical Thought* (Oxford, 1985), pp. 39–57.

branch of Protestantism rooted in Wittenberg. Unlike some of his English contemporaries for whom Luther was a closed book, Foxe championed the man, and promoted his ideas – at least those of which he approved. Both early and late in life, the martyrologist encouraged and assisted in the translation of Luther's works.[53] Foxe honoured the German reformer with a red-letter entry in his calendar of martyrs, and his story of Luther's life in the *Acts and Monuments* was highly complimentary. No other Reformation leader received such a lengthy or such a glowing report. In Foxe's greater scheme of church history, Luther was given a pivotal role. He provided the key turning-point in the progress of the True Church, becoming in effect the chief instrument in God's campaign to restore His church to its original purity.[54]

In the particular case of the Lutheran calendars, it is evident that Foxe knew and approved of at least one of them. He referred to Paul Eber's calendar for those of his own readers requiring more ample accounts of the martyrdom of Henry Sutphen. But the English martyrologist differed from both Eber and Goltwurm in the saints and martyrs whom he celebrated. No place could he find for any saints except the most pure and primitive, a distinction most striking in the contrasting treatments of Thomas Becket. Foxe exiled the Archbishop from the calendar in *Acts and Monuments*, and went to considerable pains in his text to discredit the status of his sainthood. In Foxe's view, something of Thomas's reputation and popularity still lingered on despite the draconian measures taken against the cult by Henry VIII. Eber and Goltwurm on the other hand cheerfully included the martyr in his traditional position on 29 December, with a relatively positive presentation of his cause.[55]

---

[53] Foxe's main periods of activity were the late 1540s, and mid-1570s. See William A. Clebsch, 'The Elizabethans on Luther', in J. Pelikan (ed.), *Interpreters of Luther* (Philadelphia, 1968), pp. 97–120, esp. pp. 107–11.

[54] Given the emphasis that William Haller has put upon Wyclif as the turning-point in Foxe's scheme of history, it is worthy of note that Foxe devoted neither as lengthy a treatment to Wyclif, nor gave him as prominent a position as his German counterpart. See William Haller, 'John Foxe and the Puritan Revolution', in Richard F. Jones (ed.), *The Seventeenth Century: Studies in the History of English Thought and Literature from Bacon to Pope* (Stanford, CA, 1951, repr. 1965), pp. 209–24, esp. pp. 210–16 for Wyclif's alleged centrality and Luther's relatively peripheral status. For Foxe's own portrayal of the reformers see *Acts and Monuments* (1583), vol. 1, pp. 424–50, 463–4 on Wyclif, and for Luther, vol. 2, pp. 841–63.

[55] See Goltwurm, *Kirchen Calendar*, f.135ª; and Eber, *Calendarium historicum*, p. 411. For Foxe on Thomas Becket see *Acts and Monuments* (1583), vol. 1, pp. 205–26, esp. pp. 224–6 on Thomas's claims to sanctity – or lack of them. For the banning and expunging of the Becket legend from Henrician missals see Duffy, *The Stripping of the Altars*, pp. 412, 418–19.

Interpreting pre-Lutheran history, Foxe, unlike Eber and Goltwurm, advocated an ecclesiastical history inhabited almost exclusively by a succession of medieval groups, formerly tainted by popish accusations of heresy, but now washed clean of all suspicion of heterodoxy. The martyrologists Foxe, Crespin and Rabus heard – or chose to hear – strong echoes of their own convictions amongst Waldensians in Savoy, Lollards in England, and Hussites in Bohemia. Not only did these medieval groups provide a past for Protestants, free of popish contamination, they also provided a common history for all Protestants, one in which both Lutherans and Swiss reformed could unite around a collective heritage. Thus a zealous Calvinist like Crespin, and a rabidly anti-Calvinist Lutheran such as Rabus both adopted a similar outline of history, at least as far as the outbreak of the Reformation. Foxe took this Protestant ecumenism one step further in his own calendar, celebrating the medieval forerunners of Protestantism, alongside the post-Reformation martyrs of both the Lutheran *and* reformed traditions. By appropriating the calendar, and placing his martyrs in such a familiar and well-used symbol, Foxe hammered home the point that his martyrs were a worthy inheritance for the reformed church, and a suitable answer to the perennial Catholic question of where the Protestant Church had been located before the advent of Luther, and since.[56]

The attempt to create an alternative calendar in England was not confined to *Acts and Monuments*. Many Elizabethan Puritans detested the calendar, yet if they were to remain within the established framework of the Elizabethan church they could not simply abolish the liturgical role of the calendar; the Act of Uniformity and the Queen's inclinations stood in the way. There might be room for manoeuvre however, and the so-called Puritan Prayer Book of 1578 pushed the possibilities for annotation, judicious rewriting and generous omission to their limits. This edition of the *Book of Common Prayer* was published and bound in conjunction with the Geneva Bible, and notable amongst its many changes were the alteration of 'priest' to 'minister', and of 'matins' and 'evensong' to 'morning prayer' and 'evening prayer'.[57]

---

[56] On the construction of a medieval past for the Protestant Church see Euan Cameron, 'Medieval Heretics as Protestant martyrs', in Diana Wood (ed.), *Martyrs and Martyrologies* (SCH, 30, 1993), pp. 185–208.

[57] There were over 20 editions of 'Puritan' Prayer Books. They contained a range of annotations, which tended to become increasingly marginal compared to the original boldness of the 1578 changes. See the *Book of Common Prayer*, STC 2123 (London, 1578), and subsequent entries. Editions continued to be produced until 1616. A. Elliott Peaston provides a limited bibliography of the various editions in *The Prayer Book Tradition in the Free Churches* (London, 1964), pp. 22–34. Also see Clay, *Liturgical Services*, pp. xv-xix; F. Procter and W. H. Frere, *A New History of the Book of Common*

It was the calendar which underwent the most extensive rewriting of all in the 'Puritan' Prayer Book, or at least the most comprehensive annotation. The calendar itself remained unchanged, but beneath it grew up a large number of additions, separate from the daily record of the saints, yet by implication to be read in conjunction with it. Most entries gave the relevant date, and used the form of words 'as upon this day' to introduce their extra historical information. Much of this new material was surprisingly secular in its nature, emphasizing the great moments of the Ancient (and pagan) world. Almost every entry in September was taken up with Roman history, from Caesar's defeat of Antony and Cleopatra at Actium, to the deaths of the Emperors Titus and Domitian, and the unfortunate demise of Crassus from pleurisy.[58] Such material had no particular religious connotations. Its ostensible purpose was simply to add historical detail, and for those engaged in humanistic education the episodes might also serve a pedagogic purpose, as another means to inculcate ancient history into the minds of the young. But their very presence emphasized the historicity of the remaining calendar entries, and diluted any sense that certain days, particularly black-letter days, were to be set aside or canonized by their presence in the calendar.

Even stronger than the historicization of the 1578 calendar, was its Protestantization. Great moments from the Reformation were selected to plot the development of the reformed faith, and the continuing fight against Antichrist. At first Luther was given most prominence amongst the reformers, with days to record his birth, the *Thesenanschlag* of 1517, his death and translation. A day was also allotted to his fellow worker, Philip Melanchthon.[59] At the same time, the important roles of Zwingli and of the town of Geneva were not forgotten, though they enjoyed less prominence than Luther and his followers.[60]

The ecumenical unity of the calendar was swiftly cast aside after 1578. Later editions of the calendar subtly changed the mixture of Reformation figures celebrated. Of the original 120 annotations to the calendar, seven were changed. These removed all references to Luther, to Melanchthon and to Hus. Lutheranism was entirely purged from the calendar, leaving only references to Protestantism, Swiss style. The

---

Prayer (London, 1902), pp. 133–5; Collinson, *Elizabethan Puritan Movement*, pp. 165, 365; and Cuming, *Anglican Liturgy*, pp. 100, 364 n. 35.

[58] See the entries for 27 July and 26 August respectively. The references to Caesar and Alexander recall the pantheon of heroes gathered together as the 'nine worthies' and making frequent appearances in popular literature. See Watt, *Cheap Print*, pp. 212–14.

[59] See the entries for 10 November, 31 October, 18 February and 22 February. Melanchthon's birth was marked on 16 February.

[60] Zwingli and Geneva appeared on 11 October and 27 August respectively.

revisers' sympathies lay squarely in Calvinist reform, with 27 August commemorated as the day on which religion was reformed in Geneva 'according to God's expresse truth'. The investment of an almost absolute authority in Genevan opinion was unmistakable. And there was the odd side-swipe at the practices of the English Church. The date 10 October was recorded as having been the fast of the reconciliation, and highlighted as being 'the onely fast commaunded by God', in implicit contrast to the many others commanded by the Church of England. The claim was based on the authority of scripture, and inevitably readers were referred to the appropriate verse, Leviticus 23:27, to find confirmation. Since the Prayer Book containing the calendar was bound up with a Genevan Bible (with its helpful innovation of noting chapters *and* verses), inquisitive readers could satisfy their curiosity immediately.[61]

V

Skilful propaganda Foxe's calendar may have been, but it was certainly not a practical tool for navigating through the pages of his martyrology. The calendars in the 'Puritan' Prayer Book, in the official Church of England Prayer Book, and in Catholic publications, all provided direct links to the text. They led the reader straight from the day's saints or notable events to the corresponding stories. Such cross-referencing was far more difficult in *Acts and Monuments*. In theory when a martyr was named on a particular day, it should have been possible to jump to the relevant story, and mark the anniversary with a retelling of the martyrs' death and suffering. In practice there was no apparatus, either within the calendar of martyrs or amongst the prefaces, to locate individual stories. For readers wishing to follow Foxe's calendar as a kind of reformed lectionary, the only option would have been to cross-reference each entry in the calendar with its page number in the index, if it was recorded at all. With such monstrous volumes the task would have been almost unfeasibly cumbersome for all but the most dedicated (and determined) of readers.

Yet Foxe's calendar was not completely redundant. It was printed as only one of ten prefaces, and it is in conjunction with these other prefaces that it can be best understood. In the course of his extensive prefatory material, the martyrologist introduced his text, and the multiplicity of its themes. One recurring idea was the unsung significance of

[61] For the altered version of the calendar see the 1585 edition, STC 2144.

these Protestant heroes. In typically humanistic tones, Foxe complained that while contemporaries celebrated soldiers and statesmen, the martyrs were left unacknowledged. Similar sentiments had been expressed by, amongst others, Vives, who had lamented the lack of good accounts of Christians, when the Romans had so successfully commemorated their great generals, philosophers and sages. The only difference between the Catholic writer and the Protestant was that Vives was reflecting on hagiography, Foxe on martyrology. Foxe's intention was remarkably similar to those Catholic rewriters of the saints' legends, who attempted to produce historically respectable narratives, amongst them Surius, Baronius and, ultimately, Bolland.[62] These Catholic hagiographers, like Vives, cavilled at the colourful miracles contained in the traditional legends of the saints, particularly the *Legenda aurea*. Vives referred to the legend as 'ferrei oris, plumbei cordis' (that is, iron-mouthed and leaden-hearted), and the sentiment was later echoed by Foxe.[63]

Catholic and Protestant approaches to the saints remained distinct however. Where the hagiographers tried to cleanse the stories of their supposedly fantastical elements, to transform legenda into historically grounded saints' lives, Foxe preferred to jettison them all, along with all vestiges of veneration, in favour of his newly manufactured martyrs' stories. This was made most manifest in his calendar, where the symbolism of saints displaced by martyrs was unmistakable. The same goal was apparent throughout the sequence of prefaces however. At his most extravagant he allowed himself to dream that one day martyrs would be portrayed on cups, on walls, above arches, in fact in all the places which saints had lately inhabited.[64]

Foxe had a powerful vision, and a bold one. In the martyrologist's mind, martyrs were to become part of the warp and woof of everyday experience, acting as powerful ambassadors inside every household for the reformed faith, as their saintly forebears had been for the Catholic before them. Nowhere is the iconographic zeal of early Protestantism clearer than in Foxe's hope that a whole new industry would sprout up, reproducing the images of the martyrs in silver, wood and stone. For Foxe and like-minded contemporaries, the pulling down of 'popish' idols and defacement of superstitious hagiographies was to be matched

---

[62] See Evelyn Birge Vitz, 'From the Oral to the Written in Medieval and Renaissance Saints' Lives', in Renate Blumenfeld-Kosinski and Timea Szell (eds), *Images of Sainthood in Medieval Europe* (Ithaca and London, 1991), ch. 5, esp. p. 110.

[63] See 'ad doctum lectorem' in *Acts and Monuments* (1583), sig. *2ᵃ ('magis dicam plumbeae').

[64] See 'The Utilitie', in *Acts and Monuments* (1583), sig. *6ᵃ⁻ᵇ.

by a putting up of new images and the publishing of a newly purged martyrology. Even as Foxe rejected (and reviled) popish saints, he was attempting to reform the calendar. For early Elizabethan Protestants, uprooting the old was not an end in itself, but the first step in a programme of replanting from reformed stock.

The story of Foxe's calendar is a tale of lofty ambition, partially fulfilled. It is perhaps best understood as typifying the ambiguities inherent in Elizabethan Protestantism. On one side, Foxe was reacting against the survival of 'popish' vestiges in the shape of black-letter saints in the official Church of England Prayer Book. On the other he was offering a personal vision of how the calendar could be reformed for the Elizabethan church. In the event the Church of England's calendar, complete with medieval saints, was to survive, whilst images of martyrs did not become the ubiquitous objects of decoration which the martyrologist had once hoped. Nor did the calendar of martyrs ever achieve the popularity of its Lutheran equivalents. Still, the martyrologist's version did continue as a parallel, autonomous and essentially private alternative to the official Prayer Book version. Foxe's creation constituted part of an 'alternative' calendar tradition which may not have triumphed but was never entirely suppressed.

On a grander scale, Foxe's religious aspirations, symbolized by his calendar of martyrs, may not have been realized in their entirety. There was to be no 'martyrization' of popular culture as Foxe had hoped. But on a more modest scale, there was a steady and significant addition of martyrological stories and images to the common store of popular symbols, albeit the calendar itself was not one of them. The martyr stories, to which Foxe's calendar pointed, were reproduced in woodcuts, ballads and abridgements, and in bringing Foxe's heroes to a wider audience these forms achieved a remarkable popular success.

CHAPTER SIX

Defining the Church of England: religious change in the 1570s[1]

Caroline Litzenberger

Writing to the Privy Council in the 1570s, Richard Cheyney, Bishop of Gloucester, described three types of recusants: those who 'savour of papistry', but allege sickness; those whose debts keep them away for fear of proceedings against them; and 'the third sorte, communelie called puritans, [who] wilfullie refuse to come to churche, as not lyking the surplas, ceremonies and other services now used in the churche'.[2] In presenting this typology of recusancy, Bishop Cheyney may have been influenced by the problems in Cirencester, which involved recusant laypeople at both ends of the religious spectrum and occupied much of his time and attention in the 1570s.

The emergence of these issues and opinions in the diocese of Gloucester in the 1570s was neither an accident nor an isolated occurrence. That decade was an important time in the development of English Protestantism, as events and pronouncements combined to construct the institutional identity of the church in England, if not yet of Anglicanism.[3] Crucial to the policies by which this identity was created, was the developing understanding of recusancy – not just Catholic as most historians have assumed, but also Protestant, the 'sectary recusants' of whom Diarmaid MacCulloch has written.[4] In addition, while historians of the English Reformation have typically seen religious change in England as an ongoing process, the means by which a more clearly defined national church emerged in England in the 1570s seems to have replicated some aspects of the process of 'confessionalization', which had begun in Protestant regions of continental Europe as early as the

---

[1] I would like to thank Eric Carlson for his helpful comments on this chapter.

[2] Cheyney to the Privy Council from the Vineyard in Gloucester, 24 October 1577, PRO, SP 12/117/12.

[3] For a discussion of Protestant identity formation across Europe based on theology, history and precedent, see Bruce Gordon (ed.), *Protestant History and Identity in Sixteenth-Century Europe*, 2 vols (Aldershot and Brookfield, VT, 1996).

[4] Diarmaid MacCulloch, 'Catholic and Puritan in Elizabethan Suffolk', *ARG*, 72 (1981), p. 248.

1550s.[5] Was this then the English 'second reformation', the confessionalization of English Protestantism?[6] This chapter will examine these and related issues as it explores the means by which the crown created and defined the institutional Church of England.

Religion in England in the 1570s has only recently begun to receive much attention. This may be due to the towering influence of two prominent historians, G. R. Elton and A. G. Dickens, who joined with others in asserting that England was for all intents and purposes Protestant by the time of Edward's death in July 1553.[7] According to this historiographical tradition, the Marian Restoration of Catholicism and the rather messy and confusing return to Protestantism during Elizabeth's first decade on the throne were merely detours on the highway to a Protestant England. That tradition was challenged by historians who came to see 1570 rather than 1553 as the crucial milepost, prompting a flurry of research activity which centred on the 1560s, studies which aimed to describe and analyse the final steps in the introduction of Protestantism.[8] Most recently historians have begun to suggest that even that date is too early if we look beyond official policy. Commenting not on 1570 or even 1580, but on the end of Elizabeth's reign, Patrick Collinson borrowed a line from Winston Churchill when he declared, 'It is not the end. It is not even the beginning of the end. But it is, perhaps, the end of the beginning.'[9]

This most recent wave of revisions in English Reformation history has prompted a re-examination of the nature and dynamics of religious

---

[5] For a detailed discussion of this topic, see Bodo Nischan, *Prince, People, and Confession: the Second Reformation in Brandenburg* (Philadelphia, PA, 1994) and R. Po-Chia Hsia, *Social Discipline in the Reformation: Central Europe 1550–1750* (London and New York, 1989).

[6] In his Stenton Lecture given in 1985, Patrick Collinson stated that the second Reformation began in England in about 1580 'between the first and second generations of English Protestants', but his focus was on the cultural changes which occurred with that first ascendancy of the godly to positions of prominence in both church and state. He made a similar reference in his discussion of 'The Cultural Revolution' during his Anstey Memorial Lectures delivered the next year. Patrick Collinson, *From Iconoclasm to Iconophobia: the Cultural Impact of the Second English Reformation* (Reading, 1986), p. 8; Patrick Collinson, *The Birthpangs of Protestant England* (New York, 1988), p. 98.

[7] A. G. Dickens, 'The Early Expansion of Protestantism in England 1520–1558', *ARG*, 78 (1987), p. 189; G. R. Elton, *Reform and Reformation: England, 1509–1558* (Cambridge, MA, 1977), p. 371.

[8] See Norman Jones, *The Birth of the Elizabethan Age: England in the 1560s* (Oxford and Cambridge, MA, 1993); Norman Jones, *Faith by Statute: Parliament and the Settlement of Religion* (London and New Jersey, 1982); and Winthrop Hudson, *The Cambridge Connection and the Elizabethan Settlement* (Durham, NC, 1980).

[9] Patrick Collinson, 'The Elizabethan Church and the New Religion', in Christopher Haigh (ed.), *The Reign of Elizabeth I* (Basingstoke and London, 1984), p. 194.

change in England in the later sixteenth century. Patrick Collinson, Christopher Haigh and Diarmaid MacCulloch have contributed significantly to this development, although the unanimity of their focus contrasts sharply with the divergence of their conclusions.[10] Many of the chapters in this volume, including this one, also contribute to our understanding of the ways in which Protestantism was not only established as the official religion of the realm, but also gained definition as an institution and was accepted by a majority of the English people.

English Protestantism, like the early Christian Church, came into being gradually through a series of steps which differed in size and took it in contradictory directions. During the short reign of Edward VI, the Henrician Catholicism of his father was transformed into a form of the new religion which owed much to reformers on the Continent, both in Germany and in Switzerland. However, when one considers unofficial as well as official religion, the actual process of religious change is always complex. It involves both the policy-makers and the objects of the policies, and the latter, the laity and local clergy, seldom receive what is proclaimed without modifying it to some degree. Individuals respond to change in a variety of ways depending on their experience, knowledge, preferences and personalities, and religious change can be particularly difficult to accept. The process by which even the most conforming individuals adopted Edwardian Protestantism was then gradual and involved the integration of valued vestiges of traditional religion with each person's particular worship experience and understanding of the newly established faith. A similar pattern can be seen at the corporate level, as parishes sought to come to terms with the new religion in light of local liturgical traditions. The result was a wide array of countless shades of belief so complex that the linear image of a religious spectrum, helpful as it may be, can only provide a simplified representation of English beliefs in the sixteenth century.[11] Some people and parishes may indeed have been practising some form of Protestantism by mid-1553, but most either had held on to the old religion or were practising a faith which combined elements of both the new and the old. Hence, when Edward's Catholic sister Mary succeeded him on

---

[10] See Patrick Collinson, *The Religion of Protestants: the Church in English Society, 1559–1625* (Oxford, 1982); Christopher Haigh, *English Reformations: Religion, Politics and Society under the Tudors* (Oxford, 1993); and Diarmaid MacCulloch, *The Later Reformation in England 1547–1603* (Basingstoke, 1990). Most recently, cf. Kenneth L. Parker and Eric Josef Carlson, *'Practical Divinity': the Works and Life of the Revd Richard Greenham*, (Aldershot and Brookfield, VT, 1998).

[11] For further discussion of the complexity of lay religion in sixteenth-century England, see Caroline Litzenberger, *The English Reformation and the Laity: Gloucestershire 1540–1580* (Cambridge, 1997).

the throne and restored Catholicism in England, many, perhaps most, people welcomed the return to the familiar pious practices and beliefs of the past. Official religion may have become fully Protestant under Edward, but at the unofficial local level in parish churches and in the hearts and minds of the people Protestantism was much slower to take hold. As a result, Elizabeth's accession in 1558 was greeted with mixed feelings of anxiety and optimism.

The first decade of Elizabeth's reign has been described by Patrick McGrath as the 'years of uncertainty', and by Norman Jones as 'a time of fear, confusion, hope and despair'.[12] Catholics began the decade hoping that even though England had returned to the Protestant fold shortly after Elizabeth became queen, ultimately Catholicism would be restored. Meanwhile, those Protestants who had chosen exile during Mary's reign were returning to England in droves, assuming that the re-establishment of the new religion would be just the first step in a thorough reform of English religion. But a third group also sought to influence Elizabethan religious policy: those 'Nicodemites' who had chosen to remain in England during Mary's reign.[13] Their religious beliefs seem to have been less fully reformed, less radical than their counterparts who had been in exile, and it was this third group which controlled the centre during the early years of the reign.[14] This contingent, after all, included the Queen, her secretary William Cecil, most of her Privy Council and the Archbishop of Canterbury.[15] None the less, a number of former exiles were appointed to key positions in the Church and some Catholics continued to serve in other prominent positions in Elizabeth's government. One result was significant ambiguity in official religious policy.[16]

---

[12] Patrick McGrath, *Papists and Puritans under Elizabeth I* (New York, 1967), p. 47; Jones, *The Birth of the Elizabethan Age*, p. 17.

[13] Andrew Pettegree, 'The Marian Exiles and the Elizabethan Settlement', in *Marian Protestantism: Six Studies* (Aldershot and Brookfield, VT, 1996), pp. 86–117, *passim*. Cf. Alexandra Walsham, *Church Papists: Catholicism, Conformity and Confessional Polemic in Early Modern England* (Woodbridge, 1993), pp. 37–8.

[14] Pettegree, 'The Marian Exiles and the Elizabethan Settlement', pp. 129–50, *passim*.

[15] Numerous historians have attempted to discern the Queen's religious preferences, but no clear consensus has emerged. Patrick Collinson describes her as a religious conservative, while Andrew Pettegree likens her to other prominent Protestants who found ways to stay in England during Mary's reign. Patrick Collinson, 'Windows in a Woman's Soul: Questions about the Religion of Queen Elizabeth I', in P. Collinson, *Elizabethan Essays* (London and Rio Grande, OH, 1994), pp. 87–118.

[16] Conflicting directives in the Prayer Book and Act of Uniformity of 1559, on the one hand, and in the Royal Injunctions of the same year, on the other introduced ambiguity. These concerned the approved form of communion bread (wafers or loaf bread) and the official policy on images. John E. Booty (ed.), *The Book of Common Prayer, 1559: the*

To make matters worse, specific policies were not the only sources of official religious ambiguity during those years when both Catholics and radical Protestants found reason to hope that the Elizabethan church would move in their direction. The unresolved question of the Queen's marriage also confused the religious picture as her reign began. It was of course assumed that she would marry and that her husband would influence matters of policy, as had Philip during his brief reign as king with Mary. Established religion, in particular, was seen as vulnerable to change, depending on the Queen's choice of a mate, and speculation on that assumed eventuality enhanced the impression that English religion was in a state of flux.

Meanwhile, for the Queen and her closest advisers those early years of her reign may well have been a time devoted to consolidating her power and establishing her authority as queen regnant. An analysis of drafts and fair copies of her speeches by Allison Heisch certainly supports that theory. Heisch notes that the tone of the speeches changed over time. She finds both a growing level of self-assurance and an increasing lack of patience with radical Protestants. She suggests that as Elizabeth gained confidence and a sense of her very real power and authority, she also increasingly focused on radical Protestants. The key issue was uniformity, and the hotter sort of Protestants kept insisting on more reform; furthermore, they were continually changing their demands. At least, the Catholics were fairly predictable.[17] Andrew Pettegree has also asserted that the key motivation for Elizabeth's religious policy during the 1560s was her need to establish her authority; however, he focuses on her response to the publication of John Knox's *First Blast of the Trumpet against the Monstrous Regiment of Women*. He declares that Knox's association with Calvin and the fact that the volume was published in Geneva led the Queen to distrust returning exiles who wanted to push for a more Calvinist religion in England: hence her resistance to repeated pressure to remove the images from her chapel altar. However, another subtext may be at play here as well according to Pettegree: Elizabeth may have also been determined to ensure the independence of English religion from continental influences. Thus as each of these scholars has demonstrated, Elizabethan religious policy was linked to monarchical authority.

Elizabethan Prayer Book (Folger Shakespeare Library, 1976), p. 267; 'Announcing Injunctions for Religion' in Paul L. Hughes and James F. Larkin (eds), *Tudor Royal Proclamations* (hereafter *TRP*) (New Haven, CT, 1964), vol. 2, pp. 118, 123, 131. Cf. Margaret Aston, *England's Iconoclasts: 1. Laws against Images* (Oxford, 1988), pp. 302–24.

[17] Allison Heisch, 'Queen Elizabeth I: Parliamentary Rhetoric and the Exercise of Power', *Signs: Journal of Women in Culture and Society*, 1 (Autumn 1975), pp. 31–55. I would like to thank Marianne Novy for this reference.

By the end of the 1560s the lack of clarity in religious policy had fostered a climate where it was difficult to discern the limits of acceptable religious practice. This was the situation which existed across much of England as the first decade of Elizabeth's reign drew to a close, and she found the resulting disorder intolerable. The tension which had resulted from stretching the 'walls' of the Elizabethan church to accommodate both those who favoured the old religion and those who preferred the most reformed of the new was becoming too great, and religious policy began to change. In the view of many former Marian exiles, the English Reformation was in danger of ending long before reaching the state of purity in belief and practice they had experienced on the Continent and had hoped to bring to England. Their hopes for the Convocation of 1563 had not been realized, their attempts to eliminate 'popish' vestments had been rebuffed, and the Crown did not approve of their prophesying or preaching in combination. But still they persisted. Thomas Cartwright voiced the views of many in 1570 when he delivered a series of sermons which promoted a Presbyterian system of church polity in place of the existing hierarchical episcopal structure with its bishops and archbishops. In each of these instances the Protestants persistence in advancing their cause was perceived as a threat to good order.[18]

The Catholics too were still hoping for change, albeit in the form of the restoration of their religion in England, and they were growing impatient. In 1569 the northern earls rose up against the Crown and demanded among other things a return to the old religion. A year later the Pope issued the bull *Regnans in Excelsis* excommunicating Elizabeth and placing English Catholics in a very difficult position. Their allegiance to their church and their monarch were now in conflict, and the penalties were great on both counts. The responses to this dilemma varied. Some chose church papistry, while others became determined recusants.[19] The final attempt to restore Catholicism to England, the

---

[18] Edmund Grindal, Archbishop of York and future Archbishop of Canterbury was involved in this effort. PRO SP 12/88/5. Another group of fairly radical Protestants, however, still believed the bishops could be agents of additional reform rather than impediments to it. In May 1572 the House of Commons debated a bill that would have authorized bishops to allow deviations from the established rites of the Book of Common Prayer within their dioceses. It failed and later that same year the godly submitted their Admonition to Parliament, which Patrick Collinson has described as 'the first popular manifesto of English presbyterianism'. Patrick Collinson, *The Elizabethan Puritan Movement* (London, 1967, repr., 1991), pp. 111–12; Patrick Collinson, 'John Field and Elizabethan Puritanism', in S. T. Bindoff, J. Hurstfield and C. H. Williams (eds), *Elizabethan Government and Society: Essays Presented to Sir John Neale* (London, New York and Toronto, 1961), p. 136.

[19] For a comprehensive discussion of church papistry, see Walsham, *Church Papists*.

ill-fated Ridolfi Plot, came to light just a year after *Regnans in Excelsis*, in 1571. It would have replaced Elizabeth with her Catholic cousin, Mary Stuart, who was in turn to have married the Duke of Norfolk and made him king. These three Catholic attempts to undermine or over-throw the existing regime prompted a more vigilant watch over papists by the Crown.

Hence, as the 1570s began the Crown and Council moved to carve a significantly clearer policy out of the middle of the broad spectrum of beliefs and practices which had been tolerated during the previous decade. The efforts to curtail and discipline both Catholics and Protes-tants focused on outward actions, not private faith, as the recusancy statutes were the main means of enforcing conformity to the established faith at both ends of the religious spectrum.

The first definition of 'recusant' in the *Oxford English Dictionary* reads, 'one, especially a Roman Catholic, who refused to attend the services of the Church of England'. The second definition tells us that the term was also 'applied to other religious dissentients'.[20] Beginning as early as the sixteenth century, a number of writers, including theologians and legal authorities, adopted the first of these definitions. They dated the use of the term from 1570, the year of the papal bull excommunicating Elizabeth, and have equated it with 'refusing papists'. This was the definition Gervase Babington gave in a treatise published in 1583; Sir Edward Coke made a similar deduction when writing on the subject in 1607.[21] However, the term was actually used almost 30 years earlier in a statute of Edward VI which refers to 'the Certificate of Recusauntes made by any of the said Archebyshoppes'.[22] The ecclesiastical commissioners also used it in 1561 to describe the Marian clergy who refused to accept Elizabethan Protestantism.[23] In each case the first, or Catholic, definition was applied to the term. Similarly, many modern historians have assumed that Catholicism was the sole reason for all Elizabethan recusancy and have equated 'recusant' with practising Catholics.[24] In fact the survival of Catholicism with its concomitant resistance to official religious policy may have prompted the Crown and Parliament to pass the recusancy statutes beginning in the 1560s. However, the persistent and even in-creasing pressure from zealous Protestants resulted in those same laws

---

[20] See 'recusant' in the *OED*.

[21] Walsham, *Church Papists*, p. 10.

[22] 7 Edward VI, c. 4, sec. 2.

[23] *Calendar of State Papers Domestic, 1547–1565 with addenda* (1870, repr., Nendeln, Liechtenstein, 1967), p. 514.

[24] Diarmaid MacCulloch's use of the term 'sectary recusants' to describe those who were 'at the opposite pole' from Catholic recusants is the exception. MacCulloch, 'Catholic and Puritan', p. 248.

being used to discipline them as well.[25] The even-handed use of the recusancy statutes, which emerged as official policy in the 1570s, combined with the generally stricter enforcement of other aspects of conformity, had a significant impact on the religion of the laity.

This was the decade when zealous Protestants joined Catholics among those reported for absence from their parish churches, and thus the period when reasons for recusancy varied most widely. Catholics, motivated by official exhortations and personal beliefs that Protestant worship was heretical, justified their absence by claiming to be 'out of charity' with their neighbours or by attending a nearby church or chapel which was more congenial to their beliefs than was their parish church.[26] On the other hand, refusal to have one's child baptized was a common way for hotter Protestants to demonstrate their refusal to accept Elizabethan Protestantism. Such individuals viewed as superstitious the blessing of the water to be used in the baptism and the making of the sign of the cross during the baptismal rite. In addition, there were other liturgical actions which they labelled similarly, including the use of even the simplest vestment, the surplice.

The newly emerging religious policy manifested itself in various ways as those at the centre sought to define official religion both in terms of what it was and what it was not. The more positive sense of its identity was based in the continued use of the Book of Common Prayer combined with the passage of the Articles of Religion in 1571. As the people gained familiarity with the prescribed form of worship, the Articles of Religion gave them a partial explanation of the theological implications and interpretations of that liturgy. In addition, a more distinct line was being drawn to delineate the boundary between acceptable and unacceptable beliefs and practices.

One result was that it was becoming more difficult to maintain one's Catholicism in Elizabethan England. Some people were like Edmund Campion, a protégé of Richard Cheyney, and Thomas Alfield, a resident of Gloucester, who travelled to Douai to become Jesuits in the 1570s and later returned to England as Jesuit missionaries.[27] Others were like John

---

[25] 13 Elizabeth I, c. 2, 3, 13. Cf. J. J. LaRocca, 'Time, Death and the Next Generation: the Early Elizabethan Recusancy Policy, 1558–1574', *Albion*, 14 (1982), pp. 103–17.

[26] Walsham, *Church Papists*, pp. 11–49, *passim*; GRO, GDR vol. 29, p. 71; Haigh, *Reformation and Resistance in Tudor Lancashire* (Cambridge, 1975), pp. 269–75.

[27] Edmund Campion became quite impatient with his former patron. In a letter from Douai, Campion tried without apparent success to persuade Bishop Cheyney to return to Catholicism, describing him as 'the hatred of heretics, the pity of Catholics, the talk of the people, the sorrow of your friends, the joke of your enemies'. 'Campion the martyr to Cheyney, Anglican bishop of Gloucester,' *The Rambler: a Catholic Journal and Review*, new series, 8 (1857), pp. 61–2.

Pauncefoote, who hosted Thomas Alfield on his return in 1582. Pauncefoote fled England in 1584 with his son John, and over the next two years his wife Dorothy and a second son Richard were both imprisoned for recusancy and attempting to flee from prosecution.[28] Other less prominent but equally faithful Catholics were subject to more conventional pressure to conform. Their names, like those of the Pauncefootes, appeared in lists of recusants sent to the Privy Council. One name, which appeared on such a list in 1577, was that of William Meredith of the city of Gloucester, whom his parish priest and wardens suspected of being 'an horrible papiste, and one that hathe not received the communion at anie time'. They also alleged that 'the common fame goethe that he is a maintainer of papistes beyonde the seas, and that of late he hathe byn there to have conference with theim'.[29] Beginning in the 1580s such recusants were also fined for their continued absence from their parish churches.[30] Hence, James Butler of Cirencester, William Bradstock and his wife of Corse, and John Campe of Cowley, were all fined for being absent from their respective parish churches for several months. Similarly, a number of wives of husbandmen and gentlemen of Gloucestershire, and three single women – Jane Dennis and Alice Hibbard, both of Leckhampton, and Alice Harwood of Mickleton – were also fined for their absences.[31] However, not all Catholics were that determined to remain recusant. After making their point many chose to attend their parish churches as required by statute, although perhaps as church papists rather than as fully conforming English Protestants.[32]

Some suspected Catholics were the objects of less direct pressure to conform. The poaching of numerous deer on the Berkeley estates may

---

[28] J. N. Langston, 'Robert Alfield, Schoolmaster, of Gloucester; and his sons', *TBGAS*, 56 (1934), pp. 148–51; J. N. Langston, 'Old Catholic Families of Gloucestershire: I. The Pauncefootes of Hasfield', *TBGAS*, 71 (1953), p. 139; Patrick McGrath, 'Gloucestershire and the Counter-Reformation in the Reign of Elizabeth I', *TBGAS*, 88 (1970), pp. 16–17, 25–6; PRO STAC 5/K13/9.

[29] PRO, SP 12/118/24.

[30] 23 Elizabeth I, c. 1.

[31] T. J. McCann (ed.), *Recusants in the Exchequer Pipe Rolls 1581–1592* (Southampton, 1986), pp. 22, 26, 32, 33, 35, 50, 79, 82, 126, 133, 137, 200. The inclusion in the recusancy roles of wives but not their husbands is consistent with the evidence presented by both Marie Rowlands and Alexandra Walsham. Marie Rowlands, 'Recusant Women, 1560–1640', in Mary Prior (ed.), *Women in English Society, 1500–1800* (London, 1985), pp. 151–2; Walsham, *Church Papists*, pp. 77–81.

[32] GRO, P329 CW 2/1, pp. 9, 14, 31, 45; printed in Caroline Litzenberger (ed.), *Tewkesbury Churchwardens' Accounts, 1563–1624* (Gloucestershire Record Series, vol. 7, 1994), pp. 5–6, 10, 20, 29. Cf. Walsham, *Church Papists*; F. R. Raines (ed.,) 'A Description of the state, civil and ecclesiastical of the County of Lancaster about the year 1590' in *Chetham Miscellanies V* (Chetham Society, old series, vol. 96, 1875), p. 3.

be a case in point. While on a royal progress in Gloucestershire in 1574, the Queen and the Earl of Leicester, a champion of Protestantism, led a poaching party which killed 27 deer in one day and more the next. Probably Lord and Lady Berkeley's suspected Catholicism contributed significantly to the decision to put pressure on them in this way, despite other points of contention between Leicester and Lord Berkeley. Most of the prominent Protestants in the county provided the leadership to continue the 'campaign' begun during the royal progress. Also, Lady Berkeley was the Duke of Norfolk's sister, and he had been executed for his role in the ill-fated Ridolfi Plot. Roger Manning has suggested that such poaching among royal, noble and other élite individuals served as a surrogate for armed conflict during this time. However, in this instance it appears that it may have also served as a surrogate for battles over religion and as an alternative means of enforcing conformity or at least discouraging further treasonous activity on the part of Catholics.[33]

Efforts to effect conformity within communities could often be just as complex as those among the élite. The allegations and accusations hurled back and forth by inhabitants of Cirencester in Gloucestershire beginning in 1570 are illustrative of this. In June of that year members of one faction within the town sent a letter to the Privy Council describing three of the chief inhabitants, Nicholas Phillips, Robert Strange and Christopher George, as 'wicked and traitorous papists'.[34] While the charge was probably accurate – Phillips had been a servant to Sir Henry Jerningham, the Marian Privy Councillor, and Strange and George left Catholic wills – the fact that a group of laymen sent such a letter to the Privy Council may signal an awareness of the shift to a more definitive, less tolerant religious policy.[35] Those sending the letter seem to have expected that accusing someone of papistry would now gain the attention of those in authority. In any event, this was just the opening round in a long series of declarations and pronouncement concerning conformity to the established religion in Cirencester. Between 1570 and 1574, 43 parishioners, including both Catholics and radical Protestants, were presented either for absence from worship or for not receiving Holy Communion.[36] This may have begun as a feud between factions within the town, but it soon became an example of the new 'even-

[33] Litzenberger, *The English Reformation*, pp. 126–8. Cf. Roger Manning, *Hunters and Poachers: A Cultural and Social History of Unlawful Hunting in England 1485–1640* (Oxford, 1993), pp. 48–9, 137; J. H. Cooke, 'The great Berkeley law-suit of the 15th and 16th centuries', *TBGAS*, 3 (1878), p. 321.

[34] PRO, SP 12/71/30.

[35] PRO, PROB 11/72, fos 33–3v; 11/93, fos 323–5.

[36] GRO, GDR vol. 26, pp. 135–7, vol. 28, pp. 168–70, vol. 31, pp. 81–7.

handed' policy to enforce religious conformity. The Catholics included Thomas Rastell and Andrew Phelpes, who later left Catholic wills and who, along with several others, explained their absence from church by their priests' lack of precise conformity to every provision of the Book of Common Prayer.[37] This group of individuals appeared before the Church courts, gave the reasons for their transgressions and promised to mend their ways; they then disappeared from the records. Not so some of those motivated by their radical Protestantism.

The most determined transgressors were five radical Protestants: Agnes Long, Anna and Thomas Bradford, and Elizabeth and William Whiting. They all refused to come to church but, in addition, Elizabeth Whiting also refused to have her child baptized in the parish church. She objected to the minister using the baptismal font 'for that it is supersticion'. Other complaints from this group included the wish that 'malefactors and papistes [be] excluded out of the churche', and the assertion that the minister 'dothe followe mens tradicion and do not minister nor teache the word accordinge to Godes word'. Eventually, Elizabeth Whiting had her child baptized in another Gloucestershire parish some distance to the south of Cirencester, but she still refused to attend church.[38] Her husband was so obstinate in his refusal to attend church, and so obstreperous in court that he was gaoled and eventually sent to London. Meanwhile, Anna and Thomas Bradford also stayed away from their church, and Thomas was presented with William Whiting in 1576 for using conventicles rather than attending the local parish. No amount of pressure could get these Cirencester inhabitants to change their opinion of Elizabethan Protestantism. As late as March 1587 Anna Bradford and Elizabeth Whiting were still being cited as recusants. Interestingly, 12 years earlier two unnamed women had been sent to London to appear before the Privy Council; those two were probably Elizabeth Whiting and Anna Bradford.[39]

---

[37] PRO, PROB 11/59, fos 197–8. However, some parishioners seem to have continued to hope for a return to Catholicism, as in 1576 there were 'divers vestimentes and other superstitious plate remayninge in sondrie mens handes' within the parish. GRO, GDR vol. 40, fo. 164.

[38] Elizabeth Whiting had her child baptized in the parish of Hawkesbury by Mr Woodland, the minister there. GRO, GDR vol. 35, p. 48, printed in F. Douglas Price (ed.), *The Commission for Ecclesiastical Causes within the Dioceses of Bristol and Gloucester, 1574* (Bristol and Gloucestershire Archaeological Society, Records Section, vol. 10, 1972), p. 70.

[39] GRO, GDR vol. 26, pp. 135–7; vol. 28, pp. 168–70; vol. 29, p. 71; vol. 31, pp. 81–7; vol. 35, *passim*; vol. 35 printed in Price (ed.), *Commission*, pp. 68, 70, 74–8, 80, 83, 106; GRO, GDR vol. 40, fo. 164v; McCann (ed.), *Recusants*, pp. 25, 189; J. R. Dasent (ed.), *Acts of the Privy Council*, new series (London, 1894), vol. 9, pp. 93, 95.

The 'sectary recusants' in Cirencester were not, however, the earliest radical Protestants to come to the attention of the authorities in Gloucestershire. In 1569 Edmund Batte of the parish of Moreton Valence near the city of Gloucester was presented, because he would neither 'come to the churche nor eate or drynke withe them that [did] '. He was repeatedly presented for being absent and was required to appear in court. Eventually, his case was referred to the Commission for Ecclesiastical Causes within the Dioceses of Bristol and Gloucester. There, in August 1574, he asserted that he had not attended his parish church because the minister 'wereth a sarples and other popish robes not correspondent to Godes worde'. Six months later he was still absent and defended himself, saying that 'the churche the which is so termed in these daies ought not to be so called, for it is nothing else but a place of supersticion and idolatrie'. His spirited defence was of no avail, and he was placed in the custody of the sheriff. The Commission gave him one more chance to recant, but he only asserted that he had not changed his mind, and so was returned to gaol.[40]

A couple from St Nicholas Church in the city of Gloucester, just to the north of Moreton Valence, expressed reasons similar to Batte's for staying away from church; however, they came to the attention of the Commission because, like Elizabeth Whiting, they refused to have their baby baptized in their parish church. Additionally, like both Batte and the radical Protestant recusants from Cirencester, this couple was openly defiant of both the bishop and the Commission. (The Catholic recusants who appeared before the consistory court and the Commission in the diocese of Gloucester, in contrast, seem to have been anxious to placate those in authority and disappear from public view as quickly and quietly as possible.) When William Drewett of St Nicholas in Gloucester first appeared before the Commission, he 'scoffinglie ... called the busshopp of Gloucester sittinge in commission, goodman pope that sittes there with whitt sleves', an outburst that resulted in his being gaoled. After his release, he and his wife appeared before the Commission again, but still refused to have their child baptized. On this occasion, the mayor and sheriffs of the city, 'and the hedd men of the parishe' were ordered to enter the Drewett's house 'and take the chylde and bring yt to churche ... and there the minister [was to] christen it'. However, the Drewetts insisted that if their child was taken from them and baptized by force 'they wolde never receave yt againe nor take yt for their chylde any more', but the matter did not end there. Some three weeks later the couple was back before the Commission, only this time the father carried the baby in his

---

[40] GRO, GDR vol. 26, p. 31; vol. 29, p. 88; vol. 35, pp. 4, 9, 24, 64, 80; vol. 35 printed in Price (ed.), *Commission*, pp. 49, 52, 60, 78, 85.

arms. A midwife who was present was ordered to take the child from him, but he resisted. The Commission then informed Drewett that they intended to commit him and his wife to separate prisons and ordered him to give the child to his wife 'to remayne with her that she maie geve yt sucke in prison', but he refused. Next the Commission told Sir David Walter, curate of the neighbouring parish of St Michael's, to ask Drewett to give him the child so that he could baptize it, but he refused, saying that 'the father of the chylde ought to requyre him for to christen yt'. The commissioners tried once more to force Drewett to give his child to his wife, but he continued to resist. They then ordered the churchwardens of Drewett's parish, St Nicholas, to take the child from him and give it to the mother, 'but Drewett wolde not lett yt goe'. Finally, they gave up and committed him (and the child) to one prison and his wife to another. Two days later both father and infant were released, but the father had not changed his mind. (The mother had vanished from the records.) Subsequently, Drewett was sent to London, along with William Whiting (and possibly Elizabeth Whiting and Anna Bradford), to appear before the Privy Council to answer for his actions.[41] Several years later he had still not conformed. In November 1581 two recusants 'of the precise sort' were being held in Newgate Prison in London: William Drewett and a man from another diocese.[42]

There was a clear shift in official religious policy during the years around 1570 prompted in part by the demands and actions of both Catholics and godly Protestants, but also perhaps coming as a result of the maturation of the Queen as reigning monarch. Perhaps she had 'found her feet', and assured of support from both the Council and a substantial part of the ecclesiastical hierarchy, she felt ready to move to take tighter control of religion in her realm. There is evidence that she took action to target Catholics and radical Protestants more evenly beginning in the mid-1570s. When Edmund Freke became Bishop of Norwich and John Aylmer became Bishop of London, each seems to have received specific instructions from the Queen to give equal attention to all recusants, whether Catholic or radically Protestant.[43] Perhaps

---

[41] GRO, GDR vol. 35, pp. 65, 110–11, 114, 116–17; printed in Price (ed.), *Commission*, pp. 78, 103, 105, 107–8.

[42] PRO, SP 12/150/74.

[43] Collinson, *The Elizabethan Puritan Movement*, pp. 201–2; Diarmaid MacCulloch, *Suffolk and the Tudors: Politics and Religion in an English County, 1500–1600* (Oxford, 1986), pp. 193–7; A. H. Smith, *County and Court: Government and Politics in Norfolk, 1558–1603* (Oxford, 1974), pp. 211–15, 225; *DNB*, vol. 1, p. 754; vol. 7, pp. 670–71.

Cheyney had received a similar directive, although he had been Bishop of Gloucester since 1562, and his beliefs and behaviour in administering his diocese indicate that he probably would not have needed any prodding, unless it was to pay more attention to Catholics.[44]

But are these changes more than merely the results of changing circumstances in England? Historians of the continental Reformation have described a 'second reformation' or process of confessionalization which they see as having taken place in the churches of Germany and Switzerland beginning in the 1550s. R. Po-Chia Hsia has defined confessionalization as 'the interrelated *processes* by which the consolidation of the early modern state, the imposition of social discipline, and the formation of confessional churches transformed society'.[45] Might we apply that term to the developments in England in the 1570s? Certainly, the English nation-state was coming into its own during Elizabeth's reign, and one of the catalysts for the changes in religious policy was the perceived need to curb disorder and exert tighter control over the behaviour of society, but what about a confessional church? Here too, England seems at first to fit the definition, as the passage of the Articles of Religion and the stricter administration of the laws pertaining to religious conformity demonstrate. However, there is a key difference between the English church and continental Protestant churches.

Many historians have asserted that the genius of English Protestantism and a key to its survival was that it was not in the first instance a doctrinal church: there were to be no windows on peoples' minds.[46] As it evolved in the sixteenth century the English church focused on its liturgical rites as a vehicle for expressing acceptable beliefs, rather than the other way around. On the Continent it was primarily theology, which at least initially defined each regional manifestation of the new religion. By stressing the importance of the objects, actions and symbols of worship as its defining aspects, the English church opened its doors to a wide range of beliefs. Public participation in the established rites of the Church, rather than personal beliefs, would be the measure of the acceptance of English Protestantism. Thomas Cranmer, the key religious leader of the English Reformation, was after all a gifted liturgist,

---

[44] For a discussion of Richard Cheyney's theology and episcopal administration see Caroline Litzenberger, 'Richard Cheyney, Bishop of Gloucester, an Infidel in Religion?', *SCJ*, 25 (1994), pp. 567–84.

[45] Hsia, *Social Discipline in the Reformation*, p. 5.

[46] Even though that phrase originated with Francis Bacon rather than the Queen, it accurately summarizes the overall philosophy of much Elizabethan religious policy. Patrick Collinson, 'The Elizabethan Church', p. 178.

not a gifted theologian.[47] However, the negative outcome of that approach was the lack of a clear definition of English Protestantism, and that imprecision combined with the changing religious policies of successive monarchs to produce religious instability, rather than a clear end of the Reformation in England. Thus, while historians point to approximately 1550 or 1555 (the date of the Peace of Augsburg) as marking the end of the 'first reformation' on the Continent, no similar date can be found for England. The decisions and actions of Elizabeth and her advisers in the period around 1570 was just another step in bringing the 'first reformation' to fruition, rather than the beginning of the second.

The strategies the Queen and Council chose to employ were intended to lead to a stable and widely accepted form of Protestantism in England to be characterized by outward actions, not inward beliefs. Furthermore, they were intended to transform the English church into a strong institution with a clear identity. Interestingly, some of the means employed to achieve those goals were reminiscent of the ways in which the early Christian Church had defined and established itself as an institution. Both chose to articulate a theology consistent with and supportive of the existing liturgy and polity of the Church. Additionally, in each instance those creating the institutional identity chose to demonize the 'Other', labelling as outside the margins of acceptability those actions and tenets of faith it did not espouse in order to clarify what it did practice and believe. For the early church the 'Other' was represented by the various sets of beliefs it declared to be heretical, and eventually it would prove necessary for the Church of England to look to the Continent to establish a broader frame of reference. But the Elizabethan church did not need to look beyond the realm for its 'Others'; English Catholics and radical Protestants served that function quite well.[48]

Thus, in the 1570s English Protestantism and the established church gained a clearer definition and identity through the policies and actions of those at the centre, and that trend would continue, albeit with some modifications, at least through the end of Elizabeth's reign. By the mid-1580s the recusancy statutes were being used almost exclusively against Catholics, but radical Protestants were still subject to scrutiny and punishment for behaviour deemed beyond the bounds of tolerance. In

---

[47] See Diarmaid MacCulloch, *Thomas Cranmer, a Life* (New Haven, CT and London, 1996) for the definitive biography of Thomas Cranmer.

[48] For further discussion of the interplay between heresy and orthodoxy in early Christianity, see W. Bauer, *Orthodoxy and Heresy in Earliest Christianity*, eds R. A. Kraft and G. Kodel (Philadelphia, PA, 1971). For further discussion of the use of the constructs of heresy and orthodoxy in defining belief systems, see L. R. Kurtz, 'The Politics of Heresy', *American Journal of Sociology*, 88 (1983), pp. 1085–115.

1590 Lord Burghley was still urging the Queen to take appropriate measures 'to suppress all the turbulent precisians, who do violently seke to chang the eternall government of the chyrch'.[49] As the reign came to a close, it would seem that Patrick Collinson's reference to it as 'the end of the beginning' is quite accurate. The gradual and ongoing construction of the identity of the Church of England would continue to be shaped by the 'Others' at each end of the religious spectrum and by those conforming, supportive laypeople and clergy who comprised the vast and broad middle of this diverse institution well into the next century and beyond.

Elizabeth's reign had begun rather tentatively. Her disagreements with members of the ecclesiastical hierarchy had resulted in issuing conflicting definitions of conformity during the first year of her reign. In addition, the government held some policies in abeyance while waiting to see whom the Queen would marry. The lack of either clear guidelines or consistent enforcement over the next ten years merely aggravated an already difficult situation. None the less, both the more godly Protestants and their Catholic neighbours may have welcomed that lack of clarity. The former saw benign neglect as their opportunity to worship as they wished, emphasizing preaching of the lively Word over ceremony and the Eucharist, while the latter were buoyed by the hope that the re-establishment of Protestantism would be only temporary. By the dawn of the new decade people had not been confronted by a swing of the religious pendulum in over ten years. Those on the religious margins were growing impatient, but those at the centre had finally had a chance to become familiar with at least some aspects of the established religion, however vague. After the ambiguity of the 1560s, official religion in the second decade of Elizabeth's reign was more clearly defined and more energetically enforced that it had been previously. The emphasis was on actions rather than thoughts, public worship rather than private prayer. Thus, attending church was more important to the Crown than taking communion, and the priests' attire was more important than their theological knowledge (at least if one is to judge by the penalties for transgressing those rules).[50]

As the Crown's vision of the established church then gained further definition, many of those who wanted to conform were relieved to have a clearer view of the established faith. However, some were probably distressed to learn where the boundaries of acceptability actually lay and may have joined their co-religionists at the ends of the spectrum in

---

[49] PRO, SP 12/231/103.

[50] 1 Elizabeth, c. 1, *passim*. Cf. LaRocca, 'Time, Death and the Next Generation', pp. 103–17, *passim*.

urging further change. The more definitive religious policy certainly did not bring either immediate ecclesiastical uniformity or religious conformity. The Crown and Council would continue to contend with recalcitrant clergy and laypeople. Those who clung to the old religion did so with increasing tenacity, and the more radical among the godly Protestants continued to resist the pressure to conform. Meanwhile the conforming majority was growing in numbers as more people became increasingly familiar with the essential elements of worship as prescribed by the Book of Common Prayer of 1559, and as a result of that 'osmotic process' became more accepting of English Protestantism.[51] Many contentious moments and stages of acceptance lay ahead, but during the second half of Elizabeth's reign the institutional church gained a clearer sense of its identity and the people became more accepting of the religion promoted by that church.

---

[51] Patrick Collinson suggests the 'osmotic process' was one of the ways in which the *Homilies* and The Book of Common Prayer contributed to the internalization of Protestantism. Collinson, 'The Elizabethan Church', pp. 179–80.

CHAPTER SEVEN

The 'Cambridge Boies': Thomas Rogers and the 'Brethren' in Bury St Edmunds

John S. Craig

It is unusual to comment upon a scholar's footnotes, except if one is on the attack,[1] but as this chapter had its genesis in a footnote, it is perhaps fitting that in a volume celebrating the scholarship and instruction of Patrick Collinson a word be said about footnotes, for as students of early modern English Protestantism can attest, Collinson's footnotes are as fertile for thought as is his prose. A typical Collinson footnote is both generous and gracious, invariably packed with information, a microcosmic reflection of his wide reading with his infectious sense of humour occasionally glancing through.[2] One of the more intriguing and hitherto elusive references to appear in his various essays on aspects of Puritanism in Suffolk was the citation of a sale on 6 June 1859 by Messrs Puttick and Simpson of a volume of so-called 'Ecclesiastical Miscellanies' which, according to the sale catalogue, included a 'Narrative of an exercise or disputation held apparently amongst certen ministers assembled at Bury St Edmunds, 1 April, 1590', and 'articles drawn according to the verie thoughts of the classical brethren for the wel managing of theire Mondaie exercise at Burie'.[3] Having invested some time working on Bury St Edmunds in the latter half of the sixteenth century, I had long wanted to find this manuscript and a little detective work succeeded in identifying the lost volume of ecclesiastical miscellanies as Chicago University Library Codex MS 109,[4] a manuscript which, once seen, proved as rich as the details in

---

[1] See Mark Kishlansky, 'Saye what?', *Historical Journal*, 33 (1990), pp. 917–37; Mark Kishlansky, 'Saye no More', *Journal of British Studies*, 30 (1991), pp. 399–448.

[2] See for example the footnotes in Patrick Collinson, *The Religion of Protestants* (Oxford, 1982); and P. Collinson, *The Birthpangs of Protestant England* (Basingstoke, 1988). See in particular n. 76 in Patrick Collinson, *English Puritanism* (London, 1983).

[3] Patrick Collinson, 'The Beginnings of English Sabbatarianism', in his *Godly People, Essays on English Protestantism and Puritanism* (London, 1983), p. 441; Patrick Collinson, 'Lectures by Combination, Structures and Characteristics of Church Life in 17th Century England', in ibid., p. 479.

[4] I am in the process of editing this text for publication.

the sale catalogue intimated. The items of interest are the work of the Suffolk clergyman and author Thomas Rogers, whose tidy hand fills up 42 pages of closely written text. What was described by the sale catalogue as a 'narrative of an exercise or disputation ... ' is in fact a very detailed rebuttal or confutation by Rogers of a letter sent to the Bishop of Norwich on 1 April 1590 by ten Suffolk clerics – John Knewstub, Reginald Whitfield, Walter Alen, Thomas Seffray, John Warde, Nicholas Bownde, Richard Grandidge, Robert Lewis, Leonard Greaves and Lawrence Whittaker[5] – all members of the combination lecture, explaining why they have excluded Thomas Rogers from the company of preachers. Historians have long been aware of Rogers's exclusion from the Bury exercise at this time and of his embattled relations with his clerical colleagues,[6] but the Chicago MS tells us for the first time the detailed story. And thanks to the manner of Rogers's confutation, in which he contends with the substance of the letter to the Bishop of Norwich almost line by line, both sides of the story can be told. At one level this is the tale of a tempest in a clerical teapot, a squabble amongst some Suffolk clergy in the early 1590s. It is also a tale that not only discloses much about the way in which the famous Monday exercise at Bury St Edmunds was ordered and maintained, but also illuminates aspects of clerical conflict and collegiality, as the divisions between conformity and nonconformity became acute in the midst of Whitgift's attack on the classical movement and the Marprelate controversy.

Comparatively little is known of Thomas Rogers, who is perhaps best remembered as the author of an exposition of the Thirty-nine Articles first published as *The English Creed* in 1585. It was substantially revised in 1607 as *The Faith, doctrine and religion professed and protected in the realm of England*, which was edited and republished by the Parker Society as *The Catholic Doctrine of the Church of England*.[7] A

---

[5] John Knewstub, Rector of Cockfield, Reginald Whitfield, Rector of Barrow, Walter (Gualter) Allen, Rector of Rushbrooke, Thomas Seffray, Rector of Depden, John Warde, preacher in Haverhill, Nicholas Bownde, Rector of Norton, Richard Grandidge, Rector of Bradfield St Clare, Robert Lewis, Rector of Little Waltham, Leonard Greaves, Rector of Thurston and Lawrence Whittaker, Rector of Bradfield St Clare. Knewstub, Whitfield, Seffray, Grandidge, Lewis and Greaves were all noted on a list of clergy drawn up in 1603 as 'scismatically affected heretofore'. NRO, VIS 3/3, fos 91–115.

[6] The fullest account is to be found in Patrick Collinson, 'Lectures by Combination', pp. 476–80.

[7] Thomas Rogers, *The Catholic Doctrine of the Church of England, An Exposition of the Thirty-Nine Articles*, ed. J. J. S. Perowne (PS, 1854). Perowne has a useful but brief introduction on Rogers and his work is derived mostly from Anthony Wood and Thomas Fuller.

native of Cheshire and a graduate of Christ Church, Oxford, Rogers was inducted into the living of Horringer or Horningshearth, a parish 2 miles from the town of Bury St Edmunds, on 13 May 1582.[8] He married Bridget Wincol, the daughter of an Essex clothier in 1588, and their only child, a son Robert, died in infancy. He served as Rector of Horringer until his death in 1616 when he was succeeded by William Bedell. He became chaplain to Sir Christopher Hatton and Richard Bancroft, although the details of these appointments are not known. Much of his time was spent in translating and writing books. The *Short-title Catalogue* gives us 12 of his original works and 11 translations, 18 of which had been published by 1590. He translated several works by contemporary Lutheran divines and mystical works ascribed to St Augustine. Patrick Collinson has drawn a convincing portrait of this 'most prolific author among the Suffolk clergy of his generation, but an Oxford man and a conformist, at odds with his puritanical Cambridge neighbours', 'a learned, diverse but ambitious churchman', chaplain to Archbishop Bancroft, sedulously seeking preferment yet remaining rector of Horringer until his death.[9]

When Rogers came to Suffolk, the town of Bury St Edmunds was wracked with religious controversies.[10] The early 1580s were the years of the 'Bury stirs' which involved, not only the confrontation between the Bishop of Norwich and the preachers and Puritan gentry of West Suffolk, but the challenge from a group of radical Brownists in the town.[11] Whitgift referred to the stirs as the time 'when the pretended Reformation was begun there, without staying for the magistrate, as the term was then'.[12] No doubt Rogers was aware of the divisions within the town between a group of conservative conformists and more zealous Protestants over the ministry of the two nonconformist town preachers, John Handson and Richard Gayton, both of whom left Bury

---

[8] SROB, Index of Inductions, HD 1149/1. This date corrects the information found in *Alumni Oxonienses: the members of the University of Oxford (1500–1714)* (4 vols Oxford, 1891–92), vol. 3 , p. 1272 and in the volume by S. Hervey, *Parish Registers of Horringer* (Suffolk Green Book), pp. 341–2.

[9] Collinson, *Godly People*, pp. 440–43; 478–9. Cf. Kenneth Parker, 'Thomas Rogers and the English Sabbath: the Case for a Reappraisal', *Church History*, 53 (1984), pp. 332–47; Kenneth Parker, *The English Sabbath* (Cambridge, 1988), esp. ch. 4; and for Rogers's Calvinism see Nicholas Tyacke, *Anti-Calvinists* (Oxford, 1987), pp. 25–7.

[10] J. S. Craig, 'Reformation, Politics and Polemics in Sixteenth Century East Anglian Market Towns' (PhD, Cambridge 1992), pp. 80–104.

[11] The situation in Bury has been examined by a number of historians. See in particular Patrick Collinson, 'The Puritan Classical Movement in the Reign of Elizabeth I' (2 vols, PhD, London 1957), pp. 860–930; Diarmaid MacCulloch, 'Catholic and Puritan in Elizabethan Suffolk', *ARG*, 72 (1981), 269–78; Craig, 'Reformation', pp. 80–104.

[12] CUL, Baker MS. Mm.1.47, p. 333.

in 1582 amidst charges of favouring separatists. The more dramatic events of 1583 in which two local Brownists, John Copping, a shoemaker and Elias Thacker, a tailor, were hung at the Summer Assize; a bonfire was made of Brownist literature; and an inquiry was made into the defamatory verses from the book of Revelation painted around the Queen's arms in the parish church of St Mary's (implying that Elizabeth was another Jezebel), must have been much discussed.[13]

It was into this already heated atmosphere in which the lines between conformity, nonconformity and sectarianism were easily blurred, that Whitgift's policy against the godly Nonconformists, 'our wayward and conceited persons', and drive for subscription to the Prayer Book as containing 'nothing contrary to the word of God' were initiated.[14] It is difficult to say how Rogers negotiated his way with his Cambridge colleagues, many of whom, under the bishop-like leadership of John Knewstub, the senior Puritan and Rector of Cockfield, a few miles south of Bury St Edmunds, were Nonconformists and members of the classical movement in Suffolk.[15] An entry into Rogers's position may be found by way of his exposition of the Thirty-nine Articles published in 1585 as *The English Creed*.[16] Dedicated to Edmund Scambler, Bishop of Norwich, Rogers's preface was written with Whitgift's drive for subscription clearly in mind: 'of the great subscription urged from the Pastors and ministers of the worde and sacraments in a great part of this land the last yeare, yee cannot lightlie be ignorant'. And his tone throughout, though written 'in most loyal maner to the Glorie of God, credit of our Church, and displaieng of all haeresies and errors' was moderate, even sympathetic to the call for further reformation of the Church. Although Rogers aligned himself firmly with those who believed that Whitgift's policies had 'made not a little unto the glorie of God, and comfort of his servants', he noted that 'some are of the opinion that much hurt therby hath redounded to the church of God' and argued, no doubt with his godly colleagues in mind, that no one challenged the Queen's supremacy or condemned the Book of Common Prayer, and that he believed that all clergy would subscribe if

---

[13] Craig, 'Reformation', pp. 94–9.

[14] Patrick Collinson, *The Elizabethan Puritan Movement* (London, 1967, repr., 1991), pp. 243–72.

[15] Collinson, *Elizabethan Puritan Movement, passim*.

[16] Thomas Rogers, *The English Creede, consenting with the true auncient catholique and apostolique Church in al the points and articles of Religion which everie Christian is to know and beleeve that would be saved*, (London, 1585, 1587) covering articles 20–39. It is dedicated to Sir Christopher Hatton. All of the quotations are taken from the opening preface.

that which is offensive, reformed and that which is crooked, made streight; and that which is doubtfull, made evident and plaine. Which things also are for number but verie fewe, and therefore maie the more easilie be removed; and remaine for the most part, in the directions and rubricks, and therefore with lesse offence maie be taken awaie.[17]

The enemies to the English Church were not the 'boys, babes, princocks [and] unlearned sots' as Whitgift would describe the opponents of the Prayer Book,[18] but Papists and Anabaptists. It is true that in Rogers's catalogue of the opponents of the Thirty-nine Articles he included 'Enthusiasts' and 'Schismatikes', but it is clear that he meant by these terms separatists such as the Brownists or members of the Family of Love, variously described as 'Communaltie of Love' and 'Nicholaitans of Harrie Nicholas' . Not a single error is ascribed even once to 'Puritans' and he takes pains to stress the common ground that exists, or might exist, between conformity and nonconformity alike:

For we, all of us, allowe her Maiestie's auctoritie in causes ecclesiastical and civil; we, all of us either simplie subscribe unto the forme of public praier prescribed or humbly (which libertie the lawe giveth) desire resolution in some fewe things; we, all of us, jointlie both embrace the Articles of the English creed, and renounce all haeretical opinions contrarie thereunto; we, all of us acknowledge the good things that we do enjoie and that the Church would florish much better, if that good lawes already made were faithfulie put in execution, and the true discipline of Christ so greatlie and so long wished were firmelie established, who doth not acknowledge? A thing evident enough these manie yeeres, but never so apparent as by this great, and late trial of the ministers.[19]

The 'unquenchable malice' of enemies on every side – 'Catholics, Arians, Pelagians, Jewes, Turks, Anabaptists and Familists' – is turned by Rogers into a reason and a plea for 'holy unitie'. 'What shal deterre us from loving one another with moste firme and Christian love? Shal petie and trifling things of no waight or of smal importance? Yea or anything els that can be conceived in harte or expressed by mouth or penne? God forbid.' And if the Papists should triumph, the fault lay with practice not belief:

it will not be to our griefe that we have beleeved, preached and professed the truth which the Church of England at this daie doth hold, but that we have not lived there-after, we shal repent; and publishing the Gospel of peace, have yet bine contentious, we shal repent; and being servants to one and the same Lord and master,

---

[17] Rogers, *The English Creede*, Preface.
[18] Collinson, *Elizabethan Puritan Movement*, p. 254.
[19] Rogers, *The English Creede*, Preface.

have not onlie railed upon, but also beaten and pursued one another, we shal repent; and being watchmen, have not bine more
vigilant and resident in our places we shal repent; our negligence,
our coldnesse, we shal repent; and if we have either kept out of the
Lord his vine-yard, such as both for abilitie could and for their
zeale would, either implant this Faith in the ignorant, or confirme
it in the learned; or to the certaine destruction of themselves and
manie others depending upon them either brought or kept in the
idle, and idol shepherds, that shal we repent also, and that with
teares.[20]

These passages are a far cry from the bitter polemics of the revised
edition of 1607 in which the text on the title-page was Romans 16:17, 'I
beseech you brethren, mark them diligently which cause divisions and
offences, contrary to the doctrine which ye have received and avoid
them.'[21] In this revised work, dedicated to Archbishop Bancroft, Rogers
rarely misses an opportunity to rail against 'Puritans', 'disciplinarians'
'our home faction' the 'schismaticall brethren', and 'sabbatarians' whose
Presbyterian platform is as tyrannical as popery and as divisive as Familism
or Brownism.[22] The subscription controversy of 1584 is now dismissed
peremptorily: 'This of the brethren was termed the woeful year of subscription, but that they should so do there was no cause, unless they are
grieved that factious spirits and malcontented ministers and preachers
were discovered and their erroneous and schismatical opinions brought
into light.' The dedicatory preface was transformed into an account of
the ways in which learned and godly men sought to establish the peace,
unity and uniformity of the Church of England in the face of the opposition and machinations of the 'brethren' whose views on discipline are
dismissed as 'strange and strong delusions', 'the fancies of troubled brains',
even 'frenzies', and who were once again seeking to wrest power from the
bishops through their Sabbatarian principles. The new Rogers, now in his
fifties and grey haired, is strikingly pugnacious and bitter, the sympathetic tone of 1585 utterly forgotten:

> The whole work expresseth aswell my detestation, and renuncia-
> tion of old adversaries and errors, opposite, crossing, or
> contradicting the doctrine professed by us, and protected by our
> king, or any article, or particle of truth of our religion; as my
> approbation of that truth which in our Church by wholesome
> statutes, and ordinances is confirmed.[23]

---

[20] Rogers, *The English Creede*, Preface.
[21] Thomas Rogers, *The faith, doctrine, and religion, professed and protected in the
Realme of England and dominions of the same* (Cambridge, 1607).
[22] Rogers, *Faith, doctrine, and religion*, pp. 78, 100, 111–12, 114, 133, 134–5, 162,
169, 191–2, 195, 198, 200, 206, 208, 220.
[23] Rogers, *Faith, doctrine, and religion*, p. 37.

How is the difference between the two works to be explained?

The answer lies in part in the detailed story disclosed by Rogers's account of the events that took place in 1589 in the celebrated combination lecture or exercise on Mondays in Bury St Edmunds. As is well known, the Monday exercise, held on market day in Bury St Edmunds can be traced back to the 'godlye exercise of expounding the scriptures by the way of prophecie' allowed by Bishop Parkhurst in 1573.[24] With the exception of a period of time when all prophesyings were officially suppressed in the late 1570s, the tradition of a Monday lecture was well established, and by the mid-1580s this had evolved into a popular occasion at which perhaps as many as 30 clergymen assembled together with an unknown number of townsfolk and neighbouring gentry. Both Rogers and his opponents make it clear that the ordering of the Monday exercise was ultimately at the behest of the Bishop of Norwich. Rogers speaks of the exercise having 'begunne' at the direction of Bishop Scambler 'at his first comming unto the Bishoprick', whereas the letter sent by Knewstub and his colleagues speaks of having had by the Bishop's direction 'an exercise continued upon the Mondaie at Burie ever since your L. comming to the diocesse'.[25] The difference between 'begun' and 'continued' was not insignificant but both views acknowledged the importance of the bishop's oversight. Rogers, as a learned cleric, was almost certainly a member of the combination lecture from the time of his coming to Suffolk. He wrote of 'having taken great pains among you (referring to the company of preachers) not a yeere or two but almost the tyme of a prenteship',[26] which would place his entry into the combination lecture to 1583 or 1584. Prior to 1587, there appears to have been an extremely informal arrangement of who might preach and when. Knewstub,[27] the long-serving rector of Cockfield and 'principall Senior praesent at the boorde' clearly dominated the proceedings and together with 'his table of consultacion' determined who preached. There was no rota, just an informal process of being nominated and approved 'with moste voices'. Rogers complained that before the lecture was reorganized, that 'some preached often, yee knowe, some sildome, some not at all'. Worst of all, 'no man ever knewe his turne, nor anie (whatsoever his businesse were, and the matter he had to handle never so waightie) had more than 7 daies at the moste, and

---

[24] Collinson, 'Lectures by Combination', p. 477.

[25] ChUL, Codex MS 109, fo. 1r.

[26] ChUL, Codex MS 109, fo. 2v.

[27] For Knewstub see Patrick Collinson, *Elizabethan Puritan Movement*, *passim*; and Peter Lake, *Moderate Puritans and the Elizabethan Church* (Cambridge, 1982), pp. 37, 298.

sometime not 4 to provide for the place'. This situation was rectified in 1587 when a 'set and certaine number of Preachers with free voices and choise were appointed, successivelie and in theire knowen courses to preach',[28] a division which included Thomas Rogers in its company. This appears to have been a local initiative carried out by Knewstub and his colleagues and ratified in turn by the Bishop of Norwich. The lecture itself was an exercise in biblical exegesis and expository preaching. Rogers mentions that 'the two epistles of S. Paull unto the Thessalonians ... have fully and wholie bine expounded' since Scambler's arrival in 1585 and that the preachers were currently working their way through Paul's letter to the Romans. Following the sermon, there was a short time for questions and discussion before the preachers retired for dinner at Michels 'according to the custome'.[29] It was in this context of clerical exposition and collegiality that divisions arose.

Comparing the letter sent by the ten members of the exercise to the Bishop of Norwich and Rogers's response to the same appears to tell the following story. In the weeks before Christmas 1589, the Monday exercise, was working its way through the book of Romans, when it came to the sixth, seventh and eighth verses of the twelfth chapter, a particularly controverted passage, the controversy heightened by the anonymously published but avowedly Presbyterian work from the press of Robert Waldegrave, entitled *A fruitful sermon* and attributed to Laurence Chaderton, Master of Emmanuel College, Cambridge.[30] The passage in question concerns the differing gifts given within the Church, which Chaderton had interpreted to refer to a prescribed form of church government consisting of pastors, doctors, elders, deacons and widows. Some of the heavyweights in the exercise, men like John Knewstub, Walter Allen, the Rector of Rushbrooke, and Lawrence Whittakers the Rector of Bradfield, decided that this passage needed to be handled 'responsibly' and although the passage fell by course to 'some of oure younger men (men of good giftes, but not the fittest, as we thought to handle that matter)', it was decided that 'the handling of those verses should be committed to the auncientest and discreetest of our companie'. (Rogers denied this claiming that the passage 'fell orderlie unto them which did handle that Scripture'.)[31] In the event, the responsibility was shared amongst Walter Allen,

---

[28] ChUL, Codex MS 109, fos 1r–2v.

[29] ChUL, Codex MS 109, fos 3r, 5v, 13v.

[30] Laurence Chaderton, *A fruitful sermon upon the 3, 4, 5, 6, 7, and 8 verse of the 12 chapter of the epistle of St Paule to the Romanes* (London, 1584). Cf. Collinson, *Elizabethan Puritan Movement*, p. 274; Lake, *Moderate Puritans*, pp. 26–35.

[31] ChUL, Codex MS 109, fo. 3v.

Knewstub, Mr Holt[32] and Mr Whitfield, each of whom preached a sermon on the passage, and in such a way 'as that no question [arose] among the people concerning discipline: a speciall part of [their] speech tending to this issue, viz to beate doune those which [do] wante of the discipline that theie desired, did condemne [the] Church of England, and would separate themselves from [us]'. Rogers claimed not to have been at the sermons preached by Allen or Knewstub and to have registered his dissent with some of the interpretations put forth by Holt and Whitfield, and that so plainly that Knewstub rebuked him for being in error. Rogers's turn came next. Instead of continuing with verse 9 as all expected ('Let love be without dissention … ') , he pulled out of his pocket a copy of the *Fruitful sermon* (he claimed later not to have known the author) and launched into a comprehensive attack upon the same, 'cleane leaving his texte and so spending his time contrarie to all good order'. What appears to have irritated his fellow ministers most of all is that Rogers 'reproached the author of that Sermon comparing [him] the penner thereof firste to H. N. the familist,[33] and afterward to Campion and Reignoldes, two traiterous Papistes … as that the mislike of th'auditorie did openlie appeare therein, judging by his manner of dealing that he came rather to make an invective than a Sermon'.[34] The audience was agog, and a group of ministers later claimed to have 'lovinglie and gentlie admonished' Rogers 'for his strange and unusual manner of dealing', although they noted that 'since which time he hath wholie absented himselfe from our companie, as if we had done him injurie'.[35] Fearing another such sermon, the senior ministers of the combination artfully 'secluded' Rogers under the guise of reorganizing the exercise yet again by presenting Bishop Scambler with another list of names which he then authorized as constituting the Bury exercise; the name of Thomas Rogers being carefully omitted.[36]

Rogers was deeply angered. His exclusion from the exercise was a bitter pill and followed hard upon the death of his first and only child. He obviously wrote to the bishop complaining of this unfair treatment, and in turn wrote to the Bury ministers seeking an explanation which prompted the letter of 1 April 1590. The date coincided with the first day of the general Assizes prompting a scornful comparison from Rogers:

---

[32] John Holt was Rector of Bradfield Combust. SROB, HD 1149/1.

[33] Richard Bancroft levels the same charge against Cartwright in *A Survay of the Pretended Holy Discipline* (London, 1593). Where the manuscript is torn, I have supplied the missing words and placed the same in brackets.

[34] ChUL, Codex MS 109, fo. 9r.

[35] ChUL, Codex MS 109, fo. 11v.

[36] ChUL, Codex MS 109, fos 14r, 16v.

The firste of Aprill, it seemeth, the honourable Judges with the rest of the Gentlemen and Commons of the contrie were not so occupied at Burie St Edmunds in one kind, for the go[od of some?] but at the same verie time and toune yee were as much busied in another kinde for the hurt of some. Theie met openlie, yee secretlie and classically. The fructes of theire assembling is notable knowen to the greate good of the contrie: and this letre (brought to my sight by Gods providence, contrarie to your expectation) testifieth in part th'end of your meeting at Burie St Edmundes 1 Aprilis.[37]

Whether or not Rogers intended to publish an account of his seclusion from the combination, or whether he was preparing a detailed refutation of the case made against him in the letter sent to the bishop, is not known. The manuscript is carefully written with a number of emendations but not so many that it could not stand as a fair copy. His detailed defence concluded with a satirical set of 'articles drawen (according to the verie thoughte of the classical Brethren, (the Informers above mentioned) for the wel managing of theire Moondaie exercise at Burie, and such like els-where in Marcate townes, on Mercate daies', in which Rogers caricatured his opponents as men that would 'pull the raines of government from the nowe and alwais received eclesiastical; and put them into the handes of certaine newelie devised consistorial and laical Elders and States-men in everie parish'. The proceedings against Rogers were to be an example to 'those of his minde, following his steps, what theie maie expect at our handes; and to our successors, with what endlesse and perfect hatred theie are to be pursued, that shal dare to thwart, and crosse us, or our Brethren wheresoever in our political courses and discourses about Discipline'.[38]

Although the name of John Knewstub appears at the head of the list of signatories, Rogers believed that the real villain behind his 'shameful secluding' was not so much Knewstub as Miles Mosse, the preacher of the parish of St James in Bury St Edmunds. Mosse was one of the Cambridge boys and everything that Rogers was not. Mosse was an insider, Suffolk born, undoubtedly a protégé of Knewstub and Chaderton, the son of a yeoman from Chevington, who proceeded from the grammar school in Bury to Caius College, Cambridge, and eventually via a charge in Norwich back to Bury in 1586 where he served as the preacher of the parish of St James from 1586 to 1598, possessing a handsome stipend from 1589 of £40 per annum. It initially puzzled Rogers that Mosse's name was nowhere to be found among the names of the ten ministers who complained of Rogers's 'strange and unusuall manner of dealing':

---

[37] ChUL, Codex MS 109, fo. 19v.
[38] ChUL, Codex MS 109, fos 21r–21v.

> I see John Knewstub, Reginald Whitfield Gualter Alen, Thomas
> Seffray etc. I looke for Miles Mosse and I cannot spie his name
> neither firste nor laste. Wil not he justifie the truth hereof, as yee
> will, because his hand is not heere? Will he that was the firste and
> foremost in this action against Thomas Rogers, be neither the firste
> nor last nor at all in this writing?[39]

But it eventually dawned on Rogers that 'we have his hande for this (the
letter) was his handie worke'.[40] One can sense Rogers's deep dislike for
Mosse in his sarcastic denunciation of the way in which he was admonished for his sermon:

> Neither lovinglie nor gentlie did yee admonish him. M. Mosses
> grinning at him in moste disdainful manner before moste of you,
> and objecting so often unto him the Cambridg boies,[41] maie tell
> you howe lovinglie and gentlie he was admonished. Successe Mar-
> ten and all yoe Martinistes[42] from charging our Bishops with hard
> using of the ministers: Bend yourselves henceforward against the
> Brotherhood. Yee cannot from all the Bishops proceedings their 32
> yeeres, all circumstances waied, produce an example of so injuri-
> ous dealing against theire infereiors, as this the Bretheren against a
> fellow minister. Theire roughnes is mildnes in comparison of theis
> mens gentle dealing.

This was but the beginning of the quarrell between Rogers and Mosse
which took a curious turn. Shortly after Rogers had been excluded from
the exercise and had put his sermon confuting Chaderton's into print,[43]
Mosse published, or rather republished the extremely popular catechism
by John More and Edward Dering with a short preface dedicated to the
Bishop of Norwich in which he complained that 'men will speak before
they have learned' and that 'manie ministers of the word write much

---

[39] ChUL, Codex MS 109, fo. 20r.

[40] ChUL, Codex MS 109, fo. 20r. Rogers's first attempt at this was 'Though we have
not his hande, yet we have his hed saith another. The cause is secret, saith a third, he was
our secretarie and his hart is with us, and this sufficeth.'

[41] The term is reminiscent of Whitgift's angry outbursts against some of the ministers
from Kent in 1585: 'Thou boy, beardless boy, yesterday bird, new out of the shell.'
Robert Beale also spoke of Whitgift's 'common and wonted place of boying' the ministers. See Collinson, *Elizabethan Puritan Movement*, pp. 254–5. Cf. Bancroft's comment
about those that run 'uppe and downe after every young start up, hether and thether, to
seeke new platforms of church government in this place or that place ... ': Bancroft, *A
Survay of the Pretended Holy Discipline*, 'to the reader'.

[42] The Marprelate controversy was at its height in 1589. W. Pierce (ed.), *The Marprelate
Tracts 1588, 1589* (London, 1911), p. 238. Cf. W. Pierce, *An Historical Introduction to
the Marprelate Tracts* (London, 1908).

[43] Thomas Rogers, *A sermon made upon the 6. 7. and 8. verses of the 12 chapter of S.
Paules Epistle unto the Romanes ... made to the confutation of so much of another
sermon* (London, 1590).

but preach little', statements which the suspicious and sensitive Rogers interpreted as an attack upon his own efforts as a writer.[44] Rogers responded at length and once again, paragraph by paragraph, line by line, in a bitter attack upon Mosse's preface under the title *Miles Christianus or a just Apologie of all necessarie writings and writers speciallie of them which by their labored writings take pains to build up the Church of Christ* the opening lines of which wished Mosse 'more soundnes of judgement, more substance of learning with more wisdome and discretion in all his actions'.[45] The polemics continued for another 36 pages in a similar vein. It is doubtful that the two men were ever reconciled. The last that is heard of this particular affair is found in a letter written by Rogers in the summer of 1591 to John Still, the archdeacon of Sudbury in which Rogers wrote that

> I finde that M. Mosse is much grieved at me for two thinges, viz 1. for my sermon wch I made last at Burie (and since through bad dealing offend me for the same, I have bine urged to imprinte) and for an answer unto his epistle prefixed to that catechisme by him published. What he wil object against either or bothe of these bookes I know not: and though unto whatsoever he can object, or might answere, I have donn nothing which is not sufficientlie approved by thauctoritie of our Church ... .

Mosse's grinning response to Rogers's attack upon Chaderton was remembered with bitterness as Rogers complained to Still that Mosse had attacked his sermon 'with most reprochful speiches ... and in the hearing of divers both godlie and learned ministers of the Word depraved the same exceedinglie'. 'Hence that shameful (as themselves call it) secluding me from the Burie exercise; Hence the conspering of no lesse than tenn of the chiefest ministers of the faction in Suffolk in a lettre against me and my sermon unto my Lord of Norwich', which Rogers deemed 'a prasident of greater audacitie I verilie think since your worships coming into Suffolk you never knewe' and promised to tell the full story 'with thanswere thereunto at large'.[46] It is not clear why Rogers

---

[44] The More–Dering catechism was variously entitled *A briefe and necessary instruction*, *A briefe and necessary catechisme* and *A short catechisme for householders*. See Ian Green, '"For Children in Yeeres and Children in Understanding": the Emergence of the English Catechism under Elizabeth and the Early Stuarts', *JEH*, 37 (1986), p. 399.

[45] Thomas Rogers, *Miles Christianus or a just Apologie of all necessarie writings and writers speciallie of them which by their labored writings take pains to build up the Church of Christ in this age And in a publique and diffamatorie Epistle lately set forth in Print are unjustly depraved* (London, 1590). The copy in the British Library (C 124.c.7) belonged to Thomas Rogers and is interleaved with many notes in Rogers's hand.

[46] All of the above can be found in 'The true copie of a certen leter unto the right

made his appeal to Dr Still. Perhaps he thought that Still would be more sympathetic to his stance[47] than Scambler's officials as it was clear that some kind of investigation by the diocese had been initiated. 'Midsomer is at hande, before which time our matters muste be heard and ended or els Mr Chancelour himself will resume into his owne handes and set such order as in justice he shall think most meete.' Nothing is known of the order presumably set.

Why did Rogers take it upon himself, at that time and in that place to attack the Presbyterian principles enunciated in Chaderton's sermon? Can Rogers have been quite so innocent as he protested, simply a zealous conformist exercising his right of free speech? His claim not to have known the author of *A fruitful sermon* is surely disingenuous. When Rogers, referring to the previous four sermons preached in the combination by Knewstub, Allen, Holt and Whitfield, denied that he had given 'his consent and approbation to that which had bine spoken', he wrote the following:

> He well remembreth that in your hearing he publiquelie before you all testified his dislike of that interpretation, which M. Holt ~~following therein I knowe whom~~ gave concerning prophecieng mentioned in the 6 verse ... He disliked also divers thinges tuching the doctor and his office ~~as namelie that he was onlie to teach, and neither to entreat, nor to applie his doctrine, nor to administer the sacrament~~ which M. Whitfield delivered.

The deleted passages are significant for, although they do not mention Chaderton by name nor necessarily refer to the author of *A fruitful sermon*, they indicate that Rogers was careful not to reveal too much. The collusion in Chaderton's anonymity was on both sides. The indignant response of the godly brethren against Rogers's attack upon the author of *A fruitful sermon*, is explicable in part because they knew precisely who had written this sermon and sprang to his defence, although the most they were willing to reveal was that he was 'thought to be a godlie and learned man'.[48] Although Chaderton is never once

---

Worshipfull D. Stil in defense of Miles Christianus' penned into the British Library copy of Thomas Rogers, *Miles Christianus or a just Apologie of all necessarie writings and writers* ... . Although the letter is dated 'from Horringer the 8 of June', and the year is missing, it must be dated no earlier than 1591.

[47] It is notable that Still's sermon to the Parliament that met in February 1589 appears to have been along the lines of Christopher Hatton's attack on both 'papists and puritans'. Collinson, *Elizabethan Puritan Movement*, p. 397.

[48] The links between Chaderton and Knewstubs were strong. Both were spokesmen of the Puritan party at the Hampton Court Conference. See William Barlow, *The summe and substance of the conference* (London, 1604), pp. 126–7. Cf. the references in Collinson, *Elizabethan Puritan Movement*.

mentioned by name, it seems certain that both Rogers and his opponents knew very well who was being attacked and defended.

It is the timing of the events in Bury together with the slender straws of evidence concerning Rogers's relationship with Richard Bancroft, that relentless detective of the classical movement, which proves so intriguing. The larger context for the sermons in Bury must have been the Marprelate tracts appearing as they did with effective and rollicking satire between October 1588 and June 1589. Six months before the first of the Marprelate tracts appeared, John Udall, preacher of Kingston, had published a stinging dialogue, *The state of the church of England*, in which Udall had placed the following words in the mouth of the godly preacher,

> I pray you therefore when you come to London, see if you can get these bookes: *the Ecclesiasticall Discipline*; *A lerned discourse of Ecclesiasticall governement*: *The counterpoyson*: *A sermon upon the 12 to the Romanes* and *Mr Cartwrites last reply*: some of which bookes have been extant this dozen yeeres, and yet are none of them answered ... .[49]

Was it Bancroft's idea, as part of his answering of the Marprelate tracts, that Rogers pen a response to Chaderton's sermon and deliver it among Chaderton's friends and protégés?[50] The testimonial drawn up for Bancroft that secured his appointment as Bishop of London spoke of his energy in organizing not only the anti-Martinist tracts but also 'to have the Slanderous Libels, against her Majestie answered'.[51] We do not know enough about the relationship between Bancroft and Rogers to do more than speculate, although the points of similarity between Rogers's sermon and Bancroft's own works are striking. Rogers's comparision of Chaderton to H. N. the Familist, is parallelled by the comparison drawn by Bancroft of Cartwright in his *A Survey of the Pretended Holy Discipline* published in 1593.[52] If Rogers's sermon

---

[49] John Udall, *The state of the church of England, laide open in a conference betweene Diotrephes a Bishop, Tertullus a Papist, Demetrius an usurer, Pandocheus an In-keeper, and Paule a Preacher of the word of God* (n.d., n.p.). Cf. Collinson, *Elizabethan Puritan Movement*, p. 391. Rogers makes mention of the claim by Udall in his published version of the sermon.

[50] I owe the suggestion of Bancroft's involvement to Patrick Collinson. See also Patrick Collinson, 'Ecclesiastical vitriol: religious satire in the 1590s and the invention of Puritanism', in John Guy (ed.), *The Reign of Elizabeth I, Court and Culture in the Last Decade* (Cambridge, 1995), esp. pp. 156–7. See also the discussion by Dr Brian Vickers of Francis Bacon's response to the controversies of 1589–91, *An Advertisement touching the Controversies of the Church of England*, in Brian Vickers (ed.), *Francis Bacon* (Oxford, 1996), pp. 494–501.

[51] A. Peel (ed.), *Tracts Ascribed to Richard Bancroft* (Cambridge, 1953), pp. xviii–xix.

[52] Bancroft, *A Survey of the Pretended Holy Discipline*, pp. 1–2.

against Chaderton was indeed part of an orchestrated campaign masterminded by Bancroft against the Suffolk Puritans, this would not have
been the first time that Bancroft had organized the preaching of conformist sermons in Bury to check the perceived strength of the godly.[53]

I have argued elsewhere that the strength of conformist feeling in
Elizabethan Bury St Edmunds has tended to be overlooked in part
perhaps because at a public, literary level, Bury was gaining a reputation for radical Puritanism. Martin Marprelate boasted in print of the
register that he kept at Bury, an ambiguous claim that revealed as much
about the success of the ecclesiastical authorities in suppressing nonconformity as it did the presence of the godly.[54] By 1590, Thomas Nashe
was writing caustically of the 'preaching brothers of Bury' and, in
challenging Martin Marprelate to a public disputation, wrote, 'Truly I
am afraide that this Generall counsaile must be holden at Geneva when
al is done, for I know no place in England holy inough for their fare
except it be some barne or outhouse about Bury, or some odde blinde
cottage in the heart of Warwickshire ... .'[55] Nashe's satirical critique
was based largely upon a certain familiarity with the Brownist movement in Bury, and elsewhere he repeats an inaccurate account of the
'badde practise of your brother the Booke-binder and his accomplishes
at Burie' and their 'newe Posie to her Majesties armes'.[56] Yet these
literary snapshots, hearkening back as they did to the Brownist movement and the 'stirs' of the early 1580s, were far from the whole picture,
for the town was also home to important elements that remained strongly
conservative. Rogers could speak confidently in 1591 of the number of

---

[53] Bancroft himself had preached sermons in Bury together with his Jesus College
colleagues, Oliver Phillips and Andrew Boardman at the height of the Bury Stirs in
1582–83: Craig, 'Reformation', p. 91. Cf. Peel, *Tracts Ascribed to Richard Bancroft*,
esp. pp. 69–74; and the visitation sermon preached at Towcester in June 1588 by John
Beatniffe, Vicar of Brackley and dedicated to Whitgift, Hatton, Burghley and Sir
Christopher Wray, published as *A sermon preached at Torceter in the Countie of Northampton* (London, 1590). (Northampton like Suffolk was a county where such sermons
were needed.) Beatniffe preached,

> You looke now peradventure, that I should make some bitter invective
> speeches against Byshops, which of some are thought not to be so careful
> as their office requireth: but truly I am not so determined, for indeede they
> be reverend fathers, Fathers of the Church, and they be brethren. I came
> not hether to accuse any, I love it not, I leave it to the devill ...

I owe this reference to the kindness of Patrick Collinson.

[54] W. Pierce (ed.), *The Marprelate Tracts 1588, 1589* (London, 1911), p. 283.

[55] Thomas Nashe, 'An Almond for a Parrat' (1590), in R. B. McKerrow (ed.), *The
Works of Thomas Nashe* (5 vols, Oxford, 1958), vol. 3, p. 373, 370.

[56] Nashe, 'An Almond for a Parrat', p. 352.

those who were on his side: 'though yee are nowe tenn to on, M. Rogers is not alone. He hath his favorers, and mo[r]e coadjutors than yee thinke, or than yee would he had. He is not single, nor singled from all, nor yet singular'.[57] Earlier in the manuscript, Rogers argued,

> Are all the people of one minde? And are the people, thinke yee, so ignorant that theie perceave not unto what side the discreetest among you do incline? Do all the people favor that part? Assure your selves so manie of theire auditors, as in the matter of discipline dissented from them [the preachers], were theire adversaries, and moved questions enough about discipline, and those verses too, as yee thinke, the grounde of your devises.[58]

The history of conformity in Elizabethan Suffolk, both clerical and lay, is yet to be written.

What is clear is that, despite the collapse of the classical movement, the strength of the 'Cambridge boies' in the Bury exercise grew even stronger in the 1590s and once again in a way that involved books. Bury St Edmunds had long been a place for learning closely connected to Cambridge University and many of the clergy in and around Bury were Cambridge graduates.[59] The town's grammar school was well thought of with strong ties to Gonville and Caius and St John's Colleges.[60] It is noteworthy that the only non-Cambridge autographs among the distinguished Cambridge scholars and fellows who inscribed their names in Anthony Weddeo's 'album amicorum' are those of Nicholas Martin and Rowland Wilson, master and usher respectively of the Bury school.[61] Books were plentiful in Bury with strong links to continental publishers. Thomas Gibson, who had separatist leanings, was a Bury bookbinder and the prosecution of the Brownists in 1583 demonstrated how quickly books might travel from the Low Countries to West Suffolk. Copies of Robert Harrison's *Three Formes of Catechismes*, published in the beginning of 1583, were circulating in Bury by the spring and burnt publicly at the Summer Assizes in June of that year.

---

[57] ChUL, Codex MS 109, fo. 19v.

[58] ChUL, Codex MS 109, fo. 4v.

[59] In 1618, Robert Reyce in his 'breviary of Suffolk' spoke of the 'great number of religious, grave, reverend and learned ministers of Gods holy word which are planted in this shire.' S. Hervey, *Suffolk in the XVIIth Century* (London, 1902), p. 21.

[60] S. Hervey, *Bury St Edmunds Grammar School List 1550–1900* (Suffolk Green Book, 13, 1908), Introduction.

[61] CUL, Add MS 7761, fols 7–8. Anthony Weddeo was from the Palatinate and collected autographs and aphorisms in his 'album amicorum' between 1598 and 1599. Of 51 separate inscriptions, those of Thomas Playfair, John Overall, James Montagu, William Perkins, Lawrence Chaderton, Abdias Ashton, William Bedell, Joseph Hall, Andrew Downell and Leonard Mawe are a few of the most notable.

Yet in the absence of surviving runs of probate inventories, information about books is limited to the snippets found in runs of registered and original wills.[62] Between 1550 and 1625, only 21 wills make either direct or implied mention of books. This is clearly the most visible tip of a much greater mass of printed material all too often obscured behind the phrases 'other goods' or 'household goods' which served as 'catch-alls' for scriveners. Furthermore, there are clear examples of book ownership which receive no mention in wills. Thomas Andrews, a wealthy conservative gentleman and magistrate, made no mention of any books when he drew up his will in 1585, but his bequest of 116 volumes to the grammar school by 1570 was the largest ever received by the school.[63]

Not surprisingly, most of those who made specific mention of books in their wills often held occupations which virtually required book ownership, or possessed strong religious convictions. Clerics, lawyers, teachers and scriveners hold pride of place in this small group. In 1552, John King, the schoolmaster of the grammar school, bequeathed copies of Pliny, Virgil, Horace and Ovid to the school.[64] In the same year, William Graye, 'clercke' left 'all my bokes of holye scripture' to 'Mayster Starman' and 'all my bookes of cyvyll and canone law' to 'Thomas Rowght notary'.[65] Public notaries like William Alman, gentlemen like Augustine Steward, preachers like George Estye, and common lawyers such as William Cooke, all bequeathed books in their wills.[66] Protestants such as William Bretten bequeathed Bibles, or Geneva Bibles, and less frequently works by Thomas Becon or copies of the Book of Common Prayer.[67] Conservatives bequeathed singing books or left their books to known recusants such as the mathematician and physician, Thomas Oliver.[68] Tremellius Bibles were favoured by the gentry as gifts. In 1581 Frances Jermyn gave ten preachers each a Tremellius Bible. The following year William Markaunt bequeathed £40 worth of godly books for poor scholars of divinity at Cambridge, especially Tremellius Bibles,

---

[62] Cf. Peter Clark, 'The Ownership of Books in England, 1560–1640: the Example of Some Kentish Townsfolk', in L. Stone (ed.), *Schooling and Society, Studies in the History of Education* (Baltimore 1976), pp. 95–111.

[63] Craig, 'Reformation', p. 94. All of the books from the Bury grammar school are kept at Cambridge University Library.

[64] SROB, IC 500/2/8, fol. 247v: '*Pline de naturali historia, Vigilius cum commento, Oratius cum commento, Ovidius cum commento.*'

[65] SROB, IC 500/1/21/205.

[66] Alman: NRO, NCC Hinde, fol. 229v; Steward: PRO, PCC 45 Cobham; Estye: SROB, IC 500/1/59/84; Cooke: SROB, IC 500/1/75/74.

[67] Bretten: SROB, IC 500/2/8, fol. 387r; Cf. SROB, IC 500/2/51, fols 370v–373v; SROB, IC 500/2/8, fol. 403v.

[68] Thomas Lacy left all of his books to the recusant Thomas Oliver, SROB, IC 500/2/42, fol. 343r. Cf. SROB, IC 500/1/36/201; SROB, IC 500/1/18/30A.

and left copies of Calvin's *Institutes* and Beza's translation of the New Testament.[69]

By 1595 this zeal for learning was given a particular twist by Miles Mosse with the establishment of a library in the parish church of St James.[70] This was very probably the first post-Reformation parochial library of its kind in the country, as distinct from collections of pre-scribed texts or schoolbooks.[71] The venture was organized by Miles Mosse, and within four years of its inception, possessed no fewer than 200 volumes complete with book plates commemorating donors. Many of the book plates have perished but of the 41 known donors who gave books to the library between 1595 and 1596, at least eight were gro-cers, clothiers, mercers, drapers and maltsters, 14 were gentlemen and another ten were clerics. Henry Hammond, a clothier, gave a copy of *Bernardi Opera Omnia* (Basel, 1566) on 2 November 1595. John Man, a grocer, gave a folio volume of *Cyrilli Alexandrini Opera* (Basel, 1566) and another clothier, John Lansdale, gave Bucer's *Enarrationes in Sacra Quatuor Evangelia* (Geneva, 1553). There is no telling how many other townsmen supported the library with their donations.

The purpose of this library can be discerned through an analysis of the earliest catalogue, drawn up in 1599, which gives some interesting details concerning both the volumes held by the library and the physical layout.[72] All the books were kept in a single room in the parish church of St James. As one entered the room, ten classes of books were shelved on the right and ten on the left. The books on the right were works of the Church Fathers: Augustine in class 2, Chrysostom in class 10 and in

---

[69] When Frances Jermyn, sister to Sir Robert Jermyn, made her will on 10 September 1580, (SROB, IC 500/1/40/30) she gave money to establish two scholarships at Cam-bridge, one each at St John's and Trinity colleges, and gave Bibles to ten preachers: to 'Mr Lovell, Mr Knewstubbes, Mr Hanson, Mr Gayton, Mr Whittakers, Mr Grandishe, Mr Wyllson, Mr Coppinger, Mr Dr Crooke and Mr Pricke, to everye of them a Tremelius bible fayer bound'. William Markaunt: PRO, PCC 12 Rowe.

[70] J. A. Fitch, 'Some Ancient Suffolk Parochial Libraries', *Proceedings of the Suffolk Institute of Archaeology and History*, 30 (1967), p. 44.

[71] N. Ker (ed.), *The Parochial Libraries of the Church of England* (London, 1959), gives primacy of place to a library in the belfry of the church mentioned in the church-wardens' accounts of St Martin's, Leicester in 1587, but this 'library' was a result of the generosity of the Earl of Huntingdon and quite unlike the combined efforts that estab-lished the Bury library. Cf. M. C. Cross, *The Puritan Earl* (London, 1966), p. 126.

[72] Craig, 'Reformation', appendix 4. It would appear that the prototype of what Mosse and his colleagues established in Bury can be found in the link between Bullinger's library and the *Prophezei* in Zurich, with its collection of works by the Church Fathers, all in uniform binding, borrowed we know by students. Dr Urs Leu of the Zentralbibliothek in Zurich has been painstakingly reconstructing Bullinger's library. I owe this reference to the kindness of Patrick Collinson.

between Ambrose, Hilary, Irenaeus, Athanasius, Bernard, Origen and others. On the left were the standard works of the Continental Reformers with John Calvin's works dominating classes 2 and 3, coming just behind class 1 which consisted of a variety of Bibles. Completing this side were the works of Beza, Mercer, Bucer, Zanchius, Melanchthon, Bullinger (see Figure 7.1), Peter Martyr and others. Finally, there were three classes of 'other', one of dictionaries and two of miscellaneous items. The miscellaneous items were a mixture of medieval theology, history, the odd herbal, a chronicle of the Turks, Polydore Vergil, Bodin's *Republic*, a copy of English statutes, Munster's *Cosmography* and much else. The miscellaneous quality of these books suggests that these books were true donations, whereas the two sections of Patristics and Reformed theology suggest a more systematic process of either requesting specific titles from donors or the money to acquire specific texts.

Despite the rag-bag appearance of the miscellaneous texts, there can be little doubt about the central purpose of the library. Its theological character betrays its essentially clerical function. Here was a working library, probably modelled after Cambridge college libraries, for the resident clergy and other ministers who came to Bury on Mondays. The organizing role of Miles Mosse and the specific donations from neighbouring ministers clearly indicate that the library was an offshoot of the Monday exercise. We know that members of the combination lecture, such as Nicholas Bownde of Norton, Robert Prick of Denham, Anthony Rous of Hesset, Jacob Wallais of Stowlangtoft, and Mosse himself all donated books to the library. And so too did Laurence Chaderton,[73] a particularly satisfying piece of evidence cementing the close links between the Bury exercise and the Cambridge godly.

It would be wrong to depict the library as only for the clergy of the combination. This was, after all, a *parish* library and neither the combination lecture, nor the weekly lectures in Bury on Wednesdays or Fridays had ever been the exclusive preserve of the clergy. Rogers himself noted that a certain preacher was 'woont to say in his Sermons (which I have not heard a great while) that your Townsmen of Burie are such diligent hearers of the word on the Monday exercises, that they may easely be singled out from other men'.[74] In like manner, there is evidence that the parish library was used by some townsmen as well as clergy. Although the majority of works were in Latin with a handful in Greek, there were a few works in English which enabled those whose Latin was too rudimentary, rusty or non-existent to use the library.

---

[73] Chaderton gave a copy of Claudius Guillandus, *In Evangelium secundum Ioannem Enarrationes* (Paris, 1550). Cf. Craig, 'Reformation', appendix 5.

[74] Rogers, *Miles Christianus*, p. 17.

SERMONVM

Decades quinque, de potissimis
Christianae religionis capitibus,
in tres tomos digestae, authore
Heinrycho Bullingero,
ecclesiae Tigurinae
ministro.

Cum Indice vario & copiosissimo.

TOMVS PRIMVS.

IESVS.

HIC est filius meus dilectus, in quo placata est
anima mea. Ipsum audite. Matth. 17.

TIGVRI IN OFFICINA CHRISTOPH.
FROSCHOVERI. ANNO M.D.LXVII.

Miles Mosse
Sacrae Theologiae apud Cantabrigienses
Baccalaureus et verbi divini in hac
Ecclesia iam per annos novem
completos Praedicator, dono
dedit huic Bibliotheca
Octob +
1595

7.1 Title-page with book plate from Bullinger's *Decades*, donated by Miles Mosse, in the parish library of St James, Bury St Edmunds. Reproduced by kind permission of the Provost and Chapter of St Edmundsbury Cathedral.

There was a copy of the statutes in English, Jewel's *Apology* and *Reply to Harding*, Calvin's *Sermons* on Deuteronomy and on Timothy and Titus, Peter Martyr's *Commonplaces*, a Rhemish Testament in English, Dodoens's *Herball* and a few others. Notes scribbled in some of these works indicate that some townsmen borrowed them for rather lengthy periods before they were brought back into the library.[75] The townsmen's support for the library was seen not only in gifts of books but also more lasting bequests. Two townsmen, James Baxter, a baker, and Edward White, a clothier, made provision for the library of St James in their wills. In 1612, Baxter bequeathed an acre of land lying in the Bury field to the Guildhall feoffees on the condition that 'the yssues and profites therof shall from tyme to tyme be imploied towardes the repayringe of that parte of St James his churche in Bury aforesaid which is nowe called the Liberarye'.[76] Edward White's bequest was no less specific. In 1625, he gave

> the sume of fyve markes of England to be bestowed upon a booke to be kepte as the rest of the Bookes are kept in the lybrarie of St James his Churche in Bury St Edmunds aforesaid such a Booke as shalbe thought most meete and necessarie for the same place by the discretion and advysement of the preachers and ministers of bothe the churches of St James and St Marye.[77]

What was Thomas Rogers's relationship to the new library? There is no evidence that Rogers donated any books to the library, and the marginal references in a number of his published works would indicate he owned a sizeable personal collection.[78] But it seems hard to believe that a literary cleric such as Rogers would have made no use of, or have had no interest in the Bury library. Rogers was dogged by parochial troubles in the late 1590s with an inquiry into the legality of his induction to his living, a protracted tithe suit and an ugly case involving a parishioner who accused him of preaching false doctrine.[79] The

---

[75] A note in Dodoen's *A Niewe Herball* (London, 1578) reads 'This book belonged to the Librarie and found in Mr Gol[ding's] studdie and brought in again by F[rancis] P[inner].'

[76] SROB, IC 500/2/48, fols 151v–152v.

[77] SROB, IC 500/2/53, fols 538r–539v.

[78] See in particular the books mentioned in his own copy of *Miles Christianus* (BL, C 124.c.7), a work to which he obviously returned well past its initial appearance in 1590. He cites works by Cartwright, Bucer, Calvin, Eusebius, Ovid, Ascham, Nashe, Buchanan, Bownde, Penry, Greenham, Stow, Hooker, Greene, Mosse, Melanchthon, Cranmer, Erasmus, Junius to mention but a few.

[79] SROB, HD 1149/1, Index of inductions. There appears to have been an inquiry in February 1596 and April 1601 as to whether Thomas Rogers had been properly inducted into the living of Horringer. Cf. NRO, Reg 14/ book 20, fos 72r–v. Earlier in the

parishioner, Thomas Scott, suspended for brawling in the church and churchyard, was found by the Bishop of Norwich to have acted maliciously and was ordered to 'reconcale himselfe unto Mr Rogers'.[80] There is no evidence of Rogers preaching in the Monday exercise again until 1599, significantly the year after Mosse had left his post in Bury for the neighbouring rectory of Coombs. Once again, the report that survives is of a contentious sermon, in which Rogers attacked the Sabbatarian principles enunciated by Nicholas Bownde, one of the ten ministers, it may be recalled, who 'conspired' against Rogers.[81] Clearly he was taking his place again but just when and how this was effected is not known. But Rogers never forgot his 'seclusion' by the hands of the Bury ministers. His printed work 'post-seclusion' is marked by an abiding hatred for the 'schismaticall company' and specifically against the group of Bury ministers who had effected his removal from the exercise. This explains his attack on Miles Mosse in *Miles Christianus* (1590), his attack on 'mine Antagonist' Thomas Seffray, another of the Bury ministers in *Two dialogues or conferences (about an old question lately renued and by the schismaticall company, both by printed pamphlets and otherwise to the disturbance of the Churchs quiet and of peaceable minds, very hotly pursued) concerning kneeling in the very act of receiving the sacramental bread* ... (1608), and his attack on Nicholas Bownde's book the *Doctrine of the Sabbath*. This was his most notable triumph resulting in the suppression of Bownde's work, and in the preface to his revised edition of *The English Creede*, Rogers crowed with sweet revenge, 'It is a comfort unto my soul and will be till my dying hour, that I have been the man and the means that these sabbatarian errors and impieties are brought into light and knowledge.'[82] Just how he was regarded at this time by his clerical colleagues is hard to say, but one cannot but feel that perhaps Rogers obtained a degree of malicious delight in using the library of the 'Cambridge boies' of Suffolk to expose and confute their works. But then again, perhaps they never issued him with a reader's ticket.

Drawing to a close, we are left with loose ends, tantalizing leads and much that is shrouded in obscurity. If this account has seemed to stress the play of personalities at the expense of a detailed analysis of Rogers's

---

1580s, Rogers had appealed a case into the consistory court in Norwich against one Robert Froste for unlawful detention of tithes. NRO, Con 3/1.

[80] NRO, Act/31, fo. 101r.

[81] BL, Add MS 38492, fol. 104. 'Mr Rogers sermon preached at Bury the 10 Dec. 1599'.

[82] Rogers, *Faith, doctrine, and religion*, preface. Cf. Kenneth L. Parker, *The English Sabbath: a Study of Doctrine and Discipline from the Reformation to the Civil War* (Cambridge, 1988), pp. 92–7.

substantive opposition to what he believed were the dangerous innovations of closet Presbyterians, a larger difficulty remains of assessing the ways in which clerical conformists like Rogers lived and worked with their nonconforming, or partially conforming colleagues. Given the prevalence and popularity of combination lectures throughout the country, the question takes on even greater force. Were combination lectures the occasion for harmonious clerical conference and collegiality or the context for bitter disputes for control between groups with ultimately differing goals for the Church? Both possibilities must have been present in every combination. Even though scripture spoke famously of 'love for the brethren' as a true mark of salvation, and the psalmist had likened the pleasant unity of brethren to precious ointment flowing down Aaron's garments, these sentiments were being increasingly hard pressed in the last decade of the Queen's reign.[83] And although Rogers, in the printed version of his sermon confuting Chaderton, used the term 'brethren' inclusively, speaking of 'two of our godlie brethren', this was to run against the tide for the term had been taken over in a new way by the polemicists. Led by Bancroft, the charge was now levelled that such usage smacked of a 'newe brotherhood' desirous of a pure discipline, 'thereby shewing themselves to be most notorious Schismatickes'.[84] This was certainly not the first time that 'brethren' possessed a polemical charge,[85] but from the early 1590s the term was politicized in a way that made it easier to think in terms of division rather than cohesion. But perhaps the very fact that the Bury exercise survived the 'nasty nineties' – not only the small explosions set off by Thomas Rogers in 1589 and 1599, but the 'sedicious Sermon' preached by Thomas Greenwood in the exercise on 20 September 1596[86] – and persisted well into the 1630s, attests to the truth of one of Collinson's arguments that the endurance of such lectures within diocesan structures reflected a Church 'still largely intact and sure of its integrity'.[87]

---

[83] 1 John 3:14; Psalm 133. Cf. Sears McGee, *The Godly Man in Stuart England* (New Haven, CT, and London, 1976), pp. 171–208.

[84] Richard Bancroft, *Daungerous positions and proceedings, published and practised within this Iland of Brytaine, under pretence of Reformation, and for the Presbiteriall Discipline* (London, 1593), pp. 120–24.

[85] Cf. its use disparaging early Protestants in John Craig, 'The "Christian Brethren" in Suffolk', in David Chadd (ed.), *Religious Dissent in East Anglia III* (Norwich, 1996), pp. 33–4.

[86] NRO, Act/31, fo. 133r.

[87] Patrick Collinson, 'Lectures by Combination', p. 497.

CHAPTER EIGHT

'A Glose of Godlines': Philip Stubbes, Elizabethan Grub Street and the invention of Puritanism

Alexandra Walsham

'Starch', declared Philip Stubbes in his notorious *Anatomie of Abuses* first published in 1583, was 'the devils liquore'. Used to stiffen the 'great and monsterous ruffes' flaunted by the fashion-conscious women of Elizabethan England, it was but 'one arch or piller wherby his kingdome' of pride and wickedness was 'underpropped'. Equally insupportable was that 'stinking Ydol', the maypole, erected and bedecked by rural parish communities each spring. The 'superintendent and Lord' over the 'cursed' and 'hethenical' games conducted beneath and around it was none other than 'Sathan, prince of hel'. As for the 'horrible Vice of pestiferous dauncing' – that 'quagmire or puddle of all abomination', that 'preparative to wantonnes', 'provocative to uncleanes', and 'introite to al kind of lewdenes' – it too 'sprang from the teates of the Devils brest, from whence all mischeef els dooth flow'.[1] Blustering invectives like these have made Stubbes something of a household name among early modern historians. His immoderate zeal against the customs and pastimes of 'Merrie England' has long marked him out as an arch-enemy of leisure, pleasure and 'popular culture'. Nineteenth-century literary critics saw him as a symbol of the 'sour' and 'splenetic spirit' of puritanism, a 'narrow-sould', strait-laced fanatic, the 'forerunner of that snarling satirist Prynne'.[2] Careless passing references in scholarly

---

[1] Philip Stubbes, *The Anatomie of Abuses: Containing A Discoverie, or Brief Summarie of ... Notable Vices and Corruptions*, ed. Frederick J. Furnivall (London, 1877–79), pp. 70, 51–2, 149, 168, 154, 169. All subsequent references are to Furnivall's text, which collates the four contemporary editions of 1583 (2), 1585 and 1595 (hereafter cited as Stubbes, *Anatomie*).

[2] These phrases can be found in the introduction to W. B. D. D. Turnbull's edition of the *Anatomie* (Edinburgh, 1836); Furnivall's defensive 'Forewords' to his edition, p. 36*; and T. F. Dibdin, *Bibliomania; or Book Madness* (London, 1811), pp. 366–7. I owe the latter reference to T. P. W. Pearson, who generously made available a copy of her unpublished MA dissertation on 'The Life and Works of Philip Stubbes' (Westfield College, University of London, 1958) and shared with me her valuable knowledge of Stubbes.

monographs, no less than in undergraduate essays, have perpetuated this impression up until the present day. He is regularly wheeled out by textbook writers and lecturers to play the part of the typical 'puritan' spoil-sport and killjoy.[3]

In this chapter, however, I want to suggest that Philip Stubbes is a far more shadowy, amphibious and interesting individual. Careful investigation reveals a man whose motivations and convictions are by no means as transparent as they initially appear, a man who in some ways seems more at home among the denizens of the Elizabethan literary underworld than in the select circles of godly preachers and laypeople forever striving for assurance of their own salvation and fraught with scruples of conscience about a church they regarded as 'but halfly reformed'. Indeed, it reveals a man who challenges enduring clichés about the starkly antagonistic relationship between these two milieu. Stubbes, as we shall see, is a slippery figure who stubbornly defies categorization, but his career still may have much to tell us about the dynamic process of religious identity formation and labelling in the post-Reformation period, and about what Patrick Collinson has recently described as the 'invention or reinvention of puritanism' in the last decade of Elizabeth's reign.

I

We know remarkably little about Philip Stubbes's life and lineage. The bare biographical details which can be gleaned from the prefaces and title-pages of his books, supplemented by snippets of information from parish registers and other contemporary sources, leave us with only a very partial picture. Stubbes was probably born in the 1550s, possibly in Cheshire in the Congleton area, where the surname was common, and where, before 1586, he appears to have been in possession of a messuage or tenement. Although he invariably styled himself 'Gentleman' in his published works, this may have been mere literary pretension, and it seems far more likely that he ranked among the 'middling sort'. While his family background remains all too obscure, the suggestion

---

[3] For only a few recent examples, see William Hunt, *The Puritan Moment: the Coming of Revolution in an English County* (Cambridge, MA, 1983), p. 69; David Underdown, *Revel, Riot and Rebellion: Popular Politics and Culture in England 1603–1660* (Oxford, 1987), p. 48; Ronald Hutton, *The Rise and Fall of Merry England: the Ritual Year 1400–1700* (Oxford, 1994), pp. 131–2; David Cressy and Lori Anne Ferrell (eds), *Religion and Society in Early Modern England: a Sourcebook* (London, 1996), pp. 105–7.

that he was a near relative of John Stubbs, author of that explosive protest against the Anjou match, *The Discoverie of a Gaping Gulf* (1579), can be swiftly dismissed.[4] His education is also rather a mystery. Anthony Wood stated that Stubbes had studied for a time at both universities, but being 'a restless and hot head' left them without obtaining a degree. Yet there is no record of his matriculating at either Oxford or Cambridge, and he is elsewhere alleged to have been 'nourst up onely at Grammer schoole'.[5] This would have been sufficient to supply him with the smattering of Latin and Greek and the repertoire of classical proverbs he paraded proudly in his books. It is not until 1586 that any incontrovertible facts can be established about his home life: in that year, a resident of the parish of St Mary at Hill, he was licensed to marry one Katherine Emmes, a spinster living with her mother and stepfather, and daughter of a substantial citizen and cordwainer of Fleet Street, St Dunstan in the West, recently deceased. His wife, who was no more than 15 on her wedding day, died four years later, shortly after giving birth to a son at Burton-on-Trent in Staffordshire.[6] By 1592 he seems to have been living once again in London, from whence he set out on a three-month tour of England on horseback to acquaint himself with 'the maners and dispositions of the people' and to inspect the schools, almshouses, highways, churches and other ancient monuments which 'our good Ancestors have left behind them'. This journey, which was undertaken 'partly for my private pleasure and recreation' and 'partly for avoidance of the plague', provided Stubbes with the raw material for his long commentary on the cold charity of his age, *A Motive to Good Workes* (1593). In November of that year he can be found 'lodging by Cheape side' and in 1595 he 'corrected and inlarged'

---

[4] See the accounts in Anthony Wood, *Athenae Oxonienses*, ed. Philip Bliss (4 vols, London, 1813–20), vol. 1, pp. 645–7; *DNB*, s.n. Philip Stubbes, 'puritan pamphleteer'. Both are unreliable on a number of points. For the Congleton tenement, see the bond cited in the 'Foretalk' to Philip Stubbes, *The Second Part of the Anatomie of Abuses, Containing the Display of Corruptions*, ed. Frederick J. Furnivall (London, 1882), p. xxv† (hereafter Stubbes, *The Display of Corruptions*). This refers to him as of Benefeild or Beningfeilde in Northamptonshire. [John Stubbs], *The Discoverie of a Gaping Gulf Where into England is like to be swallowed by an other French marriage* ([London], 1579).

[5] Wood, *Athenae Oxonienses*, vol. 1, p. 645; Cuthbert Cunny-catcher, *The Defence of Conny–Catching* (London, 1592), sig. C4v.

[6] The marriage licence and the entry of John Stubbes's baptism in the parish register of Burton-on-Trent are transcribed in Furnivall's 'Forewords' to Stubbes, *Anatomie*, p. 51*. A record of Katherine's burial has been inserted by a different hand between the lines of the Burton-on-Trent register on the day of her death, 14 December 1590. It seems likely that this was a later interpolation. I owe this point to Terry Pearson.

the fourth edition of his *Anatomie*. After 1610 he disappears from the historical record completely.[7]

However else he occupied his time and supported his household, during the early 1580s and early 1590s Stubbes carved out a career for himself as a semi-professional writer. Eight of his works are extant, and the titles of three others can be traced in booksellers' lists and the Stationers' register. Stubbes's earliest writings were in verse: a pair of moralistic poems about God's 'wunderfull' and 'undeferred' judgements on impenitent offenders and a metrical jeremiad entitled *A View of Vanitie, and Allarum to England*. His prose publications range from patriotic anti-Catholic pamphlets and tracts like *The Theater of the Popes Monarchie* and *The Intended Treason, of Doctor Parrie*, through miniature collections of prayers and meditations such as his *Perfect Pathway to Felicitie*, to the colourful catalogue of complaint for which he is now most famous. Augmented and reprinted four times in the 12 years after its first appearance, the *Anatomie* was soon joined by a sequel subtitled *The Display of Corruptions*. This, however, was not Stubbes's most successful work. *A Christal Glasse for Christian Women*, a pious account of the godly life and untimely death of his teenage bride, ran through at least 28 impressions to 1664 and established itself as one of the most popular religious chapbooks of the later seventeenth century, becoming part of the stock-in-trade of Restoration publishers like William Thackeray.[8]

---

[7] Philip Stubbes, *A Motive to Good Workes* (London, 1593), sigs A3r–6r. The possibility that Stubbes was alive in 1610 is inferred from the enlarged edition of his *A Perfect Pathway to Felicitie* (London, 1592) which appeared in that year.

[8] See STC 23376–99.7: *Two wunderfull and rare examples of the undeferred judgement of God* (London, [1581]). *The Theater of the Popes Monarchie* (London, 1585); *The Intended Treason, of Doctor Parrie. With a Letter from the Pope* (London, [1585]); *A Perfect Pathway to Felicitie, Conteining Godly Meditations, and Prayers* (London, 1592); *The Anatomie of Abuses* (London, 1583, 2 edns, 1585, 1595); *The Display of Corruptions* (London, 1583, 2 edns); *A Christal Glasse for Christian Women. Contayning an Excellent Discourse, of the Life and Death of Katherine Stubbes* (London, 1591). For post-1640 editions, see Wing S6074–7. For its presence in the stock of William Thackeray *c.* 1689, see Margaret Spufford, *Small Books and Pleasant Histories : Popular Fiction and its Readership in Seventeenth-Century England* (Cambridge, 1981), p. 266. Terry Pearson informs me that 27 editions are extant, the last dating between 1709 and 1714. *The View of Vanitie, and Allarum to England, or Retrait from Sinne* (London, 1582) is no longer extant, but is listed in Andrew Maunsell, *The First Part of the Catalogue of English Printed Bookes* (London, 1595), p. 111, along with another lost book by Stubbes entitled *The Rosarie of Christian Praiers and Meditations for Divers Purposes, and also at Divers Times, as well of the Day as of the Night* (London, 1583), p. 87. The latter was assigned and reprinted in 1594: Edward Arber (ed.), *A Transcript of the Registers of the Company of Stationers of London 1554–1640 A.D.* (5 vols, London, 1875–94), vol. 2, p. 651 (hereafter *SR*). Wood, *Athenae Oxoniensis*, vol. 1, p. 646, adds

Stubbes dedicated several of his books to godly magistrates and leading lights among the Protestant nobility and gentry, though in a world
in which the exercise of patronage was rapidly changing these dedications do not necessarily provide evidence of the social networks in
which he moved. While Mr and Mrs William Milward, who bore 'the
whole charges' of printing his *Perfect Pathway*, may have been personal
friends, Cuthbert Buckle, Lord Mayor of London, and the Essex
puritan magnate, Robert Lord Rich, later 1st Earl of Warwick, are more
likely to have been people he respected from afar than people he actually knew.[9] These men make strange bedfellows with Philip Howard,
Earl of Arundel, a suspected Catholic soon to be under house arrest and
interrogated regarding the Throckmorton Plot, to whom he humbly
presented both parts of his *Anatomie*. Why Stubbes did so is still
something of a puzzle and it sits uneasily alongside the fact that he
wrote eight Latin lines on the 'Papist Bloodsuckers or Leeches' which
appeared among the commendatory poems prefixed to the 1583 edition
of Foxe's *Actes and Monuments*. It is possible that these may disclose a
slight acquaintance with the great martyrologist, but overall it is clear
that he was not well connected.[10]

Stern moralist, strongly committed Protestant and ardent social reformer and critic, Stubbes was a layman whose writings read like those
of contemporary preachers and practical divines. Signing himself 'Thine
in the Lord', he certainly sought to present himself as firmly on their
side, a stalwart ally of the clergy in the battle between piety and profanity he perceived to be taking place at the heart of the Elizabethan book
trade. He thundered against the bawdy ballads, scurrilous books and
'hethnical pamphlets of toyes & bableries' which daily poured from the
presses: these were 'invented & excogitat by Belzebub, written by
Lucifer, licensed by Pluto, printed by Cerberus, & set a-broche to sale
by the infernal furies themselves, to the poysoning of the whole world'.
Better esteemed and more quickly snapped up from the stalls in Paul's

---

to Stubbes's output an undated work entitled *Praise and Commendation of Women*,
which also cannot now be traced.

[9] Dedications to *Perfect Pathway*, esp. sig. ¶4r; *Motive to Good Workes* and *The
Theater of the Popes Monarchie*.

[10] Dedications to *Anatomie* and *The Display of Corruptions* (not included in the
Furnivall edition). In the latter he claims to have received 'bountifull remuneration' from
Arundel (sig. A4r). The 1595 edition of the *Anatomie* was rededicated to the 'Christian
Magistrates and godly Governors of England'. 'In sanguisugas Papistas, Philippus Stubbes'
in John Foxe, *Actes and Monuments* (London, 1583), unpaginated prefatory matter. (I
am grateful to Dr Thomas Freeman for a discussion on this point.) Stubbes also wrote an
epistle recommending H. D[od?]'s *A Godlie and Fruitfull Treatise of Faith and Workes*
(London, 1583) to 'the Christian reader', sig. A4r.

Churchyard than the 'godlyest and sagest' treatises, they corrupted men's minds, infected their souls and brought them to the gulf of destruction. All who played a part in their production had the blood of those who thereby perished on their hands and would answer for it at the Last Judgement.[11] Here Stubbes was echoing a polemical commonplace. It was a clerical convention to condemn cheap print as the product and embodiment of the irreligious culture that revolved around the tavern and alehouse, a tool of the Pope to keep the populace imprisoned in superstition and ignorance and a ploy of the devil to undermine the efficacy of that supreme organ of Protestant evangelism, the sermon. He vocally dissociated himself from the 'drunken sockets and bawdye parasits' who peddled these wares and the motley crew of pot poets and scribblers from whose pens such ephemera so readily flowed.[12]

And yet there is much to suggest that Stubbes had closer links with an emerging breed of untalented hacks, freelance journalists and 'Englishers' of foreign news than he cared, or was publicly prepared, to admit. In a context in which capitalism and the new technology of print was transforming the book into a profitable commodity and gradually liberating the profession of letters from near total dependence on aristocratic patronage, dozens of aspiring writers flocked to the metropolis. Some, like Gabriel Harvey and Thomas Nashe, achieved a measure of fame and artistic autonomy, but most were forced into a form of literary prostitution to the unrefined tastes of the reading public in order to eke out a living. Sacrificing their self-respect for the sake of security, many became the hirelings of entrepreneurial publishers like John Wolfe and John Danter, turning out catchpenny tracts in return for (at most) 40 shillings and a bottle of inferior wine.[13]

These writers were no less notorious for their facile versatility than their dissolute tippling. 'Red-nosed rhymsters' like William Elderton and Thomas Deloney could as quickly compose sonnets about the

---

[11] Stubbes, *Anatomie*, pp. 185–6.

[12] For some examples, see Edward Dering, *A Briefe and Necessary Instruction* (London, 1572), sig. A2v; T[homas] W[hite], *A Sermon Preached at Pawles Crosse* (London, 1578), sigs A3r–v; Laurence Chaderton, *An Excellent and Godly Sermon* (London, 1580), sig. A3r. Stubbes, *Anatomie*, p. 171.

[13] See generally Phoebe Sheavyn, *The Literary Profession in the Elizabethan Age*, ed. J. W. Saunders (Manchester, 1967), esp. chs 3–5; Edwin Haviland Miller, *The Professional Writer in Elizabethan England* (Cambridge, MA, 1959), esp. p. 154 and chs 5, 7; Sandra Clark, *The Elizabethan Pamphleteers: Popular Moralistic Pamphlets 1580–1640* (London, 1983), introduction; and Lawrence Manley, *Literature and Culture in Early Modern England* (Cambridge, 1995), esp. ch. 6. For Nashe and Harvey, Charles Nicholl, *A Cup of News: The Life of Thomas Nashe* (London, 1984) and Virginia F. Stern, *Gabriel Harvey: his Life, Marginalia and Library* (Oxford, 1979), pt 1.

divine penalties dealt out to evildoers as merry jests and unctuous love-songs, and the same was true of those who specialized in prose. Educated celebrities denounced the hypocrisy of these 'three halfpenny pamphleteers' who wrote solemn commentaries on earthquakes, storms and monstrous births and chauvinistic exposés of Catholic conspiracies, Italianate romances and racy tales of the exploits of rogues and playboys – all with equal speed and ease. Many authors, including Anthony Munday, also had a foot in the door of the increasingly sophisticated and commercialized world of the theatre. Second-rate playwrights often had to resort to translation and other types of literary hackwork to supplement their income, or find a temporary substitute for it when dramatic entertainments were suspended due to the outbreak of plague. Perhaps most demeaning of all was the preparation of 'scissors and paste books' – compilations of extracts from other works, roughly stitched together and sent to the press with precipitate haste. Some were employed by unscrupulous stationers such as John Trundle to update stale news or edit and repackage old books simply by adding a fresh preface or epistle. The term Thomas Dekker coined to describe these exploitative tricks and techniques was 'falconry' and they drew forth many expressions of snobbish contempt from the self-styled literati.[14]

But the fact is that many of these Masters of Arts were hardly less flexible and mercenary themselves: Robert Greene 'yarkt' up repentance tracts as well as cony-catching pamphlets and Nashe too could turn his hand from social satire and novelistic burlesque to the dour apocalyptic didacticism of *Christs Teares over Jerusalem*, which literary scholars now regard as the low point of his career. Sometimes the supercilious scorn these wits poured on lesser writers was a blatant form of self-advertisement, designed to draw attention to their own verbal ingenuity. As Lawrence Manley has argued, it was also a symptom of anxiety about their own marginal status in an urban environment where traditional social relationships were in a profound state of flux.[15]

It is probably in this light that we should interpret the disparaging remarks about Philip Stubbes made by Nashe and Harvey in the course of their famous flyting in the early 1590s. Each invoked him among the

---

[14] In addition to the works cited above, see my 'Aspects of Providentialism in Early Modern England' (PhD, Cambridge, 1995), pp. 31–49, 74 (shortly to be published as *Providence in Early Modern England* by Oxford University Press). For Munday, see Celeste Turner, *Anthony Mundy: an Elizabethan Man of Letters* (Berkeley, CA, 1928). For Trundle, see Gerald D. Johnson, 'John Trundle and the Book-Trade 1603–1626', *Studies in Bibliography*, 39 (1986), pp. 177–99. Thomas Dekker, *The Non-Dramatic Works*, ed. A. B. Grosart (London, 1884–66), pp. 224–46.

[15] See Charles W. Crupi, *Robert Greene* (Boston, 1986), esp. ch. 2; Nicholl, *A Cup of News*, esp. chs 11–12; Manley, *Literature and Culture*, p. 322 and ch. 6 *passim*.

'common Pamfletters of London' as a weapon with which to deflate and discredit the other. In *Strange Newes* (1592), Nashe classed him with a troupe of drunken rhymsters and clowns whom, he claimed, had far more literary ability than Master Harvey, pretentious former fellow of Pembroke College in Cambridge. 'Hough Thomas Delone, Phillip Stubs, Robert Armin, &c. Your father Elderton is abus'd'. 'One cup of perfect bonaventure licour will inspire you with more wit and Schollership than hee hath thrust into his whole packet of Letters.' In *Pierces Supererogation* (1593) Harvey turned the tables and insisted that it was Nashe who could not compete with this 'rablement of botchers in Print'. Nashe disdained them 'bicause they stand in his way, hinder his scribling traffique, [and] obscure his resplendishing Fame'.[16]

Through these acid exchanges and oblique attacks we catch a glimpse of a rather different side to Stubbes's character than that which emerges from a superficial glance at his entry in the *Short-title Catalogue* – a Stubbes whose natural habitat appears to have been Elizabethan Grub Street rather than the godly household and vicarage parlour. There is no reason to suppose that Nashe and Harvey were doing more than slightly embellishing the truth in the interests of stirring up their acerbic dispute. Nor, I think, should the allegations Nashe made in his *Anatomie of Absurditie* (1589) be dismissed as spiteful aspersions with no foundation in fact. In this youthful, euphuistic lampoon, Nashe singled out Stubbes and his *Anatomie of Abuses* for a satirical beating, alluding to him in a long passage inveighing against those 'who make the Presse the dunghill whether they carry all the muck of their mellancholicke imaginations, pretending forsooth to anatomize abuses and stubbe up sin by the rootes'. Such men, he declared, assumed 'a coloured shew of zeale', 'a glose of godlines' and 'a pretence of puritie'. Though they 'never tasted of anything save the excrements of Artes' and their 'thredde-bare knowledge' was 'bought at the second hand', though 'the sum of their divinitie' consisted in 'two pennie Catichismes', still they presumed to enquire 'most curiouslie into every corner of the Commonwealth' and reprehend vices 'wherwith they are corrupted themselves'.[17] Even when due allowance is made for rhetorical hyperbole, we are confronted with a Philip Stubbes of considerable ambivalence. His individual works now demand closer inspection.

---

[16] Thomas Nashe, *Strange Newes, of the Intercepting Certaine Letters* (London, 1592) reprinted in R. B. McKerrow (ed.), *The Works of Thomas Nashe* (5 vols, Oxford, 1958), vol. 1, p. 280; Gabriel Harvey, *Pierces Supererogation Or A New Prayse of the Old Asse* (London, 1593), reprinted in *The Works of Gabriel Harvey, D. C. L.* (3 vols, London, 1884–85), vol. 2, pp. 280–81.

[17] Thomas Nashe, *The Anatomie of Absurditie* (London, 1589), reprinted in *Works*, vol. 1, pp. 19–22.

II

Stubbes's first entrée into the world of print seems to have been a six-page pamphlet containing two ballads about the supernatural punishments visited upon stiff-necked sinners. One related the story of Joan Bowser, a callous and covetous dame from Castle Donnington in Leicestershire who refused to forgive a poor man his debt as he lay on his deathbed and was subsequently haunted by Satan in the guise of 'the sayd John Twell, in corporall lyneament', who smote her as he vanished out of her horrified sight. Thereupon 'her whole body became as black as pitche', 'replenished with filthy scurffe' and disgorging 'dregges most fettulent ... which modestie ... commaunds me not to penne'. The second told of the 'thunderbolt of dread' which had recently befallen a foul-mouthed young servingman from Boothby near Grantham who habitually swore by God's blood and died with his own gushing from all his orifices and joints.[18] These dreadful ditties were typical of the cautionary tales published in profusion in the Elizabethan and early Stuart period to satisfy the thirst of the sensation-seeking populace. Godly Protestants by no means claimed a monopoly on gory anecdotes of retributive justice of this kind. Even renowned collections like Thomas Beard's *Theatre of Gods Judgements* (1597) drew examples from the popular yellow press,[19] as did later editions of Stubbes's own *Anatomie*. Not only did he incorporate the fate of the Lincolnshire blasphemer whose 'tragicall discourse I myself penned about two yeares agoe', but a number of other fascinating cases of moral delinquents receiving their just rewards which had already been narrated in cheap pamphlets and broadsides. These included the sordid ends of Anne Averies, a widow who denied stealing a ball of twine, and seven Swabian drunkards who lived to regret the day they invoked the devil in their oaths.[20] Stubbes seems to have taken the trouble of obtaining the

---

[18] Stubbes, *Two wunderfull and rare examples*, quotations at sigs B3v–4r, A3v, B1v. The well-known ballad scholar and literary forger J. P. Collier claimed to have owned a copy of a broadside relating the fate of the swearer, which he reprinted in his *Broadside Black-letter Ballads* (London, 1868), pp. 42–7, but which does not appear to survive. It is possible, however, that this is simply another instance of Collier sleight of hand, though note Furnivall's 'Forewords' to the *Anatomie*, p. 57*.

[19] Walsham, 'Aspects of Providentialism', pp. 73–4 and ch. 2 *passim*.

[20] Stubbes, *Anatomie*, p. 135. For Anne Averies and the Swabian drunkards, see pp. 136 and 111–13 respectively. Stubbes probably derived these stories from the lost pamphlet of 1576 referred to in Edmund Bicknoll, *A Swoord Agaynst Swearyng* (London, 1579), fol. 36r–v and the ballad entered in *SR*, vol. 2, p. 354. For other similar insertions and their sources, see Terry P. Pearson, 'The Composition and Development of Phillip Stubbes's "Anatomie of Abuses"', *Modern Language Review*, 56 (1961), pp. 321–32.

signatures of witnesses to the two incidents he immortalized in doggerel verse,[21] but the second bears too remarkable a resemblance to an episode recounted in the Brigittine monk of Syon Abbey Richard Whytforde's *Werke for Housholders* [1531?] for it to be a mere coincidence. This Henrician exemplum was also about an inveterate swearer, one Mr Baryngton from the Hertfordshire village of Standon who likewise expired unshriven with blood pouring from his ears, eyes, nose, wrists and 'his navyll and foundement'.[22] Some might explain the similarities as the consequence of unconscious oral transmission; an alternative interpretation is that Stubbes borrowed the basic structure of the story, embellished it with fresh details and altered the names and dates. Protestant ministers themselves did not scruple to 'improve' providential tales to make them more edifying; nor were they above plundering the homiletic literature of the Roman Catholic era for compelling cases from which doctrinally incompatible elements could be silently excised. But the active recycling of motifs from medieval hagiographical and devotional literature was also a practice employed by a number of opportunistic publishers in this period, and the inferior wordsmiths who were their subordinates.[23]

Equally suggestive of Stubbes's status as one of the 'common Pamfletters of London' is his short account of *The Intended Treason, of Dr Parrie*, probably published in the immediate wake of the assassination scare in 1585. Printed for Henry Carr, a specialist in ephemera, this black-letter tract shows tell-tale signs of the hurried composition that was a hallmark of the work of hacks. A patriotic denunciation of the infernal designs of the 'traiterous papists' and 'the Pope that great Antechriste, and rose coullored whore of Roome', it is indistinguishable from the dozens of rabidly anti-Catholic reports of plots and treasons which appeared during Elizabeth's reign. Authors like Anthony Munday fed the insatiable public appetite for these jingoistic effusions with quarto and octavo pamphlets about Edmund Campion and the Babington

---

[21] BL, MS Lansdowne MS 819, fol. 87r. The author of the *DNB* entry suggests that this note is evidence that legal proceedings were instituted against Stubbes by Joan Bowser. This mistake derives from the fact that it follows two folios (85r–86r) of legal opinions disputing the validity of the statute upon which John Stubbs and his associates were prosecuted for the publication of *The Gaping Gulfe*.

[22] Richard Whytforde, *A Werke for Housholders* ([London, 1531?]), sigs C3v–4r. Stubbes may have drawn on the version of this story recounted in Stephen Batman, *The doome warning all men to the judgemente* (London, 1581), p. 418.

[23] Walsham, 'Aspects of Providentialism', pp. 70 and n. 33, 78–9. Cf. Roger Chartier's revealing case study of this process at work in two French pamphlets: 'The Hanged Woman Miraculously Saved: an *Occasionnel*', in R. Chartier (ed.), *The Culture of Print: Power and the Uses of Print in Early Modern Europe* (Cambridge, 1989), pp. 59–91.

conspirators;[24] and the same species of bigotry found an outlet in scurrilous descriptions of the political, ecclesiastical and sexual corruptions of the papacy and priesthood. Stubbes's own *The Theater of the Popes Monarchie* was a publication in this vein – full of Foxeian platitudes about the late medieval church as 'the synagogue of Satan' and the Pope as a proud usurper, 'cruel Tartarian' and 'gresie prelate' and outrageous allegations concerning the 'uncleane Lives' of the College of Cardinals, bishops, monks, begging friars and 'dounghill Jesuites'.[25] This, like other books of its kind, had minimal theological content, but *A Motive to Good Workes* shows Stubbes manipulating polemical commonplaces about purgatory and salvation by faith alone adeptly enough. As for his lost work, the *View of Vanitie, or Alarum to England*, there can be little doubt that this was an entirely conventional exhortation to the nation to prove itself worthy of God's mercies and avoid annihilation by repenting its sins. Such 'warnings', 'lanthornes' and 'larum bells' were a well-established formula of balladmongers from the 1560s onwards – not to mention pamphleteers, playwrights and preachers. It was not difficult to mimic the national morality sermons delivered from Paul's Cross nearly every week and distil their familiar message into verse or prose. Semi-professional writers, among whom Stubbes seems to have numbered, slavishly imitated the homiletic discourse of the London clergy.[26]

They also took full advantage of the vogue for portable books of private devotion. It is becoming increasingly clear that tiny collections of scriptural sentences and spiritual meditations were not the work of men in holy orders alone. The publication of these duo- and sextodecimo manuals – which merit no mention in Dr Tessa Watt's magisterial survey of cheap religious print – appears to have been as much the product of an alliance between piety and profit as the 'penny godlinesses' pioneered by the ballad partner John Wright in the 1620s.[27] Stubbes was one of a number of laymen who assembled miniature

---

[24] Stubbes, *The Intended Treason, of Doctor Parrie*, quotations at sig. A2r–v. Similar publications by Munday include *A breefe and true reporte, of the execution of certaine traytours at Tiborne* (London, 1582); *A breefe discourse of the taking of Edmund Campion* (London, 1581); and *A watch-woord to Englande to beware of traytours* (London, 1584).

[25] Stubbes, *The Theater of the Popes Monarchie*, quotations at sigs A3r, A7r, A8r, H3v (sic 2v).

[26] See Walsham, 'Aspects of Providentialism', p. 267 and the references cited therein; E. D. Mackerness, '"Christes Teares" and the Literature of Warning', *English Studies*, 33 (1952), pp. 251–4.

[27] Tessa Watt, *Cheap Print and Popular Piety, 1550–1640* (Cambridge, 1991), ch. 8, esp. pp. 303–15.

compilations of prayers fit for 'divers purposes' and 'times', and suitable for hanging from a girdle or slipping into a capacious pocket. Such compilations were the accessories of the fashionably pious. His *Perfect Pathway* can be compared with John Phillips's little handbook with an almost identical title dated 1588 and *Crumms of Comfort*, an early Stuart favourite which was the brainchild of the bookseller Michael Sparke.[28] The anonymous *Godly Garden* first printed by Henry Middleton in 1574 also appears to have had a businessman rather than a minister behind it.[29] All these small books are close cousins of the *Flowers, Pomanders* and *Preparatives to Prayer* put together by Protestant reformers and vicars such as Thomases Becon and Tymme, as well as the semi-official primers produced by John Day. Like them, they adapt traditional Catholic materials to new ideological conditions, while preserving the distinctive rhythms of an older devotional idiom.[30] Stubbes's *Rosarie* and *Perfect Pathway* need to be seen as part of a wider attempt to tap the growing market for 'guides to godliness' and 'helps unto devotion' among the 'middling' and 'common sort'. Even that jack-of-all-literary-trades, Anthony Munday, can be found publishing a *Godly Exercise for Christian Families, containing an order of Praiers for Morning and Evening, with a little Catechisme between the man & his wife* in 1586.[31]

In view of what we have discovered so far, conventional assessments of Philip Stubbes's bestselling book, *A Christal Glasse for Christian Women*, begin to seem just a little too straightforward. This is generally regarded as an early example of the kind of godly life by which Samuel Clarke, curate of St Bennet Fink, later made his name, and linked with the edifying biographies appended to funeral sermons printed following the death of notable seventeenth-century puritans – in particular that of

---

[28] The *Perfect Pathway* was 16mo and the *Rosarie* was 12mo. John Phillips, *The Perfect Path to Paradise: Contayning Divers Most Ghostly and Wholsome Prayers* (London, 1588); Michael Sparke, *Crumms of Comfort* (6th edn, London 1627), the first extant edition.

[29] *A Godly Garden out of the which most Comfortable Herbs May be Gathered* (London, 1574).

[30] Thomas Becon, [*The Flower of Godly Prayers*] (London, [*c.* 1550]); Thomas Becon, *The Pomander of Prayer* (London, 1558); Thomas Tymme, *The Poore Mans Pater Noster, with a Preparative to Prayer* (London, 1598); Robert Hill, *The Pathway to Prayer, and Pietie* (1609; retitled version of a tract of 1606). For primers and prayer-books, see Helen C. White, *The Tudor Books of Private Devotion* (Madison, 1951) and Eamon Duffy, 'Continuity and Divergence in Tudor Religion', in R. N. Swanson (ed.), *Unity and Diversity in the Church* (SCH, 32, 1996), pp. 187–205.

[31] See Louis B. Wright, *Middle-Class Culture in Elizabethan England* (Chapel Hill, 1935), ch. 8. Munday's *Godly Exercise* is now lost, but is listed in Maunsell, *Catalogue*, p. 86.

Katherine Brettergh, sister of the godly Cheshire squire John Bruen, who died in 1601 at the age of just 22.[32]

And certainly Stubbes's obituary of his 19-year-old spouse does share many of their salient features. The first part narrates her parentage, childhood and early married life, emphasizing her modesty, courtesy and kindness as a mistress and her meek humility as a wife, but highlighting above all the 'fervent zeale' which she bore to the Gospel. Rarely would one find her 'without a Bible, or some other good booke in her Hands' and she abstained soberly from foolish pastimes, pride of apparel, idle gossip and gluttonous indulgence in 'strong drinke' and 'delicate meates'. Katherine Stubbes, in short, was 'a perfect paterne of true Christianitie' and 'a mirrour of womanhood'. Next we are told of the lingering sickness which followed the birth of her son ('a quotidian ague' she correctly prophesied would be fatal), along with various 'glorious visions' she experienced and her homiletic exhortations to the kith and kin who clustered round her deathbed. Spying her pet puppy lying on the coverlet, she sternly pushed it away and lamented her former 'vanity' in loving it. The following section is a thoroughly Protestant, if not positively Calvinist confession of faith. 'Set downe word for word as Shee Spake', so the title-page claims, it covers the resurrection of the body and fate of the soul, predestination, the sacraments and the tenet of *sola scriptura*. Good works are denounced as 'filthie dung' and she is equally vehement against transubstantiation and the invocation of saints. Finally we are treated to an account of her heroic combat with Satan and 'valiant conquest' of 'the same by the power of Christ' very much in the manner of the *Ars moriendi* and morality plays of the late Middle Ages.[33]

This element of continuity with the Catholic past needs to be stressed.[34] So too does the implicit parallel with the lives of the saints: Katherine

---

[32] It is discussed in these terms in Ralph Houlbrooke, 'The Puritan Death-bed, *c.* 1560–*c.* 1660', in Christopher Durston and Jacqueline Eales (eds), *The Culture of English Puritanism, 1560–1700* (Basingstoke, 1996), pp. 122–44. Cf. the lives of Mrs Jane Ratcliffe, Mrs Margaret Ducke, Mrs Margaret Corbet and Mrs Elizabeth Wilkinson in Samuel Clarke, *The Lives of Thirty-Two English Divines* (3rd edn, London 1677), pp. 377–91, 408–13, 414–18, 419–29; and *The Christian Life and Death of Mistris Katherin Brettergh*, appended to William Harrison, *Deaths Advantage Little Regarded, and the Soules Solace against Sorrow. Preached in Two Funerall Sermons at Childwal in Lancashire* (2nd edn, London, 1602), reprinted separately in 1612, and later incorporated into Clarke. My thinking about the *Christal Glasse* has been assisted by an unpublished essay by Jason Yiannakhou of Queens' College, Cambridge, and I am grateful to him for sharing it with me.

[33] Stubbes, *A Christal Glasse for Christian Women* (1612 edn), quotations at sigs A2v, A3r, A3v, A4v, title-page, B2v, and B3r (*sic* C3r).

[34] For the medieval *Ars moriendi*, see Eamon Duffy, *The Stripping of the Altars: Traditional Religion in England 1400–1580* (New Haven, CT, and London, 1992), ch. 9, esp.

Stubbes helped fill the gap left by the banishment of holy women like Bridget of Sweden and Catherine of Siena from the Reformed universe. Along with Anne Askew and the Duchess of Suffolk, she met the need for new Protestant heroines. Her biography, moreover, assimilated some of medieval hagiography's most distinctive motifs: trances, prophecies and temporary transcendence of the inferior status patriarchal society imposed upon the 'weaker sex' in that liminal phase between life and death. The 'filthie cur' ascetically ejected from Katherine's affections also has literary and legendary forbears: it curiously echoes the stories which circulated about the Renaissance magus Henry Cornelius Agrippa, who allegedly dismissed his black spaniel on his deathbed with the words 'Depart from me thou wicked beast, which hath destroyed me.' Symbolizing Agrippa's renunciation of the occult sciences, the repudiation of the dog (alias familiar spirit or demon) was an allegory of triumph over the Tempter and a theme with a venerable heritage.[35]

The later accounts of pious puritan ladies which Stubbes's tract fore-shadows have essentially the same narrative structure. They too depict not so much a person as a paragon. Synthesizing personal details with prescribed traits, they present paradigms of ideal feminine behaviour as laid out in contemporary conduct books – they are in a sense guides to living, and dying, well.[36] It is a curious and significant fact that Philip Stubbes's book seems, as Patrick Collinson once remarked in a foot-note, to have inaugurated a literary fad. It shaped and perhaps even sparked off a genre later appropriated and dominated by ordained Protestant ministers, who gradually remoulded it in line with the classi-cal encomium.[37] This apparent pattern of development has some

---

pp. 313–27. Michael MacDonald and Terence R. Murphy argue that Protestants incorpo-rated the tropes and imagery of medieval moralities into Reformed religious psychology: *Sleepless Souls: Suicide in Early Modern England* (Oxford, 1990), esp. pp. 35–6.

[35] Watt, *Cheap Print and Popular Piety*, pp. 90–96. Nor is the *Christal Glasse* so far removed from the water-poet John Taylor's *Life and Death of … the Virgin Mary* (1620). This was based on 'an old printed Booke in prose' he had acquired in Antwerp and out of which he had '(like a Bee) suck't the sacred hony of the best authorities of Scriptures', leaving 'the poyson of Antichristianisme to those where I found it': sig. A5r–v. For Agrippa, see the preface to James Sanford's translation of *Of the Vanitie and Uncertaintie of Artes and Sciences* (London, 1569), fo. 3v. I am grateful to Terry Pearson and my colleague Gareth Roberts for discussions on this point.

[36] Jacqueline Eales, 'Samuel Clarke and the "Lives" of Godly Women in Seventeenth-Century England', in W. J. Sheils and Diana Wood (eds), *Women in the Church* (SCH, 27, 1990), pp. 365–76; Alison Wall, 'Elizabethan Precept and Feminine Practice: the Thynne Family of Longleat', *History*, 75 (1990), pp. 23–7.

[37] Patrick Collinson, '"A Magazine of Religious Patterns": an Erasmian Topic Trans-posed in English Protestantism', in P. Collinson, *Godly People: Essays on English Protestantism and Puritanism* (London, 1983), p. 523 n.110 and *passim*.

interesting similarities with the process by which puritan clergymen hijacked the popular murder pamphlet and adapted it for evangelical ends.[38] Reissued by mid-seventeenth-century publishers who inherited it as part of their stock and widely alluded to in plays as a standard item in the pedlar's pack, *A Christal Glasse* may testify to a far more intimate and intricate relationship between clerical propaganda and 'popular literature' than many historians tend to assume.[39]

And so we come at last to the *Anatomie of Abuses*, upon which Stubbes's modern reputation almost solely rests. Framed as a dialogue between Philoponus (who has just spent seven years touring the exotic island of Ailgna) and Spudeus (a passive listener who supplies the chief interlocutor with cues), the book is a thinly disguised diatribe against the customs, manners and vices of the inhabitants of his own native England. This fictional device, which Stubbes dispensed with in the edition of 1595, permitted him to take up the pose of a detached anthropological observer and thereby provide us with one of the richest and most vivid of all evocations of that world of May games, Lords of Misrule and parish wakes and ales, which we have now lost – the generic link between Protestant polemic against pastimes and later antiquarianism like John Aubrey's *Remaines of Gentilisme and Judaisme* should not be overlooked. The *Anatomie* is a highly readable account of Elizabethan fashions, sexual habits, linguistic and behavioural conventions, and forms of sociability and seasonal festivity – and it sometimes betrays more than a hint of relish at the salacious details it is hell-bent on denouncing. Space permits a single example:

> What clipping, what culling, what kissing and bussing, what smouching & slabbering one of another, what filthie groping and uncleane handling is not practised every wher in these dauncings? yea, the very deed and action it selfe, which I will not name for offending chast eares, shall be purtrayed and shewed foorth in their bawdye gestures.[40]

---

[38] See the two recent essays by Peter Lake: 'Deeds against Nature: Cheap Print, Protestantism and Murder in Early Seventeenth Century England', in Kevin Sharpe and Peter Lake (eds), *Culture and Politics in Early Stuart England* (Basingstoke, 1994), pp. 257–83, and 'Popular Form, Puritan Content? Two Puritan Appropriations of the Murder Pamphlet from Mid-Seventeenth-Century London', in Anthony Fletcher and Peter Roberts (eds), *Religion, Culture and Society in Early Modern Britain: Essays in Honour of Patrick Collinson* (Cambridge, 1994), pp. 313–34.

[39] For allusions to the *Christal Glasse* in plays, see Richard Brome, *The Antipodes: A Comedie* (London, 1640), sig. F2r; William Cartwright, *The Ordinary*, act 3, sc. 5, in *Comedies, Tragi-Comedies, with other Poems* (London, 1651), p. 52.

[40] Stubbes, *Anatomie*, p. 155. I owe the point about the link between antiquarianism and polemic to Dr Alison Shell. For Aubrey, see James Britten (ed.), *Remaines of Gentilisme and Judaisme* (Publications of the Folk-Lore Society, 4, 1881).

Notwithstanding his concessions to delicacy, Stubbes's prudish Victorian critics and editors were evidently offended by some of his more purple passages: Thomas Frognall Dibdin hoped that 'every virtuous dame' would incinerate copies which came into her hands, while John Payne Collier thought some of his epithets too coarse to quote in 'all Companies'.[41] But the *Anatomie* is no more racy and indecorous than early editions of Foxe's *Actes and Monuments*,[42] and censorious moralism is undoubtedly the predominant tone.

First published in 1583, it can be seen as part of an evolving literature of complaint in which authorial indignation was exaggerated for stylistic effect. Tracts like the Bristol minister John Northbrooke's *Treatise wherein Dicing, Dauncing, Vaine Playes or Enterludes ... are Reproved* (1577), the clergyman Christopher Fetherston's *Dialogue agaynst Light, Lewde, and Lascivious Dauncing* (1582) and the leading Presbyterian Thomas Wilcox's *Glasse for Gamesters* (1581) took particular exception to metropolitan pastimes such as bowling, cards, and commercialized bear-baiting. But the rural diversions which exercised Stubbes – fêtes, fairs, football and summer games – also received their fair share of hostile attention. The practical sabbatarianism which underpins these clerical texts is equally prominent in the *Anatomie*, as are the deep concerns of pastors and preachers about the dangers associated with dramatic entertainment.[43] This latter subject was discussed in a relatively short chapter comprising six pages out of the total of 208, which students of the Elizabethan stage have allowed to balloon out of all proportion to its actual importance and used to justify Stubbes's inclusion in a black pantheon of anti-theatrical writers.[44]

---

[41] Dibdin, *Bibliomania*, p. 367; J. P. Collier, *The Poetical Decameron* (2 vols, Edinburgh, 1820), vol. 2, p. 238.

[42] See Patrick Collinson's remarks in 'Truth and Legend: the Veracity of John Foxe's Book of Martyrs', in A. C. Duke and C. A. Tamse (eds), *Clio's Mirror: Historiography in Britain and the Netherlands* (Zutphen, 1985), esp. pp. 49–50.

[43] John Northbrooke, *Spiritus est Vicarius Christi in Terra. A Treatise Wherein Dicing, Dauncing, Vaine Playes or Enterluds with other Idle Pastimes ... are Reproved* (London, 1577); Christopher Fetherston, *A Dialogue agaynst Light, Lewde, and Lascivious Dauncing* (London, 1582); T[homas] W[ilcox], *A Glasse for Gamesters* (London, 1581). Cf. Humfrey Roberts, *An Earnest Complaint of Divers Wicked and Abused Exercises* (London, 1572) and the anonymous *A Treatise of Daunses* (London, 1581). For discussions of this literature of complaint, see Patrick Collinson, *The Religion of Protestants: the Church in English Society 1558–1625* (Oxford, 1982), ch. 5; Hutton, *The Rise and Fall of Merry England*, pp. 128–34.

[44] Stubbes, *Anatomie*, pp. 140–46. See, for example, Elbert N. S. Thompson, *The Controversy Between the Puritans and the Stage* (1903; repr., 1966), ch. 5; Jonas Barish, *The Antitheatrical Prejudice* (Berkeley, CA, 1981), ch. 4. Stubbes's *Anatomie* and *Display of Corruptions*, and a number of other works cited in n. 43, are reprinted in

In fact, Stubbes conceived of the *Anatomie* principally as a tractate on pride. This, he declared in the dedicatory epistle, was its 'chiefest argument', being 'the verie efficient cause of all evills'. And, indeed, a damning indictment of doublets and ruffs, Venetian hose and costly 'netherstocks', earrings, extravagant head gear and other newfangled items of dress does occupy a third of the book.[45] Taken together with his strictures against coveous enclosers, rack-renting landlords, grasping barristers and greedy usurers, Stubbes's emphasis on sumptuary excess is strongly reminiscent of a much older tradition of moral complaint. This can be traced through manuscript sermons and vernacular treatises of the late Middle Ages like Robert of Brunne's *Handlyng Synne* (*c.* 1303) and the famous fifteenth-century dialogue between *Dives and Pauper*, later printed by Richard Pynson and Wynkyn de Worde.[46] Like Protestant commentators, medieval writers and preachers also condemned swearing, fornication, and boisterous recreations, though these offences were often integrated into the older schema of the Seven Deadly Sins rather than the alternative moral system of the Decalogue, towards which, as John Bossy has argued, Western society was gradually moving in a major paradigm shift.[47] In some senses the *Anatomie* itself lies in limbo between these two ethical codes: the accent falls as much on transgressions against charity and communal solidarity as on manifestations of spiritual apostasy and idolatry. Revealingly, Stubbes's overriding concern about the use of cosmetics, elaborate hairstyles and male and female finery seems to have been not fear that they stirred up lust and led to prostitution or a conviction that they were inherently wrong, but anxiety about preserving traditional distinctions of rank and upholding the established social order. He stressed in the preface that 'I wold not be so understood, as though my speaches extended to any, either noble, honorable, or worshipful': 'they both

---

facsimile in the Garland series, Arthur Freeman (ed.), *The English Stage: Attack and Defense 1577–1730*.

[45] Stubbes, *Anatomie*, pp. viii, 27. The section on pride runs from p. 26 to p. 87.

[46] For usurers, enclosers, lawyers and landlords, see Stubbes, *Anatomie*, pp. 114–29. Frederick J. Furnivall (ed.), *Robert of Brunne's 'Handlyng Synne', AD 1303* (EETS, old series, 119, 1901); Anon., *The Riche and the Pore [The Dialogue of Dives and Pauper]* (London, 1493). Cf. John Peter, *Complaint and Satire in Early English Literature* (Oxford, 1956), esp. ch. 4; G. R. Owst, *Literature and Pulpit in Medieval England* (Oxford, 1961), esp. ch. 7; Bernard Lord Manning, *The People's Faith in the Time of Wyclif* (Cambridge, 1919), chs 8–9 (who notes the many similarities between the themes of fourteenth-century tracts and seventeenth-century 'Puritan' literature, esp. p. 113).

[47] John Bossy, 'Moral Arithmetic: Seven Sins into Ten Commandments', in Edmund Leites (ed.), *Conscience and Casuistry in Early Modern Europe* (Cambridge and Paris, 1988), pp. 214–34.

may, and for some respects ought, to wear such attire (their birthes, callings, functions, and estats requiring the same'. It was only the vain presumption and pretension of the 'inferiour sorte' which demanded reform.[48]

The suggestion that, as a moralist, Stubbes was actually rather old-fashioned is borne out by the second part of the *Anatomie*, *The Display of Corruptions*, which is far more like classic estates satire than the Elizabethan clerical literature of complaint. Its colourful taxonomy of classes and types – unscrupulous lawyers, crooked merchants, dishonest tradesmen, rapacious farmers and forestallers of corn – reads very much like the parades of corrupt professionals and personified vices in such late medieval works as the 'Speculum Laicorum'.[49] Of course, humanism had transmuted many of these themes into the new discourse of the 'Commonwealth' and elements of this native strand of critique were reworked in the writings of Edwardian Protestant reformers. It would be a mistake to ignore the extent to which Stubbes's tract echoes works like Henry Brinkelow's *The Complaint of Roderyck Mors* (c. 1542), Thomas Starkey's 'Dialogue between Cardinal Pole and Thomas Lupset' (1533–38), and the sermons of Latimer and Lever.[50] Yet I would still maintain that there is something distinctly unreconstructed about his social thinking.

A certain conservatism also emerges in *A Motive to Good Workes*. In documenting the nationwide decay of the charitable foundations and public amenities established by earlier generations, Stubbes reveals a Stow-like nostalgia for the passing of an age of munificence, hospitality and plenty. He expresses admiration for the 'bountifull liberalitie of our predecessors' and complains that contemporaries are outdone in meritorious deeds by their 'good forefathers' who lived in the time of superstition and popery. And his lament for the neglect of ecclesiastical buildings (too many of which lay 'like barnes', 'beastly' and unkempt) foreshadows sentiments which would flower in the Laudian and pre-Laudian programme for embellishing churches in the early seventeenth

---

[48] Stubbes, *Anatomie*, p. xii. Cf. Bernard Capp's similar verdict on John Taylor: *The World of John Taylor the Water-Poet 1578–1653* (Oxford, 1994), p. 131.

[49] As Patrick Collinson has noted: 'Elizabethan and Jacobean Puritanism as Forms of Popular Religious Culture', in Christopher Durston and Jacqueline Eales (eds), *The Culture of English Puritanism, 1560–1700* (Basingstoke, 1996), p. 34. See Peter, *Complaint and Satire*, ch. 4; Owst, *Literature and Pulpit*, ch. 6; and the comments of Clark, *The Elizabethan Pamphleteers*, pp. 142–5.

[50] Helen C. White, *Social Criticism in Popular Religious Literature of the Sixteenth Century* (New York, 1944), esp. chs 6–7; John N. King, *English Reformation Literature: the Tudor Origins of the Protestant Tradition* (Princeton, 1982), esp. pp. 49–51; Manley, *Literature and Culture*, ch. 2.

century.[51] When combined with his fierce attack on Catholic works righteousness and progressive views on differential poor relief, these attitudes make Stubbes a strangely Janus-faced figure – both forward – and backward-looking – almost as much of a walking contradiction as John Taylor, the water-poet, is portrayed in Bernard Capp's latest book.[52]

To return to the 'reformation of maners and amendement of life' for which Stubbes called in the first part of his *Anatomie*,[53] recent research has greatly downplayed the novelty of the sixteenth- and seventeenth-century campaigns to correct moral abuses and transform the festive culture of urban and rural communities. A number of scholars have stressed that the imposition of 'godly discipline' was a routine and perennial feature of English parochial life and shown that spasms of this sort of activism were also characteristic of earlier periods of economic crisis and demographic pressure.[54] There has likewise been a tendency to dispute the connection between the early modern crusade against sin and Calvinist doctrine and zealous Protestant piety, with Margaret Spufford going so far as to declare religion and religious belief, in this instance, 'a gigantic red herring'.[55] Nevertheless as Martin Ingram has recognized, it would wrong to say that there was nothing new under the sun: the advent of Protestantism and print did coincide with 'a permanent tilt in the pattern of regulation' in England.[56] And puritans were not only especially prominent in local offensives but driven by particularly intense convictions about their duty to edify their

---

[51] Stubbes, *A Motive to Good Workes*, pp. 85, 71–2, 79–82. See Ian Archer, 'The Nostalgia of John Stow', in David L. Smith, Richard Strier and David Bevington (eds), *The Theatrical City: London's Culture, Theatre and Literature, 1576–1649* (Cambridge, 1995), pp. 17–34; Felicity Heal, *Hospitality in Early Modern England* (Oxford, 1990), ch. 3, esp. pp. 93–4.

[52] For Stubbes's views on poor relief, see *The Display of Corruptions*, pp. 41–4; Heal, *Hospitality*, pp. 133–4. Capp, *The World of John Taylor*, p. 3, 191 and ch. 5.

[53] Stubbes, *Anatomie*, p. viii.

[54] See, in particular, Martin Ingram, 'The Reform of Popular Culture? Sex and Marriage in Early Modern England', in Barry Reay (ed.), *Popular Culture in Seventeenth Century England* (London, 1988), pp. 129–65, and his 'Reformation of Manners in Early Modern England', in Paul Griffiths, Adam Fox and Steve Hindle (eds), *The Experience of Authority in Early Modern England* (Basingstoke, 1996), pp. 47–88; Margaret Spufford, 'Puritanism and Social Control?', in Anthony Fletcher and John Stevenson (eds), *Order and Disorder in Early Modern England* (Cambridge, 1985), pp. 41–57.

[55] Spufford, 'Puritanism and Social Control?', p. 57. Cf. the most recent contribution to the secondary literature, Hutton's *The Rise and Fall of Merry England*, which allocates more responsibility to religious factors than to economic and social pressures, esp. pp. 111–12, 146, 261–2.

[56] Ingram, 'Reformation of Manners', p. 77.

brethren and protect the nation from providential catastrophe.[57] Similarly misleading may be Kenneth Parker's insistence that a developed doctrine of the Sabbath predated the Reformation. Concerns about the proper observance of Sunday were shared by Protestants of all persuasions and did have medieval roots, but the sabbatarianism which emerged in the work of Nicholas Bownde and other ministers in the mid and late 1590s was theologically different and distinct.[58] All this leaves a picture which is very much more subtle and nuanced than older notions of the 'Puritan Reformation of Manners'. What we are confronted with now is a broad phenomenon marked by an alliance of heterogeneous groups animated by an eclectic mixture of motives. It is not always easy to disentangle pragmatic concerns about public disorder and expense from religious ones about divine wrath and intolerable relics of heathenism, and puritanism can be confused with 'the officious, responsible respectability' of substantial farmers and civic officials.[59]

This is the context in which Stubbes's *Anatomie of Abuses* must be situated – a context in which some other notable contributions to the literature of moral complaint seem to have been written by the commission of city fathers preoccupied perhaps primarily with issues of crowd control and health and safety. Stephen Gosson's attack on the metropolitan stage in *The School of Abuse* (1579) is almost certainly a case in point. Although he claimed to have undergone a sudden conversion and seen the evils of his former profession as an actor and playwright, there are several pieces of evidence to the effect that Gosson's pamphlet was a piece of hack work written to order – a welcome form of patronage for an impoverished dramatist who had not prospered in that trade.[60] This argument is much reinforced by the fact that the ghost writer behind *The Second and Third Blast of Retrait from Plaies and Theaters*

---

[57] See the judicious revisiting of this issue in Keith Wrightson's postscript to the 2nd edition of *Poverty and Piety in an English Village: Terling 1525–1700* (Oxford, 1995), esp. pp. 201–9; Underdown, *Revel, Riot and Rebellion*, pp. 47–63; and the remarks of Peter Lake in 'Defining Puritanism – Again?', in F. J. Bremer (ed.), *Puritanism: Transatlantic Perspectives on a Seventeenth-Century Anglo-American Faith* (Boston, 1993), pp. 10–15.

[58] Kenneth L. Parker, *The English Sabbath: A Study of Doctrine and Discipline from the Reformation to the Civil War* (Cambridge, 1988), p. 5 and *passim*. Cf. Patrick Collinson, 'The Beginnings of English Sabbatarianism', reprinted in P. Collinson, *Godly People*, pp. 429–43.

[59] Patrick Collinson, *The Birthpangs of Protestant England* (London, 1988), p. 153.

[60] Stephen Gosson, *The Schoole of Abuse, Conteining a Plesaunt Invective Against Poets, Pipers, Plaiers, Jesters, and such like Caterpillers of the Commonwelth* (London, 1579). The evidence is laid out in William Ringler, *Stephen Gosson: a Biographical and Critical Study* (Princeton, 1942), pp. 24–8, and see pp. 80–82. Cf. W. Ringler, 'The First Phases of the Elizabethan Attack on the Stage, 1558–1579', *The Huntington Library Quarterly*, 4 (1942), pp. 391–418.

published in 1580 'by auctoritie' and bearing the coat of arms of the corporation of London, was a professional wordsmith well known for his moral and generic agility, Anthony Munday.[61]

This brings us back to the murky backstreets and bedsits of the Elizabethan literary underworld, on at least the fringes of which I have already suggested that Philip Stubbes stood. One does not have to look very hard to detect him cutting, pasting and stitching passages from other works with the bare minimum of rewriting, or none at all. He lifted about two-thirds of his chapter on stage plays and interludes from Gosson's *Playes Confuted in Five Actions* (1582) and most of the rest from Northbrooke's *Treatise*, while his diatribe against 'pestiferous dancing' draws liberally on Christopher Fetherston's *Dialogue*.[62] The additions he made to the second and later editions reveal him foraging among topical news pamphlets for recent cases of retributive justice, which he sometimes inserted almost verbatim. These suggest that there is less of a gulf between Stubbes's book and Munday's *View of Sundry Examples* [1580], a patchwork quilt of previously printed accounts of murders, monstrous births and celestial omens, than is often supposed. We have tracked down some of his sources above, but John Field's *Godly Exhortation* about the Paris Garden bear-baiting disaster in 1583 can be added to the list,[63] along with Samuel Saxey's report of the horrible death suffered by the whore-mongering haberdasher William Brustar and his Bridewell 'concubine'.[64] It would be unwise and anachronistic to rest a case for Stubbes's status as a marginal figure in Grub Street on the grounds of plagiarism alone. In a period prior to the introduction of copyright laws and modern concepts of authorial rights, this was practised without any sense of shame by individuals as illustrious as the historian John Hayward and eminent divines like Thomas Beard and Samuel Clarke.[65] But I think enough has been said to suggest that Stubbes occupies a rather different echelon within the religious

---

[61] *A Second and Third Blast of Retrait from Plaies and Theaters* (London, 1580). The second blast was by the fifth-century ecclesiastical writer Salvian, the third by Munday.

[62] Compare, for example, Stephen Gosson, *Playes Confuted in Five Actions* (London, 1582), sig. C5r–v and Stubbes, *Anatomie*, p. 143. Ringler, *Stephen Gosson*, p. 125 n. 8, notes other parallel passages in Stubbes, Gosson and Northbrooke.

[63] See above, n. 20. Anthony Munday, *A View of Sundry Examples* (London, [1580]). John Field, *A Godly Exhortation, by Occasion of the Late Judgment of God, Shewed at Parris-Garden* (London, 1583) (cf. Stubbes, *Anatomie*, p. 179).

[64] Samuel Saxey, *A Straunge and Wonderfull Example of the Judgement of Almighty God, Shewed upon Two Adulterous Persons in London* (London, [1583]). Cf. Stubbes, *Anatomie*, pp. 100–101.

[65] The extent of John Hayward's plagiarism will be revealed in a forthcoming PhD dissertation by Lisa Richardson of Pembroke College, Cambridge. For Beard, see Walsham,

publishing industry. And it needs to be stressed that moralistic pamphlets like the *Anatomie* were part of the 'popular literature' of Elizabethan London. They were not only the work of idealistic evangelists and lone preachers crying in the wind, but also of semi-professional authors in touch with the preferences and whims of the reading public.

The image of Stubbes with which we began has, then, become increasingly opaque, clouded over with insights into his conduct and character which belie common assumptions. No less of a tarnish on this traditional portrait is the revelation that, when he turned to consider the 'abuses of the spirituality' in the second part of the *Anatomie*, Stubbes showed himself a staunch supporter of the institution of episcopacy. He was, in a word, no presbyterian.[66] He took a moderate conformist line on the question of the established ecclesiastical polity, declaring that the office of elder was ceremonial only, that the duties of deacons were now fulfilled by churchwardens and that individual churches could alter their internal forms of government according to prevailing conditions. His opinion on the appointment of ministers was more idiosyncratic: he argued that congregations should be allowed to nominate up to four candidates for final choice by the bishop. As for the 'reverend Byshops' themselves, they were 'most needful' and their calling 'most honorable', while those who decried them were 'either wilfull, waiwarde, or maliciouslye blinde'. Stubbes upheld the right of the prince to decide upon clerical vestments, against the claims of men 'more curious than wise' who condemned the surplice, tippet and cap as the rags of Antichrist. He sharply reproved 'precisians' who abandoned their flocks because of scruples of conscience about 'meere triffles as these garments be' and dismissed their arguments as 'simple shifts', calling upon all parties to 'agree togither in these external shadowes' and cease to 'brabble'. Needless to say, he had no time whatsoever for those 'neotericall and phantasticall spirits' and 'new phangled felows sprong up of late', the separatists. Finally, he defended 'bare reading' as a temporary substitute for a proper

---

'Aspects of Providentialism', pp. 69–70. Clarke lifted and reprinted most of his godly lives from earlier funeral sermons and spiritual biographies, including that of Katherine Brettergh. Cf. the remarks of Clark, *The Elizabethan Pamphleteers*, pp. 33, 96.

[66] In this point I have been anticipated by Professor Collinson, 'Elizabethan and Jacobean Puritanism', pp. 34, 57, and earlier writers including Pearson, 'The Life and Workes of Phillip Stubbes', ch. 7. Cf. the recent assumption by Hutton, *The Rise and Fall of Merry England*, pp. 131–2.

[67] Stubbes, *The Display of Corruptions*, esp. pp. 100–6, 109–16, 71–4. See also the passing references in Stubbes, *A Motive to Good Workes*, pp. 82, 79. Stephen Gosson, who later became a clergyman and preached at Paul's Cross, was even more fiercely anti-presbyterian; see his *The Trumpet of Warre* (London, 1598), pp. 66, 72, 75, 86.

preaching ministry.[67] This last statement acquires an interesting personal resonance if we take at face value Thomas Nashe's allegation that in his youth Stubbes had been employed as a lay reader in Cheshire.[68] Aired in the context of Archbishop Whitgift's subscription campaign and the ejection of a large number of ministers for liturgical nonconformity, these views are unequivocal proof that Stubbes was not a disciple of Travers and Cartwright. They show him wearing his colours on his sleeve.

The purpose of the foregoing analysis has not been to unmask Philip Stubbes as a fraud, defrock him as a 'Puritan' and reallocate him to the category of profane and impious scribbler. This would be to perpetuate a set of false dichotomies which he does nothing so much as undermine. His ambiguity is itself instructive, evidence of the complex dialectic between fervent, clerical Protestantism and the commercial book trade which the research of Tessa Watt, David Hall, Peter Lake and other historians has recently revealed.[69] Stubbes's career seems to epitomize the cross-fertilization between these two spheres which is now becoming apparent. It also has some surprising lessons to teach us about the making of a body of Protestant devotional literature and practical divinity.

I see Stubbes in the same light as the obscure and unfortunate John Phillips, another relatively minor writer of epitaphs, patriotic blackletter ballads, sensational news tracts and tiny duodecimo prayer-books, whom the editors of the *Dictionary of National Biography* split schizophrenically in two. Styling himself 'student of divinitie', Phillips too was earnest, devout, and probably in search of supplementary income.[70] Both bear a distinct resemblance to John Andrewes, the 'market-place

---

[68] Thomas Nashe, *An Almond for a Parrat* (London, 1590), in *Works*, vol. 3, p. 357. The context of this remark is discussed below.

[69] Watt, *Cheap Print and Popular Piety*; David D. Hall, *Worlds of Wonder, Days of Judgement: Popular Religious Belief in Early New England* (Cambridge, MA, 1990), chs 1–2; Lake, 'Deeds against Nature' and 'Popular Form, Puritan Content?'; Manley, *Literature and Culture*, ch. 6; Eamon Duffy, 'The Godly and the Multitude in Stuart England', *The Seventeenth Century*, 1 (1986), esp. pp. 41–9; and Walsham, 'Aspects of Providentialism'. Cf. Patrick Collinson, *From Iconoclasm to Iconophobia: the Cultural Impact of the Second English Reformation* (The Stenton Lecture, Reading, 1986), restated in Collinson, *Birthpangs*, ch. 4.

[70] See *DNB*, s.n. 'John Phillips' and 'John Philip'; STC 19862–77. The error is corrected by W. W. Greg in 'John Phillip – Notes for a Bibliography', *The Library*, 3rd series, 1 (1910), pp. 302–28, 396–423. Stubbes and Phillips may have numbered among the 'private persons ... bolde in the pride of their wittes [who] upon the reading of a fewe bookes, or the hearing of a fewe Sermons, ... thrust foorth a Pamphlette unto the worlde ... ' about whom William Cupper complained in *Certaine Sermons* (London, 1592), sig. A4v.

200 BELIEF AND PRACTICE IN REFORMATION ENGLAND

theologian' who was described on the title-pages of his best-selling
penny godlies as 'Minister and Preacher of the Word at Barwicke Basset
in the County of Wilts', but who seems to have been a man on the edges
of the ecclesiastical mainstream and may never in fact have been ordained. Manufactured by means of a marriage between business initiative
and evangelical zeal, his name became a trademark and a signpost to
the reader.[71] Stubbes also has parallels with John Taylor, water-poet
and 'cultural amphibian', and Miles Huggarde, the Marian Catholic
controversialist and layman-cum-preacher.[72] Hotter sort of Protestant
or three halfpenny pamphleteer? The further one probes the more difficult it becomes to place Stubbes in a particular pigeon-hole and to
determine whether one is looking at an historical personage or a literary
persona. We know too little about his private life to draw any hard and
fast conclusions about the theological temperature and flavour of his
piety; we have no notebooks like those which enabled Paul Seaver to
make windows into Nehemiah Wallington's soul; and we lack sufficient
evidence to reach a firm verdict about his religious subjectivity and
ideological outlook.[73]

III

But an interesting problem remains. How, when and why did Stubbes
come to acquire his reputation as a 'puritan' – and, indeed, the nickname? To ask this question is to venture into treacherous waters: defining
puritanism is a reef on which many a historian has already foundered.
The concept is 'an elusive protean beast' and 'a dragon in the path of
every student of the period'; the debate about it rather like letting a
group of blindfolded scholars loose in a darkened room with an ele-
phant; and the word itself 'an admirable refuge from clarity of thought',
which some have insisted should be banished completely from scholarly
discourse.[74] As Patrick Collinson has taught us, 'puritan' was above all

---

[71] Watt, *Cheap Print and Popular Piety*, pp. 306–11. Andrewes was not the incumbent
at Berwick Bassett. Cf. Phillips, who was identified as 'preacher of the Word of God' on
the title-page of the posthumous 1626 edition of his *Perfect Path to Paradice*. For other
similar figures, see Hall, *Worlds of Wonder*, pp. 49–50.

[72] See Capp, *The World of John Taylor* and J. W. Martin, 'Miles Hogarde: Artisan and
Aspiring Author in Sixteenth-Century England', reprinted in Martin, *Religious Radicals
in Tudor England* (London, 1989), pp. 83–105.

[73] Paul Seaver, *Wallington's World: a Puritan Artisan in Seventeenth Century London*
(Stanford, CA, 1985).

[74] See respectively W. J. Sheils, *The Puritans in the Diocese of Peterborough 1558–
1610* (Northamptonshire Record Society, 30, 1979), p. 2; Christopher Hill, *The Economic*

a term of abuse, 'a broad and sticky brush' with which to tar one's opponents, 'a weapon of some verbal finesse but no philosophical precision'. 'Puritans' were people who earned this opprobrious epithet from their neighbours and peers, Protestants as they were perceived in a particular set of circumstances, individuals whose utterances and/or conduct profoundly irritated those who encountered them. And 'Puritanism' was 'not a thing definable in itself but only one half of a stressful relationship' – a fluid and unstable situation involving friction and confrontation between rival moral economies and world views.[75]

To understand how Philip Stubbes became a 'puritan', then, it is necessary to recapture some sense of the theological, cultural and social tension and estrangement of which the term is an index. We must also be sensitive to the extent to which the meaning of the word became inflated over time and evolved in the course of its use. Probably first employed by exiled Catholic polemicists in the mid-1560s, 'puritan' was soon extended to clergymen who could not stomach the surplice, tippet and bishops. Thereafter it gradually moved beyond the boundaries of ecclesiastical debate and was applied indiscriminately to wound and insult. By 1600 it had acquired common currency at the grass roots, as well as strong connotations of moral fastidiousness, officiousness and above all hypocrisy.[76] In the context of the Arminian and Laudian challenge to Calvinist orthodoxy and the policies of Charles I's Personal Rule, the term dilated and mutated yet further, becoming synonymous at the same time with doctrinal deviance and political

---

Problems of the Church (London, 1956), p. xii ; Patrick Collinson, 'A Comment: Concerning the Name Puritan', *JEH*, 31 (1980), p. 484; Christopher Hill, *Society and Puritanism in Pre-Revolutionary England* (London, 1964), p. 6. It was famously Thomas Fuller who wished that the word might be banished from common discourse: *Church History of Britain* (Oxford, 1842), vol. 2, p. 475.

[75] Patrick Collinson, 'Ecclesiastical Vitriol: Religious Satire in the 1590s and the Invention of Puritanism', in John Guy (ed.), *The Reign of Elizabeth I: Court and Culture in the Last Decade* (Cambridge, 1995), p. 155; P. Collinson, *Elizabethan Puritanism* (London, 1983), p. 10 and pp. 7–11; Collinson, *Birthpangs*, p. 143. For perhaps the most extreme version of his position, see P. Collinson, *The Puritan Character: Polemics and Polarities in Early Seventeenth-Century English Culture* (Los Angeles, 1989). Peter Lake 'Defining Puritanism – Again?', however, suggests this case has been overstated and insists upon the existence of 'a central core' and 'distinctive style of piety and divinity' which can legitimately be identified as 'Puritan'. The most recent attempt at synthesis and definition is Christopher Durston and Jacqueline Eales's introduction to *The Culture of English Puritanism, 1560–1700* (Basingstoke, 1996), pp. 1–31.

[76] See Collinson, *Elizabethan Puritanism*, pp. 7–11; Basil Hall 'Puritanism: the Problem of Defintion', in G. J. Cuming (ed.), *Studies in Church History*, 2 (London, 1965), pp. 283–96; Thomas H. Clancy, 'Papist-Protestant-Puritan: English Religious Taxonomy 1565–1665', *Recusant History*, 13 (1975–76), pp. 238–41.

sedition.[77] Particularly relevant here is the extent to which the reproclamation of the Book of Sports in 1633 politicized the issue of seasonal pastimes and sabbath observance, making zeal against Maygames, morris dancing and other 'idle' Sunday recreations an earmark of 'puritanism'.[78] Surely no less important in explaining Stubbes's metamorphosis into a 'puritan' is the gargantuan encyclopaedia of antitheatrical lore, *Histriomastix*, for which William Prynne famously lost a portion of his ears. Prynne listed the *Anatomie* among the literally thousands of other authorities he piled up in support of his claim that stage plays were 'sinfull', 'heathenish' and 'lewde', 'the very Pompes of the Divell', and impossible to countenance in any form at all.[79] Ironically, unlike Prynne, Stubbes does not seem to have regarded the dramatic medium as intrinsically evil. In the preface to the 1583 edition (mysteriously removed in the next and later impressions), he had acknowledged that 'some kind of playes, tragedies and enterluds' were very 'honest' and 'commendable', yielding 'wholsome instruction' and 'conducible to example of life and reformation of maners'.[80] But, by 1633, as Prynne complained, condemnation of stage plays, along with alehouse-haunting and diceplay, extravagant fashions and traditional festive customs, however qualified, was widely recognized as 'one grand badge' and 'eminent character' of a 'Puritan' – and the association was one which *Histriomastix* and *The Unlovelinesse, of Love-lockes* did much to cement. No word in the language had 'passed through the mouthes of all sorts of unregenerate men with more distastefulnesse and gnashing of teeth' and become so widely misapplied 'as a very Motto ... of disgrace' than this.[81] As Henry Parker lamented in 1641, in this 'Ethical sense' it enjoyed 'a vast circumference' and was used 'to cast dirt in the face of all goodness'.[82]

There is one further strand in the story of Stubbes's evolution into a 'puritan' which must be unravelled. And that is the way in which the

---

[77] Nicholas Tyacke, *Anti-Calvinists: the Rise of English Arminianism c. 1590–1640* (Oxford, 1990), pp. 7–8 and *passim*.

[78] Parker, *The English Sabbath*, ch. 7 and p. 158.

[79] William Prynne, *Histriomastix: the Players Scourge, or Actors Tragaedie* (London, 1633), title-page.

[80] Stubbes, *Anatomie*, p. x.

[81] Prynne, *Histriomastix*, pp. 799–807, 827; William Prynne, *The Unlovelinesse, of Love-lockes* (London, 1628).

[82] Henry Parker, *A Discourse Concerning Puritans* (London, 1641), reprinted in Lawrence A. Sasek (ed.), *Images of English Puritanism* (Baton Rouge, LA, 1989), pp. 167–68. Cf. the argument of Jeremy Goring, *Godly Exercises or the Devil's Dance? Puritanism and Popular Culture in Pre-Civil War England* (Friends of Dr Williams's Library, 37th Lecture, London, 1983).

concept and stereotype was partly invented, or reinvented, by the theatrical and literary underworld itself. As Professor Collinson has compellingly demonstrated in two recent essays, the figure of the stage puritan, familiar to us from the comedies of Shakespeare and Jonson in the guise of Malvolio and Zeal-of-the-Land-Busy, was very largely a by-product of the Marprelate Controversy in the late 1580s and early 1590s. It grew out of a vigorous popular and semi-official backlash against the evasive and irrepressible Martin and his anti-episcopal pamphlets. These hilariously iconoclastic tracts were the last desperate measures of the presbyterians in their drawn-out war with the prelates and they drew upon a lively oral and vernacular tradition of defamatory 'ballading'. In due course Martin was answered 'after his own vein' by a group of literary hacks including Thomas Nashe, John Lyly, Robert Greene and probably Anthony Munday in a propaganda campaign sponsored and masterminded by Richard Bancroft, Bishop of London. The biting satire and doggerel broadsides which flowed from the pens of 'Cuthbert Curryknave', 'Mar-Martin', 'Pasquil' and 'Pappe Hatchet' also fed off the mocking rhymes and libels that were the stuff of England's 'street wars of religion': they were parasitical upon an established repertoire of anti-puritan motifs. In addition to, and perhaps even before his lampooning in print, Martin was mercilessly ridiculed on the professional stage, appearing in a series of lost jigs and plays with intriguing titles like *The Maygame of Martinisme*. It was these pamphlets and spectacles which perfected and released into the public domain the perennial stock character of the 'puritan' which is instantly recognizable even today – the moral and sexual hypocrite and carping precisian who condemns cakes and ale and tears down the idol of the maypole only to set up the Bible in its place.[83]

The career of Philip Stubbes adds a nuance or two to this extraordinary tale of 'traffic between the academic and the demotic', and of 'ecclesiastical vitriol' poured out by university wits.[84] It is by no means insignificant that Stubbes's name appears in the final phases of the Marprelate affair and the opening stages of the Nashe–Harvey flyting,

---

[83] Patrick Collinson, 'Ecclesiastical Vitriol' and 'The Theatre Constructs Puritanism', in David L. Smith, Richard Strier and David Bevington (eds), *The Theatrical City London's Culture, Theatre and Literature, 1576–1649* (Cambridge, 1995), pp. 157–69. But note Lake's objections to some aspects and implications of this argument in '"A Charitable Christin Hatred"': the Godly and their Enemies in the1630s', in Christopher Durston and Jacqueline Eales (eds), *The Culture of English Puritanism, 1560–1700* (Basingstoke, 1996), pp. 178–9, 307. For Puritan satire and the evolution of the stage Puritan, cf. William Holden, *Anti-Puritan Satire 1572–1642* (New Haven, CT, 1954), chs 2–3, esp. pp. 101–44.

[84] Collinson, 'Ecclesiastical Vitriol', pp. 150, 155.

which in many respects was a spin-off from it. In *An Almond for a Parrat*, now confidently attributed to Nashe, and one of the last volleys from the anti-Martinist camp, he is subjected to a particularly vicious piece of character assassination. Cuthbert Curryknave mischievously, but also sarcastically, suggests that 'brother Martin' should commandeer Philip Stubbes to help prop up his ramshackle cause, his own 'witte' being 'welny worn thredbare' and his 'banquerout invention cleane out at the elbowes'. Stubbes was, Nashe assured Martin, 'a tall man for that purpose'. 'What his *Anatomy of Abuses*, for all that, will serve very fitly for an Antipast before one of Egertons Sermons; I would see the best of your Traverses write such a treatise as he hath done against short heeld pantoffles.' Nashe proceeded to allege that although Stubbes railed against diceplay he had been overheard arranging a game for the next sabbath ('by the grace of God ... if it shal so seeme good to his providence'), and although he kept 'a stirre' against 'dumb ministers', like all 'privy Martinists' he had 'in his minority plaide the Reader ... for five marke a yeare and a canvas dublet'. And the following passage is worth quoting in full:

> What need more words to prove him a protestant? did not he behave himselfe like a true Christian when hee went a wooing for his friend Clarke, I warrant you hee saide not God save you, or God speed you, with good even or good morrow, as our prophane woers are wont, but stept close to her, with peace bee with you, very demurely, and then told her a long tale, that in so much as widowhoode was an uncleane lyfe, and subject to many temptations, shee might doe well to reconcile her selfe to the Church of God, in the holy ordinance of matrimony. Manye wordes past to this purpose, but I wotte well the conclusion was this, that since she had hitherto convert with none but unregenerate persons, and was utterly carelesse of the communion of Saints, she would let him, that was a man of God, put a newe spirite into here, by carnall copulation, and so engraft into the fellowshippe of the faithfull; to which that shee might more willingly agree, hee offered her a spicke and spanne new Geneva Bible, that his attendant Italian had brought with him, to make up the bargaine. But for all the Scripture he could alledge, it should not bee, Phil. Stu. Was no meate for her tooth, God wote he could not get a penyworth of leachery on such a pawne as his Bible was, the man behinde the painted cloth mard all, and so, O griefe, a good Sabaoths day work was lost.[85]

Here, in what reads like a summary of a scene from a comedy, we have nearly all the key ingredients of the classic stage Puritan –

---

[85] Nashe, *An Almond for a Parrat* in *Works*, vol. 3, p. 356–8. For Nashe's role in the Marprelate affair, see Nicholl, *A Cup of News*, ch. 6. For a survey of publications during the Marprelate and Nashe–Harvey controversies, see Peter Milward, *Religious Controversies of the Elizabethan Age: a Survey of Printed Sources* (London, 1977), pp. 86–93.

hypocrisy, lasciviousness, sanctimonious piety and cosening. Nashe had etched the rest in his *Anatomie of Absurditie*, published the previous year. There we find Stubbes depicted in another conventional pose:

> It is not the writhing of the face, the heaving uppe of the eyes to heaven, that shall keepe these men, from having their portion in hell. Might they be saved by their booke, they have the Bible alwaies in their bosome, and so had the Pharisies the Lawe embroidered in their garments.[86]

A remarkably similar comic caricature was incorporated in a tract of 1592 entitled *The Defence of Conny-Catching*, the work of a writer calling himself 'Cuthbert Cunny-catcher'. This purported to be a confutation of Robert Greene's series of pamphlets exposing urban rogues and criminals, but should probably be seen instead as a sequel to them, designed to swell their sale. Among other amusing anecdotes about knaves and swindlers related by the author (who may have been Lyly, Nashe or even Greene himself) was the 'pleasant tale' of 'Maister P.', one of the 'poetical Brethren' of Grub Street and a 'pure Martinist' – a 'learned Hypocrite' who could 'brooke no abuses in the Commonwealth' and who had recently 'put an English she Saint in the Legend, for the holiness of her life: and forgot not so much as her dogge'. This 'holy brother' – who was without doubt Philip Stubbes – had 'cunningly conny-catcht ... for a Wife' by pretending to be 'a Gentleman from Cheshire', insinuating himself into the affections of an eligible young heiress and pulling the wool over the eyes of her unsuspecting stepfather and mother.[87]

Whether or not these allegations contained more than a grain of truth is largely irrelevant; there was enough circumstantial similarity with the facts of Stubbes's marriage to Katherine Emmes to make the slander stick. Such satiric vignettes illustrate the existence of a stereotype to which Stubbes was actively being assimilated and which he, in turn, helped to shape and to stimulate. He seems to embody the ease with which puritans and stage puritans came to be confused.[88] It makes sense

---

[86] Nashe, *The Anatomie of Absurditie* in *Works*, vol. 1, p. 22. It is tempting to think that Stubbes's call for the suppression of 'railing libels & slaunderous pamphlets' and the execution of their authors reflects his own bitter experience: *A Motive to Good Workes*, pp. 184–8.

[87] Cuthbert Cunny-catcher, *The Defence of Conny-Catching*, sigs C4r–D1v. The first to suggest the identification of 'Maister P.' with Philip Stubbes was R. B. McKerrow in a review published in 1916. See Terry P. Pearson, 'The Defence of Conny Catching', in *Notes and Queries*, new series, 204 (1959), pp. 150–53.

[88] See Collinson, 'The Theatre Constructs Puritanism', p. 157. Like Katherine Emmes, the innocent bride in this 'pleasant tale' had been left property by her father, and lived with her mother, now remarried, 'in Fleetstreet or thereabouts'.

to see him as a pawn and a football in a quarrel conducted by and between men who flattered themselves they were his literary superiors: 'liminary luminaries' who had a vested interest in perpetuating and reviving a controversy that had boosted their incomes.[89] He may also perhaps help to solve a paradox noted by Professor Collinson: that the stereotype unleashed by the Marprelate episode bore little resemblance to the picaresque figure of Martin.[90] Could it be that Stubbes and other vociferous critics of leisure and the theatre provided a model for the deep suspicion of pleasure and ludicrously intemperate attack upon recreations and pastimes which were such indispensable and entertaining features of the stage puritan? Would that the play in which Gosson's *School of Abuse* and its author were held up to contempt in 1580 had survived, and the long line of performances which made the glancing reference to the *Anatomie* as 'a zealous Brothers booke ... full of fables' in John Fletcher's *The Night Walker* (1640) instantly understandable to its metropolitan audience.[91] It was not just the Protestant busybodies of later Tudor villages and towns who became templates for the cardboard cut-outs of moral austerity which appeared on the stage, but also the literary personae adopted by the authors of the popular literature of complaint.

Philip Stubbes remains something of a riddle, a cultural chameleon. Even so, his career has proved very revealing. It has served to undercut the assumption that any kind of apartheid existed between committed Protestants and the pot-poets and scribblers of the metropolis, and to show that the circles in which they moved were not mutually exclusive. It has also demonstrated that puritanism derived its substance and meaning not merely from polemical interchanges which took place in market squares and streets and scholars' studies and texts, not merely from the inner psychological wranglings of experimental predestinarians, but also from altercations within the seedy, Bohemian and muck-raking world of Elizabethan Grub Street. Maria's equivocal comment on Malvolio in *Twelfth Night* seems a suitable epitaph for Stubbes and an appropriate note on which to close: 'sometimes he is a kind of puritan'.[92]

---

[89] Manley, *Literature and Culture*, p. 300.

[90] Collinson, 'Ecclesiastical Vitriol', pp. 157, 168.

[91] As noted in Gosson, *Playes Confuted*, sigs D5r, F1v–2r; Ringler, *Stephen Gosson*, pp. 38, 73. John Fletcher, *The Night Walker, or the Little Theife. A Comedy* (London, 1640), sig. F3v.

[92] William Shakespeare, *Twelfth Night*, eds Roger Warren and Stanley Wells (Oxford, 1994), act 2, sc. 2, l. 130, p. 131.

CHAPTER NINE

Laurence Chaderton and the Hampton Court Conference

Arnold Hunt

In January 1566 Robert Beaumont, master of Trinity College, Cambridge, wrote a long *apologia* to his former comrade-in-exile Anthony Gilby, explaining why he had subscribed to the Prayer Book:

> For myne owne parte, desirous to teache our ignorant Bretheren so long as I may, I weare the Cappe and Surplesse, the which if I refused to do, I coulde not be suffered to preache. I wishe with many mo godly Bretheren, that they may spedely be taken awaye. The which sholde shortly be brought to passe, if I were the publike person for suche matters lawfullie authorised. But nowe my hands are tyed ... [1]

Beaumont's letter shows that as early as the 1560s, a split had opened in the ranks of the 'godly Bretheren' over the issue of conformity to the Prayer Book. Moderates like Beaumont acknowledged their dislike of some of the ceremonies, but argued that they were 'lawfullie authorised' by the magistrate and that ceremonial scruples should not be allowed to interfere with the work of the ministry. Yet – as the defensive tone of Beaumont's letter demonstrates – they were uneasily aware that some of their old comrades regarded this as a betrayal. For radicals like Anthony Gilby, the ceremonies were not merely indifferent: they were illicit additions to the form of Christian worship laid down in scripture, and the magistrate had no right to impose them. Academic as this debate may seem – particularly to present-day members of the Church of England, accustomed to a far greater degree of diversity within the Anglican communion than either Beaumont or Gilby could possibly have imagined – one should not underestimate its importance. The stability of the Elizabethan settlement depended on the ability of moderate puritans to persuade their radical brethren to remain in communion with the Church of England rather than lapsing into separatism.

Although the arguments used to justify it became more subtle and sophisticated, the essence of the moderate puritan position outlined by

---

[1] CUL, MS Mm.1.43 (Thomas Baker's collections), p. 429.

Beaumont in 1566 remained unchanged for the next 75 years. The continuity of the moderate tradition can be seen most clearly in the long career of Laurence Chaderton, fellow of Christ's College, Cambridge, from 1568, master of Emmanuel College from its foundation in 1584 until his resignation in 1622, the grand old man of Cambridge puritanism until his death in 1640 at the age of 104, and latterly canonized as the patron saint of moderate puritanism, the 'central point of ideological reference' in Peter Lake's book, *Moderate Puritans and the Elizabethan Church* (1982). As a Cambridge Head of House, Chaderton (like Beaumont) acted as an academic talent-spotter, recruiting godly young men to tutor the sons of the puritan gentry, eventually placing them in vacant livings controlled by sympathetic patrons, and – if they got into trouble for nonconformity – using his influence at court to protect them from deprivation. Here again he could have echoed Beaumont's words to Gilby: 'How hote I am in urging mans traditions, I dare make them Judges, for whom I have bene & am a Sutor to my Lord of Canterbury & Mr Secretarie, that their refusall of Surplesses notwithstanding, they may remaine in their Livings still.' Chaderton's position as a mediator between nonconformity and authority – as it were, the acceptable face of puritanism – explains why he was one of the four ministers chosen to appear before the King at the Hampton Court Conference in January 1604 to put the puritan case for ecclesiastical reform.

It has long been recognized that the puritan speakers at Hampton Court – Chaderton, John Knewstub, John Reynolds and Thomas Sparke – opted for a moderate approach. After the Conference, disgruntled radicals like Henry Jacob accused them of having failed to attack the Prayer Book ceremonies in sufficiently strong terms.

> Most of the persons, appoynted to speake for the Ministers, were not of their chosing, nor nomination, nor of their judgment in the matters then and now in question, but of a cleane contrary. For being intreated at that time by the Ministers to dispute against these things, as things simply evill and such as cannot be yeelded unto without sinne; they professed to them, that they were not so perswaded, and therefore could not so doe. Being then requested, to let his Maiesty understand that some of their brethren were further perswaded touching the unlawfulnes of these things, then themselves were, they refused that also.[2]

Jacob's sense of grievance is understandable. The effect of the moderate approach adopted at Hampton Court was to render the radical agenda

---

[2] [Henry Jacob], *A Christian and modest offer of a most indifferent conference, or disputation*, STC 14329 (1606), D3r.

politically unfeasible: Jacob's demand for another conference was wholly impractical, wrote his moderate puritan opponent John Burges, because

> the State would never suffer these things to be questioned of unlawfulnesse, which Doctor *Raynold*, Doctor *Chadderton*, Doctor *Sparke*, and the rest the most eminent men of this nation, which seemed to favour that partie, would neither affirme to be unlawfull, nor bee knowne that any of that side were so weake as to think so.[3]

What is less clear, however, is whether this outcome was actually sought or desired by the puritan speakers at the conference. To put it another way, were they genuine in their moderation, or was it assumed for self-protection in circumstances where, as Reynolds complained, their opponents were only too eager to smear them with 'the imputation of Schisme'?

This uncertainty is compounded by the inadequacy of the evidence. As Patrick Collinson has remarked, 'the historian of Hampton Court faces formidable difficulties': contemporary accounts of the conference, though numerous, are 'episodic and selective', and the most important of them, William Barlow's *The Summe and Substance of the Conference ... in his Maiesties Privy-Chamber, at Hampton Court* (1604), has long been recognized as a tainted source, 'a skilfully tendentious piece of propaganda' designed to discredit the puritan clergy who participated. As for Chaderton, Peter Lake has described the available sources – principally drawn from the sole surviving volume of Chaderton's papers, now Lambeth Palace Library MS 2550 – as 'interesting without being comprehensive', permitting a detailed but 'rather patchy' account of the moderate puritan position.[4] This chapter will introduce a new source of evidence which helps to fill in some of the gaps: a group of books from Chaderton's library, annotated in his hand, including a copy of Barlow's *Summe and Substance* corrected against his own recollections of the Hampton Court Conference. In many respects, this new material simply reinforces and sharpens the picture of Chaderton that emerges from the existing sources. But whereas the papers in Lambeth MS 2550 are, for the most part, drafts of letters and sermons, these annotations are of a more private nature, consisting as they do of the raw material out of which Chaderton's controversial writings were

---

[3] John Burges, *An Answer reioyned to that much applauded pamphlet* (London, 1631), B6r.

[4] Patrick Collinson, 'The Jacobean Religious Settlement: the Hampton Court Conference', in Howard Tomlinson (ed.), *Before the Civil War: Essays on Early Stuart Politics and Government* (London, 1983), pp. 36–7; Peter Lake, *Moderate Puritans and the Elizabethan Church* (Cambridge, 1982), p. 5.

The text explaned.

Ætus vos posuit episcopos. In which the holy ghost hath placed you Bishops.) The discussing whereof, shall be like the trial of an *Ephraemite*, by *Shiboleth* and *Siboleth*, to see whether it *lisp* for the *Presbyterie*, or speak fully for the *Prælacy*. The first is coniecturall, becaufe whom verse 17. hee calleth *Presbyters*; them in this verse he intituleth *Bishops*, their names not distinct, their offices therefore are not different: that is *their* conclusion. The second, I thinke, is direct, these words describing fully every part of the *outward* function of *Bishops*. First, their *preeminent superioritie* in the word (*Episcopos*) for as there are ⲟⲝⲃⲁⲩⲧⲉⲥ *seers* Philip. 3.17. which expresseth the duty of each *Pastour* ouer his flock, (so are there 1.Pe.5,2 ⲉⲡⲉⲝⲛⲟ̄ⲧⲉⲥ (ⲟ̄ⲧⲉⲛ Ⲗⲉⲥⲟⲝⲟ̄ⲭⲟⲩⲧⲉⲥ) such as must visit & ouerlook both the *Flocke* and the *Seers*. 2. in the word (*posuit*) both their *Cathedrall Seate*, this word onely distinguishing a *Bishop* from an *Apostle* (setting aside their extraordinary indowments, and immediate calling) the *Apostles* function being an *vnlimited* *Circuit*, *Ite in vniuersum orbem* Mat.28.19. the *Bishops* a fixed or *positiue residence* in one citty : as also (*posuit*) not a change of regencie like the *Leuiticall seruice*, a weekely, monethly, or annuall course, but (*posuit*) setled in their persons during life. Thirdly, their *Diocesan Iurisdiction* (*In quo vniuerse*) for a *Parochian* assemblie, a petty parish, came not within S. *Pauls cognisance* for a *Bishop*. Fourthly, the *author* of these all (*spiritus sanctus*) this calling being no *humane inuention* : for *euery plant which my heauenly Father hath not planted shall bee rooted out*. Fifthly, the *manner* thereof, that is also in the

B 3   word

*a. If the holie ghost hath made you (presbyters) by ... this flock, then ...
heed to yr selues & to all that flock: to feed ... of god
But the holy gh. hath made you (presb.) BB. in this flock. Ergo.
Agayne. If god hath purchased this church wth his owne blud*

9.1 A page from William Barlow's *One of the foure Sermons preached before the Kings Maiestie* (1606), with Chaderton's annotations. The text under discussion is Acts 20:28, 'in which the Holy Ghost hath placed you bishops' (or 'overseers', as the Authorized Version translates it). Barlow argues that this proves the existence of episcopal government in the early church. In response, Chaderton asserts the equality of bishops and presbyters ('their names are distinct, not their office, or function') and accuses his opponent of dishonesty: 'is not this to add to the text? & to make it serv the purpose'. Reproduced by permission of the Master and Fellows, Trinity College, Cambridge.

developed. If, as Peter Lake has argued, moderate puritanism tended to define itself in relation to the views of its opponents, then Chaderton's annotations reveal the moderate puritan position in the process of definition, a process that was inevitably messier and more confused than his finished writings make it appear.[5]

Chaderton employed at least two distinct styles of annotation. From the notes in his copy of John Reynolds's *Sex theses* (1602) summarizing the main topics and supplying running-titles at the head of each page, we can deduce that Chaderton read the book closely, referred to it frequently and saw no reason to dissent from its conclusions.[6] In other books from his library, the marginalia are much more adversarial in character: a series of laconic but decisive interventions, aimed very precisely at particular words or sentences in the text, often indicating disagreement indirectly by pointing out faults in the logic of the argument.[7] In a man who was schooled in the formal syllogistic logic of the academic disputation, this is hardly surprising; but it is of some significance in assessing Chaderton's response to the Hampton Court Conference. Even after the conference's failure to produce any major reforms, puritans still clung to the belief that a conference between the bishops and the puritan ministers could reach a mutually satisfactory conclusion as long as it was conducted in the manner of a formal disputation, the arguments framed 'in strict forme of Syllogisme only', the replies made 'directly to the premises, either by denying or distinguishing', and the whole proceedings copied down and 'subscribed by all parties of each side in the conference, as their joynt act'. Hampton Court had failed not because this method was in any way flawed or impractical, but merely because the participants had not kept the rules: 'the Prelats took unto them selves liberty to interrupt, at their pleasure, those of the other side', and Barlow's report of the conference had not been agreed by all parties.[8] The King seems to have regarded the conference rather differently, telling the bishops in his opening speech that they were there 'severally by themselves, not to bee confronted by the contrary opponents' but to be consulted individually as occasion arose; and Patrick Collinson is right to point out that in practice, largely because of James's idiosyncratic style of chairmanship, the Conference

---

[5] Lake, *Moderate Puritans and the Elizabethan Church*, p. 7.

[6] John Reynolds, *Sex theses de sacra Scriptura & Ecclesia* (London, 1602). Chaderton's copy: Emmanuel College, Cambridge, MSS 4.3.1. All the annotations occur in the second section, the *Apologia thesium*, which implies that Chaderton owned and had already read the text of the theses themselves in the edition of 1580 (STC 20624).

[7] On styles of annotation, see William H. Sherman, *John Dee: the Politics of Reading and Writing in the English Renaissance* (Amherst, 1995), pp. 65–78.

[8] Jacob, *Christian and modest offer*, A2v.

was 'a kind of round-table conference on a variety of ecclesiastical topics' rather than anything more formal. Chaderton, however, may have expected the Conference to take the form of a disputation between opposing parties, with the King acting as an impartial moderator. He may therefore have shared the radicals' sense of frustration that the puritan cause had not been given a proper hearing.

When it came to justifying his own conduct, however, it was in Chaderton's own interests to portray the Conference in the King's terms, as a consultation exercise in which he and the other puritan clergy had been speaking for themselves and not as the delegates or representatives of any party. This enabled him to counter Jacob's charge of having betrayed the puritan cause, as well as Barlow's mischievous insinuation that the puritan speakers, for all their moderation, had been covertly pursuing a radical agenda. Barlow had, for example, described them as 'Agentes for the Millenarie Plaintiffes'. 'Patientes rather', replied Chaderton,

> being commanded to attend, nor but to heare his maiesties pleas-
> ure. God forbyd we should be agentes for any sect in religion or for
> any faction. Nether could we bee for these, seing none ever re-
> quired this at our handes. No learning therfore can iustifie this, nor
> excuse the breach of charitie.

When Barlow wrote that the second day's Conference was 'appointed ... for the Opponents to bring in their Complaintes', Chaderton responded forcefully: 'thei knew no such appoyntment'. And when he and the other puritan speakers, 'the most grave, learned, and modest of the aggreeved sort', were said to have been summoned by the King, Chaderton pounced triumphantly on the contradiction: 'Being sent for how could thei be agentes for others? Being willed to speak how could thei be plentives?'[9] Barlow's choice of vocabulary was clearly designed to serve a polemical purpose, but Chaderton's efforts to dissociate himself from the puritan radicals were equally disingenuous. A group of nearly 30 puritan ministers, including Stephen Egerton and Henry Jacob, the organizers of the Millenary Petition, appear to have been present at Hampton Court, 'at [the Conference] but not in place', and Jacob's testimony suggests that they were in close touch with Chaderton and the other puritan speakers. A list of proposals addressed 'to our reverend brethren, chosen to deal for the cause in the conference', which calls for the disputed ceremonies to be 'abolished, or at least left free to

---

[9] William Barlow, *The Summe and Substance of the Conference, which, it pleased his Excellent Maiestie to have with the Lords, Bishops, and other of his Clergie ... in his Maiesties Privy-Chamber, at Hampton Court* (London, 1604), B1v, D2r, D4r. Chaderton's copy: Trinity College, Cambridge, C.9.125.

use or refuse according to the conscience and discretion of the faithful minister', may represent a compromise between moderates and radicals; and many of the items on the list, such as the request 'that better order may be taken for the observation of the Sabbath', were indeed raised at the Conference.[10] Chaderton's depiction of the Conference as a royal audience, with the puritan ministers summoned to wait upon the King and 'to heare his maiesties pleasure', was a convenient simplification which ignored these intricate negotiations behind the scenes.

In his summing-up at the end of the Conference, the King ordered the puritan speakers to set a good example to 'all their sorte' by conforming to the Prayer Book, 'Obedience and Humilitie being markes of honest and good men'. Chaderton in particular was taken to task for allowing 'sitting Communions in Emanuel Colledge', to which he replied rather lamely that 'they had some kneeling also'. Finally, he and the other puritan speakers made a formal act of submission, promising (in Barlow's words) 'to bee quiet and obedient, now that they knew it to be the Kinges mind, to have it so'.[11] The Conference was over; but for Chaderton and the other Puritan participants, the most delicate part of the proceedings still lay ahead: persuading their radical brethren to accept what, on the face of it, looked like near-total defeat. They were not the only people trying to put a positive spin on the result. The account of the Conference drawn up by Patrick Galloway for Scottish circulation, and approved by the King himself, presents it as a major reforming enterprise involving the commissioning of a new translation of the Bible, the revision of the Prayer Book, the overhaul of the High Commission and the church courts, new restrictions on the importation of popish books, the removal of unlearned and scandalous clergy and a resolution that 'as manie learned ministers as may be had, with convenient maintenance for them, may be placed in suche places where there is want of preaching, with all haste'. But if James hoped that the Scots

---

[10] *HMC Montagu of Beaulieu* (London, 1900), pp. 32–4. Patrick Collinson's comment on the Montagu manuscripts ('The Jacobean Religious Settlement', p. 38) that the disputed ceremonies were condemned 'as absolutely unlawful rather than merely indifferent' results from a confusion between two separate documents, the list of proposals 'to our reverend brethren' (p. 32) and the more radical paper on 'the use of the surplice ... and sundry other offensive ceremonies in our church' (p. 34).

[11] Barlow, *Summe and Substance*, O1v, O4r. The best analysis of these concluding events can be found in Frederick Shriver, 'Hampton Court Re-visited: James I and the puritans', *JEH*, 33 (1982), p. 61, which stresses that although the King was 'trying to appear well disposed to the puritan representatives' he did not grant them any substantial concessions. Even this very limited show of support for the Puritans may, as John Morrill has suggested to me, have had more to do with sending signals back to Scotland than with any real sympathy for the puritans in England.

would welcome these measures, he was to be disappointed. When Galloway's report was read to the Edinburgh presbytery on 29 February 1604, James Melvill called on those present to express their solidarity 'with manie godlie and learned brethrein in our nighbour countrie, who, having expected a reformatioun, are disappointed and heavilie greeved', adding darkly that they should take great care 'that no perell or contagioun come from our nighbour kirk' to compromise the Reformed cause in Scotland.[12] Chaderton and his colleagues evidently faced an uphill struggle in trying to convince their puritan allies, whether in Scotland or in England, that the Conference had not been a disaster.

Chaderton's annotations to one of the puritan pamphlets published in the immediate aftermath of the Conference, the anonymous *Certaine Demandes with their grounds, drawne out of holy Writ* (1605), represent part of that process, in which Chaderton defended the use of the surplice in Emmanuel College chapel for what was probably the first time since the college was founded. The wearing of the surplice, Chaderton argued, was justified by 'Christian libertie warranting as well the wearing, as not wearing', depending on circumstances such as 'the law, use, and custome of this church'. Christ did not institute it, 'yet he left all free' so that the Christian magistrate 'may be licensed bothe to commaund and forbyd it'. When the authors of the *Certaine Demandes* declared that the surplice was 'falsly ... called indifferent', Chaderton retorted: 'prove this falsly, and take all'. When they condemned the use of 'popish and Idolatrous rites and ceremonies', Chaderton threw down a challenge: 'have you proved or can you prove them Idolatrous? 2°. can you prove them to be popish? 3°. being popish can you conclude that therefore thei may not be ordayned? 4°. can you prove them to be relicks monuments or memorialls of Idolatrie? si, eris mihi magnus Apollo'.[13]

Assembled in this way, Chaderton's annotations amount to the standard moderate conformist position, justifying the ceremonies as things indifferent, unnecessary but not unlawful. When the authors of the *Certaine Demandes* argued that the preaching of the word was 'in its owne nature more precious, more needfull and more profitable for the people' than the wearing of the surplice, Chaderton skilfully turned the argument against them: to be sure, the surplice was intrinsically unimportant, yet it was 'commaunded by authoritie upon condition of not

---

[12] David Calderwood, *The History of the Kirk of Scotland*, ed. Thomas Thomson (Wodrow Society, Edinburgh, 1842–49), vol. 6, pp. 241–7.

[13] *Certaine Demandes with their grounds, drawne out of holy Writ, and propounded in foro conscientiae by some religious Gentlemen*, STC 6572.5 (1605), A2v, B1r, B2r, B2v, B4r, H4v. Chaderton's copy: Trinity College, Cambridge, C.9.126. The Latin tag ('if so, I shall honour you as Apollo himself') comes from Virgil's Eclogues, 3: 104. (My thanks to Neil Hopkinson for this reference.)

preaching', and expediency therefore demanded that it be worn. Whether
authority was justified in imposing such a condition was a question he
did not choose to ask.[14] All this is fully consistent with the view of
Chaderton as a moderate for whom, as Peter Lake comments, the
Hampton Court Conference 'was far from a disaster. At worst it was a
tie: but most importantly it was a tie from which the puritans had
emerged to fight another day'. One of Chaderton's few recorded utterances at the Conference was a request 'that the wearing of the *Surplis*,
and the use of the *Crosse in Baptisme*, might not be urged upon some
honest, godly, and painefull ministers in some partes of *Lancashire*', to
which the King replied that if they were 'quiet of disposition, honest of
life, and diligent in their calling' they would not be forced to conform,
or at least not immediately. Having extracted this concession, Chaderton
could now carry on working behind the scenes, in the way that he and
other moderate puritans in positions of influence had always done,
buying time for nonconformist clergy while trying to persuade them to
conform.[15]

But Chaderton's moderation needs to be qualified. His annotations to
the 1559 Ordinal, unfortunately undated, show that he had once held
staunchly presbyterian views. Bishops, he believed, were no different
from the 'overseers' mentioned in Acts 20:28, and 'the worke and
ministerye of a Byshope' was therefore 'all one ministerie with the
priest'. Episcopacy was 'no ministerie ordayned by christ'. He also
maintained that clergy were to be chosen by the people, according to
the practice of the early church (Acts 6:5), and objected to the rubric
that 'the Archedeacon shall presente unto the Bysshop all them that
shall receive the order of Priesthode', noting that 'to present (before the
church where thei must minister have elected, or others that have
interest therein) is preposterous, and contrarie to thapostolick practise'.[16] It has been argued that by the time of the Hampton Court
Conference, Chaderton had abandoned his earlier presbyterianism,
or was at any rate less insistent on the prescriptive authority of apostolic practice.[17] Yet his annotations to William Barlow's sermon of

---

[14] *Certaine Demandes*, B3r.

[15] Lake, *Moderate Puritans and the Elizabethan Church*, p. 248. Barlow, *Summe and Substance*, O2r.

[16] *The fourme and maner of making and consecratyng, bisshops, priestes, and deacons* (1559, part of STC 16292). Chaderton's copy: LPL, MS 2550, fols 201–13.

[17] Collinson describes Chaderton as 'once, but perhaps no longer, a theoretical presbyterian' ('The Jacobean Religious Settlement', p. 38), while Lake suggests that Chaderton had retained his presbyterianism 'in a slightly modified form' which no longer laid claim to *iure divino* status (*Moderate Puritans and the Elizabethan Church*, pp. 260–61).

September 1606 'concerning the Antiquitie and Superioritie of Bishops' suggest that his views remained unchanged. Chaderton's marginal comments are unambiguously presbyterian: 'No episcopall calling different from the calling of presbyters ... their names are distinct, not their office or function, as the function of the Apostles was the same before and after the resurrection.' When Barlow describes the apostle Timothy as 'ordeined' bishop of Ephesus, Chaderton substitutes 'elected'; and in reference to Titus 1:5 ('and ordain elders in every city') he comments: 'these presbyters weare Bishops, vers. 7. and must not be made otherwyse then Paule had appoynted hym'.[18] These annotations put a very different complexion on Chaderton's presence at Hampton Court. The moderation of the puritan speakers at the Conference may have been tactically necessary, but it cannot be taken as an accurate guide to Chaderton's own views. Indeed, Chaderton may well have been the one speaker exempted from the strictures of the unrepentant presbyterian Humphrey Fen on 'that shew of a dispute in the cause at Hampton Court, wherein men were purposely chosen to undertake our cause, who (excepting one reverend Father) never tooke the cause to heart'.[19]

As a man with a radical past, Chaderton's readiness to justify the wearing of the surplice was more likely to impress other puritan radicals; in that sense, his presbyterianism simply made him a more valuable asset to the moderate cause. But his initial defence of the surplice was remarkably limited in its scope. In the immediate aftermath of Hampton Court, Chaderton can be found arguing that the surplice was a 'scholastical or Academicall habit' which could be lawfully worn in a university setting. This resembles the distinction drawn by John Foxe in 1576 between popish vestments (the chasuble, alb, amice, stole and maniple) and scholarly garments (the gown, academic cap, and surplice); but it was peculiarly appropriate to the special circumstances of 1604–05, when Chaderton had agreed to use the surplice in Emmanuel College but when it was still unclear how strictly it would be imposed elsewhere.[20] It was an argument which enabled Chaderton to justify his own conformity without committing himself to the general enforcement of the ceremonies. Writing to Chaderton in January 1606, Thomas Brightman also distinguished between the use of the surplice 'which is injoyned us in the country' and its

---

[18] William Barlow, *One of the foure Sermons preached before the Kings Maiestie, at Hampton Court* (1606), B2v, B3r, C2v, C3r. Chaderton's copy: Trinity College, Cambridge, C.9.113.

[19] *The Last Will and Testament, with the Profession of the Faith of Humfrey Fen, sometimes Pastor of one of the Churches of Coventry* (London, 1641), A4r.

[20] LPL, MS 2550, fol. 58r. For Foxe's argument, see C. M. Dent, *Protestant Reformers in Elizabethan Oxford* (Oxford, 1983), p. 59.

use 'in Colleges', though, unlike Chaderton, he denied the validity of the distinction: 'There seemeth to be some difference, yet the nigh similitude of an evill thing, as also the former generall reasons, maketh this also to seem a poyson not to be touched.'[21]

At the same time as Chaderton was experimenting with this severely qualified defence of the surplice 'after the manner of the universitie', he was also showing himself extremely unwilling to defend another of the disputed ceremonies, the sign of the cross in baptism.[22] In his annotations to *Certaine Demandes*, he was prepared to justify the lawfulness of the surplice on the grounds that what was unlawful was 'not the things but the abuse'. However, in his annotations to Samuel Gardiner's *A Dialogue or Conference ... about the rites and ceremonies of the Church of England* (1605) he turned this argument on its head. Gardiner declared that the sign of the cross should not be abolished merely because it had been superstitiously abused. 'Why not?' responded Chaderton, 'seing thabuse can not be removed from us, onless the thing be.'[23] This was not as inconsistent as it may seem. The crucial difference between the surplice and the sign of the cross, in Chaderton's opinion, was that the surplice had the practical function of clothing the body, whereas 'the cross is not commaunded, nor ordayned by god for any such necessarie use of soule or bodie'. But while it may not have been inconsistent, it was suspiciously convenient for Chaderton's own ministry at Emmanuel, where he was obliged to wear the surplice but would not have had occasion to baptize or to use the sign of the cross, and may not have been required to subscribe to the Prayer Book.[24] It is hard

---

[21] Brightman to Chaderton, 10 January 1605–06: LPL, MS 2550, fol. 176.

[22] The cross in baptism was widely regarded as the least defensible of the disputed ceremonies: 'none of the other are more evill then this', declared one writer (*An Answere to a Sermon preached the 17 of April Anno D. 1608, by George Downame*, STC 20605 (1609), 7*1r). John Downe, a former fellow of Emmanuel who at the time of the Hampton Court Conference was vicar of Winsford, Somerset, was prepared to wear the surplice but refused to use the cross in baptism 'because he taketh it to be a matter unlawful' (Somerset Record Office, Taunton, D/D/Ca 134).

[23] Samuel Gardiner, *A Dialogue or Conference betweene Irenaeus and Antimachus, about the rites and ceremonies of the Church of England* (London, 1605), C4v. Chaderton's copy: Trinity College, Cambridge, C.9.132.

[24] John Reynolds was not required to subscribe (see Dent, *Protestant Reformers in Elizabethan Oxford*, pp. 227–8), and the same indulgence may have been extended to Chaderton. One puritan writer admitted in 1605 that the bishops were flexible in their enforcement of conformity, 'accepting of some the use of the crosse, and surplice onely. Of others the use of the surplice alone; of others a promise to use them onely; and of some the profession of their judgment onely that they may be used, without pressing them to the use of them, at all.' [Samuel Hieron], *A short dialogue proving that the ceremonies ... are defended, by none other arguments then such as the Papists have heretofore used*, STC 6814 (1605), A4v.

to avoid the suspicion that Chaderton's defence of the surplice was an exercise in pragmatism: he was prepared to conform, and to justify his conformity, only so far as authority required him to do so, and no further.

As it became clear that the ceremonies were to be enforced across the country, Chaderton was forced to revise his earlier arguments, and to fall back on the familiar defence of conformity as part of the obedience due to the magistrate in matters of indifference. 'If the lawes had not beene in these cases alreadie made,' wrote Gardiner, 'I should never, for my owne part, wish to have them made: but seeing wee have now such prescription for them, and they are still enjoyned us, I shall not be one to marre them.' Chaderton concurred. 'Nor I: but to pray for the chang.'[25] The implication was that change would come about from above, by royal decree or by a replay of the Hampton Court Conference, rather than by the pressure of nonconformity from below. Yet even this defence of the ceremonies was hedged with qualifications. 'We must beware', wrote Chaderton in his position paper *De licitis*, 'that we use them not with a repugning or doubting conscience but with a mynd fully persuaded of the lawfulnes and indifferencie thereof for els we synn being condemned of our owne conscience. Yea to such an one yndifferentes (though otherwyse cleane of them selves) are uncleane'.[26] The one point where Chaderton registered agreement with the authors of *Certaine Demandes* was when they enquired whether it was lawful to use the ceremonies 'doubtingly'. His answer was definite: 'no'. It was true that 'the synn cometh from the doubt of the conscience, and not from the impuritie of the garment, or unlawfulnes of the usage', but it was sin nevertheless.[27] It was also true that it arose from 'ignorance' and was therefore capable of refutation; but if a man failed to be persuaded by Chaderton's arguments about the lawful use of indifferent ceremonies, neither Chaderton nor anyone else had the right to force him to conform.[28]

There were thus strict limits on the lengths to which Chaderton would go in co-operating with the authorities to enforce the ceremonies. Nor was this the end of them. 'We must use them without geving offence to any present that shall signifie his weaknes in fayth unto us or which otherwyse shall be made knowne to us. For in the use of these we must seeke to please as well the weake as the strong, yea all men.' Even

---

[25] Gardiner, *Dialogue*, E3v.

[26] LPL, MS 2550, fol. 58v.

[27] *Certaine Demandes*, G3v, B3r.

[28] *Certaine Demandes*, H2v; see also Chaderton's notes on Gardiner, *Dialogue*, E3v, and Lake, *Moderate Puritans and the Elizabethan Church*, p. 255.

if a minister was personally convinced of the lawfulness of the ceremonies, he should still refrain from using them if they were likely to offend other members of the congregation.[29] This had obvious implications for Chaderton himself, which was why he was so anxious to justify his conduct in the eyes of the godly, why he apparently required the fellows of Emmanuel to sign a declaration 'that there is no just cause why any should be offended' with the use of the surplice in the college chapel, and why, despite these precautions, he refrained from wearing the surplice until the last possible moment. Samuel Ward's diary gives 18 January 1604, the final day of the Hampton Court Conference, as the date when the surplice was officially ordered to be worn in Emmanuel, but reveals that the college was still holding out in August, when Magdalene and Sidney Sussex had succumbed. Not until November, when the King personally gave order 'to remove him if he continue obstinate', did Chaderton finally submit.[30]

Behind the debate on ceremonial conformity, as the authors of the *Certaine Demandes* were aware, lay a more fundamental and troubling question: could the conscience of the supreme magistrate, 'be he never so Christian', satisfy the conscience of 'him that obeyeth doubtingly'? Chaderton described this as 'a great poynt, full of difficultie and perill', but his own opinion is made plain by his marginal comment that 'conscience ruleth not conscience but superior inferior. As for the commaund it reacheth not to conscience.' For the puritan speakers at Hampton Court, this was a point of immediate practical importance: in his annotations to Barlow's *Summe and Substance*, Chaderton originally wrote that their duty was 'to heare and obey his maiesties pleasure', then – apparently feeling that this threatened the autonomy of the individual conscience – crossed out the words 'and obey'. There was no absolute necessity to obey the magistrate: when Gardiner wrote of the ceremonies that 'the Christian Magistrate commanding them, whom wee stand bound to obey for conscience sake, I hold them necessarie to be observed', Chaderton objected: 'doth not this necessitie remove th'indifferencie?' There is, admittedly, one point in *De licitis* where Chaderton appears to admit such a necessity, when he declares that just as Christ paid tribute-money (Matthew 17:27) 'least he should offend the profane kings', so 'we must use [the ceremonies] lest we geve offence to our superior governors'. The risk of offending our brethren by using the ceremonies is thus counterbalanced by the risk of offending the magistrate by not using them, a dilemma which Chaderton does not

---

[29] LPL, MS 2550, fol. 58v. See also Chaderton's notes on Gardiner, *Dialogue*, E2v.

[30] M. M. Knappen (ed.), *Two Elizabethan Puritan Diaries* (Chicago and London, 1933). *HMC Salisbury*, vol. 16 (London, 1933), pp. 366–7.

attempt to resolve. However, he immediately contradicts himself by saying that we 'may' (not 'must') use the ceremonies 'to manifest our obedience to our superiors', citing Romans 12:18, Paul's exhortation to keep the peace 'if it be possible, as much as lieth in you'. Obedience to the magistrate is thus presented as an additional motive for conformity, but not as an overriding necessity.

Chaderton's doctrine of obedience is developed in more detail in a slightly later set of annotations, to David Owen's loyalist tract *Herod and Pilate Reconciled* (1610). Not surprisingly, Owen's ferocious anti-puritan invective found little favour with Chaderton, who jotted down a few of the more colourful passages on a blank page at the beginning of the book: 'Puritans ... their unquiet hartes, & seditious disposition ... Parish Popes. Lordlie consisterie. Polytyque puritans ... Brethren in sedition will sett the church on fyre & state in an uprore, robb wyddows houses &c.' More serious than these allegations was Owen's claim that puritans asserted a 'nationall soveraigntie' which allowed kings to be deposed by their own subjects. 'Quote express words or els', responded Chaderton; and on the following page, when Owen named Christopher Goodman, Lambert Danaeu, Theodore Beza and the 'English Sectarie' Dudley Fenner as the four leading proponents of resistance theory, he retorted: 'none of these 4 once nameth nationall suveraygntie to dispose of kings & their kingdoms.'[31] As always, Chaderton was quick to spot the weak links in his opponent's chain of reasoning. Owen had argued, with impeccable logic, that 'particular instances' of kings being deposed did not prove that deposition was lawful: one could not reason '*a facto ad ius*', from a particular deed to a general rule. Chaderton commented that by the same token, one could not deduce a rule from the not doing of a deed ('*a non facto*'), which, as he pointed out, was precisely what Owen was trying to do. 'Who questioned *David* for his murther and adulterie?' asked Owen:

> Who censured *Salomon* for his idolatrie? though their crimes were capitall by the law of God. After that kingdome was divided, all the Kings of *Israel*, and most of the Kings of *Judah*, were notorious idolaters: yet during those kingdomes, which endured above 200. yeares, no Priest did chalenge, no States-men did claime power from the highest, to punish or depose their Princes.

But the fact that neither David, Solomon nor any of their successors had been deposed did not prove that deposition was unlawful.[32]

---

[31] David Owen, *Herod and Pilate Reconciled* (Cambridge, 1610), ¶3r. Chaderton's copy: Trinity College, Cambridge, C.10.126.
[32] Owen, *Herod and Pilate*, A1v, F1v.

As a response to Owen's charges of puritan disloyalty, this is remarkably half-hearted. Were there any circumstances under which a king might lawfully be resisted or deposed? While Chaderton is understandably reticent on this subject, he does drop a few hints. In his annotations to *Certaine Demandes*, he declares that while the magistrate may lawfully suspend nonconformist clergy from preaching or administering the sacraments, 'yet he may unjustlie forbydd these exercises'; and in his annotations to Owen, he permits passive resistance to an unjust command. Owen cited various examples of early Christians who had refused to obey the emperor but who 'resisted not his soveraigne power' and 'yeelded themselves to his mercy and pleasure'. Chaderton underlined the words 'refused to obey' and enquired sharply: 'is not this to resist?'[33] Thus it is reasonable to suppose that Chaderton would, for example, have supported Grindal's non-compliance with the royal order to suppress the prophesyings. This, in itself, is not particularly surprising; but Chaderton's concept of resistance does not stop here. When Owen argued that kings 'can by no compulsion of law, be drawne to punishment', Chaderton responded: 'what yf he be elected on that condition? or be sworne?' And when Owen declared that even if the king was impious or unjust, 'the subiect must endure him … and no mortall man hath authoritie to disturbe or displace him', Chaderton posed the awkward question: 'what must the state doe?' The conditions under which the king exercises his office, and the persons or institutions through which the state acts, are left conveniently vague; but it is hard to interpret Chaderton's remarks as anything other than an affirmation of the State's power to depose the king. Elsewhere, Owen quoted the teaching of Daneau that 'in case the king deserve to be deposed … that ought to be done by the publike Councell, the Parliament of the kingdome, or by the Estates of the land', to which Chaderton commented: 'yf there be any such fundamentall laws of a kingdome to which all are obliged by othe'. This is Chaderton's strongest hint that a king who has sworn to obey the 'fundamentall laws', and who then breaks his oath, may lawfully be deposed.[34]

Chaderton was not the only person in Cambridge to harbour doubts about Owen's doctrine of obedience. In January 1618 Owen, who was a fellow of Clare Hall, fell into conversation with Ralph Brownrigg, a fellow of Pembroke Hall, who criticized *Herod and Pilate Reconciled* and put the following questions to him: '1. Whither a Kinge breaking fundamentall Lawes maye be opposed? 2. What is to be thought of the

---

[33] *Certaine Demandes*, A2r. Owen, *Herod and Pilate*, C1r.
[34] Owen, *Herod and Pilate*, ¶4r. I am grateful to Alan Cromartie for discussing the implications of this passage with me.

Noblemen when they opposed King John making him feudarye to the Pope?' For proposing these 'two scandalous Questions' Brownrigg was suspended from his degrees, and the case was referred to the King by the vice-chancellor, John Richardson, 'and some other of the heads'.[35] As a Head of House, Chaderton was notionally involved in the censure of Brownrigg and the endorsement of *Herod and Pilate Reconciled*, a book printed in Cambridge under the vice-chancellor's imprimatur, as the official doctrine of the university. His annotations, however, show that he and Brownrigg were thinking along similar lines, and lend support to Richard Cust's suggestion that 'in certain godly circles ideas of resistance represented part of a continuing tradition'.[36] It was a tradition that tended to run underground, only occasionally breaking cover; it is significant that both Brownrigg and Chaderton preferred to express their opinions indirectly, by way of objections to Owen's doctrine, and in private. One of the few occasions when it surfaced in print was in Andrew Willet's commentary on the first book of Samuel, in which he debated 'whether it be not lawfull to kill a tyrant, seeing David spared Saul'. Willet declared that although there was no warrant for a private individual to kill a tyrannical ruler,

> yet tyrants and wicked governours may be remooved by the whole state ... but this must be understood of such kingdomes where the kingdome goeth by election; as in Polonia, and Venice ... but where kingdomes goe by succession, the reason is otherwise: unlesse the Prince by oath be tied unto certaine conditions ... which seemeth to be the question at this day, between the Archduke and the States of the united Provinces.[37]

Willet's application of this principle to the situation in Holland conveniently diverts the reader's attention from its potential application to England, where the monarch, though not elected, was undoubtedly 'tied unto certaine conditions' by the coronation oath. Willet was a former fellow of Christ's College and knew Chaderton well; his discussion of resistance theory not only helps to flesh out Chaderton's typically laconic remarks, but also suggests that there was a received tradition of teaching on the subject in Cambridge.[38]

---

[35] CUL, University Archives V.C.Ct. I. 9 (Acta Curiae 1617–21), fols 22–4.

[36] Richard Cust, *The Forced Loan and English Politics 1626–1628* (Oxford, 1987), p. 184.

[37] Andrew Willet, *An Harmonie upon the First Booke of Samuel* (London, 1614), N2v. William Dowsing's copy of this work (now in CUL, Bassingbourn 48) shows that he paid close attention to this passage.

[38] On Willet's links with Chaderton, see Anthony Milton, *Catholic and Reformed* (Cambridge, 1995), p. 13.

The picture of Chaderton that emerges from these annotations – a lifelong presbyterian, a reluctant semi-conformist and a student of resistance theory; in short, a man of radical views – is not altogether surprising. As I suggested above, his efforts during and after the Hampton Court Conference to disengage himself from his radical brethren need to be regarded with a certain amount of scepticism; *via media* rhetoric in this period is rarely as innocent as it seems. But this puts a sharper edge on the question of Chaderton's response to the Conference. How far would Chaderton have shared Jacob's dissatisfaction at the failure of the radical agenda to get a proper hearing? There is no doubt that Hampton Court was a fairly comprehensive defeat for the puritan cause. Admittedly, Barlow's narrative may exaggerate the scale of that defeat, as Mark Curtis has suggested and as one of Chaderton's annotations appears to confirm. According to Barlow, the King said of the Puritan speakers that 'they did ... traduce the present well setled Church governement'; *'nihil istiusmodi memini'* (I remember nothing of the sort), was Chaderton's reply. While the King was hardly the impartial chairman that Chaderton might have wished for, he was neither as partisan nor as forthright in his anti-puritan views as Barlow's account suggests.[39] But what Chaderton says here is arguably less significant than what he fails to say elsewhere. The crucial events of the second day's Conference – the King's brisk dismissal of the puritan objections to the Prayer Book, his famous remark 'no bishop, no king' and his parting threat that if the puritans did not conform 'I will harrie them out of the land, or else doe worse' – attracted no marginal comment from Chaderton, implying that on these points Barlow's account is a tolerably accurate record of what actually took place.[40] This bears out Frederick Shriver's argument that while the Conference was a sincere attempt to conciliate puritan opinion, James profoundly distrusted puritan nonconformity and never seriously contemplated any major alterations to the Elizabethan settlement.

In matters of doctrine, the puritan speakers scored a few successes. On the issue of lay baptism, for example – the one issue debated at the conference on which the King was in substantial disagreement with the bishops – Chaderton's annotations reveal his approval of James's stance. Bancroft, speaking in support of baptism by laypersons in case of necessity, had declared that a Christian man would wish to have his child baptized 'by any meanes'. 'What', wrote Chaderton, scandalized, 'by a woman? or boy?' Bilson's argument in favour of lay baptism was

[39] Barlow, *Summe and Substance*, E2v. M. H. Curtis, 'Hampton Court Conference and its Aftermath', *History*, 46 (1961), pp. 1–16.
[40] Barlow, *Summe and Substance*, M1v, M2r.

that 'the minister is not of the *Essence* of the sacrament', to which the King answered that 'though he be not of the Essence of the sacrament, yet is he of the Essence of the right and lawfull ministrie of the sacrament'. Chaderton's rebuttal was even more decisive: 'Minister not of the essence. Is not everie precept of god of the essence of the thing commaunded?'[41] The consequent alteration of the Prayer Book rubric to forbid lay baptism was of considerable doctrinal significance, since it effectively denied the absolute necessity of baptism as a precondition of salvation. Frederick Shriver believes that 'only very small changes' were made to the Prayer Book as a result of the Conference, but Chaderton's attention to the question of lay baptism suggests that he would not have regarded this as a trivial concession.[42] He may, indeed, have regarded it as an indication of the King's soundness on the crucial issue of predestination. When Barlow reported that James had 'very well approved' the Church of England's doctrine of predestination, as set down in the Articles, Chaderton responded crisply, 'not to my memorie', and went on to gloss James's dictum that 'we may often depart from Grace' in an orthodox Reformed fashion, as a departure 'from the measure, not from the gift', thus contradicting Barlow's claim that the King had expressed his 'utter dislike' of the doctrine of perseverance.[43]

But while these annotations show that there were significant areas of agreement between the King and the puritans, other annotations suggest that Chaderton was deeply dissatisfied with the outcome of the Conference. It is clear, for example, that he had hoped for a major revision of the confirmation service to turn it into a stringent examination 'whether the baptized have kept their promiss'; while the King's assertion that 'none shold preach without [episcopal] licence' prompted the query '*denique quid non?*' (which should probably be paraphrased 'what, then, do they say no to?'), a reflection on the failure of the bishops to reject unlearned clergy. Here, Chaderton pinpointed two of the major administrative weaknesses in the Church of England, neither of which was adequately addressed at Hampton Court. Elsewhere, he noted the failure to put into practice the reforms which had been agreed at the conference. Barlow acknowledged that the puritan proposal for a crackdown on the profanation of the Sabbath 'found a generall and

---

[41] Barlow, *Summe and Substance*, C4v, D1v.

[42] Shriver, 'Hampton Court Re-visited', p. 62. C. M. Dent has also argued that the conference failed to provide any of the 'additional doctrinal safeguards' which the puritans desired (*Protestant Reformers in Elizabethan Oxford*, p. 229); but for the significance of the decision on lay baptism, see the comments of Nicholas Tyacke, *Anti-Calvinists: the Rise of English Arminianism c. 1590–1640* (Oxford, 1987), p. 25, and Seán Hughes, *Journal of Theological Studies*, new series, 45 (1994), p. 407.

[43] Barlow, *Summe and Substance*, E3v.

unanimous assent'; 'yet not executed', commented Chaderton sourly. Chaderton's annotations to Matthew Sutcliffe's *Treatise of Ecclesiasticall Discipline* (1591) show that he also wanted the sanction of excommunication to be limited to cases of 'contumacie joined with impenitent obstinacie' instead of being exercised indiscriminately; another reform that was generally supported at the Conference but never acted upon.[44]

Subsequent conformist apologetic depicted Hampton Court as an almost theatrical show of obedience in which 'D.D. Rainoldes, Sparkes, M. Chadderton, and Knewstubs ... were not so wedded to theire owne opinions, and other mens examples at the first, but theie afterwardes, upon better advisement, and conference with most godlie, and worthie men, altered theire mindes, and promised conformitie even to al thinges required'.[45] Quite apart from being the sort of *ad hominem* argument for conformity that Chaderton, with his belief that 'conscience ruleth not conscience', would have detested, this is a profoundly inaccurate interpretation of Chaderton's response to the Conference. Not only was he frustrated by the failure to initiate major reforms, but his conformity was, at most, half-hearted, and his obedience to the King was qualified by the demands of conscience. Significantly, he was prepared to defend the notes in the Geneva Bible against the King's attack on them as 'very partiall, untrue, seditious, and savouring, too much, of dangerous, and trayterous conceipts: As for example, *Exod.* 1. 19. where the marginall note alloweth *disobedience to Kings*'. Chaderton underlined the last three words, and commented: 'being an obedience to god, not otherwyse'. In circumstances where he and the other puritan speakers were being required to submit to the King's judgement, and at the very point in Barlow's account where Puritan loyalty was being called into question, Chaderton exposed the potential conflict between obedience to God and obedience to the magistrate, and – by implicitly upholding the individual's right to arbitrate between these competing claims on obedience – articulated a doctrine of conscience very much at odds with that of James.[46]

Peter Lake has questioned the validity of the distinction between 'radical' and 'moderate' puritanism, particularly when applied to Chaderton.

---

[44] Matthew Sutcliffe, *A Treatise of Ecclesiasticall Discipline* (London, 1591), T2r. Chaderton's copy: Trinity College, Cambridge, C.9.11.

[45] 'Certaine objections with answeres and replies for the finding out of the truth touching Kneeling in the act of receiving the Lords Supper' (1607), Beinecke Library, Yale, Osborn MS b.191, p. 26.

[46] On James's doctrine of conscience, see Kevin Sharpe, 'Private Conscience and Public Duty in the Writings of James VI and I', in John Morrill, Paul Slack and Daniel Woolf (eds), *Public Duty and Private Conscience in Seventeenth-Century England* (Oxford, 1993), pp. 77–100.

'Committed ... to the national church' yet 'unwilling to denounce as sectaries those who pushed their protestant principles to more radical conclusions', Chaderton embodies the tension between the radical and moderate positions, but without coming down firmly on one side or the other: his teaching on the ceremonies 'provided a basis for both the control of precisian excess and a critique of the ecclesiastical establishment', neatly combining moderate and radical aspects. His newly discovered annotations are equally even-handed in criticizing the advocates of nonconformity for their misguided dogmatism and the defenders of episcopacy for their unscriptural pretensions. But Lake's argument does not mean that Chaderton the Elizabethan radical evolved easily or naturally into Chaderton the Jacobean moderate. Chaderton was unsympathetic to a great deal of Jacobean conformist argument, even when it was couched in very moderate language. He rebuked Samuel Gardiner for suggesting that the surplice could be regarded as a symbol of purity; for 'is it no religion to signifie puritie and dignitie?' and as he argued elsewhere, 'no religiouse use of the ceremonies is urged by our church, nether ought any to use them religiously as any partes of divine service or worshyp, but as maters of order, conformitie, and testifications of obedience to the church, and prince'.[47] When Robert Sanderson, Lake's archetypal 'Calvinist conformist', tried to draw a distinction between two types of *jure divino* ceremonies, those that could not be altered at all and those that might be altered in case of necessity, Chaderton (by now in his nineties) would have none of it, annotating Sanderson's tract in a tremulous but still vigorous hand: 'Yf this be, in deed, jus divinum, it byndes no less then the other.'[48] These passages, and Chaderton's annotations, reveal the difference between Elizabethan and Jacobean styles of conformity, the one regarding the ceremonies merely as things indifferent, the other more receptive to the notion of 'significant ceremonies' and with a more flexible definition of *jure divino*. In these matters Chaderton, as might be expected, was an unreconstructed member of the Elizabethan old guard.

Lake questions the distinction between radical and moderate puritans on the grounds that their shared commitment to an 'evangelical protestant world-view' was far more significant than their disagreements over ceremonial conformity. Such disagreements were not trivial, but 'amongst men who recognised the sincerity and zeal of each other's protestantism'

---

[47] Gardiner, *Dialogue*, C1v; Chaderton's notes on Thomas Brightman's letter, LPL, MS 2550, fol. 176.

[48] Robert Sanderson, *A Soveraigne Antidote against Sabbatarian Errours* (London, 1636), D1r. Chaderton's copy: Trinity College, Cambridge, C.26.34. On Sanderson, see Peter Lake, 'Serving God and the Times: the Calvinist conformity of Robert Sanderson', *JBS*, 27 (1988).

they were 'not of prime importance'. Nicholas Tyacke has argued that at the Hampton Court Conference, doctrinal questions took precedence over ceremonial grievances, and that the King and many of the bishops, while stopping short of adopting the Lambeth Articles as an official confession of faith, supported the Calvinist doctrines put forward by the puritan speakers. The accommodation between the bishops and nonconformist clergy that held good for most of James's reign rested on the 'long-standing assumption that in matters of doctrine Puritans and their opponents were in fundamental agreement'. Patrick Collinson also believes that the 'rising tide of consensual, evangelical Calvinism all but submerged the old differences between conformity and nonconformity', and that the ceremonies 'assumed minor importance in the perceived priorities of the religious public'.[49] I suggest that this view needs to be revised. Even a man like Chaderton, for whom the ceremonies were indifferent, was extremely reluctant to conform, not just out of respect for the feelings of his radical brethren but out of a personal commitment to a reformed discipline – polity as well as liturgy – that could not be laid aside merely for the sake of a doctrinal consensus. Any attempt to enforce ceremonial conformity, as in the aftermath of the Hampton Court Conference, could easily have shattered that consensus. That this did not happen had a lot to do with Chaderton's diplomatic skills; but simply because it did not happen, one should not assume that the radical and moderate shades of puritan opinion were inseparable or that Chaderton, if he had had to choose between them, would necessarily have chosen moderation.

Some commentators have argued that the Hampton Court Conference did represent a parting of the ways, and that Chaderton did indeed choose the path of moderation. Patrick Collinson regarded the Conference as 'the end of the story' for the Elizabethan style of puritanism: the King had ruled out any possibility of further reformation, the puritan clergy were forced either to conform or to leave the Church of England, and the majority of them chose to remain. Peter Lake has suggested that this was the more far-sighted choice. He contrasts Chaderton with the radical nonconformist (and product of Chaderton's Emmanuel) William Bradshaw, pointing out that whereas Bradshaw's ministry was confined to the protected enclave of a godly gentry household, Chaderton's ministry could be exercised over a much wider sphere of influence 'in less contentious, but in the long run no less significant, ways'.[50] But this is

---

[49] Lake, *Moderate Puritans and the Elizabethan Church*, p. 281. Tyacke, *Anti-Calvinists*, pp. 22, 186. Collinson, 'The Jacobean Religious Settlement', p. 50.
[50] Patrick Collinson, *The Elizabethan Puritan Movement* (London, 1967), p. 465. Lake, *Moderate Puritans and the Elizabethan Church*, pp. 277, 281.

to underestimate Chaderton's radicalism. With hindsight, it is easy to see the Hampton Court Conference as a decisive rejection of the Elizabethan puritan programme, but Chaderton continued to await a magisterial reformation and, in his own words, 'to pray for the chang', an expression of that half-hearted conformity which we have already encountered in Beaumont, reluctantly donning the cap and surplice but still hoping 'that they may spedely be taken awaye'. Chaderton's conformity was qualified and partial; like Bradshaw, he was fortunate to live in a protected enclave where the limits of his conformity were not immediately obvious. And it was as a radical, not as a moderate, that he proved to be most influential. By the time of his death in 1640, the moderate, conformist puritanism of the Jacobean period had been discredited by its association with Laudianism, and presbyterianism had re-emerged as a viable alternative. It is, of course, possible to regard Chaderton as a sort of puritan coelacanth: an Elizabethan who outlived his own time, and as such an exceptional figure. But one is forced to wonder whether the real accident of survival may not be Chaderton's annotated books rather than Chaderton himself, and whether other Jacobean 'moderates' might not, but for the loss of their private papers, prove to have held unfashionably Elizabethan and unexpectedly radical beliefs.

CHAPTER TEN

'The Problem of "Calvinism"': English theologies of predestination *c.* 1580–1630

Seán F. Hughes[1]

In 1985 Patrick Collinson in his essay 'England and International Calvinism, 1558–1640' raised some crucial questions about the use of the term Calvinism for the study of the Church of England from the reign of Elizabeth I to the English Civil War.[2] He believed that 'the extent to which English Protestantism in the age of its maturity can be properly called Calvinist is one of some delicacy. "Calvinist" is a stereotype and too blunt an instrument for any discriminating purpose'.[3] For Collinson the term had the added danger of implying a subjection of English Protestantism to 'some Genevan magisterium' which was not the case.[4] The use of the term 'Calvinism' tended to exaggerate the impact of Calvin and his successor at Geneva, Theodore Beza, and to obscure the diverse theological traditions of the Reformed churches of Switzerland, south-west Germany, France, the Low Countries, England and Scotland. Collinson acknowledged in passing that the term Reformed with a capital 'R' would be better than Calvinist, but despite his serious misgivings, he felt the continued use of 'Calvinism' and its cognates was unavoidable.

Collinson's remarks were an intervention in a long-running debate about the existence of a 'Calvinist consensus' in England. Nicholas Tyacke has argued that 'Calvinism, centring on the belief in divine predestination both double and absolute' was the 'characteristic theology' of English Protestantism, and its acceptance by virtually the entire clerical élite

---

[1] I am deeply indebted to Patrick Collinson, Arnold Hunt, Lori Anne Ferrell and A. S. McGrade for their invaluable comments on various drafts of this chapter. I am particularly grateful to the editors, Caroline Litzenberger and Susan Wabuda for their superb editorial skills, endless patience and indispensable suggestions.

[2] Patrick Collinson, 'England and International Calvinism, 1558–1640', in M. Prestwick (ed.), *International Calvinism* (Oxford, 1985), pp. 197–223.

[3] Collinson, 'International Calvinism', p. 214.

[4] Collinson, 'International Calvinism', p. 214.

provided an important bond of stability.[5] In reply, Peter White has denied the existence of a 'Calvinist consensus' and argued that Calvinism, defined 'with reference to the doctrine of predestination', was alien to the Church of England.[6] However, their debate was not over terminology: Tyacke and White both accepted the validity of the term Calvinism, even though they disagreed vehemently about its applicability to English Protestantism. Collinson's concerns about the dangers inherent in the term should therefore have set alarm bells ringing in both camps.

Instead the debate has continued to focus on the predestinarian theology of English divines, and whether it does or does not merit the label 'Calvinist'. The inevitable reaction has now begun: Peter Lake has criticized what he describes as the 'bizarre obsession with predestination'.[7] Indeed, the intrinsic importance of theology has been called into question. 'Religion may have been the central discourse of 1642', wrote Kenneth Fincham, 'yet we must acknowledge that it embodied and mediated a host of secular concerns and values'.[8] In my view, the frustration and bewilderment of many historians, confronted by what they perceive as a sterile debate, has a great deal to do with the misuse of the term 'Calvinism', and there is a great risk that religion will again be sidelined in the current historiography unless historians develop a keener sense of the perils of 'Calvinism' as well as its obvious convenience.

Tyacke and White have both been misled by the widely held thesis of 'Calvin against the Calvinists', which holds that Reformed Protestantism underwent a sea-change in the late sixteenth century.[9] According to

---

[5] Nicholas Tyacke, 'Puritanism, Arminianism and Counter-Revolution', in Conrad Russell (ed.), *The Origins of the English Civil War* (London, 1973), pp. 119–43; N. Tyacke, 'The Rise of Arminianism Reconsidered', *Past and Present*, 115, May (1987), pp. 201–16; N. Tyacke, *Anti-Calvinists: the Rise of English Arminianism c. 1590–1640* (Oxford, 1987); N. Tyacke, 'Archbishop Laud', in K. Fincham (ed.), *The Early Stuart Church 1603–42* (London, 1993), pp. 51–70.

[6] Peter White, 'The Rise of Arminianism Reconsidered', *Past and Present*, 101, November (1983), pp. 34–54; P. White, 'A Rejoinder', *Past and Present*, 115, May (1987), pp. 217–29; P. White, *Predestination, Policy and Polemic: Conflict and Consensus in the Church of England From the Reformation to the Civil War* (Cambridge, 1992); P. White, 'The *via media* in the Early Stuart Church', in K. Fincham (ed.), *The Early Stuart Church 1603–42* (London, 1993), pp. 211–30.

[7] Peter Lake, 'The Laudian Style', in K. Fincham (ed.), *The Early Stuart Church 1603–42* (London, 1993), p. 162.

[8] Kenneth Fincham, 'Introduction' in K. Fincham (ed.), *The Early Stuart Church 1603–42* (London, 1993), p. 22.

[9] The most influential advocates of 'Calvin against the Calvinists' in the historiography in question are Basil Hall, 'Calvin against the Calvinists', in G. E. Duffield (ed.), *John Calvin* (Abingdon, 1966), pp. 19–37; Brian G. Armstrong, *Calvinism and the Amyraut Heresy: Protestant Scholasticism and Humanism in Seventeenth-Century France* (London, 1969); R. T. Kendall, *Calvin and English Calvinism to 1649* (Oxford, 1979).

this influential account, Calvin's own theology was Christocentric, rooted in scripture – a theology in which predestination was important, indeed a crucial doctrine, but not the central controlling concept. Calvin's successors, however, created a deterministic system in which all theology was controlled by and deduced from the absolute decrees of election and reprobation. Just as for Lutherans, the central organizing principle was justification by faith, so in this formulation, predestination becomes the central controlling principle of Reformed orthodoxy. All other doctrines – the Trinity, Christology, ecclesiology and the sacraments – become appendages to the doctrine of predestination. This scholastic codification of Calvinism is held, in many respects, to have contradicted the thought of Calvin himself. For example, R. T. Kendall has argued that Calvin's careful emphasis on the universality of the atonement was replaced by a doctrine of limited atonement logically deduced from the doctrine of predestination.[10]

The teaching of Theodore Beza was supposedly the most influential version of Reformed scholasticism, in the period we are examining. Kendall even calls it 'English Calvinism' because of its influence on England. The debate about 'Calvinism' in the English church is really a debate about Beza's interpretation of predestination. Tyacke and White may disagree about whether the Church of England is 'Calvinist' or not, but despite their differences, they are both locked into the same false assumption, that 'Calvinism' basically means the thought of Theodore Beza. White claims to recognize Reformed diversity, yet he maintains, in effect, that because the Church of England was not Bezan, therefore it was not 'Calvinist'. Tyacke holds that there is a basic identity of doctrine between the Church of England and the continental Reformed churches, yet he sometimes seems to argue that because a particular divine was not sufficiently Bezan, therefore he must have been an anti-'Calvinist'. All of this is particularly bizarre because the Bezan form of the doctrine of predestination always remained a minority position in the Reformed churches, and never achieved confessional status.[11]

Tyacke and White are only the latest in a long line of scholars who have accepted the thesis of 'Calvin against the Calvinists' and identified Calvinism with the thought of Theodore Beza. Where does this interpretation come from? The most convincing answer to this question can be found in the recent work of Richard Muller, particularly in his *Christ and*

---

[10] Kendall, *Calvin and English Calvinism*, esp. pp. 1–28.

[11] Richard A. Muller, *God, Creation and Providence in the Thought of Jacob Arminius* (Grand Rapids, MI, 1991), p. 19.

the Decree.[12] He has traced the roots of the focus on Beza's interpretation of predestination to a group of nineteenth-century German Reformed theologians. They took a very positive view of what they perceived as the increasing centrality of predestination in the theologies of late sixteenth- and seventeenth-century Reformed divines.[13] Through their work Theodore Beza came to be regarded as the person largely responsible for establishing predestination as the central controlling concept of Reformed theology. But later Reformed scholars took an increasingly unfavourable view of this supposed development in their tradition.[14] English-speaking writers have taken these criticisms even further by perceiving in Reformed orthodoxy a radical distortion of Calvin's thought, the alien importation of scholasticism and the adoption of metaphysical determinism: hence 'Calvin against the Calvinists'.[15]

I believe that it is still legitimate and indeed very important for historians to study the doctrines of grace current in the late sixteenth and early seventeenth centuries. Virtually every Christian tradition in this period, including the Roman Catholic and Eastern Orthodox Churches, had profound debates on the doctrine of grace.[16] What we must not do, however, is to assume that predestination was a peculiarly Reformed doctrine, or to treat any one formulation of that doctrine, Bezan or otherwise, as the only serious expression of it. In many people's minds, predestination automatically implies the so-called 'five points of "Calvinism"': total depravity, unconditional election, limited atonement, irresistible grace, and perseverance of the saints. Two remarks

---

[12] Richard A. Muller, *Christ and the Decree: Christology and Predestination in Reformed Theology from Calvin to Perkins* (Durham, NC, 1986), esp. pp. 1–13, and *passim*.

[13] The works cited by Muller, *Christ and the Decree* include Alexander Schweizer, *Die Glaubenslehre der evangelisch-reformierten Kirche* (2 vols, Zurich, 1847); F. C. Baur, *Lehrbuch der Christlichen Dogmengeschichte* (Tübingen, 1858), pp. 314 ff; F. C. Baur, *Theologisches Jahrbuch* (Tübingen, 1847), pp. 309–42; Wilhelm Gass, *Geschichte der Protestantischen Dogmatik* (Berlin, 1854), vol. 1, pp. 7–9. On Schweizer, see the fascinating account of his theology in B. A. Gerrish, *Tradition and the Modern World: Reformed Theology in the Nineteenth Century* (Edinburgh, 1978), pp. 119–36.

[14] Heinrich Heppe, *Reformed Dogmatics*, ed. E. Bizer, trans. G. T. Thomson (London, 1950).

[15] Brian G. Armstrong, *Calvinism and the Amyraut Heresy* (London, 1969), *passim*.

[16] 'Baius and Baianism', in *New Catholic Encyclopedia* (New York, 1967), vol. 2, pp. 19–21; 'Congregatio de Auxiliis', in *New Catholic Encyclopedia* (New York, 1967), vol. 4, pp. 168–71; N. J. Abercrombie, *The Origins of Jansenism* (London, 1936); 'The Confession of Metrophanes Kritopoulos' (1625), 'The Confession of Cyril Lukaris' (1631) and 'The Orthodox Confession of Mogilas' (1643), in Philip Schaff, *The History of the Creeds of Christendom* (London, 1878), pp. 50–67; 'The Confession of Dositheus' (1672), in J. H. Leith, *Creeds of the Churches* (rev. edn, Richmond, VA, 1973), pp. 485–517.

need to be made about these 'five points'. First, the theological issues underlying them are not exclusively 'Calvinist' and comparable ideas can be found in many other Christian traditions. Secondly, the Reformed tradition was dynamic and highly diverse. Attempts to fix the boundaries of Reformed thought in a rigid way soon run into difficulties. Even Muller, much as I am indebted to his work, tends to iron out many of the paradoxes and discontinuities in the Reformed tradition.[17] We need to keep in mind the sheer range of the tradition – taking in the formative impact of Peter Martyr, Heinrich Bullinger and Martin Bucer as well as Calvin and Beza – and the powerful but often unacknowledged contribution of Roman Catholic ideas.[18]

I

In my view scholars have paid insufficient attention to the broader comparative context of Reformed theology in the early modern period, particularly its complex relationship to Roman Catholic theology. This comparative context will be explored by examining two documents which give us an intriguing 'snapshot' of early Stuart English theologies. The first text is *Appello Evangelium* by John Plaifere, fellow of Sidney Sussex College, Cambridge.[19] The title of the work suggests that it may have been drawn up in the 1620s, during the controversy over Richard Montagu's *Appello Caesarem* (1625).[20] Plaifere died in 1632, but the

---

[17] See for example his rather negative account of hypothetical universalism: Richard A. Muller, *Dictionary of Latin and Greek Theological Terms* (Grands Rapids, MI, 1985), pp. 319–20.

[18] For a study of the enormous diversity of the developing Reformed tradition, which concentrates on predestination and Christology, see Muller, *Christ and the Decree*, pp. 39–75, 97–125; on the highly significant impact of Roman Catholic theology, see John P. Donnelly, 'Calvinist Thomism', *Viator*, 7 (1976), pp. 441–55; J. P. Donnelly, 'Italian Influences on the Development of Calvinist Scholasticism', *SCJ*, 7 (1976), pp. 81–101; Richard A. Muller, *Post Reformation Reformed Dogmatics: Vol. 1 Prolegomena to Theology* (Grand Rapids, MI, 1987), *passim*; Muller, *Arminius, passim*.

[19] John Plaifere [or Playfer or Playford] was admitted as a sizar at Emmanuel College, Cambridge in 1595. The title of the work in the 1651 edition is *Appello Evangelium for the true doctrine of the divine predestination, concorded with the orthodox doctrine of God's free-grace and man's freewill*. I have used a 1718 edition in an anonymous collection of reprinted works, *A Collection of Tracts concerning predestination and providence and the other points depending on them* (Cambridge, 1718). I have compared this edition with the 1651 original and the changes have been found to be stylistic and orthographical. All further references will be to the pagination and text of the 1718 reprint.

[20] Richard Montagu, *Appello Caesarem: A Just Appeal from two Unjust Informers* (London, 1625).

work did not appear in print until 1651. The second text will be better known. It is *The Collegiat Suffrage of the Divines of Great Britaine* which was drawn up in Latin in 1619 and translated into English in 1629.[21]

Appello Evangelium is a work of polemic, written (strictly speaking) from an *Arminian* point of view. One of Plaifere's aims, as we shall see, was to rescue Arminianism from the charge levelled against it by opponents, that it made election conditional upon human response and consequently limited God's providential control of creation. What is unusual is the care which Plaifere takes to delineate the views of his opponents. I have found that his definitions of opposing positions, while often unsympathetic, are in the main accurate. For many of Plaifere's contemporaries, attention to the diversity of opinions held by their opponents, and accuracy in describing them, were less important than polemical effectiveness. For example, William Perkins, the fashionable Cambridge divine of the late sixteenth century in his 'View of the distribution of the causes of salvation and damnation as the Church of Rome would have it' makes the false claim that all Roman schools teach predestination on the basis of foreknowledge of works.[22] Plaifere is a notable exception, although his studied fairness and rhetoric of moderation should not blind us to his fundamentally polemical purpose.

Appello Evangelium is particularly interesting for two reasons: first, because it aims to show the diversity within the Reformed and other Christian traditions on the doctrine of predestination, and can therefore be used in conjunction with the work of modern scholars who share that aim; secondly, because it shows that some contemporaries perceived that diversity. It is, of course, important to be aware of polemical positions, but on their own these will not suffice. Tyacke and White have rightly been criticized for mistaking polemic for reality, but even among their critics there is a tendency to assume that polemic constituted reality. [23] Many English divines, including Plaifere, were extremely well read in continental theology. If Plaifere was capable of disentangling

---

[21] *Suffragium Collegiale theologorum Magnae Britanniae de quinque controversis remonstrantium articulis* (London, 1629); *The Collegiat Suffrage of the Divines of Great Britaine, concerning the five articles controverted in the Low Countries. Which Suffrage was by them delivered in the Synod of Dort, March 6, Anno. 1619. Being their vote or voice foregoing the joint and publique judgement of the Synod* (London, 1629).

[22] William Perkins, *A Golden Chaine*, in *The Workes of ... Mr William Perkins* (Cambridge, 1616), vol. 1, p. 95. See also the Lutheran Saxon visitation Articles of 1592 with their fascinating but wholly negative account of the 'False and erroneous doctrine of the Calvinists concerning the predestination and providence of God' in Philip Schaff, *The Creeds of the Evangelical Protestant Churches* (London, 1877) p. 189.

[23] Peter Lake, 'Lancelot Andrewes, John Buckeridge, and Avant-garde Conformity at

the polemic from the reality, it is important that we should try to do the same.

The five doctrines of predestination Plaifere presents can be very crudely summarized as follows:[24] first, supralapsarian predestination; secondly, predestination based on God's foreknowledge; thirdly, predestination based on God's 'middle knowledge'; fourthly and fifthly, infralapsarian predestination. One way (and most certainly not the only way[25]) of discerning the Church of England's relationship to the 'Calvinist' or Reformed tradition is to find doctrines that were distinctive to that tradition, and that were not held in common with Roman Catholics or Lutherans. This is the approach that will be adopted here.

The first of the five opinions, supralapsarianism or as it is sometimes known, 'full double absolute predestination' is summarized by Plaifere as follows:

1. God from all eternity decreed to create human beings.
2. He elected some and reprobated others.
3. In this act he respected nothing other than his own will.
4. To bring about this end he permitted sin and decreed to send his Son to redeem the elect.

According to Plaifere,

> This opinion hath for its defenders Beza, Piscator, Whitacre [sic], Perkins, and other Holy and learned Men; But is rejected by the Reverend Divines of our Church that were at Dort, by Peter Moulin, Robert Abbot, Bishop of Salisbury and others: it is detested by the

---

the Court of James I', in L. L. Peck (ed.), *The Mental World of the Jacobean Court* (Cambridge, 1991) p. 123.

[24] For the sake of clarity in my argument I have departed from Plaifere's own rather wordy formulations and altered his numbering of the positions. Using my numbering the original order is: 1, 4, 5, 2, 3.

[25] I am deeply indebted to Peter Lake's seminal article 'Calvinism and the English Church 1570–1635', *Past and Present*, 114 (1987) pp. 32–76. Lake showed how helpful the distinction between credal and experimental predestinarianism could be in untying some of the Tyacke–White knots and it was also one of the earliest pieces to emphasise the fluidity of English 'Calvinist' thought. I have not used the credal-experimental division in my analysis, although it will be clear to anyone familiar with Peter Lake's work that the *Collegiat Suffrage* is an almost classic exposition of a credal position. Also, Anthony Milton's *Catholic and Reformed: the Roman and Protestant Churches in English Protestant Thought, 1600–40* (Cambridge, 1995) is without a doubt one of the most important works to appear in this field in many years. Milton argues that the increasing subtlety of mainstream Jacobean Calvinist ecclesiology was a necessary development away from the crudity of earlier positions, but paradoxically that very subtlety made it polemically very difficult to establish 'clear blue water' between English moderate Calvinist positions and those of Rome. It is my intention in this chapter to draw a rough sketch which will allow us to see why analogous problems developed for the Jacobean mainstream over the doctrine of predestination.

Papists and Lutherans; and was that which Arminius and his followers, chiefly opposed in the Low Countries.[26]

In this doctrine the eternal decrees of the election and reprobation of
individuals are prior to the eternal decrees of the fall and the redemption
– *supra lapsum* means before the fall. The decree to permit the fall and
the decree to bring about redemption are means to the end of election
and reprobation. Plaifere neglects to mention that in many supralapsarian
accounts creation itself, as well as redemption, is a means to the end of
manifesting divine justice and mercy.[27] Supralapsarianism is usually
characterized as determinist and yet many of its exponents, such as
Perkins, used concepts like secondary causality and divine permission.[28]
Plaifere admits of this first opinion that God 'decreed to *permit* sin to
enter in upon all men'. Nor did this position necessarily imply a sym-
metrical mirroring of election and reprobation.[29] The opposing Reformed
position is infralapsarianism – *infra lapsum* means below or after the
fall – or so-called 'single predestination', in which the divine decrees to
create human beings with free choice and to permit the fall are prior to
the election of some to salvation.[30]

Plaifere makes clear that all five of his opinions deal with the eternal
logical order of God's decrees, not with their temporal order. God is not
conceived of as changing his mind. This is common ground for practically everyone. Also, whether election is founded on a form of divine
knowledge or purely on the divine will, all schools of thought hold that
the number of the elect and reprobate is fixed from eternity. The elect,
by definition, cannot cease to be elect.

Beza's position, supralapsarianism is the classic 'Calvinist' position,
as assumed in much of the historiography. Yet there is not a single
Reformed confession that incorporates supralapsarianism. Dort is often
perceived as a quintessential example of rigid 'Calvinism', yet it is
emphatically infralapsarian.[31] Another often quoted example of

---

[26] Plaifere, *Appello Evangelium*, p. 7.

[27] Thus, we have no need for a new category of 'creabilitarian' theologians as Peter
White suggests. White, *Predestination, Policy and Polemic*, p. 16. Cf. Heppe, *Reformed
Dogmatics*, pp. 146–9, 159–62.

[28] Calvin rejected the concept of divine permission. See Muller, *Christ and the Decree*,
p. 172. On secondary causality, see '*causae secundae*' and on permission see '*permissio*'
in Muller, *Dictionary*, pp. 63, 222.

[29] Muller, *Christ and the Decree*, pp. 170–72.

[30] See 'predestinatio' and 'supra lapsum' in Muller, *Dictionary*, pp. 233–5, p. 292.

[31] *The Judgement of the Synod Holden at Dort* (The English Experience, 678, Amster-
dam, 1974), Article V, p. 4; Article XV, p. 9, but esp. Article VII, p. 5:

Now election is the unchangeable purpose of God, by which, before the
foundation of the world, according to the most free pleasure of his will,

'Calvinist' extremism, the *Helvetic Consensus Formula* of 1675, is scrupulously infralapsarian: 'So indeed, God, determining to illustrate his glory, decreed to create man perfect, in the first place, then, permit him to fall and at length pity some of the fallen, and therefore elect those, but leave the rest in the corrupt mass and finally give them over to destruction.'[32] More surprising still is the fact that in the Geneva of Beza supralapsarianism did not hold exclusive sway. Beza does not seem to have claimed 'confessional' status for his doctrine, but rather, recognized infralapsarianism as the confessional norm; it was Heinrich Bullinger's *Second Helvetic Confession* that became the basis for the 'Harmony of the Reformed Confessions' developed in Geneva in 1580 under the supervision of Beza.[33]

The second doctrine in Plaifere's scheme is predestination based on God's foreknowledge, which he attributes to Melanchthon, Nils Hemmingsen, the Lutherans of the *Formula of Concord*, the Remonstrants and 'many papists'.

1. God decreed to create human beings, to permit their fall, and to send Christ to redeem the world.
2. God made a general decree of predestination under the condition of faith and perseverance; a special absolute decree of election of those whom he foreknew would persevere; and a special absolute decree of reprobation of those whom he foreknew would remain impenitent.[34]

Plaifere's reasons for disliking this doctrine reflect common objections to all such views of election: first, a general conditional predestination is seen as none at all; secondly, it implies that God gives no more grace to the elect than to the reprobate; thirdly (and most importantly from our perspective), the decree of special election appears to make the human being choose God, rather than God choose the human being.[35] Plaifere seems to be aware of the profound theological uneasiness which can be evoked by any theory that seems to possit a 'God with twiddling thumbs, waiting patiently in eternity' as human beings make their decisions in time.

---

and of his meere grace, out of all mankinde, fallen, through their owne fault, from their first integrity into sinne and destruction, he hath chosen in Christ unto Salvation a set number of certain men, neither better nor more worthy than others, but *lying in the common misery with others* ... ' (emphasis added).

[32] Leith, *Creeds of the Churches*, p. 311. Cf. Schaff, *Creeds of Christendom*, pp. 477–89 for a very full discussion of the background of the *Helvetic Consensus Formula*.

[33] Muller, *Arminius*, p. 19; Schaff, *Creeds of Christendom*, p. 554.

[34] Plaifere, *Appello Evangelium*, p. 25.

[35] Plaifere, *Appello Evangelium*, pp. 25–6.

Plaifere writes that the Lutherans of the *Formula of Concord* follow this opinion.[36] The reality was not so simple. Some Lutheran dogmaticians such as Aegidius Hunnius (1550–1603) came up with accounts of predestination that are close to Plaifere's summary. However, more conservative Lutherans, who remained committed to the inconsistencies and agnosticism of the *Formula of Concord* on predestination, felt that the view defined by Plaifere had a grave tendency to slip into a subtle but deadly synergism, that is into an understanding of God and humanity co-operating as partial causes of salvation.[37] It could, they felt, lead to an undermining of the Lutheran tenet of the unconditional and exclusive nature of God's activity in the process of salvation.

Many orthodox Lutherans came eventually to adopt positions like that of Hunnius as the best bulwark against the evils of 'Calvinism'. These 'Hunnian' Lutherans tried vigorously to distinguish their position from that of the Dutch Arminians by claiming that the Arminians, in common with Melanchthon, taught 'the ability to attach oneself to grace'.[38] They rejected this formulation in favour of 'the ability to turn oneself away from grace'.[39] To see why such a subtle distinction should be seen as so important we need to look at the Lutheran view of regeneration. Lutherans held that human free choice was enslaved before regeneration, and used much stronger language than the Reformed to express this enslavement: the faculty of decision-making, as they put it, was like a log or a stone.[40] Such extreme phraseology was rejected by the Second Helvetic Confession, and indeed by the Reformed in general.[41]

Plaifere also asserted that 'many papists' held this opinion. However, in the post-Tridentine period this position became increasingly rare among Roman Catholic theologians. After the acrimonious disputes of the late sixteenth century between the Dominicans and the Jesuits, there developed a theological consensus that truly Catholic doctrines of

---

[36] Plaifere, *Appello Evangelium*, p. 25. T. G. Tappert (ed.), *The Book of Concord: the Confessions of the Evangelical Lutheran Church* (Philadelphia, 1959): 'The Formula of Concord', pp. 494–7, 616–32.

[37] Muller, *Dictionary*, 'synergismus', pp. 158, 294.

[38] Plaifere, *Appello Evangelium*, p. 24 describes Melanchthon and the Remonstrants as holding the same position as the Lutherans. Vigorous attempts to distinguish positions should not always be taken at face value. The differences, as in this case, can often be quite minor.

[39] Muller, *Dictionary*, p. 113.

[40] Schaff, *Creeds of Christendom*, pp. 313–14; Tappert, *Concord*, pp. 469–72, 519–39.

[41] A. C. Cochrane, *Reformed Confessions of the 16th Century* (London, 1966), pp. 237–40.

predestination had in some way to affirm that predestination was not dependent on human response. The Council of Trent's decree on justification had rather paradoxically taught that the state of final perseverance could not itself be merited, even though obtaining one's own eternal life could be the object of merit.[42] None the less, there is no doubt that many Roman Catholic clergy in popular polemic, catechesis and preaching often abandoned the subtle distinctions of the schools in favour of straightforward predestination based on foreknowledge of merits.

The third doctrine of predestination was Plaifere's own and he claimed to share this view with Arminius, with many Jesuits and with the Greek and Latin fathers before Augustine.[43] Here is Plaifere's account of this view:

1. God from all eternity knew all things that could possibly exist.
2. Among all the other possibilities, he conceived the world as it is now, and every individual person in it, as possible.
3. He knew how to alter any part of humanity or person, in order to bring forth other effects.
4. But he considered it to be good, for the manifestation of his wisdom and power, justice and mercy, to bring this particular frame of the world and this particular order of humankind into being.
5. He foreknew that, if he brought this universe into being, particular persons would inevitably be saved and others, by their own fault and by God's justice, would inevitably be damned.
6. Yet he determined to bring all this into being, and in so doing, to predestine all human beings either to eternal life or to eternal death.[44]

This is a very clever and subtle presentation of the doctrine that predestination is based on what is termed God's middle knowledge. Middle knowledge falls between the two generally accepted categories of divine knowledge: first, 'the absolute unbounded knowledge by which God perfectly knows himself and the whole range of possibilities for the world', and secondly, 'knowledge of actual things brought freely into existence by the divine will operating within that range of possibility'. For Roman Catholic followers of Thomas Aquinas and St Augustine, as for Lutherans and the mainstream Reformed, nothing falls outside these aspects of God's knowledge, because all things rest ultimately on the divine will.[45] But certain Jesuits proposed the idea of divine middle

[42] N. P. Tanner, *Decrees of the Ecumenical Councils* (London, 1990), vol. 2, p. 681.
[43] Plaifere, *Appello Evangelium*, p. 27.
[44] Plaifere, *Appello Evangelium*, pp. 27–9.
[45] Muller, *Dictionary*, pp. 274–6.

knowledge. This was, crudely, God's knowledge of how human beings would freely choose to act or not to act in all possible hypothetical contexts, indeed alternative universes. Middle knowledge was violently rejected by its opponents, most of whom argued that the notion was incoherent, as well as erroneous.[46]

Richard Muller has convincingly demonstrated the correctness of Plaifere's thesis that Jacob Arminius and many of his disciples used this Jesuit notion in their doctrines of predestination and providence.[47] This is in stark contrast to the previously dominant view of Arminius which held that Arminius's doctrines on predestination grew out of the residue of an early Dutch Protestantism with its simple evangelical concerns and a distaste for speculation on election.[48] But Arminius's use of the concept of middle knowledge is important for another reason. Arminius was deeply concerned to deny that he taught some form of conditional predestination. Plaifere supported Arminius's concerns. According to Plaifere, this position protected the gratuity of predestination, because the divine will chose this world rather than millions of others. Thus 'it acknowledgeth the deepness of God's judgements, and the unsearchableness of his counsels; for who can tell why God by his divine decree resolved upon Peter, rather than upon Judas; why he loved Esau less than Jacob'.[49] One of the main Jesuit proponents of middle knowledge is mentioned by Plaifere. His name is Luis de Molina. Molina's followers, who were vehement opponents of Dominican teaching on predestination, came to be known as Molinists.[50] Molina, like Plaifere, was also convinced his view ensured that predestination was gratuitous. Even though Molina's view is usually characterized as making predestination dependent on divine foreknowledge of human response to grace, he believed that there was absolutely no causal influence on the part of rational creatures that influenced God in choosing this particular world over any other possible world.[51]

Now we come to the last two positions on predestination articulated by Plaifere, both of which can generally be described as versions of

---

[46] Brian Davies, *Thinking about God* (London, 1985), pp. 183, 189; Kathryn Tanner, *God and Creation in Christian Theology: Tyranny or Empowerment?* (Oxford, 1988), pp. 141–52.

[47] Plaifere, *Appello Evangelium*, p. 27; Muller, *Arminius, passim*.

[48] Carl Bangs, *Arminius: a Study in the Dutch Reformation* (Nashville, TN, 1971), *passim*.

[49] Plaifere, *Appello Evangelium*, p. 36.

[50] See 'Molinism' in *New Catholic Encyclopedia* (New York, 1967), vol. 9, pp. 1011–13 and 'Scientia Media', in vol. 12, pp. 1224–5.

[51] See 'Predestination (in Catholic theology)' in *New Catholic Encyclopedia* (New York, 1967), vol. 11, pp. 717–18; Luis de Molina, *On Divine Foreknowledge*, trans. A. J. Freddoso (*Concordia*, pt 4, 1988), *passim*.

infralapsarian predestination. The first of these last two positions holds that

1. God from all eternity decreed to create human beings holy and good.
2. God foresaw that humanity would fall into sin unless he hindered it, and he decreed not to hinder it.
3. Out of fallen humanity he elected some and rejected the rest.
4. God decreed to send his Son to redeem his chosen and his Spirit to call them; the rest he decreed to foresake.[52]

The last is the opinion attributed to John Overall, bishop of Norwich (1561–1619):

1. God decreed to create humanity good.
2. God foresaw the fall and permitted it.
3. God decreed to send his Son to die for the world and his Word to offer salvation to all human beings with a common and sufficient grace in the means to work faith in human beings.
4. God foresaw that none would believe by this common grace and decreed to add a special and effectual grace to whomsoever he pleased, by which they would believe.[53]

These opinions are highly significant because, as Plaifere points out, they were shared by many Roman Catholics and many Reformed. Of the fourth of our positions Plaifere writes, 'Many do say that St. Austin was the author of this opinion, since whom it hath had for its defenders the Dominicans, Bellarmine, Cajetan and many other papists; and among Protestants the Synod of Dort, P. Moulin, Dr. Abbot Bp of Salisbury, Dr. Carleton Bp of Chichester and others.'[54] Of the fifth and last position he says, 'This seems to be defended by the Reverend and learned Bishop of Norwich, Dr. Overal and Richard Thompson his diligent Auditor and familiar; as may be gathered out of the Bishop's Judgement concerning the five articles controverted in Holland and out of Thompson's *Diatribe de Intercissione Justitiae*.'[55] These two positions are so similar that it will be helpful to consider them together. Plaifere places the Dominicans in the fourth group, and Bishop John Overall in the fifth, but, as we shall see, on a number of related issues the close connections between Overall and the Dominicans are very striking.

As Plaifere notes, the fourth position was adopted by the Dominicans, some Jesuits like Robert Bellarmine and 'many other papists', who drew

---

[52] Plaifere, *Appello Evangelium*, p. 12.
[53] Plaifere, *Appello Evangelium*, pp. 16–17.
[54] Plaifere, *Appello Evangelium*, p. 12.
[55] Plaifere, *Appello Evangelium*, p. 17.

their inspiration directly or indirectly from Thomas Aquinas.[56] However, the foundation of the separation of the elect from the non-elect was a matter of some delicacy and much controversy for Roman Catholics, not just because opinion was divided, but because a number of opinions came very close to Reformed doctrines. This emerges very clearly if we examine the doctrine of reprobation in more detail. Plaifere holds that the fourth position 'supposeth original sin the cause of reprobation'.[57] But for Roman Catholics who regarded predestination as independent of foreseen merit, the situation was more complicated. For rigorist Thomists the sole motive for reprobation was the sovereign will of God. This is stronger language than many Reformed infralapsarians would have tolerated and is, if anything, closer to supralapsarianism.[58] A second and larger group of Roman Catholics held a view which was basically the same as the confessional Reformed position, namely, that the motive for reprobation was original sin, in which God in his justice could leave as many as he saw fit. A third group were uncomfortable with the language of direct exclusion from heaven, and held that the reprobate were excluded not from heaven but from the means necessary to attain heaven.[59]

All these opinions caused immense polemical problems. Their Roman Catholic defenders tried desperately to distinguish their positions from that of the Reformed. They sought, rather unconvincingly, to describe Reformed doctrines of reprobation, whether infralapsarian or supralapsarian, as involving absolute reprobation to hell, as distinct from Roman Catholic doctrine, which merely involved absolute exclusion from heaven. This distinction can only be sustained on the basis of gross distortion of Reformed orthodoxy; the reality is that the vast majority of the Reformed also taught absolute exclusion from heaven, not absolute reprobation to hell.[60] In any case, as far as Roman Catholic opponents of this teaching were concerned, there was little difference between those two positions: to one reprobated by God it would be all the same, because in either case he would be inevitably lost.[61]

---

[56] In the late sixteenth century the correct interpretation of Aquinas's teaching on predestination was disputed, but most theologians then, as all scholars do now, accepted that he taught predestination independent of divine prevision of human merits. Thomas Aquinas, *Summa Theologiae*, Vol. 5 *God's Will and Providence* (Blackfriars edn), 1a. 23. 5, p. 129.
[57] Plaifere, *Appello Evangelium*, p. 13.
[58] J. Pohle, *Grace Actual and Habitual: a Dogmatic Treatise* (St Louis, MO, 1915), p. 216.
[59] Pohle, *Grace Actual and Habitual*, pp. 216–20.
[60] Pohle, *Grace Actual and Habitual*, pp. 212–16; *New Catholic Encyclopedia* (New York, 1967), vol. 11, pp. 719–20.
[61] Pohle, *Grace Actual and Habitual*, p. 221.

II

What then of Reformed opinion? Plaifere claims that the fourth position is defended by a number of English divines, including the influential Robert Abbot, and by the Synod of Dort.[62] We can test this claim by examining *The Collegiat Suffrage* drawn up in 1619 by the English delegates at Dort. Peter White has tried to distance this document from the Canons of the Synod of Dort.[63] However, while it is true that the Canons are a compromise between various strains of the Reformed tradition, and that the British did not succeed in getting all their requests incorporated, the fact remains that the British were considered orthodox by the other delegates at Dort. Their opinions were treated with great respect, and their signatures to the Canons come immediately after those of the synodical officers.

The *Suffrage* is scrupulously infralapsarian. Infralapsarians are extremely careful in their language about reprobation, and the *Suffrage* has a preference for terms like non-electing or passing over.[64] The Canons of Dort, the Irish Canons of 1615 and the Westminster Confession all share the same reticence in discussing reprobation.[65] Infralapsarians are emphatic, as Plaifere observes, that the human subjects of the decrees of election and non-election are viewed by God in eternity as created and fallen. In his justice, God can leave the non-elect to their punishment; in his mercy, he rescues the elect from 'the damned lump' of fallen humanity. This defence of the righteousness of God in electing some and not others is adopted by the *Suffrage*:

> Neither is it any inclemency or cruelty, to deny to any man, which is in no way due unto him; especially, when in the person presented there is found the highest demerit or desert of punishment, which is so farre from expecting free gifts, that it cannot choose but call for most just judgement of which sort is the whole state of mankind represented to God, when hee was to choose, or refuse whom he would among them.[66]

Thus it seems to make no sense to describe such a position as 'the Calvinist doctrine of double predestination'.

Now let us draw some general conclusions from all this. There is obviously no simple dichotomy between Reformed doctrines of

---

[62] Plaifere, *Appello Evangelium*, p. 12.
[63] P. White, *Predestination, Policy and Polemic* (Cambridge, 1992), pp. 175–202.
[64] Muller, *Dictionary*, p. 243.
[65] For Dort see *Judgement*, p. 9; on the Irish Articles and the Westminster Confession see Schaff, *Creeds of Christendom*, pp. 763, 792.
[66] *The Collegiat Suffrage*, p. 30.

predestination and Roman Catholic doctrines of freewill. It is some-times held that Roman Catholics who teach absolute predestination rather than conditional predestination differ from the Reformed in two ways: first, because they affirm the universal saving will of God, and the genuine offer of salvation to all; and secondly, because they teach that freewill is not destroyed by either concupiscence or grace.[67] But does Reformed orthodoxy reject these positions, and in what senses do Roman Catholics hold them?

Let us look first at the universal saving will of God. There was in fact great variation in the strength with which this teaching was held by Roman Catholic theologians, and a few even took the unorthodox line of rejecting it.[68] Among orthodox divines, some Thomists even went so far as to describe the universal saving will of God as an ineffectual wishing. They believed that they were following the teaching of Thomas Aquinas who writes in the *Summa Theologiae*:

> God antecedently wills all human beings to be saved, but conse-quently wills some to be damned, according to the requirements of his justice. Now that which is antecedently willed is not willed outright but only in a manner of speaking. Things are only downrightly willed when all their surrounding circumstances are taken into account: this is called consequent will ... Whatsoever God simply wills, that he does; whatsoever he wishes, that may not come about.[69]

However, Thomists did, of course, accept the Tridentine dogma that God does not command the impossible: hence God's universal saving will must mean that all human beings are capable, through grace, of observing God's commandments. The concept of sufficient grace – grace that gives human beings the power to perform God's commandments, but not the salutary acts themselves – plays a crucial part in preventing any contradiction between God's universal saving will and the doctrine of predestination.

But the doctrine of God's universal saving will was not peculiar to Roman Catholicism. Many Reformed held a similar doctrine which is known as hypothetical universalism, and while some Reformed churches were suspicious of or openly hostile to it, it was never formally condemned as incompatible with the Canons of Dort except by the

---

[67] Pohle, *Grace Actual and Habitual*, p. 218.

[68] For an exploration of the universal saving will, which is extremely hostile to Catholic doctrines of absolute predestination, see Pohle, *Grace Actual and Habitual*, pp. 152–67.

[69] The translation in the text is from T. Gilby, *St Thomas Aquinas: Theological Texts* (Oxford, 1955), p. 178; Thomas Aquinas, *Summa Theologiae, Vol. 5 God's Will and Providence* (Blackfriars edn), 1a. 19. 6, pp. 28–31.

short-lived and locally authoritative *Helvetic Consensus Formula*.[70] Two of the British delegates at Dort, Samuel Ward and John Davenant, accepted hypothetical universalism, and by the mid-seventeenth century their example was being widely followed.[71]

But even those Reformed, such as the remaining British delegates at Dort, who rejected hypothetical universalism were often equally insistent that the Gospel could be preached sincerely to all human beings. As the *Suffrage* makes clear,

> There is no mortal man, who cannot truly and seriously bee called by the ministers of the Gospel to the participation of remission of sinnes and eternal life by this death of Christ ... There is nothing false, nothing fained in the Gospell, but whatsoever is offered or promised in it by the Ministers of the word, is after the same manner offered and promised unto them by the Author of the Gospell.[72]

But is not this just a verbal ploy? How can the reprobate be genuinely called, if they do not receive the means by which to respond?

Here, at last, we come to a genuinely distinctive Reformed position. All through the *Suffrage* a classical Reformed teaching is stated: regeneration, saving faith, justification, sanctification, and final perseverance are all part of an unbreakable golden chain which only applies to the elect.[73] For Roman Catholics, the only 'grace' which is unique to the elect is the divinely ordained condition of dying in a state of grace, rather than mortal sin (that is, final perseverance). I have already mentioned that final perseverance cannot be properly merited according to the teaching of the Council of Trent. In other words, a person, whom God has eternally decreed to exclude from heaven, might, however, still be predestined to the graces of true justification for a period of time or indeed a number of times in his or her life, but God has eternally ordained that this person will inevitably die in a state of unrepented mortal sin and therefore he or she is not nor can be one of the elect. A few English Protestants take the same line: John Overall, while adhering to absolute predestination, also maintains that justifying grace can be lost, and his distinction between common and special grace resembles the Roman Catholic distinction between sufficient and efficacious grace. This rejection of the 'golden chain' by Overall is a very significant departure from Reformed orthodoxy.

---

[70] Schaff, *Creeds of Christendom*, pp. 480–83.

[71] W. Robert Godfrey, 'Reformed Thought on the Extent of the Atonement to 1618', *Westminster Theological Journal*, 37, Winter (1975), pp. 133–71.

[72] *The Collegiat Suffrage*, pp. 46–7.

[73] *The Collegiat Suffrage*, pp. 7, 30, *passim*.

However, it is interesting that a version of the distinction between common and special grace does exist in the mainstream Jacobean Reformed tradition. While the orthodox are emphatic that 'speciall graces' are given only to the elect, many of the non-elect do receive temporary graces. These 'initial', 'exciting' or 'enticing' graces arise from the preaching of the word and the genuine offering of the gospel. They are common to the preparatory stages of regeneration in the elect and the temporary gifts of the reprobate. As the *Suffrage* makes clear, they are not counterfeit imitations of grace: 'When the Gospell of its owne nature calls men to repentance and salvation, when the incitements of divine grace tend the same way we must not suppose anything is done fainedly by God.'[74] Nevertheless, these graces can be resisted, and the non-elect will always eventually fall from them. It is these temporary graces which leave the reprobate utterly responsible for their impenitence and without excuse: 'Some in whose hearts by the vertue of the word and the Spirit, some knowledge of divine truth, some sorrow for sin, some desire and care of deliverance have been imprinted, are changed quite contrary, reject and hate the truth.'[75] Yet it is human beings who are responsible for this rejection, not God.[76] So these two graces, 'initiall' and 'speciall', have a similar function to the Roman Catholic distinction between sufficient and efficacious grace. But for orthodox Roman Catholics, sufficient graces were more comprehensive and salvifically significant than Reformed initial graces (for instance, they included the infused virtues of supernatural faith and hope).[77]

So now we have uncovered the fundamentally distinctive position of the Reformed concerning the unbreakable golden chain. In the *Suffrage* a long discussion of the perseverance of the saints deals with the two crucial questions: (1) whether those who are not elect may ever come to the state of justification and sanctification and be reckoned among the number of the saints; (2) whether the elect, who are justified and sanctified, do at any time wholly fall from this estate. The orthodox Reformed answer to both these questions was the same as that of the *Suffrage*: no.[78]

But while all the Reformed believed that the opposing opinions were erroneous and contrary to the teaching of Holy Scripture, they differed in the vehemence of their strictures. At Dort the British requested that the synod refrain from an outright condemnation of those who believed in the errors of temporary regeneration and justification on these grounds:

[74] *The Collegiat Suffrage*, pp. 71–2.
[75] *The Collegiat Suffrage*, p. 74.
[76] *The Collegiat Suffrage*, p. 73.
[77] R. Garrigou-Lagrange, *Reality* (St Louis, MO, 1953), p. 306.
[78] *The Collegiat Suffrage*, pp. 102–56.

1. That Augustine, Prosper and other fathers who propounded
    the doctrine of absolute predestination and who opposed the
    pelagians, seem to have conceded that certain of those who are
    not predestinated can attain the state of regeneration and justi-
    fication ...
2. That we ought not without grave cause to give offence to the
    Lutherans churches who in this matter, it is clear, think differ-
    ently.
3. That (which is of greater significance) in the Reformed churches
    themselves, many learned and saintly men who are at one with
    us in defending absolute predestination, nevertheless think that
    certain of those who are truly regenerated and justified are
    able to fall from that state and to perish and that this happens
    eventually to all those, whom God had not ordained in the
    decree of election infallibly to eternal life.
4. Finally we cannot deny that there are some places in Scripture
    which apparently support this opinion, and which have per-
    suaded learned and pious men.[79]

John Overall was certainly one of those so persuaded.

'Credal'[80] infralapsarian Reformed were particularly concerned to
prevent the golden chain from becoming an excuse for antinomianism.
The elect could fall into serious sin, because concupiscence still remained in the regenerate and God could choose not to hinder its effects.
However virtually all Reformed theologians frowned on speculations
about the hypothetical possibility of certain of the elect dying impenitent, because they believed such ideas would call into question God's
ability to bring about the conditions of salvation for the elect and
because they held that such a doctrine would be pastorally irresponsible
and dangerous.

Now we come to a brief consideration of another supposed difference
between the Roman Catholic doctrines of predestination and Reformed
'predestinarianism', namely the supposed 'Calvinist' destruction of free
will. According to the *Suffrage* 'speciall' grace is indeed not given to
everyone, but the freedom of the will is not destroyed by this effectual
or special grace. This argument is based on distinctions such as the
appeal to secondary causality which are absolutely commonplace in
Reformed theology.[81] They are also very similar to arguments used by

---

[79] I owe the translation of this fascinating document to White, *Predestination*, p. 198,
but note his erroneous interpretation of its significance. The text refers not just to the
question of whether those who truly believe and are truly regenerate can fall totally, but
also to the question of whether they can fall finally. In other words it is dealing with the
opinion of certain divines who hold the number of the elect is a subset of the larger (and
therefore, obviously, not coterminous) set of the justified.

[80] See above, note 25.

[81] *The Collegiat Suffrage*, pp. 77, 79, 87, 88.

Thomists, who hold that, since what God wills must come to pass, the effect of efficacious grace must be infallible. Thus efficacious grace *infallibly predetermines* the human will to perform a salutary act *freely* and so the end of the efficacious grace is achieved without imposing on the will a necessity of coercion or an absolute necessity.[82] It cannot fail to elicit consent.[83] The consent of the will effected by efficacious grace cannot become dissent, though the will is still said to retain the power of dissenting, as well as consenting.[84] Roman Catholic positions like those held by Thomists are thus clearly no stronger in their defence of free will under the action of efficacious grace than the mainstream Reformed are in defending the integrity of the free will acted upon by special grace.

The last significant difference between the various adherents of Plaifere's fourth position pertains to the question of assurance or more precisely certitude of present grace and of eternal salvation.[85] Can the elect, in ordinary circumstances, be confident of their election? Both Reformed and Lutherans believe that they can, and that the doctrine of assurance is an integral part of the doctrine of grace. Lutheran dogmaticians, however, found difficulty in defending certitude of eternal salvation, because of their belief that the justified can fall totally and finally from grace. *The Collegiat Suffrage* is extremely careful, like many Reformed confessional documents, in its formulation of doctrine on this point. It accepts that such assurance of grace and salvation is above moral certitude, (which is as far as Roman Catholics are prepared to grant concerning knowledge of whether one is in a state of grace), but it recognizes that assurance is below 'dogmaticall certitude'.[86] Thus it is part of the certitude of faith, but it is not identical with that portion of faith directed to embracing the revealed truth in scripture.[87] Because of sin and the parental disciplining of God, awareness of assurance can be withdrawn. However, the authors of the *Suffrage* do show enormous pastoral sensitivity in dealing with problems of doubt and despair by emphasizing that assurance is based on a

---

[82] Muller, *Dictionary*, pp. 199, 200. See H. McSorley, *Luther: Right or Wrong?: An Ecumenical Study of Luther's Major Work, The Bondage of the Will* (New York, 1969), pp. 148–59, for discussion of different concepts of necessity in Aquinas.

[83] Most Thomists teach that there is a *praedeterminatio ad unum* of the will, but because this predetermination is supernatural it does not destroy the free will: Pohle, *Grace Actual and Habitual*, pp. 240–42.

[84] Pohle, *Grace Actual and Habitual*, p. 243.

[85] Muller, *Dictionary*, pp. 64–5.

[86] For a Thomist view of certitude see Garrigou-Lagrange, *Reality*, pp. 326–7. See also 'certitude' in *New Catholic Encyclopedia* (New York, 1967), vol. 2, pp. 408–11.

[87] *The Collegiat Suffrage*, pp. 145–8.

panoply of means of consolation from God.[88] Roman Catholic theologians vehemently opposed the doctrine of assurance in its Reformed and Lutheran forms, because they felt that it might lead some to forget that confirmation in grace was a privilege granted to only a few of the saints, and that for the rest the total and final loss of justifying grace was always a possibility. However, one would expect many of the functions of assurance to be carried in Roman Catholic theology by reflection on the supernatural infused virtue of hope.[89] In the light of this it is fascinating that the *Suffrage* at one point uses 'infused hope' as a synonym for assurance.[90]

My limited purpose in this essay has been to separate out some of the distinctive elements of Reformed doctrine on grace from those that were held in common with other Christians. I have tried to show that many Roman Catholic and mainstream Reformed doctrines of predestination were virtually identical, and that their differences lay not in the doctrines of predestination *per se*. Instead historians ought to give more attention to a crucial aspect of the doctrine of the perseverance of the saints, in its distinctively Reformed form: the 'order of salvation' linking regeneration, justification and election in an inseparable and unbreakable 'golden chain'. The *Suffrage* proclaims the 'golden chain' enthusiastically. And yet, despite the extraordinary significance and polemical power of the doctrine, John Overall's clear rejection of this uniquely Reformed tenet was viewed with ever-increasing tolerance by the great bulwarks of Jacobean moderate 'Calvinism'. If Overall could be so tolerated in his rejection of the golden chain, why should absolute predestination alone remain sacrosanct? Plaifere is an unequivocal example of someone who took up that dangerous, challenging and momentous question.

---

[88] *The Collegiat Suffrage*, p. 124.

[89] Stephanus Pfürtner, *Luther and Aquinas – a Conversation: our Salvation, its Certainty and Peril* (London, 1964), *passim*.

[90] *The Collegiat Suffrage*, p. 24.

CHAPTER ELEVEN

'The Quakers quaking':[1] print and the spread of a movement

Kate Peters

Quakers, unlike Puritans, 'papists' or ranters, have always enjoyed an enviably distinct identity. Historians are confident that the movement began in 1652, when its chief proponent, George Fox, travelled to Swarthmoor Hall in Lancashire and met Margaret Fell, thus forging links between his new followers in Yorkshire and the Seeker communities of Lancashire and Westmorland. The solidity of the Quaker movement is reinforced by the fact that we can count its members, the estimated 40,000 Quakers by 1660 suggesting a truly remarkable growth rate in the 1650s. Perhaps most impressive of all is the fact that the Quakers retain an important role in the political histories of the 1650s and later. Historians who otherwise argue against the significance of religious radicals, all agree that both in terms of their numbers and their impact, the Quakers were an important phenomenon in the interregnum period.[2]

In this chapter I will argue that one of the reasons for the Quakers' strong identity, was the alacrity with which they appropriated their own

---

[1] This was actually the title of a tract published against the Quakers in 1656: Jeremiah Ives, *The Quakers quaking and their foundations shaken* (London, 1656). Many other tracts made similar play on the nickname: see for example Ralph Hall, *Quakers principles quaking* (London, 1656); Ellis Bradshaw, *The Quakers quaking principles examined* (London, 1656).

[2] William Braithwaite, *The beginnings of Quakerism* (Cambridge, 1955), pp. 78–96. Barry Reay has made a retrospective study from post-Restoration records, and from Hearth Tax returns, to assess the numbers of Quakers in the 1650s: B. Reay, 'Early Quaker activity and reactions to it, 1652–1664' (PhD, Oxford, 1979), pp. 218–20. For accounts of the importance of the Quakers to the 1650s, see G. E. Aylmer, for whom the Quakers are 'the most serious and remarkable' of the sects: G. E. Aylmer, *The Interregnum: the Quest for Settlement 1646–1660* (London, 1974), p. 13; for John Morrill, they are the 'most important': John Morrill, *The Nature of the English Revolution* (London, 1993), pp. 25–6; Derek Hirst states that 'more than any other group, the Quakers made a reality of the sectarian challenge': Derek Hirst, *Authority and Conflict: England 1603–1658* (London, 1986), p. 344; Ronald Hutton also thought that the Quakers 'more than any other' were the cause of political unrest: Ronald Hutton, *The British Republic 1649–1660* (London, 1992), p. 70.

nickname, and presented it in their publications as a term which epitomized their causes and their beliefs. The ways in which they did this
reinforce much of what we already know about the labelling of religious groups in the early modern period. But the extraordinary speed
and self-confidence with which Quakers proclaimed their own identity
tell us much about the dynamics of religion in the 1650s.

The use of nicknames in the context of early modern religion is
usually seen as an indicator of the attitudes of early modern society as a
whole. Patrick Collinson's work has brilliantly described the term 'Puritan' as deeply problematic, applied at different times and in different
circumstances to different people. The impact of Collinson's insistence
that the construction of religious identity can tell us much about early
modern religion, is evident, although perhaps misconstrued, in the debates over the Ranters in the 1650s. All participants in the Ranter
debate agree that the terms 'Ranter' and 'ranting' were in origin hostile
and essentially ambiguous, attributed to people or ideas which were
understood as threatening to social norms, but without any internal
coherence.[3] Labelling of groups identified as outsiders or representing
'otherness' is thus understood as the impulse of the majority who stood
outside those groups. English society expressed itself in terms of binary
oppositions: the appearance of Puritans, 'papists' and Ranters reveals
more about society at large than about the nature or coherence of the
supposed groupings themselves.[4]

What, therefore, is interesting about the Quakers, appearing on the
scene very suddenly in the 1650s, is their own, concerted response to
their nickname, and its importance in the rapid consolidation of the
movement. Quaker authors argued that the donning of the nickname
confirmed that they were the 'people of the Lord': it enhanced their
status as true prophetic figures who were bound to be rejected by the
profane and the ungodly. In their tracts, Quaker authors devoted considerable time and effort to the significance of their denunciation as
'Quakers'. Although the term 'Quaker' already had some currency from
1647 or 1650, the initiative in publicly applying it to the people and

---

[3] Patrick Collinson, *The Puritan Character: Polemics and Polarities in Early Seventeenth-century English Culture* (Los Angeles, 1989), p. 22 and *passim*; J. C. Davis, *Fear,
Myth and History: the Ranters and the Historians* (Cambridge, 1986), pp. 17–21; J. C.
Davis, 'Debate: Fear, Myth and Furore', *Past and Present*, 140 (1993), pp. 155–6, 165,
172, 179–80, 192, 195–6.

[4] Patrick Collinson, *The Puritan Character*; Peter Lake, 'Anti-popery: the Structure of
a Prejudice', in Richard Cust and Ann Hughes (eds), *Conflict in Early Stuart England*
(London, 1989), pp. 72–106; Christopher Durston and Jacqueline Eales, 'Introduction:
the Puritan Ethos, 1560–1700', in C. Durston and J. Eales (eds), *The Culture of English
Puritanism 1560–1700*, (London, 1996), pp. 1–9.

ideas associated with Fox and his co-religionists came from the writings of a handful of Quaker authors, who carefully co-ordinated the earliest Quaker publications.

Quaker historiography has paid surprisingly little attention to the development of the term 'Quaker'. Although the Temporary Subject Catalogue at Friends' House Library considers in some detail the first usage of the rather more sober 'Society of Friends', which dates from the late eighteenth century, for the term 'Quaker' it cites from the *Oxford English Dictionary*.[5] This refers to a letter of intelligence from Secretary Nicholas, dated 1647, which records a 'sect of woemen' at Southwark who 'come from beyond sea, called quakers; and these swell, shiver and shake'.[6] The Quaker historian William Braithwaite believed that this could not be a reference to 'Friends', presumably because the real Quaker movement began in the Midlands and north of England with the followers of George Fox.[7] Nevertheless, this early reference is revealing. The women were thought to have been conversing with Muhammad's holy spirit, and were said afterwards to preach what the spirit had delivered to them: a charge also made against the ecstatic worship of the Quakers in 1654.[8] The letter of 1647 also described the 'anti-monarchical' sentiments of the army at the Putney Debates, and the upsurge in sectarian activity during the Commons' vote on toleration.[9] 'Quakers' thus made their first historical appearance at one of the more politically charged moments of English history, when fears of sectaries were very high. The label 'quaker' was generically

---

[5] The Temporary Subject Catalogue at Friends' Library (under the heading 'Friend') cites from the General Epistle of the Yearly Meeting of 1781, which referred to 'every humble member of our religious society'; and notes that the first official use of the term 'Religious Society of Friends' is thought to be in the 1793 address to George III. The Temporary Subject Catalogue also notes that the terms 'Children of light' or 'Children of God' were the earliest collective names used when addressing the outside world. Russell Mortimer has discussed eighteenth-century dictionary references to Quakers, and shows how they all identified the beginnings of the Quaker movement to 1650 or 1652: R. S. Mortimer, 'Some Notes on Early Dictionary References to Quakers', *Journal of the Friends' Historical Society*, 43 (1951), pp. 29–34.

[6] Bodleian Library, Oxford, Clarendon State Papers 2624, MSS Clarendon (hereafter MSS Clarendon) vol. 30, fos 139–40.

[7] W. C. Braithwaite, *The Beginnings of Quakerism* (Cambridge, 1955), p. 57. A short article by Henry Cadbury discusses the reference, and concludes that it is indeed the earliest reference to 'Quaker': H. J. Cadbury, 'Early Use of the Word "Quaker"', *Journal of the Friends' Historical Society*, 49 (1959), pp. 3–5.

[8] MSS Clarendon vol. 30, fo. 140r; compare this with Thomas Welde, William Cole, Richard Prideaux, Samuel Hammond and William Durant, *The perfect pharise under monkish holines* (London, 1654), p. 42.

[9] MSS Clarendon vol. 30, fos 139r, 140r.

applied to those engaged in ecstatic religious worship, and explicitly linked with political turmoil and insecurity.

The process by which Quaker leaders appropriated this nickname to their movement is illustrated in a rather bizarre entry in George Fox's *Journal*. Fox's *Journal* was compiled in the 1670s and 1680s, and published posthumously in 1694: it consists not merely of Fox's narrative of the early movement, as Fox dictated it to his step son-in-law, but is also interspersed with extracts from Fox's own writings.[10] The very first of these extracts concerns the infamous occasion in October 1650 when the term 'Quaker' was first applied to George Fox and his followers. Having spoken at length after a public lecture in Derby, Fox was imprisoned by two Derby magistrates, Gervase Bennett and Nathaniel Barton: during his examination, Gervase Bennett reputedly called Fox and his companions 'Quakers', because of Fox's insistence that they should tremble at the name of the Lord. William Braithwaite agreed with Fox that this was a decisive moment in Quaker history: 'the derisive name at once came into vogue'.[11]

In fact the immediacy with which the term took hold is far from clear. Included in Fox's *Journal*, and dated October 1650, is a paper sent by Fox to Gervase Bennett which denounced him as the father of 'Reprochers scoffers and mockers': 'for thou was the first man that gave the children of god that name of quakers, and soe it was spread over the nation ... '.[12] Yet Bennett alone could not have been responsible for the spread of the term 'through Every towne in the nation', and certainly not by October 1650, as Fox's *Journal* suggests.

It is far more probable that Fox's letter to Bennett was written in 1653 or 1654, just as Quaker pamphleteering and the movement were acquiring national significance, and that Fox, even at this early date, was establishing a landmark in its history. In 1653, two pamphleteers hostile to the Quakers remembered the stir caused by Fox and his followers in the Midlands in 1650. The Cheshire congregational leader Samuel Eaton, writing in late 1653, recalled that 'about three years since' he had travelled through Nottingham, where he had met with

---

[10] Edmund T. Harvey's Introduction in Norman Penney (ed.), *The Journal of George Fox* (2 vols, Cambridge, 1911), vol. 1, pp. xxxi–xlii; John L. Nickalls, *The Journal of George Fox* (London, 1975) pp. vii–xxxvii. Much has been written about the literary structures and devices which shaped Fox's Journal; Thomas Corns most recently has convincingly cautioned against attributing too much literary strategy to it: T. Corns, '"No man's copy": the Critical Problem of Fox's Journal', in Thomas Corns and David Loewenstein (eds) *The Emergence of Quaker Writing: Dissenting Literature in Seventeenth-century England* (London, 1995), pp. 99–111.

[11] Braithwaite, *Beginnings of Quakerism*, p. 57.

[12] Penney, *Journal of George Fox* (Cambridge, 1911), vol. 1, p. 6.

'many reports respecting a People who are called Quakers, concerning Sorcery and witchcraft that should be among them'.[13] The Westmorland minister Francis Higginson also harked back to 1650 when he described the Derby trial in a pamphlet published in 1653.[14] In response to Higginson's tract, two Lancashire Quakers, Robert Widders and James Taylor, travelled to Derby in order to collect their own slanderous accounts of Justice Gervase Bennett (now in addition having a certain political piquancy as Bennett was a member of the Barebones Assembly). Their account of this journey, and the *mittimus* by which Fox had been arrested, were then published in a tract in 1654, the main body of which was actually a response to Samuel Eaton.[15] It is more than likely that this was the occasion on which Fox saw fit to denounce Gervase Bennett as the 'father of mockers scoffers and scorners' who had 'first' coined the pejorative appellation.[16]

The process by which Quakers recognized their nickname and appropriated it, is tightly bound up with the attempts of an embryonic religious movement to establish a relationship with the outside world. A strong sense of community was expressed privately between Quaker leaders in their first surviving letters. Although significant links between Quaker leaders existed before the summer of 1652, when George Fox travelled from Yorkshire to Swarthmoor Hall, it is nevertheless this momentous journey which forms the traditional narrative for the beginnings of 'Quakerism'. In part, this is an archival beginning. Over the summer of 1652 two Quaker leaders, Margaret Fell at Swarthmoor Hall, and Fox's erstwhile travelling companion Elizabeth Hooton, now imprisoned in York gaol, began to keep copies of their letters and papers.[17] By the end of that year, the first pamphlets had been printed. The survival of these documents is in itself suggestive of a growing sense of group cohesion. In the letters themselves, the spiritual unity between Quaker leaders is very clear: 'Praise my dearest thou art mine and I am thine, lett us live together, I am with thee and thou art with mee, none

---

[13] Samuel Eaton, *The Quakers confuted* (London, 1653), sig. A4v.

[14] Francis Higginson, *A brief relation of the irreligion of the northern Quakers* (London, 1653).

[15] [John Camm], *An answer to a book which Samuel Eaton put up to the Parliament* (London, 1654), pp. 51–5.

[16] Other details in Fox's paper suggest that it was written just after the end of the Barebones Parliament, which also fits in with the chronology of the printed exchange with Samuel Eaton. Penney, *Journal of George Fox* (Cambridge, 1911), vol. 1, pp. 5–7.

[17] A lengthier account of the importance of letter writing in the development of the Quaker movement is in my doctoral thesis: Kate Peters, 'Quaker pamphleteering and the development of the Quaker movement, 1652–1656' (PhD, Cambridge, 1996), pp. 29–35.

cann break the Unyon', wrote the Yorkshire Quaker Richard Farnworth to George Fox; later on Farnworth sent his 'deare love to all deare babes and Lambes And faithfull Frends' at Swarthmoor Hall.[18] The words used by the Quaker leaders to describe the relationship with their own brethren were most often 'fellowship', 'union', 'family' and 'friends': 'You are all deare to me in the grace of god which hath united us together and given us feloship one with another', wrote Richard Hubberthorne from Chester to Margaret Fell and friends at Swarthmoor Hall.[19] 'To you all the deare famaly of love my love is rune into you all', he had enthused earlier, in the summer of 1652, 'you are my relations: father, mother, sisters and brothers, which I must now own: and dwell with in unitie and love'.[20]

The sense of themselves as 'Quakers', however, arises from their perception of their relationship with the outside world. In the late summer of 1652, Richard Farnworth described a visit to York in a letter to George Fox. 'Friends', he wrote, 'are close shutt up in prison' and Farnworth had not been allowed to see them. Although one friend in particular, John Leake, was 'at Liberty again', Farnworth reported that there was 'another simple heart with Thomas Aldam', and '2 or 3 more in prison about Tithes', as well as 'one Mr Sikes at Knollingley': 'a great man of 3 or 4 hundred a yeare by relation, he hath proclaimed against Tythes, in his proclamation he calls them theeves and Robbers and he sent a maid about to cry against them'.[21] Farnworth's letter described a relatively fluid group at York, with the allies of the Quaker Thomas Aldam being defined in terms of their stance on tithes rather than mentioned by name or proclaimed as 'Friends'. In the letter, Farnworth went on to describe how Mr Sikes had been urged by the authorities to renounce his proclamation against tithes in order to secure his release. Sikes refused to do this, insisting that he would not pay so much as sixpence for his release unless tithes were abolished, he himself

---

[18] Richard Farnworth to George Fox and James Nayler, Sedburgh, November 1652, Friends' House Library, London, Swarthmoor MSS 3: 58 (hereinafter Sw MSS); Farnworth to Margaret Fell, Balby, 8 June 1653, Sw MSS 3: 46.

[19] Richard Hubberthorne to Margaret Fell, Chester prison, [January 1654], Swarthmoor Transcripts 1: 340 (hereinafter Sw Trs). Unless otherwise stated, all manuscript references are from the Friends' House Library, London.

[20] Richard Hubberthorne to G[eorge] F[ox], [June/July 1652], Sw MSS 4: 4. Such a sense of 'family' unity with his co-religionists compares strikingly with the sentiments of William Dewsbery, who reported to Margaret Fell that his proselytizing had gone from strength to strength 'sinc my desposing of the Famally that was on mee in the outward'. William Dewsbery to Margaret Fell, [August 1654], Sw MSS 4: 133.

[21] Richard Farnworth to George Fox and James Nayler, August or September 1652, Sw Trs 2: 42.

compensated, and most significantly, 'his friends called Quakers sett at Liberty'.[22]

This is perhaps the earliest instance of the use of the term 'Quaker' in the correspondence at Friends' House. Given the fluidity of the relationships between the prisoners at York, it is interesting that Sikes was aware of a specific group of 'Quakers', to whom he felt allegiance, although Farnworth's letter is ambiguous as to whether Sikes was counted as one of their own. By the summer of 1652, a group of prisoners at York castle were perceived by outsiders to be 'Quakers', and they themselves recognized the term as an indication that they were a visibly separate group.

Although clearly an appellation used by hostile onlookers, the consolidation of the term 'Quaker' in print occurred initially in the Quakers' own tracts; and it was their use of the term in print from 1652 onwards which gave rise to subsequent printed denunciations of the 'Quakers'. Over the next four years of publications, there was a clear textual dynamic in the spread of the term. This is not to argue that 'Quakers' were purely an invention of their own literature, nor of the literature of their opponents; but rather that there was a sustained textual development of the term which occurred concurrently with the dissemination of Quaker ideas. That this was at the initiative of the Quaker leaders themselves is deeply revealing about the nature of the development of the Quaker movement, and the role of print in its consolidation.

A discussion of 'quaking' took place in the earliest extant publication of the Quaker movement. This was a broadside by George Fox, which proclaimed itself to be 'An exhortation to you who contemne the power of God, and speak evill of it; As of Trembling, and Quaking, to beware what you doe.'[23] This broadside, as the title suggests, responded to hostile criticism – presumably oral or unpublished – levelled against the ecstatic worship of Fox and his followers. Much of his broadside discussed scriptural precedents for trembling, and argued that those who rejected trembling and ecstatic worship were blind to the presence of God. Fox's broadside was a significant publication as it introduced most of the key references to biblical 'quaking' which other Quaker authors later embraced.

Fox's first point, from the Old Testament prophet Isaiah, was that trembling was a sign of openness to God and of one's prophetical status, 'for (saith the Lord) This is the man that I do regard, he that is of a broken heart, and a contrite spirit and trembleth at my Word'.[24] Fox

---

[22] Farnworth to Fox and Nayler, Sw Trs 2: 42.

[23] George Fox, *An exhortation to you who contemne the power of God* [n.p., 1652].

[24] Fox, *An exhortation to you who contemne.*

went on to argue that, just as 'trembling' indicated one's prophetical status, so the denunciation of those who trembled was a sign of profanity. The derision of those 'that trembleth at the word of the Lord', 'makes manifest that you have the Letter but in notion, neither have you the spirit that was in Isaiah'. Fox then elaborated on other instances of divine revelation which had led to trembling: 'when the Lord spoke to Moses, ... and said he was the God of Abraham, the God of Isaac and the God of Jacob; then Moses trembled and durst not behold him: will you say that this was the Devill that made Moses to tremble, and durst not behold him?' Fox referred also to Daniel, who 'trembled, and his breath and strength was gone, and he did scarce eat any meat for three weeks together'; and to Habakkuk, who, 'when he heard of the power of the Lord his lips quivered, and his belly shoke, and rottenesse entred into his bones'.

Having established scriptural precedent for trembling at God's word, Fox emphasized the parallels between the experience of the Quakers and the Old Testament prophets:

> The same power now makes to tremble, and throws down proud flesh: you never read that any of the holy men of God scorned trembling, or them that trembled at the word of the Lord; but it is the unholy and ungodly proud Priests and Professors that must be scorning, that knows not the power of the Lord, and God scorns such.[25]

Fox also demanded that his audience consider their own response to trembling and ecstatic worship. 'If you should see one now', he continued, 'their lips quiver, their bellies shake and tremble, would you not say they were bewitched, and it was the power of the Devil, and it was the voice of the Devil?' His verdict on such derision was unequivocal: 'here you shew forth your blasphemies against the Holy Ghost, and against the power of the Lord'.

At the end of his broadside Fox turned around the status of his readers. Whereas previously he had addressed 'you who contemne the power of God', and had assumed that the readers were 'of the same generation' as those who despised the prophets in the Old Testament, at the end of his work Fox directed an appeal to his readers which allowed them to turn against their 'ungodly proud Priests and Professors', and towards his own movement:

> Now if you should see a company of people trembling, your Teachers would call them fooles, and the Prophets of the Lord called

---

[25] Fox, *An exhortation to you who contemne.* For an excellent discussion of Quaker prophecy, see Leo Damrosch, *The Sorrows of the Quaker Jesus: James Nayler and the Puritan Crackdown on the Free Spirit* (Cambridge, MA, 1996), esp. pp. 69–107.

them foolish people which did not tremble at the word of the Lord. So judge you all people, whether you have the power of the Lord, and the spirit which was in his people.[26]

Although this early broadside did not refer to 'quaking' other than in the opening sentence, it established the main justifications for trembling at the word of God which would be used later with direct reference to 'quaking'. Moreover, Fox referred to a specific 'company of people'. Fox had defined his co-religionists as a peculiar group whose ecstatic worship, and subsequent derision by outsiders, clearly indicated that they were the true spiritual successors of the Old Testament prophets.

Fox's discussion of trembling appeared as a defence of 'quaking' in subsequent publications. Typically, these tracts were ones sent ahead of major Quaker infiltration of an area or town, which served to publicize the advent of Quakers and their ideas.[27] Many were more elaborate versions of Fox's broadside: 'search the Scriptures, and you shall finde that the holy men of God do witness quaking and trembling, and roaring and weeping, and fasting and tears', exhorted the Quaker James Nayler in 1653, and went on over four pages to recall the trembling of Moses, Daniel, Habakkuk and David.[28] This tract was in circulation in London in August 1653, well before any sustained Quaker presence in the capital.[29] Nayler implied that 'quaking' and a certain knowledge of the divine were intrinsically linked, promising to show his readers 'the way how all flesh comes to know the Lord and fear him, by his terrible shaking the earthly part in man, witnessed by the holy men of God in Scripture'.[30]

Other tracts which proclaimed Quaker ideas to an audience for the first time carried a far more abbreviated justification of quaking. *A message from the Lord* by Richard Farnworth in 1653 promised to show its readers, 'that those whom the world scornfully call *Quakers* ... are the only people of the Lord', and included by way of introduction the following summary of Fox's much lengthier account:

> Moses quaked, *Hebrew* the 12 ver 21. Ezekiel was commanded to eat his bread with quaking. David did tremble, and there were with

---

[26] Fox, *An exhortation to you who contemne.*

[27] The use of printed tracts in the geographical spread of the movement is discussed in Peters, 'Quaker pamphleteering', pp. 60–92.

[28] James Nayler, *The power and glory of the Lord shining out of the north* (London, 1653), pp. 16–19.

[29] The London bookseller and collector, George Thomason, dated his copy of this tract 17 August 1653: G. K. Fortescue (ed.), *Catalogue of the Pamphlets, Books, Newspapers and Manuscripts Relating to the Civil War, the Commonwealth, and Restoration, Collected by George Thomason, 1640–1661* (2 vols, London, 1908).

[30] Nayler, *The power and glory of the Lord*, sig. Ar.

him that quaked. Job his bones did shake, and his flesh did tremble, *Job* 4.14. Habakkuk his belly did shake, and his lips quivered,
and all his flesh trembled: See *Hab.* 3.16. David roared by reason
of the powerfull workings of the Lord in him; and his bones did
shake, and his flesh did tremble: See *Psal.* 38.8,9,10. and 22.1 *Psal.*
119, 120. Isaiah spoke to the people to heare the Word of the
Lord, that did tremble at it, with many others, etc. And there were
Mockers then as there are now: See *Job* 17.2, *Acts* 13.41, *Isa.*
28.22, *Isa.* 29.20, *Psal.* 50.2, 3.[31]

Although there is no precise evidence for the circulation of this tract,
it was one of a number of octavo tracts by Farnworth, described by
Aldam as 'little' books which were very effective in spreading the word.
These books were still being circulated in 1654, and distributed to the
Quaker ministers as they set out on a national preaching campaign in
the summer of 1654.[32]

The elaborate and frequent references to the scriptural significance of
quaking also became a point of contention in formal pamphlet debates
with Puritan opponents. In 1653, the minister Thomas Welde and his
colleagues from Newcastle, subjected the Quaker authors' defence of
'quaking' to their own lengthy exegesis, explaining that they did so,
'lest they should charge us with passing over that which they presume
to make so much for them'.[33] James Nayler's reply to the Newcastle
ministers was highly revealing of the textual construction of the identity
of his movement, and the control which Quaker authors sought to have
over it. The Newcastle ministers had drawn their evidence for 'quaking'
from a hostile tract by John Gilpin, which provided graphic eyewitness
reports of Quaker meetings.[34] James Nayler first reproved the ministers
for equating 'quaking and trembling', with stories taken from Gilpin's

---

[31] Richard Farnworth, *A message from the Lord* (London, 1653), p. 3. Another early
tract by Farnworth cited simply on its title-page: 'And so terrible was the fight, that
Moses said, I exceedingly fear and Quake. Hebr. 12.21'; see Richard Farnworth, *Englands
warning-peece gone forth* (London, 1653), sig. Ar. For further examples of descriptions
of 'quaking', see George Fox and James Nayler, *A word from the Lord unto all the
faithlesse generation of the world* (n.p., 1654), pp. 9–12; George Fox, *A paper sent forth
into the world from them that are scornfully called Quakers* (London, 1654), pp. 5–6;
Richard Farnworth, *The brazen serpent lifted up on high* (London, 1655), pp. 24–7;
James Nayler, George Fox, Richard Farnworth and Gervase Benson, *Several petitions
answered that were put up by the Priests of Westmorland* (London, 1653), pp. 26, 35–6.

[32] Thomas Aldam to George Fox, York Castle, [July] 1654, Sw MSS 3: 44.

[33] Thomas Welde, William Cole, Richard Prideaux, Samuel Hammond and William
Durant, *The perfect pharise under monkish holines* (London, 1654), pp. 41–4.

[34] John Gilpin described how his need for fellowship had drawn him to the Quakers at
Kendal, and after meetings with them and having read their books, recounted: 'I began
(as I had formerly desired) to tremble and quake so extremely, that I could not stand
upon my feet'. John Gilpin, *The Quakers shaken* (London, 1653), p. 3 and *passim*.

tract of 'grovelling upon the ground, and foaming at the mouth', which he denounced as 'lyes and slanders' of the ministers' own invention. Nayler went on to defend his own accounts of quaking and its significance: 'but for *quaking and trembling* we owne it, as that which the Lord hath said shall come upon all flesh'.[35] To experience quaking and announce its import to an audience was one thing; to reduce it to scholarly debate or salacious stories was quite another. Nayler denounced the ministers for discussing the tremblings in the Bible, 'but know them not within yourselves', and argued that 'what ye speake by heare-say' should be discounted.[36] Nayler was at pains to discredit accounts of foaming at the mouth, but at the same time appropriated and defended 'quaking' as a significant experience of his co-religionists.

Just as James Nayler 'owned' quakings and tremblings, so other authors were also keen to draw attention to their nickname. 'Quaking we own, else we should lay waste the Scriptures, as you do', wrote John Camm in a printed reply to tracts by Samuel Eaton and Joseph Kellett.[37] Edward Burrough wrote of the 'despised and contemned people, called Quakers (whom I do own as my Brethren in the sufferings of Jesus)'.[38] The political importance of such a statement is illustrated in its considered use by a group of soldiers in Robert Lilburne's regiment of horse in 1657. Following an instruction that lists of all Quaker soldiers be submitted to General Monck, a group of soldiers issued a statement which declared that since the name 'Quaker' was the term given by the world 'in much scorne and derision' to the Children of the Lord, they dared not use it of themselves, but went on to note: 'quakinge and tremblinge according to what the scriptures declares of wee doe owne'.[39] The soldiers recognized that to embrace the label 'Quaker' in this context, with its implications of curbed religious liberty and even political disloyalty, was to condone the worldly connotations and political ramifications of the term; in denying this, they nevertheless reiterated the scriptural significance which they themselves attached to it.

Thus a significant number of early Quaker tracts included a scriptural justification of 'quaking' or 'trembling'. We must suppose that this is evidence of public accusations that particular preachers or groups

---

[35] James Nayler, *An answer to the booke called the perfect pharisee* ([London], 1654), p. 25.

[36] Nayler, *An answer to the booke*, p. 26.

[37] John Camm, *An answer to a book which Samuel Eaton put up to the Parliament* (London, 1654), p. 45.

[38] Edward Burrough, preface to Christopher Atkinson, *The standard of the Lord lifted up* (London, 1653), sig. A3v.

[39] Sw MSS 4: 237, cited in M. E. Hirst, *The Quakers in Peace and War* (London, 1923), pp. 530–31.

were 'Quakers'. But the initiative was taken by the Quaker authors themselves, and not by their opponents, in developing the lengthy explanations of the term's significance, and appropriating it to themselves.

James Nayler's careful distinction between accusations of 'quaking' and of 'foaming at the mouth' is also important in this context. Other 'badges' of the Quakers associated with their ecstatic worship, such as swelling stomachs, writhing on the ground and speaking in tongues, were propounded initially by hostile observers of the Quakers.[40] Much of the evidence for the Quakers' ecstatic worship, and particularly for glossolalia, or speaking in tongues, comes from hostile sources, a point which their ethnographer failed to emphasize.[41] Frequently these accounts were denounced as slander by Quaker authors. The authors did attempt to explain important symbolic actions, such as going naked, the donning of sack-cloth and ashes, the use of thee and thou, and the performance of other 'signs and wonders', as further evidence of their status as prophets. One historian, Kenneth Carroll, suggests very plausibly that it was the justification of these actions in print by key Quaker authors, which was instrumental in the repeated instances of such behaviour in the 1650s and 1660s.[42] Printed justifications for 'going naked' thus functioned in a similar way to the lengthier and more common justifications for quaking.

The alacrity of the Quaker authors in owning 'quaking' was central to the rapid perception of a 'Quaker' movement. The use of the term 'Quaker' in their tracts was far more widespread than the prosaic

---

[40] Higginson, *A brief relation of the irreligion,* sig. a3r, pp. 10–23, 28–30; Gilpin, *The Quakers shaken, passim;* William Prynne, *The Quakers unmasked, and clearly detected* (London, 1655), sig. Ar, pp. 3–4, 6–7; Anon., *The Quakers dream* (London, 1655), p. 3; Anon., *The Quakers fiery beacon* (London, 1655), *passim;* Ralph Farmer, *The great mysterie of godliness and ungodliness* (London, 1655), pp. 81–2; Cole et al., *The perfect pharise,* pp. 41–5.

[41] Richard Bauman, *Let your words be few: symbolism of speaking and silence among seventeenth-century Quakers* (Cambridge, 1983), pp. 80–83.

[42] Important justifications for the use of 'thee' and 'thou' are found in Richard Farnworth, *The pure language of the spirit of the truth* (London, 1655); Richard Farnworth, *A call out of Egypt and Babylon* (London, 1653), sigs E2r–v; George Fox and James Nayler, *Several papers, some of them given forth by George Fox* ([n.p.], 1653), p. 10; James Nayler, *A few words occasioned by a paper lately printed* ([London], 1654), p. 13; James Parnell, *The trumpet of the Lord blowne* (London, 1655), pp. 1–2. For justifications of going naked and of the performance of other signs, see Farnworth, *The pure language of the spirit of the truth;* R. Farnworth, *The spirituall man judgeth all things* (London, 1655), p. 25; Francis Howgill, *A woe against the magistrates, priests and people of Kendall in Westmorland* (London, 1654), pp. 1, 3, 5; Kenneth Carroll, 'Sack-cloth and Ashes, and Other Signs and Wonders', *Journal of the Friends' Historical Society,* 53 (1975), pp. 314–25; Kenneth Carroll, 'Quaker Attitudes towards Signs and Wonders', *Journal of the Friends' Historical Society,* 45 (1977), pp. 70–84.

discussions of quaking. The small body of authors very rapidly began to subsume their individual names beneath their collective identity as 'Quakers'. This is a crucial distinction from Ranters, who never described themselves as such in their publications, and thus provoked much of the recent anxiety about the true nature of a Ranter text or Ranter beliefs.[43] Quaker authors wrote self-consciously as 'Quakers', and as such produced an immediately recognizable body of tracts through which their beliefs were – and continue to be – easily identified.

Just as the appropriation of biblical 'quaking' was nuanced to invoke both a prophetical status and the inevitable persecution that followed, so the author's description of themselves as 'Quakers' was also carefully qualified and a number of meanings attached to it. William Dewsbery declared his work to be 'From the Spirit of the Lord, written by one, whom the people of the world calls Quaker, whose name in the flesh is William Deusbery, but hath a New Name, the World knows not, written in the Book of Life.'[44] This authorial device rehearsed the argument that the epithet 'Quaker' was applied by ignorant people to the true servants of God and as such was an intrinsic indication that the Quakers were a peculiar and godly people. Yet Dewsbery's concern with his status as a Quaker also had a clearly political edge. In 1655 he protested in print that he had been arrested, and that on the warrant for his arrest 'there was not any name; but for one whom he in scorn called a Quaker'. Dewsbery claimed he had been arrested, literally, for being a Quaker: something fundamentally at odds with the relatively tolerant tone of the Protectorate's Instrument of Government. Dewsbery emphasized the political injustice of his arrest, arguing that it was 'the Liberty of the Laws in the Nation, that all that profess the faith of Christ Jesus, may walk in uprightness to their faith in him, without any Breach of the Law'.[45]

The definition of authors as 'Quakers' also gave their pamphlets a clear collective status: the authors wrote not as individuals, but under the auspices of their religious movement. The promulgation of this collective identity was orchestrated by a tiny number of the movement's leading authors. Richard Farnworth, by far the most sophisticated and prolific of the early Quaker pamphleteers, gave the lead in propounding the use of the term. His first use of the 'Quaker' authorial device, in a

---

[43] Davis, *Fear, myth and history*, pp. 17–75; Davis, 'Debate: Fear, Myth and Furore', pp. 167–70, 175–6, 179–94, 202–3, 208–10.

[44] William Dewsbery, *The discovery of mans returne to his first estate* (London, 1654), sig. Ar.

[45] William Dewsbery, *A discovery of the grounds from whence the persecution did arise* (London, 1655), pp. 6, 12.

tract which he dated 1652, is also the most elaborate. The fact that it rhymes is evidence, too, of the performative nature of Quaker tracts:

> Written from the Spirit of the Lord, by one whom the people of the world calles a Quaker,
> but is of the Divine nature made partaker:
> whom the world knows not, that are in their old nature,
> and so mock and deride:
> but wo to the wicked, it shall be ill with them.[46]

Farnworth's other early pieces also made use of the device in more abbreviated tones: 'This was written by One the World calleth a QUAKER', he proclaimed in one tract; another of his title-pages pronounced it to be: 'Written by one whom the people of the world call a Quaker, whose name is RICHARD FARNWORTH'.[47]

Notable new recruits to the movement could use the device to signal their new-found allegiance: in his first 'Quaker' publication, the former army captain George Bishop of Bristol claimed his tract was: 'Given forth for the sake of the honest-hearted ... every where spoken against, scorned, and persecuted, under the Reproachful Name of Quaking.'[48] Anonymous or composite works also used the device to identify themselves explicitly with the Quaker movement: *A Declaration of the marks and fruits of the false prophets* (1655) announced itself to be 'From them who in the World in scorn is called *Quakers*, which suffers for the Righteous Seed sake'.[49] An anonymous collection of papers, 'from them who in scorn are called Quakers', and which argued for the right of Quakers to meet, and the illegitimacy of their prosecution by magistrates and people, asserted 'There is a people in England, whom they call Quakers; the name is right, a Scripture name, and we own it ... .'[50]

The 'Quaker' identity of authors and tracts affected the nature of public responses to them. In December 1652, a petition from the gentlemen and freeholders of Worcestershire, on the initiative of Richard Baxter, was presented to Parliament, complaining about the proliferation of religious sects and demanding improvements to

---

[46] Richard Farnworth, *A discovery of truth and falshood* (London, 1653), sig. F3r.

[47] Richard Farnworth, *A brief discovery of the kingdome of Antichrist* [n.p., 1653], sig. Ar; R. Farnworth, *A call out of false worships* (n.p., 1653), sig. Ar.

[48] George Bishop, *Jesus Christ, the same today as every day* (London 1655), sig. Ar; for his earlier publishing career, see J. W. Martin, 'The Pre-Quaker Writings of George Bishop', *Quaker History*, 74 (1985), pp. 20–27.

[49] Anon., *A Declaration of the marks and fruits of the false prophets* [London, 1655], p. 1.

[50] Anon., *Some papers given forth to the world* (London, 1655), p. 32.

England's ministry.[51] By February 1653, a response to this petition had been published by three Quaker prisoners at York, Thomas Aldam, John Harwood and Benjamin Nicholson.[52] Baxter issued his own rapid response, in *The Worcestershire petition ... defended*, published in May 1653.[53] Baxter was keen to respond to the queries laid down by Aldam and his colleagues, believing that they spoke with 'the mouth of the Divel'. He was unaware of, and unconcerned by, the precise identity of his opponents: 'The Authours are many, not worth the naming, some subscribing one part, and some another: and sometimes daring thus to subscribe, Written from the spirit of God.'[54] In his autobiography, Baxter admitted, 'I knew not what kind of Person he was that I wrote against, but it proved to be a Quaker, they being just now rising, and this being the first of their Books (as far as I can remember) that I had ever seen.'[55] The prisoners at York had not written under their collective epithet, and as a consequence had not been recognized by Baxter as Quakers, but merely as part of a wider attack on the national ministry.

The perception of a national 'Quaker' presence was determined in large part by the Quaker authors' own, deliberated appropriation of the nickname, and this is reflected in the ways in which opponents themselves used it. By 1655 Richard Baxter declared his dislike of 'so wilde a Generation as the *People called Quakers* are'; John Bunyan referred to 'those pained hypocrites *called Quakers*'. Henry Haggar wrote a response to a book by Richard Farnworth, 'who is commonly *called a Quaker*'; and included some queries 'concerning those people *called Quakers*'.[56] None of these publications directly addressed the issue of the Quakers' name, nor the Quakers' insistence that their being 'socalled' was evidence of their prophetic status and persecution. That the

---

[51] *The humble petition of many thousands ... of the county of Worcester* (London, 1652).

[52] Thomas Aldam, Samuel Buttivant, John Harwood, Thomas Lawson, James Nayler and Benjamin Nicholson, *A brief discovery of the three-fold estate of Antichrist* (London, 1653).

[53] Richard Baxter, *The Worcestershire Petition to the Parliament for the ministry of England defended ... In answer to ... A brief discovery of the threefold estate of Antichrist* (London, 1653).

[54] Baxter, *The Worcestershire Petition*, sigs A2r–v.

[55] Matthew Sylvester (ed.), *Reliquiae Baxterianae*, pt 1, pp. 115–16, as cited in N. H. Keeble and Geoffrey Nuttall, *Calendar of the Correspondence of Richard Baxter* (2 vols), Oxford 1991), vol. 1, p. 94.

[56] Richard Baxter, *The Quakers catechism* (London, 1655), sig. A3r; John Bunyan, *Some Gospel truths opened, according to Scriptures* (London, 1656), p. 213; Thomas Pollard and Henry Haggar, *The holy scripture clearing itself of scandals* (London, 1655), sig. Ar (emphasis added).

critics unwittingly adopted the qualifier underlines that the Quakers' self-consciously constructed identity was deeply influential.

One contemporary at least, however, was offended by the Quakers' authorial device. In the fifth, posthumous, edition of Ephraim Pagitt's *Heresiography* (1654), which added the 'Quakers or Shakers, and the Ranters', the author was so outraged by the fact that they 'owne the title of Quakers ... that it may appeare a name imposed by themselves', that he began his description of 'The Quaker or Shaker' with a discussion of this phenomenon. James Nayler's citations 'from all the places of the Scripture which mentions either trembling or shaking' were, he argued, 'impertinent and farre from the purpose'.[57] In his careful citations from the works of Farnworth, Nayler and Thomas Aldam, the author of *Heresiography* had detected that Quakers were deliberately playing on their nickname, and was accordingly outraged. This was immediately apparent to a heresiographer in 1654, who was actively seeking to describe the Quakers from their own writings, while critics like Baxter and Bunyan, perhaps more concerned with immediate confrontations with them, unconsciously repeated the qualification of the nickname.

An important consequence of authors defining themselves as 'Quakers so-called' is that it alerted readers (and subsequently historians) to the fact that they were reading a Quaker tract. The authorial device therefore contributed to the notion that Quakers were a recognizable and coherent body: it was all the more effective because it often appeared on the title-pages of their tracts. This practice contrasted to publications by other religious groups. Baptist 'confessions' tended to be issued in the name of specific congregations or regional associations; otherwise, radical religious writings appeared most frequently in the name (sometimes contrived) of individual authors.

The description of the authors as 'Quakers' on title-pages was exploited further by the fact that the word 'Quaker' itself could appear, almost iconographically, in large capital letters on the front of a tract, confirming to readers that this was a publication of an organized, identifiable group. The earliest instance of this was also one of the most influential tracts, *Saul's errand to Damascus*, the first publication to be organized by Margaret Fell in February 1653, and which drew attention to the sufferings of 'nick-named QUAKERS' in large letters. Significantly perhaps, *Saul's errand* was also the first Quaker publication to be acquired by the London book collector George Thomason,

---

[57] Ephraim Paggit, *Heresiography* (5th edn, London, 1654), p. 137. Compare with James Nayler, *The power and glory of the Lord shining out of the North* (London, 1653), pp. 16–19.

who, like Richard Baxter, had missed earlier tracts by George Fox and Thomas Aldam which made no obvious reference to their Quaker status.[58] Subsequent publications which marked new stages of the development of the movement also made similar, deliberate reference to 'Quakers' on their title-pages. The arrival of the first Quaker preachers in London in March 1654 was marked by tracts clearly marked with the word QUAKER circulating in the capital.[59] This impulse was even more evident as a mass of Quaker ministers began converging on London in August 1654 in time for the opening of the first Protectorate Parliament, disseminating tracts dominated by the word QUAKER.[60] For a movement which so roundly rejected icons and pictorial representations, Quaker pamphlets made an impressive use of one large word to indicate spiritual unity and a cohesive identity.

The exploitation of the term 'Quaker' or 'quaking' in the printed tracts presents us with a number of features of the developing Quaker movement. The numerous references to Quakers and quaking in the early tracts indicate a tightly co-ordinated body of authors, who presented audiences with an impressively uniform body of ideas. In the wider context of how the tracts were read, the term 'Quaker' summarized many crucial aspects of Quaker belief: as the tracts explained again and again, 'Quakers' were prophets and servants of God, destined to be derided as such by outsiders who by definition would be unable to recognize God's presence. The Quakers thus drew on the same tensions and notions of a binary opposition between 'godly' and 'ungodly' which fuelled the pejorative labelling of religious groups throughout the early modern period, in order to define their own movement. Yet the alacrity and sophistication with which Quaker authors acted also has much to do with the immediate circumstances of the 1650s. The Quaker movement emerged, and flourished, at a time when religious toleration and liberty of conscience for Protestants were closer than ever before to being realized. Dewsbery's complaint on being arrested as a 'Quaker' in 1655 was a specific protest that the 'laws of the nation' had been violated. For the Quakers, their nickname and persecution were clear

---

[58] George Fox, James Nayler, John Lawson, W[illiam?] W[est?], *Saul's errand to Damascus* (London, 1653).

[59] George Fox, *The trumpet of the Lord sounded and his sword drawn* (London, 1654), circulated in London prior to the Quakers' arrival there.

[60] George Fox and James Nayler, *A word from the Lord to all the world, and all professors in the world, spoken in parables* (London, 1654), dated by the bookseller George Thomason 25 August 1654, and hence in circulation as Quaker ministers congregated in the capital; [George Fox], *A declaration against all profession and professors* (London, 1654), dated by Thomason 28 August 1654, as Quaker ministers congregated in the capital.

signs that liberty of conscience was still far from secure. Their ability to exploit the nickname as a symbol of religious persecution, rested in turn on the fact that Quakers and their contemporaries had relatively easy access to the press. Largely unconstrained by censorship, Quaker authors were able to employ sophisticated pamphleteering techniques to render their name, and what it symbolized, recognizable to literate and illiterate audiences across the country. The response of contemporaries and historians alike testifies to their success in so doing.

Afterword

Caroline Litzenberger and Susan Wabuda

Patrick Collinson's career as a historian is all the more extraordinary, because it was his second choice. In his youth, he was strongly attracted to the zoological sciences, and he has maintained a deep appreciation for bird and animal life, and their habitats. His knowledge in this area has never failed to impress his friends. Patrick's students, over the years, may have heard him rattle off the names of all of the different species of mammals that are native to the British Isles, seen the Victorian specimen of a pangolin in the living-room, or noticed a bowl of highly exotic seed pods on the coffee table.

His intellectual interest in nature is complemented by his love of the outdoors. For many years he was a keen mountain climber, and it is still hard to keep up with him as he scrambles up one of the many peaks near his Derbyshire home. He has also traced the migration of butterflies across the Alps; watched bald eagles, moose and bison in the Rockies; wandered rain forests in Australia and New Zealand; and gone steelhead fishing in the Pacific Northwest of the United States. And this last activity relates to his first career choice: above all, Patrick was drawn to ichthyology, and it was once one of his and Liz's great regrets that he was not able to pursue formally his interest in the study of fish.

Fishing has, however, figured large in some of the best advice he has ever offered to students. History does not, and should not, consist of letting preconceived theories shape one's research and writing. It would be wrong to let mere theory stand in the way of the evidence, when true scholarship demands that the nature of the evidence should lead the argument and thus the historian. One should cast one's line into the material and see what fish are drawn to the hook, or make a systematic troll through a set of documents. Or, as Izaak Walton wrote in the 1676 edition of the *Compleat Angler*:

> But he that hopes to be a good *Angler* must not only bring an inquiring, searching, observing wit; but he must bring a large measure of hope and patience, and a love and propensity to the Art it self; but having once got and practis'd it, then doubt not but *Angling* will prove to be so pleasant, that it will prove to be like Vertue, *a reward to it self*.

Each of the chapters in this volume reflects Patrick's guidance, including his urging us to cast our nets wide and see what we find. In addition, we have each brought our particular interests and expertise to the task, and the variety of topics covered in these chapters reflects both Patrick's fertile, creative and inquisitive mind and his openness to a wide range of approaches and topics. As the title of this volume indicates these chapters are about various aspects of belief and practice in Reformation England, and as Norman Jones has said in his introduction they are also about religious identity and definition for individuals, communities and the institutional Church. Whether by reading the Bible or debating theology, people took steps to further define their identity. Meanwhile, parish communities were finding new ways to re-create themselves in response to changing demands, and the printing-press was being used to promote and reflect newly developing religious norms, especially the norms espoused by godly preachers. And while all this was going on privately, locally and in the press, the institutional church was also working to define itself: in the 1560s and 1570s through Convocations and recusancy statutes; and then, after that, through the creation of a body of theological writings and debates. Religion in Reformation England was as diverse as the people, places and leaders of the Church and State whose beliefs and practices are reflected in this volume. Patrick Collinson's influence on his students is clear in the varied and complex nature of this collage of religious images. He urged us all to not only cast our nets wide, but also to examine and analyse the contents of those nets very closely with an eye to wider, more complex representations and influences. 'Speculate! Speculate!' he used to write in our margins.

Though the world lost a fine scientist when Patrick Collinson embraced history, we may rejoice in his career and in the formative influence he had on those of us who have been privileged to work with him and learn from him.

> So when I would beget *content*, and increased confidence in the *power*, and *Wisdom*, and *Providence* of Almighty God, I will walk in the *Meadows* by some gliding stream, and there contemplate ... those very many other various little living *creatures*, that are not only created but fed (man knows not how), by the goodness of the God of *Nature*, and therefore trust in him.

And let His blessing be 'upon all that are lovers of *Vertue*; and dare trust in his *providence*, and be quiet, and go a *Angling*'.[1]

---

[1] Source for quotations: Izaak Walton, *The Compleat Angler 1653–1676*, ed. Jonquil Bevan (Oxford, 1983), pp. 190, 371.

Bibliography of the published writings of Patrick Collinson, 1992–98[1]

A full listing of Professor Collinson's publications from 1957 until 1992 has already appeared in his first festschrift, *Religion, Culture and Society in Early Modern Britain*, which was edited by Anthony Fletcher and Peter Roberts (Cambridge: Cambridge University Press, 1994). This present bibliography stands as a mere extension to that, and covers only an additional five-year span. Readers must be aware that Professor Collinson's prolific output is the delight of historians, but the despair of his bibliographers.

I Books, articles, and lectures

1993

Entries for 'George Carelton' and 'Josias Nicholls', in C. S. Nicholls (ed.), *The Dictionary of National Biography: Missing Persons*. Oxford and New York: Oxford University Press.

'The Late Medieval Church and its Reformation 1400–1600', in the German translation of *The Oxford Illustrated History of Christianity*, ed. J. McManners. Original edition, 1990; Chinese translation 1996.

'Sects and the Evolution of Puritanism', in *Puritanism: Transatlantic Perspectives on a Seventeenth-century Anglo-American Faith*, ed. Francis J. Bremer. Boston: Massachusetts Historical Society, pp. 147–66.

1994

Elizabethan Essays. London: Hambledon Press. Appearing for the first time are the essays: 'Windows in a Woman's Soul: Questions about the Religion of Queen Elizabeth I'; and '"Not sexual in the ordinary sense": Women, Men and Religious Transactions'. Previously

---

[1] Susan Wabuda wishes to thank Arnold Hunt and the former Regius Professor himself for their assistance in assembling this bibliography.

published works appearing here are: 'De Republica Anglorum: or, History with the Politics Put Back' (1990); 'The Monarchical Republic of Queen Elizabeth I' (1987); 'Puritans, Men of Business and Elizabethan Parliaments' (1988); 'Truth and Legend: the Veracity of John Foxe's Book of Martyrs' (1985); 'Perne the Turncoat: an Elizabethan Reputation' (1991); and 'William Shakespeare's Religious Inheritance and Environment' (1985).

'The Elizabethan Exclusion Crisis and the Elizabethan Polity', the Raleigh Lecture on History. Printed in Proceedings of the British Academy, vol. 84, 1993 Lectures and Memoirs, pp. 51–92.

'England', in Bob Scribner, Roy Porter and Míkulaš Teich (eds), The Reformation in National Context. Cambridge: Cambridge University Press, pp. 80–94.

'Professor Sir Geoffrey Elton', an obituary in the Independent, 9 December, p. 16.

'Reformation or Deformation?', The Tablet, 22 January, pp. 74–5.

'Separating In and Out of the Church: the Consistency of Barrow and Greenwood', Journal of the United Reformed Church History Society, 5.

1995

An Address to the Clare College Commemoration of Professor Sir Geoffrey Elton, delivered 20 May 1995 at Great St Mary's Church, Cambridge. Printed in DeLloyd J. Guth (ed.), Elton ... Remembrances, for the North American Conference on British Studies, 7 October, pp. 22–5.

Archbishop Laud: a Lecture for St John's College, Oxford, May 25th, 1995, on the Occasion of the 350th Anniversary of the Death of Archbishop William Laud. Oxford: St John's College.

'Ben Jonson's Bartholomew Fair: the Theatre Constructs Puritanism', in David L. Smith, Richard Strier and David Bevington (eds), The Theatrical City: Culture, Theatre and Politics in London, 1576–1649. Cambridge: Cambridge University Press, pp. 157–69.

'The Coherence of the Text: How it Hangeth Together: the Bible in Reformation England', in W. P. Stephens (ed.), The Bible, the Reformation and the Church: Essays in Honour of James Atkinson (Journal for the Study of the New Testament, supplemental series, vol. 105), pp. 84–108.

'Critical Conclusion', to Margaret Spufford (ed.), The World of Rural Dissenters, 1520–1725. Cambridge: Cambridge University Press, pp. 388–96.

'Ecclesiastical Vitriol: Religious Satire in the 1590s and the Invention of

Puritanism', in John Guy (ed.), *The Reign of Elizabeth I: Court and Culture in the Last Decade*. Cambridge: Cambridge University Press, pp. 150–70.

A History of Canterbury Cathedral, edited with Nigel Ramsay and Margaret Sparks. Oxford: Oxford University Press. Includes 'The Protestant Cathedral, 1541–1660', pp. 154–203.

'No Popery: the Mythology of a Protestant Nation', which appeared as part 4 of the series 'Prejudice Unmasked', in *The Tablet*, 25 March, pp. 384–6.

'Protestant Culture and the Cultural Revolution', in Margo Todd (ed.), *Reformation to Revolution: Politics and Religion in Early Modern England*. London and New York: Routledge, pp. 33–52.

Tudor England Revisited: the Sixth Annual Bindoff Lecture. London: Queen Mary and Westfield College, University of London.

'The Vertical and the Horizontal in Religious History: Internal and External Integration of the Subject', in Alan Ford, James McGuire and Kenneth Milne (eds), *As by Law Established: the Church of Ireland since the Reformation*. Dublin: Lilliput Press, pp. 15–32.

1996

'Religion and Human Rights: the Case of and for Protestantism', in Olwen Hufton (ed.), *Human Rights and Historical Change: the Oxford Amnesty Lectures 1994*. New York: Basic Books.

'Christian Socialism in Elizabethan Suffolk: Thomas Carew and his *Caveat for Clothiers*', in Carole Rawcliffe, Roger Virgoe and Richard Wilson (eds), *Counties and Communities: Essays on East Anglian History Presented to Hassell Smith*. Norwich: Centre of East Anglian Studies, University of East Anglia, pp. 161–78.

Entries for 'Edward Dering', 'John Foxe', 'Edmund Grindal', 'John Jewel', 'Puritans', and the 'Vestiarian Controversy', in Hans J. Hillerbrand (ed.), *The Oxford Encyclopedia of the Reformation*. 4 vols, New York and Oxford: Oxford University Press.

'Opening Windows into Men's Souls', *Times Higher Education Supplement*, 6 July 1996, no. 1235, pp. 16–17.

'Elizabethan Puritanism and Jansenism as Forms of Popular Religious Culture', in C. Durston and J. Eales (eds), *The Culture of English Puritanism 1560–1700*. Basingstoke: Macmillan, pp. 32–57.

'William Tyndale and the Course of the English Reformation', *Reformation*, 1, pp. 72–97.

1997

'Biblical Rhetoric: the English Nation and National Sentiment in the Prophetic Mode', in Claire McEachern and Debora Shuger (eds), *Religion and Culture in Renaissance England*. Cambridge: Cambridge University Press, pp. 15–45.

'Comment on Eamon Duffy's Neale Lecture and the Colloquium' in Nicholas Tyacke (ed.), *England's Long Reformation 1500–1800*. London: London University College Press, pp. 71–86.

'The English Reformation, 1945–1995', in Michael Bentley (ed.), *Companion to Historiography*. London and New York: Routledge, pp. 336–60.

'From Iconoclasm to Iconophobia: the Cultural Impact of the Second English Reformation', originally published in 1986. Reprinted in Peter Marshall (ed.) *The Impact of the English Reformation 1550–1640*. London: Edward Arnold, pp. 278–308.

'Geoffrey Rudolph Elton 1921–1994', *Proceedings of the British Academy*, vol. 87, *Lectures and Memoirs, 1996*.

'The Monarchical Republic of Elizabeth I', originally published in 1987. Reprinted in John Guy (ed.), *The Tudor Monarchy*. London: Edward Arnold, pp. 110–34.

'Puritanismus: Puritanismus I. Puritanismus in Grossbritannien', in *Theologische Realenzyklopädie*, Band XXVIII, 1/2, pp. 8–25.

'The Religion of Elizabethan England and of its Queen', in Michele Gilberto and Nicholas Mann (eds), *Giordano Bruno 1583–1585: the English Experience/L'esperienza inglese: Atti del convegno (Londra, 3–4 giugno 1994)*. Florence: L. S. Olschki, pp. 3–22.

'Richard Hooker and the Elizabethan Establishment', in A. S. McGrade (ed.), *Richard Hooker and the Construction of Christian Community*. Medieval and Renaissance Texts and Studies, vol. 165. Tempe, AZ: Medieval and Renaissance Texts and Studies, pp. 149–81.

'Truth, Lies and Fiction in Sixteenth-century Protestant Historiography', in D. R. Kelley and D. H. Sacks (eds), *The Historical Imagination in Early Modern Britain: History, Rhetoric and Fiction 1500–1800*. Cambridge: Woodrow Wilson Center Press and Cambridge University Press, pp. 37–68.

1998

The Reformation in English Towns 1500–1640, edited with John Craig, Themes in Focus Series. Basingstoke: Macmillan. Includes 'The Shearmens' Tree and the Preacher: the Strange Death of Merry

England in Shrewsbury and Beyond', and Introduction (co-written with Craig).

II Reviews

1992

A review of Kevin Sharpe, *The Personal Rule of Charles I* in the *Observer*, 27 December, p. 34.

1993

'With a Small "r"', a review of Christopher Haigh's *English Reformations: Religion, Politics and Society under the Tudors*, *Times Literary Supplement*, no. 4725, 22 October, pp. 14–15.

'The Sense of Sacred Writ', a review of Christopher Hill's *The English Bible and the Seventeenth-century Revolution*, *Times Literary Supplement*, no. 4697, 9 April, pp. 3–4.

A review of G. J. R. Parry's, *A Protestant Vision*, *English Historical Review*, 108, pp. 453–4.

1994

'The Martyred Ghost', a review of David Daniell's *William Tyndale*, *Times Literary Supplement*, 21 October, no. 4777, pp. 3–4.

1995

'Married to her Kingdom', reviews of Helen Hackett's *Virgin Mother, Maiden Queen*, and Carole Levin's *'The Heart and Stomach of a King'*, *Times Literary Supplement*, 10 March, no. 4797, p. 11.

1996

'The Trial of Truth: Cranmer's Last Hours and the Birth of the Church of England', a review of Diarmaid MacCulloch's *Thomas Cranmer: a Life*, *Times Literary Supplement*, 24 May, no. 4860, pp. 3–4.

1997

A review of Michael A. R. Graves's, *Thomas Norton: the Parliament Man*, *Parliamentary History*, 16, pp. 231–4.

A review of Blair Worden's, *The Sound of Virtue: Philip Sidney's Arcadia and Elizabethan Politics, London Review of Books*, **19**, 3 April, pp. 26–9.

'The Last Caesars: Religious Rhetoric and Cold Political Reality in the History of the Papacy', reviews of Paul Johnson's *The Papacy*; P. G. Maxwell-Stuart's *The Chronicle of the Popes*; James Bentley's *God's Representatives*; and Eamon Duffy's *Saints and Sinners, Times Literary Supplement*, 26 December, no. 4943, pp. 3–4.

1998

'Defined by his death: a Realistic Account of the Guarded Life of a Martyr Saint and Scourge of Heretics', a review of Peter Ackroyd's *The Life of Thomas More, Times Literary Supplement*, 13 March, no. 4954, pp. 3–4.

Index